Adolescents and Risk

Adolescents and Risk

Making Sense of Adolescent Psychology

Patrick B. Johnson and
Micheline S. Malow-Iroff

Making Sense of Psychology
Carol Korn-Bursztyn, Series Editor

Westport, Connecticut
London

Library of Congress Cataloging-in-Publication Data

Johnson, Patrick B., 1944–
　　Adolescents and risk : making sense of adolescent psychology / Patrick B. Johnson and
　　Micheline S. Malow-Iroff.
　　　　p. cm. — (Making sense of psychology, ISSN 1940–3267)
　　Includes bibliographical references and index.
　　ISBN 978–0–313–33687–4 (alk. paper)
1. Adolescent psychology. I. Malow-Iroff, Micheline S., 1959– II. Title.
BF724.J64　2008
155.5′18—dc22　　2007043643

British Library Cataloguing in Publication Data is available.

Library of Congress Catalog Card Number: 2007043643
ISBN: 978–0–313–33687–4

ISSN: 1940–3267

First published in 2008

Praeger Publishers, 88 Post Road West, Westport, CT 06881
An imprint of Greenwood Publishing Group, Inc.
www.praeger.com

Printed in the United States of America

The paper used in this book complies with the
Permanent Paper Standard issued by the National
Information Standards Organization (Z39.48–1984).

10 9 8 7 6 5 4 3 2 1

This book is dedicated to our children, whose adolescent experiences reminded us of the many risks involved in growing up. Their resilience and ultimate success dealing with these challenges informed this collaborative effort.
P. B. J. & M. M. I.

Contents

Series Foreword

The "Making Sense of Psychology" series is designed to provide readers with broad perspectives on some of the greatest challenges affecting the psychological growth and development of children, adolescents, and emerging adults today. The idea for the series grows out of the need for bringing the knowledge and current findings of researchers and practitioners to a wide audience of readers who interact with young people daily, readers who are concerned about and able to impact on their growth and development. The series provides a reliable reference source for concerned parents, teachers, mental health providers, youth counselors, and others looking for basic, practical information grounded within current research and professional practice. It provides a wealth of information together with informed, professional perspectives in a readable style.

The "Making Sense of Psychology" series supports, for example, the student writing a term paper on contemporary issues in childcare, the parent seeking an understanding of a child's disability or of risky behavior in adolescence, or the teacher seeking up-to-date, reliable, and expert information on the effects of family stress on school performance. The series explores the everyday, commonplace difficulties of growing up, as well as the more complex issues that young people face at home with parents, siblings, and other family members—at school, with friends in the community, and at work.

Each volume in the series provides readers with an overview of the topic that is the subject of the book, including a concise history and overview of contemporary perspectives of the topic. Readers learn about major theories and concepts and read how these theories and approaches are applied in real-life situations. The series volumes present the most important disputes and controversies in the field and explain, in jargon-free language, the issues involved. The "Making Sense of Psychology" series provides an entry point for readers to continue their research and learning. Resources for professionals and parents, including articles, books, organizations, and appropriate and dependable web sites, are listed.

Divided into three major groups of titles, the series "Making Sense of Psychology" presents today's concerns for today's researchers, including parents, teachers, mental health practitioners, and youth counselors. Series volumes are grouped under the following: *Making Sense of Child Psychology; Making Sense of Adolescent Development and Psychology;* and *Making Sense of Emerging Adulthood.*

Researchers and practitioners in the field of psychology, social work, psychiatry, and mental health who are studying major issues and concerns regarding the healthy development of children, adolescents, and emerging adults are invited to submit manuscripts. Also invited are parents, teachers, and others who wish to submit essays that describe their experiences with children, teens, and young adults for inclusion in the series.

Carol Korn-Bursztyn, Psy.D.
Series Editor

CHAPTER 1

Introduction

When adolescents experiment with alcohol or engage in sexual experimentation, they are not necessarily behaving much differently than their peers,
from a statistical perspective. In fact, as they move through adolescence,
those who do not engage in one or more of these risky activities are
abnormal in comparison to the larger group of adolescents.

For many adults, including parents and teachers, it seems obvious that
adolescents enjoy taking risks. Their propensity for risk taking can be
seen in the apparently casual fashion in which they engage in a host of
risk-related activities, including using drugs, having unprotected sex,
and driving cars and motorcycles too fast and far too recklessly. Over
the years, a number of explanations or theories have been offered to
explain the apparent link between the adolescent life stage and risk
taking. These theories are briefly summarized in this chapter within the
context of providing some historical perspective on adolescent risk
taking—a subsequent chapter provides a more detailed discussion
of the possible causes of adolescent risk taking. A short section on self-
reported data, the primary source of information about adolescent
risk-taking behaviors, is also presented in the current chapter with more
detailed discussions occurring in subsequent chapters.

The following list summarizes selected theories that have been put
forth to explain adolescents' apparent affinity for engaging in various
risky activities.

- Rebellion—Adolescents take risks to rebel against adult authority.
- Problem Behavior Theory—Adolescents that engage in risk taking
  take multiple risks and do so as a form of their unconventionality.
- Sensation Seeking—A subset of adolescents possesses a biological
  predisposition to engage in activities associated with heightened

physiological arousal. This theory assumes a genetic component to adolescent risk taking.

- Invulnerability—Adolescents engage in risk-taking behavior because they see themselves as invulnerable to the potential risks associated with their actions.
- Conscious Decision—Adolescents consciously decide to take risks because they perceive personal benefits from doing so.
- Immaturity and Present Orientation—Adolescents take risks because they are not yet mature enough to see the potential risks associated with their actions and because they tend to live in the present moment, making it difficult for them to consider future consequences.

Common explanations of adolescent risk taking range from seemingly simplistic ideas, such as risk taking as a form of rebellion or self-definition, to somewhat more complex or sophisticated theories, such as problem behavior theory. Problem behavior theory attempts to explain multiple elements of adolescent risk taking including the fact that adolescents who engage in one problem behavior (smoking cigarettes) are more likely to also engage in other problem behaviors (delinquency or early sexual experimentation).

In addition to being characterized by their complexity, these different explanations can also be distinguished by what they see as the ultimate cause of adolescent risk taking: whether the risk taking resides within the individual adolescent or outside in the adolescent's environment. To illustrate this distinction: While explanations that focus primarily on adolescent personality traits, such as sensation seeking, view the source of the risk taking in the individual, those that focus on family stress or peer pressure view it as outside the individual in the context of specific environmental forces. These environmental forces are thought to lead the individual to engage in risky activities that would not occur in their absence.

Finally, another way to distinguish the different theories or explanations of adolescent risk taking has to do with the extent to which the individual is making a conscious decision to engage in a specific activity. On the one hand, cognitive theories argue that adolescents consciously choose to engage in risky behaviors for a variety of reasons, including the possibility that they consider themselves invulnerable to the risks or alternatively view the risks in a positive or beneficial light. On the other hand, non-cognitive theories, including the affective/emotional explanations, suggest that adolescents do not so much choose to engage in risky behaviors as inadvertently engage in behaviors that turn out to be risky. Thus affective reasons have little to do with the risk involved but more with the emotional thrill or personal enjoyment associated with risk taking.

Historical Perspective on Adolescent Risk Taking

While philosophers, including Socrates and Rousseau among others, have emphasized the selfishness and self-centered dimensions of children and their actions, a focus on adolescent risk taking had to wait until a separate period of life was created between childhood and adulthood—adolescence.

Socrates is often quoted as having lamented that youth was characterized by risky and thoughtless behaviors. But since we only have Plato's description of what Socrates said, it is probably more accurate to ascribe this position to him. Describing the youth of the day, Plato is reported to have stated, "What is happening to our young people? They disrespect their elders. They disobey their parents. They ignore the law. They riot in the streets inflamed with wild notions." A similar quote has been attributed to Hesiod in the eighth century BC, "I see no hope for the future of our people if they are dependent on the frivolous youth of today, for certainly all youth are reckless beyond words." It is probably safe to assume that young people have created problems for their caretakers since the earliest days of "civilized" human society.

Adolescence appears to be a recent cultural invention of the Western world, and discussions of adolescent risk taking, with attempts to understand it, did not seriously begin until the second half of the twentieth century. For the purposes of this book, adolescence is defined as the period of life between the onset of puberty and adulthood—where adulthood is variously defined as beginning between 18 and 21 years of age depending upon the nature of one's life circumstances.

Jessor and Jessor's (1977) problem behavior theory represents one of the first systematic attempts to develop a comprehensive understanding of adolescent risk taking. From their perspective, adolescent risk taking is not unitary but rather clusters together as those adolescents that engage in one risky behavior are likely to engage in others as well. According to the original theory, one of the central reasons for taking multiple risks is that the groups of adolescents that do so have come to define themselves in opposition to their more conventional peers precisely by engaging in these unconventional, risky activities. From this perspective, therefore, adolescent risk taking has much to do with attempts at self-definition.

While this summary fails to provide the rich and systematic nature of problem behavior theory and its subsequent iterations, it does place it squarely within the framework of other self-definition theories of adolescent risk taking, including Friedenberg's (1967) theory of adolescence. From Friedenberg's perspective, adolescence is a period of development characterized primarily by conflict and the need to define oneself in comparison to and against the adult world. From this perspective then, it is normal for adolescents to take risks and test the limits of the adult world that they will soon be entering. In testing these limits, they must necessarily engage in behaviors that have been specifically designated as "adult" activities, including alcohol and tobacco use as well as sexual intercourse.

While it is important to emphasize that some contemporary adolescent theorists reject the idea that adolescence is necessarily a period of stress and conflict as described by Friedenberg, many still consider this an apt description. One reason for this continuing view is that, despite the fact that adolescents appear to be adults in terms of physical development, they are generally not treated as such by their parents, teachers, and other authority figures. The obvious tension that results from this apparent inconsistency as well as the stress of dealing with the many physical changes that accompany puberty may make this a difficult period of adjustment for many, if not most, adolescents.

We would like to return to the idea of adolescent risk taking as normal or normative because it highlights an extremely important point. When adolescents experiment with alcohol or engage in sexual experimentation, they are not necessarily behaving much differently than their peers, from a statistical perspective. In fact, as they move through adolescence, those who do not engage in one or more of these risky activities are abnormal in comparison to the larger group of adolescents. For example, by twelfth grade over two-thirds of adolescents have experimented with alcohol.

A classic study by Shedler and Block (1990) bears directly on this point. Analyzing data from a long-term study in which adolescents were followed over an extended period and regularly interviewed, these researchers observed that adolescent drug experimentation was essentially normative behavior in which many adolescents engaged. Even more important from the perspective of normality, these researchers also found that those adolescents who had experimented with marijuana were actually healthier as determined by a battery of psychological assessment tools than their counterparts who either had abstained altogether from such experimentation or who had gone from experimentation to heavy use.

One of the most frequently employed explanations of adolescent risk taking relates to an economic risk-benefit model of human behavior. From this perspective, individuals decide to engage in specific behaviors after thoughtfully analyzing the positive and negative outcomes associated with the behavior in question. While this rational explanation may be appealing to many because it makes actions not only thoughtful, but even reasonable from the individual's perspective, it is actually hard to believe that people, especially relatively young ones, stop to consider the positive and negative aspects associated with behavior before consciously making most behavioral decisions.

Harris and colleagues' research on adolescents' "nothing to lose" attitude has found mixed support for this position (Harris, Duncan, & Boisjoly, 2002). They found that all risky behavior holds some benefits for adolescents, such as pleasure, status, and perhaps increased income. However, for many individuals the risks outweigh those benefits and individuals do not engage in those behaviors. Thus most adolescents will not become involved in a situation that has been assessed to be very risky (Rolison & Scherman, 2002). This holds for some acts but not all, as can be seen in the case of adolescents who sell drugs. For these individuals, the risks of detriment to health, loss of educational aspirations, and the illegal nature of the act are not enough to deter them—perhaps they feel they have nothing to lose and thus choose to sell drugs anyway.

Steinberg (2003) is one theorist who has criticized this decision-making explanation of adolescent risk taking. Instead, he has suggested that adolescents engage in greater risk taking due to their less-mature judgment, their greater susceptibility to peer pressure, and their greater tendency to live in the moment than to consider the broad range of immediate or long-term consequences of their actions. Instead of thinking about doing something and what might happen as a result, adolescents often "just do it" and then must confront negative outcomes not considered beforehand.

Slovic (2003) agrees with Steinberg that decision making is probably not the best way to characterize or understand adolescent risk taking. However, he has also argued that more attention needs to be given to the emotional or affective determinants of adolescents' risky actions. From his view, the motivation for adolescent risk taking can be found not in adolescents' thoughts and analyses of specific behaviors, but rather in the images associated with those behaviors and the emotions those images stimulate. Companies that advertise products frequently associated with adolescent risk taking, such as tobacco and alcohol, have long recognized the power of feelings and images to drive human behavior. In fact, a recent study summarized in the *New York Times* (Nagourney, 2006) revealed that special promotions and ads designed to lure new teens to try cigarettes were effective in doing so (White, White, Freeman, Gilpin, & Pierce, 2006). In line with that, it is hardly surprising that Slovic contends that traditionally our research studies on adolescent behavior have ignored these powerful, but sometimes less visible or recognizable forces.

The emphasis on the importance of high-intensity emotions, however, may only apply to some adolescents. Zuckerman's 1979 sensation seeking theory of adolescent risk taking highlighted the importance of high-level emotional arousal for a special subgroup of adolescents. Zuckerman categorized four dimensions of sensation seeking: thrill and adventure, disinhibition, experience seeking, and boredom susceptibility. According to Zuckerman's theory, some adolescents seek activities and experiences that gratify their unusually high need for sensations, and that involvement in activities that would be stressful for many adolescents are preferred and actively sought out by this adolescent subgroup. Research

has substantiated the relationship between sensation seeking and engagement in high-risk behaviors (Rolison & Scherman, 2002). High sensation-
seeking orientations have been found among marijuana users (Satinder &
Black, 1984) and adolescents who prefer hard rock/heavy metal music
(Arnett, 1992).

While many of these explanations were developed specifically to better
understand adolescent risk taking, more-general theories of behavior
have also been used in the same way. Bronfenbrenner's (1979) ecological
theory of development is a good example of such a broad theory that
has been used to better understand adolescent risk taking. In this theory,
the individual can be found at the middle of a series of concentric circles,
each of which represents a context that influences adolescent behavior.
While an individual's behavior can be influenced separately by each of
these separate contexts or spheres, from family, to neighborhood, to
culture/society, the model also enables an analysis of the multiple ways
in which these different spheres interconnect and influence the individual
in combination with one another. While the ecological theory can be
comprehensive and can simultaneously consider multiple factors that
produce adolescent risk taking—genetics, parental interactions, peer
influences, and cultural influences including the media—its comprehen-
siveness also means that it is cumbersome and sometimes unable to make
testable, specific predictions. In any event, attempts have been made to
use this theory to predict and understand various elements of adolescent
risk taking, including substance abuse and sexual experimentation.

One of the important strengths of Bronfenbrenner's model is that it
includes a time element that allows the incorporation of changing social
mores and intergenerational changes in values and habits. This is particularly important in some areas of adolescent risk taking such as drug
abuse, where the substances of choice may change dramatically from
one time period to the next. It is also true that the risk-taking activities
of one generation—swallowing goldfish or having toga parties—may
have little meaning or significance to another generation. In this way,
adolescent risk-taking activities contain an element of faddishness as they
may come in and quickly go out of style. Also in this way, each generation
of young people has an opportunity to define itself in its own terms.
Of course, this also ensures that there will always be some element of
incomprehensibility for the older generations as they observe the "new"
risk-taking activities of a newer generation of adolescents.

As an illustration of this point, consider two of the "new" risk-taking
activities many adolescents engage in that raise eyebrows among the
older generation: tattoos and body piercing. Although both acts have
been around for centuries, seen primarily in native cultures, observing
this type of body decoration on adolescents has created concern in many
parents and other well-meaning adults. The growing popularity of both
practices has moved these risk-taking acts into the area of generational

conformity. Thus it is hard to determine if getting a tattoo or a body piercing is simply a statement of identity that is commonly accepted by the peer group, or if it is a red flag of more troubling risk-taking behaviors. Recent research on this issue has not come to any firm conclusions. For some adolescents, a new tattoo or body piercing may be just body decoration, like a new shirt or necklace. However, for others it may be part of the constellation of adolescent risk behaviors that cluster together—multiple drug use, gambling, violence, tattoos, and body piercing (Carroll, Riffenburgh, Roberts, & Myhre, 2002; Deschesnes, Fines, & Demers, 2006). Thus it is important to look at the risk-taking act in the context of its meaning to the individual and to the peer group. Only in this way can a risk-taking act be examined for whether it represents generational conformity or is part of a movement to a high-risk life style for any particular adolescent.

Subsequent chapters will address individual risk-taking behaviors including drug use, gambling, and sexual activity, among others. While providing an overview of each area, these chapters will also include brief sections on intervention/prevention attempts that have been developed to reduce adolescent risk taking in a particular area. Some of the same theories or explanations that have been summarized here will be presented along with specific theories developed for use with a specific risky behavior. Following these chapters on individual areas of adolescent risk taking, chapters will highlight adolescent mental health, possible causes of adolescent risk taking, and prevention.

Before concluding this introductory chapter, it is necessary to highlight a potentially serious limitation in most studies of adolescent risk taking—their reliance on self-reported behavior. There are many reasons to assume that such reliance may not be justified and that there are many systematic as well as unsystematic distortions that occur when adolescents are asked to state the extent to which they have been involved with specific risk-taking and sometimes illegal activities including smoking, drinking, and gambling. More attention will be given to this problem in the subsequent chapter on teen drug use. For the reader, however, it is important to keep in mind that such distortions may raise serious questions about some of the findings presented and conclusions reached by those researchers who study adolescent risk taking.

Works Cited

Arnett, J. (1992). The soundtrack of recklessness: Musical preferences and reckless behavior among adolescents. *Journal of Adolescent Research, 7*, 313–331.

Bronfenbrenner, U. (1979). *The ecology of human development.* Cambridge, MA: Harvard University Press.

Carroll, S.T., Riffenburgh, R.H., Roberts, T.A., & Myhre, E.B. (2002). Tatoos and body piercings as indicators of adolescent risk taking behaviors. *Pediatrics, 109*, 1021–1027.

Deschesnes, M., Fines, P., & Demers, S. (2006). Are tattooing and body piercing indicators of risk taking behaviours among high school students? *Journal of Adolescence, 29,* 379–393.

Friedenberg, E.Z. (1967). *The Vanishing Adolescent.* New York: Dell Press.

Harris, K.M., Duncan, G.J., & Boisjoly, J. (2002). Evaluating the role of "nothing to lose" attitudes on risky behavior in adolescence. *Social Forces, 80,* 1005–1039.

Jessor, R. & Jessor, S.L. (1977). *Problem behavior and psychosocial development: A longitudinal study of youth.* New York: Academic Press.

Nagourney, E. (2006, March 7). Coupons lure young smokers, research suggests. *New York Times.*

Rolison, M.R. & Scherman, A. (2002). Factors influencing adolescents' decisions to engage in risk-taking behavior. *Adolescence, 37,* 585–596.

Satinder, K.P. & Black, A. (1984). Cannabis use and sensation-seeking orientation. *Journal of Psychology, 116,* 101–105.

Shedler, J. & Block, J. (1990). Adolescent drug use and psychological health: A longitudinal inquiry. *American Psychologist, 48,* 612–630.

Slovic, P. (2003). Affect and risk. In D. Romer (Ed.), *Reducing adolescent risk: An integrated approach* (pp. 44–48). Thousand Oaks, CA: Sage Publications.

Steinberg, L. (2003). Is decision making the right framework for research on adolescent risk taking? In D. Romer (Ed.), *Reducing adolescent risk: An integrated approach* (pp. 18–24). Thousand Oaks, CA: Sage Publications.

White, V.M., White, M.M., Freeman, K., Gilpin, E.A., & Pierce, J.P. (2006). Cigarette promotional offers: Who takes advantages? *American Journal of Preventive Medicine, 30,* 225–231.

Zuckerman, M. (1979). *Sensation seeking: Beyond the optimal level of arousal.* Hillsdale, NJ: Lawrence Erlbaum.

CHAPTER 2

Adolescent Drug Use

> In describing their own activities with regard to sensitive topics like drug use, study participants are asked to be accurate and truthful about behaviors where accuracy and honesty demonstrate their involvement in illegal activities. At the same time, study participants are asked to provide this information within a social context in which they are acutely aware that others will evaluate their responses and compare them to those of other respondents. Because of this, drug abuse researchers and those interpreting their findings, including parents and educators, need to evaluate and acknowledge the likelihood of dishonesty or inaccuracy in self-reported responses and attempt to create ways to maximize their accuracy. (Richter & Johnson, 2001, p. 812)

Historically, public perception of drug use has moved from tolerance to intolerance (Robert Wood Johnson Foundation, 2001). While the late nineteenth century represented a period of relative tolerance for cocaine and opiates, more recently, increasing intolerance has been the rule, partly because of the association between illicit drug use and inner city violence, and, over the last four decades, partly in reaction to the largely unsuccessful "War on Drugs."

While alcohol and drug abuse have often been stigmatized behaviors, in the past few years substance abuse has been viewed less in moralistic terms and has been viewed instead from a medical perspective, as chronic relapsing disease—that is, a disease that varies in its intensity and reoccurs from time to time, much like diabetes and hypertension.

There are many compelling reasons to take a general health perspective rather than a personal perspective when we look at substance use and abuse. In fact, Dr. Alan Leshner (2000), former director of the National Institute on Drug Abuse (NIDA) wrote that "the most immediate, extensive, and long-lasting problems caused by drug abuse, both for individuals and for society, are often medical in nature." Then, too, "NIDA research has shown that almost every drug of abuse harms some tissue or organ" (Leshner, 2000). From this perspective, it makes good sense and represents enlightened public policy to consider illicit drug use a public health problem.

This would certainly be in line with the current national zeitgeist in which smoking and obesity are viewed as major threats to public health. It is interesting to note that many of the public health threats cited over the years by the Centers for Disease Control and Prevention (CDC) have themselves been connected to illicit drug use. For example, a strong and consistent association has been observed between smoking and illicit drug use (Grant, Hasin, Chou, Stinson, & Dawson, 2004; Helstrom, Bryan, Hutchison, Riggs, & Blechman, 2004). Moreover, research has also demonstrated a connection between drug use and failure to use auto seat belts (Mathews, Zollinger, Przybyiski, & Bull, 2001). In addition, illicit drug use has been associated with driving under the influence and with engaging in violent behaviors, two other public health threats previously highlighted by the CDC.

Methodological Issues

Before laying out what we currently know about the pervasiveness of adolescent drug use, it is essential that the reader be aware of some limitations of the available data to inform us regarding drug use and its various impacts. According to Weston (1996, p. 49), "The major problem with survey methods is that they rely on subjects to report on themselves truthfully and accurately." Nowhere is this limitation more apparent than in those research studies where people are asked to report on sensitive behaviors such as illicit drug use and delinquent acts. "A question is considered sensitive if it raises concerns about disapproval or other consequences (such as legal sanctions) for reporting truthfully or if the question itself is seen as an invasion of privacy" (Tourangeau & Smith, 1996, p. 276).

In describing their own activities with regard to sensitive topics like drug use, study participants are asked to be accurate and truthful about behaviors where accuracy and honesty could expose their involvement in illegal activities. At the same time, study participants are asked to provide this information within a social context in which they are acutely aware that others will evaluate their responses and compare them to those of other respondents. Because of this, drug abuse researchers and those interpreting their findings, including parents and educators, need to acknowledge and evaluate the likelihood of dishonesty or inaccuracy in self-reported responses and attempt to create ways to maximize their accuracy (Richter & Johnson, 2001).

While researchers studying sensitive behaviors frequently and understandably cite work that supports the accuracy of self-reported substance use, some skeptics have serious concerns about whether the responses are in fact valid. In the area of drug use, for example, Harrison (1997, p. 17) emphasized that "recent validation studies conducted with criminal justice and former treatment clients using improved urinalysis techniques and hair analysis demonstrate that self-report methods miss a lot of recent drug use." These conclusions were echoed by Cook, Bernstein, and Andrews (1997) writing in the same monograph, "The findings cast doubt on the validity of self-reports as means of estimating drug use prevalence and suggest the need for multiple assessment methods" (p. 247).

Comparisons of self-reported responses among three leading national and federally-funded surveys of youth risk behaviors also raise questions regarding the accuracy of self-reported data in sensitive areas such as drug use or sexual activity. Specifically, self-reported rates of substance use are significantly higher in the anonymous Youth Risk Behavior Survey (YRBS) by the CDC, compared to those in the Office of Applied Studies' National Household Survey on Drug Abuse (NHSDA) or those in the Monitoring the Future (MTF) study (Johnston, O'Malley, Bachman, & Schulenberg, 2007), which are not anonymous.

In a recent editorial, Males (2007) pointed out that: "While Monitoring the Future....showed that drug use dropped sharply in the last decade, the National Center for Health Statistics has reported that teenage deaths from illicit drug abuse have tripled over the same period" (para. 1). He goes on to conclude: "It's time to end the obsession with hyping teenage drug use. The meaningless surveys that policy makers now rely on should be replaced with a comprehensive 'drug abuse index' that pulls together largely ignored data on drug-related deaths, hospital emergencies, crime, diseases and similar practical measures" (para. 3).

When interpreting research that attempts to demonstrate the impact of adolescent drug use, a second question to consider concerns cause and effect and our current statistical tests. Many of our most widely-used statistical procedures for analyzing the relationship between illicit drug use and various outcomes such as school failure and hospitalization cannot actually determine causal connections. Many of these procedures rely on a technique known as correlation, which only demonstrates that there is a statistical/mathematical link between two sets of numbers such as self-reported marijuana use and school grades. It is not possible for these correlational techniques to demonstrate that one variable actually causes another, to demonstrate, for example, that frequent marijuana use produces lower grades.

Despite this limitation, many researchers and policy reports leave readers with the clear impression that drugs cause rather than simply correlate with various negative behaviors. It is essential for readers to understand this limitation and to avoid the interpretative trap of confusing correlational with causal connections. As a case in point, a recent headline from the "Science Times" section of the *New York Times* reported: "Smoking Tied to Increased Risk of H.I.V." The brief summary considered a series of possible explanations for the observed relationship while completely ignoring the fact that teens who engage in one risk behavior—smoking—are also more likely to engage in another risk behavior—unprotected sex—which may have led to the statistical relationship. In this instance, both effects would have been caused by some third factor, and there would exist no real causal linkage between smoking and HIV status.

Of course, the situation is much the same when experts try to determine which factors cause or predispose American children to drug experimentation or drug abuse and which buffer them from such involvement. One leading organization suggests that parents can prevent their children from becoming involved with drugs by simply having dinner with them on a regular basis. It is hardly surprising that there is a negative correlation between the number of times a child reports having dinner with the family and his or her level of drug use. Undoubtedly a similar association could be found between having breakfast with family members or engaging in other family rituals, such as regular trips to the supermarket, and relatively low levels of self-reported drug involvement.

But the statistical relationship in question probably results from the fact that having dinner with one's family is a proxy for more general or frequent parental involvement with children. Again, this is hardly surprising, as research has long demonstrated that parental monitoring protects children from various problem behaviors including drug involvement. It is prudent to bear in mind that correlation does not equal causation.

To provide a backdrop against which to understand how drug abuse impacts key American institutions, and to understand how the drug abuse scene has changed since 1993, we now provide information about:

- the changing trends in drug use from 1993 to 2003, and
- a summary of comparative findings of youth drug use and drug-use attitudes given by the Partnership for a Drug-Free America.

Drug Use Comparisons, 1993–2003

While this chapter will highlight adolescent use of illicit drugs, brief consideration will also be given to alcohol and tobacco use as well. This is essential because these two are the drugs most used by adolescents and because, for many, poly-drug use (or the use of multiple substances) is the rule rather than the exception. Therefore, when we attempt to document or isolate the effects of illicit drug use, we need to recognize that most of the people who abuse drugs also use or abuse alcohol, and many of these same individuals also smoke cigarettes. Accordingly, when we cover drug use and abuse, we will be discussing research findings focused mainly on the use and abuse of illicit drugs or the illegal use of prescription medicine for nonmedical purposes. On the other hand, when we discuss substance abuse and its impacts, we will refer to research findings involving illicit drugs and licit drugs, including alcohol and tobacco. Of course for minors, alcohol and tobacco are both illegal substances as well.

The following list summarizes comparative data collected over a 10-year period by the Partnership for a Drug-Free America.

- Decreases in ecstasy and marijuana use were observed in 2003, which may have resulted from the Partnership for a Drug-Free America's anti-ecstasy and anti-marijuana advertising campaigns.
- Increases were observed in eighth graders' use of inhalants (from 7.7 percent to 8.7 percent) and of prescription pain relievers, including Vicodin and OxyContin.
- After rising through the 1990s, high school students' use of steroids declined slightly in 2003.
- Declines that had been occurring over time in eighth graders' use of hallucinogens, amphetamines, tranquilizers, and other drugs either halted or slowed considerably in 2003.

In discussing the declining use of many illicit drugs, this same report suggests that the reduction in use seen in previous years may be ending because of generational forgetting, which refers to new cohorts of young people not having learned the dangers and damage associated with drug use. Additional support for this contention can be taken from the report finding that over a recent five-year period the percentage of high school seniors that considered steroid use to be a "great risk" dropped from 68 percent to 55 percent.

Comparison of Youth Drug Use Attitudes in 1993 and 2003

It is important to emphasize that in terms of youth illicit drug use, the United States stands alone among Western countries. A 1999 survey of 30 European countries found that not a single country had rates of illicit drug use as high as those traditionally observed in the United States (Hibell, Andersson, Bjarnason, Ahlstrom, Balakireva, Kokkevi, & Morgan, 2003). Heroin was the one exception noted in the research findings.

The Partnership for a Drug-Free America has carried out an annual youth survey of drug use and drug attitudes since 1993. Analyses of responses on comparable items were carried out by one of the authors of this book. Comparison of these analyses revealed significant differences between youth in 1993 and the cohort in 2003. We have summarized the most significant and most illuminating in the following list.

In comparison with youth who participated in the 1993 Partnership for a Drug-Free America survey, youth who participated in the 2003 Partnership survey were more likely to support the following statements—

- Drugs help you forget your troubles.
- Drugs help kids when they're having a hard time.
- Drugs are fun.
- Parties are more fun with drugs.
- Sex is better when you're high.
- Drugs help you relax socially.
- Marijuana helps you relax.
- Being high feels good.
- There is little risk if you use cocaine once or twice.
- There is little risk of dying if you use cocaine.
- There is little risk of becoming a dealer if you use cocaine.

Youth who participated in the 2003 Partnership survey indicated the following about their use of drugs—

- Used marijuana more frequently and had done so more in the past month and past year.
- Used cocaine more frequently in the past year.

Youth who participated in the 2003 Partnership survey indicated that they had more friends who—

- Get stoned on marijuana usually.
- Use cocaine occasionally.
- Use ecstasy.
- Use heroin.

In addition, the 2003 youth cohort was also more likely to agree with the statement that commercials and ads had "given you new information or told you things you didn't know about drugs" and were less likely to agree with the statement that commercials and ads had "made you aware that America's drug problem is a problem for you and your family."

While these comparative results are certainly disappointing given the efforts directed over the years at reducing youth drug involvement, we should not forget the other progress that has been made over the same years. In many respects, the results support the suggestion by Lloyd Johnston and the other investigators associated with recent Monitoring the Future findings: "We are concerned that these changes among 8th graders may reflect generational forgetting of the dangers of drugs beginning to take place as a result of generational replacement, with newer cohorts of young people not hearing as much about the potential harm of many of these drugs" (Johnston, O'Malley, Bachman, & Schulenberg, 2004, p. 7). Our comparison of youth in 1993 and 2003 certainly supports this suggestion.

At the same time, however, the findings indicate that youth in 2003 were more likely to believe that they had learned about drugs from commercials and ads. The recent reduction in rates of marijuana and ecstasy use that these same researchers emphasized, in fact, may reflect the impact of anti-marijuana and anti-ecstasy ad campaigns by the Partnership for a Drug-Free America.

Before concluding this section, brief summaries of findings on the two drugs most widely used by adolescents—alcohol and tobacco—will be provided. An analysis of National Household Survey data (Johnson & Richter, 2002) indicated that these two behaviors are also dramatically linked in early adolescence, although the pattern of the relationship is reversed. That is, while young heavy smokers are highly likely to be binge drinkers, there are many binge drinkers who do not smoke. The connection between smoking and binge drinking first appears in early adolescence (between 13 and 16 years of age) and then seems to weaken. This suggests that early experimenters with cigarettes and binge drinking may be different in important ways from those who begin to experiment with either later in adolescence.

A press release from Monitoring the Future researchers emphasized that the decline in daily smoking in younger teens appears to have stopped (Johnston, O'Malley, Bachman, & Schulenberg, 2006). According to the Centers for Disease Control (2006), "every day, approximately 4,000 American youth aged 12–17 try their first cigarette." Should this trend continue, it is estimated that 6.4 million of our current children will die prematurely from some smoking-related disease. Still today in this country, tobacco use is the single leading preventable cause of death.

With regard to alcohol use, the CDC found that the percentage of students reporting some alcohol use has declined from 51 percent in 1991 to 43 percent in 2005. While the Monitoring the Future findings have generally observed similar declines in alcohol use over the years, their most recent findings suggest that the decline in alcohol use among younger teens may be coming to an end, although it appears to be continuing to trend lower among twelfth graders.

Current Prevalence of Drug Use in Eighth, Tenth, and Twelfth Grade Students

The following statistics are taken from the 2006 Monitoring the Future survey (Johnston, O'Malley, Bachman, & Schulenberg, 2007). A summary of the methodology used in this survey may be found at http://monitoringthefuture.org/. Following are some of the important findings from the most recently published survey results. The authors note that teen drug use continues to decline although use of prescription drugs continues at relatively high rates. The declining trend appears to be most pronounced among older teens. Results also suggested that teen use of OxyContin and Vicodin appeared to increase in 2006.

- By the time they have graduated from high school, 48.2 percent of seniors have used at least one illicit drug in their lifetime compared with 20.9 percent of eighth graders.
- 6.5 percent of seniors report they have used ecstasy and 8.5 percent report having used cocaine.
- Comparisons of eighth and twelfth grade drug-use prevalence rates of specific drugs reveal that 15.7 percent of eighth graders and 42.3 percent of twelfth graders report lifetime marijuana use; 16.1 percent of eighth graders and 11.1 percent of twelfth graders report lifetime use of inhalants, and 7.3 percent of eighth graders and 12.4 percent of twelfth graders report lifetime use of amphetamines.
- 24.6 percent of eighth graders and 47.1 percent of twelfth graders report having smoked a cigarette.
- 40.5 percent of eighth graders and 72.7 percent of twelfth graders report having consumed alcohol.
- 24.6 percent of eighth graders and 47.1 percent of twelfth graders report having been drunk.

Increasing Numbers of Drugs to Abuse

Concluding their summary of 27-year-trend data on adolescent drug use, Johnston, O'Malley, and Bachman (2003) lamented, "Finally, we note the seemingly unending capacity of pharmacological experts and amateurs to discover new substances with abuse potential that can be used to alter mood and consciousness" (p. 32). While it is likely that the introduction of LSD into the drug lexicon of the 1960s brought the most famous addition to our nation's illicit drug scene, in recent years a number of new illicit drugs have been added to this scene and, at the same time, the illicit use of prescription drugs has increased sharply. One way to demonstrate changes in the drug use scene is to simply list the new drugs that have appeared in recent years, including ecstasy and OxyContin. Another is to point out how national surveys have added questions to determine how many of our young people are using these drugs. For example, the 2000 Monitoring the Future survey added club drugs to its list, including ketamine, GHB, and Rohypnol. In 2001 the male strength drug androstenedione, a precursor of anabolic steroids, was added to the survey along with creatine, a protein supplement. The following textbox deals with performance-enhancing drugs. Recently, OxyContin, the powerful pain reliever, was also added in order to collect more specific data on the pervasiveness of the nonmedical use of this prescription drug.

PERFORMANCE-ENHANCING DRUGS

- Professional wrestler Chris Benoit's murder-suicide once again focused public attention on the serious negative consequences associated with the use of performance-enhancing drugs such as testosterone by athletes both young and old.

- A report on youth steroid use by Adler (2004) suggested the following about the players associated with the ongoing steroid scandal: "Their examples have placed a generation of teenage athletes at risk for the same mistakes, which could end their careers—if not their lives—long before they reach the big time." In the same article, a New York physician described youth steroid use as a "burgeoning epidemic."

- Adler also pointed out that the parents and families of steroid-abusing adolescents are often oblivious regarding the use, let alone abuse, of their children. If parents are unable or unwilling to recognize that a serious problem exists, how can teachers, coaches, and other involved adults be expected to recognize its existence?

The fact that new drugs and new uses of old drugs continue to appear on the American drug scene highlights the intractability and changeable nature of the drug abuse problem in this country. It also increases the difficult task that parents have in protecting their children from experimentation and subsequent abusive involvement with drugs.

The recent crisis surrounding the use of over-the-counter cold remedies containing pseudoephedrine provides yet another object lesson in the changing landscape of the American drug culture and policy makers' struggles to reduce or eliminate it (Butterfield, 2005). These over-the-counter medicines are purchased in large amounts and then used in "meth labs" to manufacture methamphetamines for private use and illegal distribution and sale. Twenty states, including Minnesota, where methamphetamine use has increased dramatically in urban as well as rural areas, have drafted legislation to reclassify these over-the-counter medicines Schedule 5 drugs, which would indicate that they possess low to moderate hazards and require some caution in handling, storage, and use.

In 2005 the Combat Methamphetamine Epidemic Act was passed as an amendment to the controversial Patriot Act. This act restricted sales of pseudoephedrine-containing products to three packages at a time. The restrictions require that anyone purchasing pseudoephedrine must have valid photo identification and sign a logbook at the time of purchase. Various retailers have enforced this act by having the products behind the counter and requiring a minimum customer age to purchase. As pseudoephedrine is available without a prescription yet still has a potential for abuse, many states would like it to be classified as a Schedule 5 drug. These legislative efforts have been motivated by the increasing spread of methamphetamine use from western states and rural areas to eastern states and more urban environments.

Pervasiveness of Illicit Drug Use: Geography

There is a quaint belief among many Americans that the drug abuse problem in this country is localized in large cities and that rural America and the suburbs have been spared. In reality, of course, drug abuse has not spared any area where Americans congregate in sufficient numbers to represent a "market" for drugs. The National Center on Addiction and Substance Abuse at Columbia University (CASA) emphatically made this point in its 2000 report on substance abuse in mid-size cities and rural America.

The CASA report observed that there were essentially NO statistically-significant differences between adults 18 years and older in their rates of past-month use of any illicit drug other than marijuana in large cities (over 1 million residents), mid-size cities (50,000– million residents), and rural communities (counties with no city over 50,000 residents). CASA did report, however, that adults in rural America were less likely to have smoked marijuana in the past month. More-detailed analyses that subdivided rural and mid-size cities led to the following conclusion: "Past month use of cocaine and amphetamines are identical in rural areas with populations less than 2500 and large metropolitan areas" (p. 6).

The picture that emerged from analyses of the 1999 Monitoring the Future survey for eighth graders in the same report revealed that, in comparison with their more urban counterparts, rural youth were at considerable risk for drug use. For example, findings indicated that rural eighth graders were more likely than eighth graders in the largest metropolitan areas to report using marijuana, cocaine, crack, inhalants, and amphetamines in the past month. No difference was observed in the two groups' past-month heroin use.

Furthermore, a report revealed that from 1992 to 2002, treatment admission rates for narcotic painkillers increased by 155 percent (Office of Applied Studies, 2004). While admission rates increased at all levels of population density, they were greatest in rural areas of the country.

Together these findings clearly demonstrate that drug use is hardly restricted to urban or suburban areas and, in fact, may be more problematic for some specific substances among rural youth. Research has also revealed that rural and urban youth report using drugs for similar purposes and report similar perceptions of risk associated with drug use (Johnston, O'Malley, & Bachman, 2000).

It should be noted that contemporary rural youth have greater access to drugs. For some time it has been clear that there has been increasing drug traffic in rural areas. One simple reason for this is that rural areas are frequently used as sites for marijuana cultivation, for locating methamphetamine laboratories, and for trafficking in prescription medicine including OxyContin (Butterfield, 2005).

The same *New York Times* article indicated that rural drugstores were more likely to use vaults with barred windows than more-traditional surveillance cameras. In some instances, employees have even begun arming themselves as a precaution against thefts. Pharmaceutical companies have also been forced to alter their procedures in response to the upsurge in rural prescription drug thefts so that medicines are now delivered in armored vehicles, accompanied by armed guards, while being tracked by satellites. The advent of the powerful pain killer OxyContin and its abuse appears to have been associated with many of these changes.

Pervasiveness of Illicit Drug Use: Gender, Race/Ethnicity, and Social Class

Drug abuse is not restricted to either gender or any specific socioeconomic or racial/ethnic group. According to Johnston, O'Malley, and Bachman (2002), "While the rate of using marijuana in the past year is slightly higher for boys, the rate for the use of any illicit drug other than marijuana is slightly higher for girls" (p. 20). At the same time, National Household data reveal that girls between 12 and 17 were equally likely to report illicit drug abuse in the past year (Office of Applied Studies, 2002).

According to a Monitoring the Future report (Johnston, O'Malley, Bachman, & Schulenberg, 2004), "For many drugs the differences in use by socioeconomic class are very small, and the trends have been highly parallel" (p. 40). While there have been some exceptions to this pattern, cocaine, for example, illicit drug use rates among our youth have been generally consistent across social classes. Another exception noted by Luthar and D'Avanzo (1999) was that affluent youth living in the suburbs were more drug-involved than youth living in inner cities.

The picture with respect to racial/ethnic differences in drug use is somewhat more complicated. The results of the National Survey of Drug Use and Health Survey (Office of Applied Studies, 2004) conducted on individuals 12 years of age and older revealed that American Indians (12.1 percent) and biracial Americans (12 percent) were most involved with drugs while Hispanics (8 percent) and Asian Americans (3.8 percent) were least involved. In contrast, Monitoring the Future results which focused on American secondary school students (Johnston et al., 2004) revealed that African Americans were far less likely than Whites to be involved with drugs while Hispanics generally fell between these two groups. However, among eighth graders Hispanics reported greater use of almost all drug categories, while among twelfth graders Hispanics only reported greater crack use and heroin use with a needle. The relatively high dropout rates of Hispanics (Spring, 2003) probably account in large measure for the different eighth and twelfth grade patterns of Hispanic students drug use. In any event, it is clear that illicit drug use certainly is found among members of each and every group.

The landscape of youth drug use has both changed and remained the same during the past decade. It has changed in that both new drugs and younger initiates have become part of the landscape for some drugs. It has remained the same in that illicit drug use remains a critical social problem despite the considerable progress that has been made in some important areas.

Prevention

Three levels or degrees of prevention, originally proposed by the Institute of Medicine, have frequently been employed in the drug use field to encompass the full range of prevention services: universal, selective, and indicated. In this model of prevention, universal approaches refer to those that could be provided to a whole population—in drug prevention this might include school-based prevention programs designed to be given to all students in a particular grade level. Selective prevention programs, on the other hand, are designed for population subgroups that possess one or more characteristics that might place them at heightened risk of becoming involved with drugs. For example, a prevention program that was only offered to students involved in delinquent activities (because such activities have been associated with the increased likelihood of drug involvement) would be a selective program. Finally, indicated drug-prevention programs have been designed for individuals (rather than subgroups) who possess one or more risk factors that place them at even greater risk of subsequent drug abuse. In this category would be programs for adolescent smokers or drinkers because such groups are at especially elevated risk for subsequent drug experimentation and/or abuse.

The adolescent drug abuse field has generally focused more attention on universal, frequently school-based, prevention programs than on selective or indicated programs, because of the assumption that these programs reach the largest number of adolescents and, thus, should have the greatest impact at preventing or reducing adolescent drug involvement. It should be noted, however, that there is disagreement among experts in the field regarding the validity of this assumption. One reason for this is that universal programs may expend valuable resources targeting large numbers of adolescents who have little, if any, chance of ever becoming seriously involved with drugs. These resources, it has been argued, could have far greater impact on reducing adolescent drug use if they were employed either in selective or indicated prevention programs because they target those most likely to become involved with drugs in the future.

Although some school-based programs have shown promising results, the National Institute on Alcohol Abuse and Alcoholism (NIAAA) reported, "effect sizes for school-based programs are not large, and it is generally conceded that school curricula....are not sufficient to make sizeable and lasting changes in alcohol use by adolescents..." (NIAAA, 2000). Others (Gorman, 1996, 1998; Skager, 2000) have also questioned their impact on substance use generally. Similarly, the surgeon general's report on youth violence (USDHHS, 2001) emphasized, "For most violence, crime, and drug-prevention programs now being implemented, there is simply no evidence regarding effectiveness." Some have even suggested that school-based substance use and violence reduction programs may create the very problems they were designed to prevent (Gorman, 1996; Mendel, 2000).

A number of prevention/intervention programs have also been developed for at-risk adolescents, including family systems approaches that work with youth and their immediate families, as well as programs that work both in schools and with youth and their families outside of school. Project Success is one of the most promising of these programs. Designed to prevent and reduce substance use and abuse among high-risk and multi-problem youth, Project Success places highly trained counselors in schools to provide a full range of services. It also provides parent programs as well (http://www.sascorp.org/).

Evaluations and recommended programs can be found through a number of sources including the Center for Substance Abuse Prevention (CSAP) and the National Institute on Drug Abuse (NIDA).

Finally, anti-drug media campaigns have been carried out both locally and nationally. The most extensive and expensive has been conducted by the Office of National Drug Control Policy (ONDCP) in collaboration with the Partnership for a Drug-Free America. To date, the results of this campaign have been quite disappointing. According to a U.S. Government Accountability Office report (USGAO, 2006), the $1.2 billion campaign was ineffective in reducing youth drug use.

Substance Abuse Resources

American Academy of Child and Adolescent Psychiatry—Facts for families
http://www.aacap.org/page.ww?section=Facts+for+Families&name=Facts+for+Families

The Center for Parent/Youth Understanding
http://www.cpyu.org/

Keeping Youth Mentally Healthy and Drug Free—Family Guide—Public
education web site developed by the Substance Abuse and Mental Health
Services Administration (SAMHSA)
http://family.samhsa.gov/

National Institute on Drug Abuse
http://www.nida.gov/

The National Resource Center for Drug Rehabilitation and Drug Treatment—Resources for young adults and parents of adolescents
http://www.drugrehabtreatment.com/

National Youth Network—Helping parents and professionals alike in
providing education and information regarding programs and services
for underachieving youth
http://www.nationalyouth.com/substanceabuse.html

Substance Abuse and Mental Health Services Administration (SAMHSA)
U.S. Department of Health and Human Services
5600 Fishers Lane
Rockville, MD 20857
301–443–8956
http://www.samhsa.gov

Troubled Teen Help Directory—Help for parents of struggling teens
http://www.teen-help-directory.com/categories/Substance-Abuse.asp

Works Cited

Adler, J. (2004). Toxic strength. *Newsweek, 954,* 44–51.
Butterfield, F. (2005, January 30). Fighting an illegal drug through its legal source.
   New York Times.
Cook, R.F., Bernstein, A.D., & Andrews, C.M. (1997). Assessing drug use in the
   workplace: A comparison of self-report, urinalysis, and hair analysis. In
   L. Harrison & A. Hughes (Eds.), *Validity of self-reported drug use: Improving
   the accuracy of survey estimates* (NIH Publication No. 97–4147, pp. 247–272).
   Rockville, MD: National Institute on Drug Abuse.
Gorman, D.M. (1996). Do school-based social skills training programs prevent
   alcohol use among young people? *Addiction Research, 4,* 191–210.
Gorman, D.M. (1998). The irrelevance of evidence in the development of
   school-based drug prevention policy, 1986–1996. *Evaluation Review, 22,*
   118–146.

Grant, B.F., Hasin, D.S., Chou, S.P., Stinson, F.S., & Dawson, D.A. (2004). Nicotine dependence and psychiatric disorders in the United States: Results from the national epidemiologic survey on alcohol and related conditions. *Archives of General Psychiatry, 61,* 1107–1115.

Harrison, L.D. (1997). The validity of self-reported drug use in survey research: An overview and critique of research methods. In L. Harrison & A. Hughes (Eds.), *Validity of self-reported drug use: Improving the accuracy of survey estimates* (NIH Publication No. 97–4147, pp. 17–36). Rockville, MD: National Institute on Drug Abuse.

Helstrom, A., Bryan, A., Hutchison, K.E., Riggs, P.D., & Blechman, E.A. (2004). Tobacco and alcohol use as an explanation for the association between externalizing behavior and illicit drug use among delinquent adolescents. *Prevention Science, 5,* 267–277.

Hibell, B., Andersson, B., Bjarnason, T., Ahlstrom, S., Balakireva, O., Kokkevi, A., & Morgan, M. (2003). *The ESPAD Report 2003: Alcohol and other drug use among students in 35 European countries.* ESPAD.

Johnson, P.B. & Richter, L. (2002). The relationship between smoking, drinking, and adolescents' self-perceived health and frequency of hospitalization: Analyses from the 1997 National Household Survey of Drug Abuse. *Journal of Adolescent Health, 30,* 175–183.

Johnston, L., O'Malley, P.M., & Bachman, J.G. (2000). *Monitoring the Future: National results on adolescent drug use: Overview of key findings, 1999.* Rockville, MD: U.S. Department of Health and Human Services, Public Health Service, National Institute on Drug Abuse.

Johnston, L.D., O'Malley, P.M., & Bachman, J.G. (2002). *Monitoring the Future national survey results on adolescent drug use: Overview of key findings, 2001* (NIH Publication No. 02–5105). Bethesda, MD: National Institute on Drug Abuse.

Johnston, L.D., O'Malley, P.M., & Bachman, J.G. (2003). *Monitoring the Future national survey results on drug use, 1975–2002. Volume I: Secondary school students* (NIH Publication No. 03–5375). Bethesda, MD: National Institute on Drug Abuse.

Johnston, L.D., O'Malley, P.M., Bachman, J.G., & Schulenberg, J.E. (2004). *Monitoring the Future: National results on adolescent drug use: Overview of key findings, 2003* (NIH Publication No. 04–5506). Bethesda, MD: U.S. Department of Health and Human Services, Public Health Service, National Institute on Drug Abuse.

Johnston, L.D., O'Malley, P.M., Bachman, J.G., & Schulenberg, J.E. (2006). *Decline in daily smoking by younger teens has ended.* Ann Arbor, MI: University of Michigan News and Information Services. Retrieved from http://www.monitoring thefuture.org/

Johnston, L.D., O'Malley, P.M., Bachman, J.G., & Schulenberg, J.E. (2007). *Teen drug use continues down in 2006, particularly among older teens; but use of prescription-type drugs remains high* [Online]. Ann Arbor, MI: University of Michigan News and Information Services. Retrieved December 21, 2007, from http://www.monitoringthefuture.org/

Leshner, A. I. (2000). Director's Column: Addressing the medical consequences of drug abuse. *NIDA Notes, 15.*

Luthar, S. S. & D'Avanzo, K. (1999). Contextual factors in substance use: A study of suburban and inner-city adolescents. *Development and Psychopathology, 11,* 845–867.

Males, M. (2007, January 3). This is your brain on drugs, Dad. *New York Times.*

Mathews, J., Zollinger, T., Przybyiski, M., & Bull, M. (2001). The association between risk-taking behavior and the use of safety devices in adolescents. *Annual Proceedings of the Association for the Advancement of Automotive Medicine, 45,* 23–36.

Mendel, R. A. (2000). *Less hype, more help: Reducing juvenile crime, what works—and what doesn't.* Washington, DC: American Youth Policy Forum.

National Center for Chronic Disease Prevention and Health Promotion. (2006). *Tobacco use.* Retrieved from http://www.cdc.gov/HealthyYouth/tobacco/index.htm

National Center on Addiction and Substance Abuse [CASA]. (2000). *No place to hide: Substance abuse in mid-size cities and rural America.* Retrieved from http://www.casacolumbia.org/absolutenm/templates/Home.aspx

National Institute on Alcohol Abuse and Alcoholism [NIAAA]. (2000). *Prevention of alcohol-related problems among adolescents* (RFA: AA-01–001). Alexandria, VA: National Institutes of Health.

Office of Applied Studies. (2002). *Detailed tables for 2000 National Household Survey on Drug Abuse: Dependence, abuse, and treatment 5.1 to 5.66: Prevalence estimates.* Retrieved December 23, 2007, from http://www.drugabustatistics.samhsa.gov

Office of Applied Studies. (2004). *Overview of findings from the 2003 National Survey on Drug Use and Health* (NSDUH Series H-24, DHHS Publication No. SMA 04–3963). Rockville, MD. Retrieved December 23, 2007, from http://www.samhsa.gov/

Richter, L. & Johnson, P. B. (2001). Current methods of assessing substance use: A review of strengths, problems, and developments. *Journal of Drug Issues, 31,* 809–832.

Robert Wood Johnson Foundation. (2001). *Substance abuse: The nation's number one health problem.* Prepared by the Schneider Institute for Health Policy, Brandeis University.

Skager, R. (2000, March). *Reinventing drug prevention education for adolescents.* Paper presented at the New York Academy of Medicine Seminar, New York.

Spring, J. (2003). *American Education* (12th ed.). New York: McGraw-Hill.

Tourangeau, R. & Smith, T. W. (1996). Asking sensitive questions: The impact of data collection mode, question format, and question context. *Public Opinion Quarterly, 60,* 275–304.

United States Department of Health and Human Services [USDHHS]. (2001). *Youth violence: A report of the surgeon general* [Online]. Retrieved December 23, 2007, from http://www.surgeongeneral.gov/library/youth violence

United States Government Accountability Office [USGAO]. (2006). *ONDCP Media Campaign* [Online]. Retrieved December 23, 2007, from http://www.gao.gov/new.items/d06818.pdf

Weston, D. (1996). *Psychology: Mind, brain, and culture.* New York: John Wiley and Sons.

CHAPTER 3

Adolescent Gambling

Considered by many the greatest poker and gin rummy player of all time, Stuey "The Kid" Ungar's story as portrayed in *One of a Kind*, a biography, offers an extreme example of the forces that shape a gambler's life and the costs that lifestyle ultimately inflicts upon the individual. Ungar's father was a bookie and loan shark; his mother, an avid card player. He began playing cards as a child, moving on from competitive games like checkers and Monopoly. He had a gift for numbers and was a natural card player. Hyperactive and extremely bright, he became bored with school early on, never graduating from high school. Stuey was making a lot of money playing gin rummy by the time he was 14 years old, much of it in games sponsored by friends from a Genovese crime family. By 16 he was too good for anybody to want to play with him anymore. He turned to poker where he is reported to have won over $30 million in his relatively short life. In his later years, he became a drug addict. He was found dead and penniless in a cheap hotel at the age of 45. Stuey's life began and ended with gambling, the pastime that consumed his life before he turned to drugs. (Dalla & Alson, 2006)

As Stuey's sad and brief life attest, drug use and gambling often go hand in hand for many American adults and teens. In 2005, 53 percent of adult Americans played the lottery, 35 percent gambled in a casino, 18 percent played poker, 6 percent bet on a race, and 2 percent engaged in internet gambling according to the American Gaming Association. Despite these substantial numbers, gambling is frequently referred to as the "hidden addiction" (Griffiths, 2003). This designation may surprise anyone who has ever visited Las Vegas or Atlantic City. However, pathological gambling was first diagnosed as a mental health problem only in 1980. Pathological gambling is characterized by "a continuous or periodic loss of control over gambling, accompanied by a progression in gambling frequency and amounts wagered" (Cox, Lesieur, Rosenthal, & Volberg, 1997, p. 4).

Shortly after being legalized in the United States in 1978, gambling acquired the status of an addictive disorder.

Many researchers have highlighted the pervasiveness of gambling throughout this country and emphasized that our society not only condones gambling, it encourages it (Volberg, 2003). Evidence for this encouragement may be found in the increasing availability of casino gambling and the general deregulation of gambling by state and local governments. Some have suggested that these changes may have led to the apparent sharp increase in rates of adolescent gambling during the past two decades. Increasing availability of and exposure to gambling are represented by the growing number and variety of state lotteries, religious-group supported gambling activities such as bingo nights, as well as college-supported gambling (Deverensky, Gupta, Dickson, Kardoon, & Deguire, 2003). In each instance, sponsors have supported these activities to generate more income.

Before being legalized in the country as a whole, Nevada was the only state with legal casino gambling. However, as mentioned, gambling does not only occur in casinos. In 1963, New Hampshire began a state lottery program and many other states followed suit. At the end of 2007, there were only two states in the United States without some form of legalized gaming: Hawaii and Utah. This does not prevent individuals from gambling in those states, however; the sharp growth of internet gambling, along with the informal gambling that takes place amongst individuals and for the support of various organizations, makes gambling easily available to all adult Americans and the vast majority of American teens as well. Thus today's adolescents are one of the first generations of teens to grow up with widespread exposure to and opportunity for legal and illegal gambling. It can come as no surprise then that one in twenty college students experience difficulty with gambling (Student Affairs Leader, 2006).

Also not surprisingly, the acceptance of gambling as a legal activity for those over the age of 18 has made gaming activities big business. In 2002 the National Council on Problem Gambling reported that legalized gambling netted over $68.7 billion, or $68,700,000,000.

Gambling's pervasiveness in American society may explain in part why people, especially teenagers, find it difficult to see that gambling can take over a person's life. This proliferation was noted in the National Research Council's review (1999) of gambling research that was conducted at the request of the National Gambling Impact Study Commission. According to Potenza (2003), the past decade has witnessed an unprecedented increase in the availability of gambling opportunities for adults.

It is estimated that over 85 percent of adults in the United States have engaged in some form of gambling during their lives; 80 percent within the past year. In fact, Americans will spend more on legal gaming activities in a year than they will on most other forms of entertainment combined. However, not all individuals who engage in gambling go on to become pathological gamblers. Most individuals who engage in gambling activities do so as a game. Unfortunately, some become addicted to various forms of gambling as one would become addicted to drugs or alcohol.

As a disorder, pathological gambling is classified in the latest edition of the American Psychiatric Association's *Diagnostic and Statistical Manual of Mental Disorders, Fourth Edition (DSM-IV),* under the category of disorders of impulse-control. According to the *DSM-IV,* pathological gambling is a persistent and recurrent maladaptive gambling behavior that is indicated by five or more instances of specific diagnostic criteria (a list of these criteria follows shortly). Individuals with this impulse-control disorder continue to gamble despite harmful consequences for them and their families. Such gambling interferes with occupational pursuits and over-rides concerns for other major life activities including nutrition and sleep. The following textbox provides specific examples of problems frequently associated with chronic and pathological gambling.

SIGNS OF A GAMBLING PROBLEM

- Gambling until you lose all of your money
- Losing sleep because you can't stop thinking about gambling
- Using your savings to continue gambling
- Being unable to stop despite serious financial losses
- Borrowing money or breaking the law—often stealing—to continue gambling
- Feeling depressed or suicidal because of continued gambling
- Gambling to win money to meet your financial requirements

The National Council on Problem Gambling estimates that two to three percent of the adults in the United States will experience a gambling problem in any given year. Although these percentages seem small, in real numbers they translate to approximately six to nine million Americans annually, with consequences ranging from domestic violence to child endangerment, increased participation in crime, mood disorders, sub-stance use, and suicide. The following list presents the diagnostic criteria that the *DSM-IV* associates with pathological gambling.

Persistent and recurrent maladaptive gambling behavior is indicated by five (or more) of the following exhibited symptoms:

1. Is preoccupied with gambling (e.g., preoccupied with reliving past gambling experiences, handicapping or planning the next venture, or thinking of ways to get money with which to gamble)

2. Needs to gamble with increasing amounts of money in order to achieve the desired excitement

3. Has repeated unsuccessful efforts to control, cut back or stop gambling

4. Is restless or irritable when attempting to cut down or stop gambling

5. Gambles as a way of escaping from problems or of relieving a dysphoric mood (e.g., feelings of helplessness, guilt, anxiety, depression)

6. After losing money gambling, often returns another day to get even ("chasing" one's losses)

7. Lies to family members, therapist, or others to conceal the extent of involvement with gambling

8. Has committed illegal acts such as forgery, fraud, theft or embezzlement to finance gambling

9. Has jeopardized or lost a significant relationship, job, or educational or career opportunity because of gambling

10. Relies on others to provide money to relieve a desperate financial situation caused by gambling

Evidence of gambling's increasing popularity with teens can be found in the growing number of teens who select gambling as the theme for their Bar or Bat Mitzvah or "sweet sixteen" party. One of the authors of this book recently attended two such celebrations where 12- to 14-year-olds were introduced to black jack, craps, and poker by professional card dealers in an environment designed to precisely mimic casino gambling. Play money that was won could then be exchanged for prizes. While a good time appeared to be had by all, at least one guest remarked that the party served as a training exercise for future members of Gamblers Anonymous. What seemed particularly unusual was the extent to which the parents and adults at the gathering were unaware of the potential problems that might stem from such an early introduction to professional gambling activities.

Types of Teen Gambling

Gambling appears to start innocently enough: watching parents gamble, playing games of chance with friends and family, or by pitching quarters in a schoolyard. For many children these activities begin before they have reached their teen years. This is a point of concern for researchers and clinicians as investigations of problem gambling indicate that such behaviors emerge during childhood and adolescence (Gupta & Deverensky, 1998; Wynne, Smith, & Jacobs, 1996). One epidemiological study that took place in Florida found that the mean age of introduction to gambling was 12.5 years (Lazoritz, 2002), while the National Council on Problem Gambling cites other research indicating that almost half of the problem gamblers in this country began before the age of 10 years. In fact, studies of problem gamblers during treatment reveal that, for many, their involvement in gambling activities began by 8 years of age or earlier (National Research Council, 1999). (See also the information on Stuey Ungar at the beginning of this chapter).

However, for many teens the biggest problems begin in high school. Playing cards with friends for money, high school betting pools, and scratch-off cards at fast food restaurants are all ways that teens develop firsthand experience with gambling. Although these activities don't involve the violation of any laws, teens have penetrated all forms of gambling, including going to racetracks, using bookies to bet on sports or other events, and even going to casinos. For example, the Council on Compulsive Gambling in New Jersey reported that an Atlantic City casino received an $85,000 fine for allowing minors to gamble.

Card games and betting on sports are the most common forms of teen gambling. Poker has become increasingly popular in association with television programs such as Celebrity Poker and the Poker World Series. Sports betting has also grown along with the American obsession with college and professional sports, with teens and adults betting frequently on their favorite teams. There is also mounting anecdotal evidence suggesting that online gambling has increased greatly. In addition, it must also be emphasized that any teen with access to the internet has access and opportunity to gamble. As explanation for this increase, the Federal Trade Commission (FTC) indicates that children and adolescents have such easy access to opportunities for online gambling because age regulations are difficult or impossible to enforce on internet gambling sites. One reason for the proliferation of internet gambling is that many of the most popular web sites for teens contain advertisements for online gambling and/or direct links to online gambling sites. Teens with credit or debit cards may be especially vulnerable to becoming involved with such sites. Although many of these web sites are technically beyond U.S. legal jurisdiction as they are administered at sites operating outside of the country, the government has recently moved to control these sites.

In response to the growing concern about online gambling and its potential impact on teens and their families, the House of Representatives recently passed anti-gambling legislation by a vote of 317–93. The legislation was designed to crack down on internet gambling and was debated within the context of the 2005 indictment of Jack Abramoff in association with Indian casino payoffs. If the law were also to be passed by the Senate and signed by the president, it would become illegal for financial institutions to process any payments associated with offshore casinos, where most internet gambling occurs. The legislation would also increase criminal penalties associated with internet gambling.

In the debate that occurred before the House vote, much of the discussion focused on skyrocketing online betting that has quadrupled in recent years to almost $12 billion. The legislation's future in the Senate is unclear at present, although the United States Justice Department has consistently taken the position that online gambling is illegal.

It is interesting to note that in the House-passed legislation, exceptions were made for Powerball and other state-sponsored gambling. It also preserved state rights to regulate gambling in the form of lotteries and horse racing. In the same legislation, players of fantasy sports would not be allowed to bet on team wins or individual players but could bet on which player, for example, was going to break Joe DiMaggio's hit-streak record. Needless to say, the legislation would still allow plenty of gambling, but it might significantly curtail the growth of online or internet gambling.

In a possible follow-up to the passage of this legislation, federal agents recently arrested the chief executive of an extremely profitable online betting site of a British-owned company operating out of Costa Rica. He was arrested in Texas as he attempted to board a plane headed for Costa Rica. The executive and 10 others were charged with fraudulently taking bets from U.S. citizens by phone and by internet and with failure to pay excise taxes on the bets.

In 2007, two Canadian citizens were arrested by American authorities having been charged "with laundering billions of dollars in gambling proceeds" ("Two Charged," 2007). What is revealing about this case is that U.S. government officials once again demonstrated their willingness to go after people involved with internet gambling even when both "assets and defendants are positioned outside the United States."

Some believe that the passing of the legislation and subsequent arrests will have a major impact on reducing the spread of internet gambling. Others, however, are convinced that it will have little impact stopping the operation of offshore casinos and suggest that media attention associated with such activities will only enhance the popularity of gambling venues such as Las Vegas, Atlantic City, and the growing number of Indian casinos.

Because of the spread of teen online gambling, the chair of the Federal Trade Commission warned parents about the dangers of online gambling and of the need for parents to monitor their teens' internet habits. An informal web site survey conducted at the request of the FTC found that minors can and do access gambling web sites and are often exposed to ads for online gambling.

Rates of Teen Gambling

Unfortunately, rates of teen gambling have increased sharply over the past two decades. According to Potenza (2003), between 1987 and 1988 approximately 45 percent of teens reported having gambled in some form. Between 1998 and 1999, the percentage reporting having gambled increased to 66 percent, while the previously mentioned 1999 National Research Council report estimated that up to 80 percent of teenagers had gambled.

According to a number of sources, adolescents are about twice as likely to have engaged in problematic gambling as adults with pathological gambling estimates of teens ranging between 3.5 and 6 percent (Chevalier, Gupta, Martin, & Deverensky, 2005; Gupta & Deverensky, 1998). Other research suggests that somewhere between 4 and 8 percent of adolescents have experienced problems associated with their gambling activities (Griffiths, 1995). In absolute numbers, this suggests that as many as 2.2 million American teens have experienced some form of personal problem associated with gambling.

It also appears that teens are twice as likely as adults to have engaged in internet gambling. Some have highlighted the link between such gambling and the fantasy games so popular with teenagers as a potential source of this difference—one of the reasons that government officials have become increasingly interested in controlling and reducing access to computer games that so many children and teens enjoy. The parallel between computer games with flashy graphics and instant feedback and internet gambling, which employs similar techniques, may be particularly appealing to teens even if they have not previously viewed gambling by significant others in their immediate surroundings.

Factors Related to Teen Gambling

As is the case with most teen risk behaviors, gambling has been linked to other risk-taking behaviors. Gambling is established early and is related to other problems (Gupta & Deverensky, 1996). The National Council on Problem Gambling indicates that teens with a gambling problem are more likely to engage in unsafe sex, binge drinking, smoking marijuana, and skipping school. Studies have found that teens that gamble excessively experience substance use disorders (Wagner & Anthony, 2002), either consuming excessive amounts of alcohol or ingesting various illicit drugs, including marijuana and cocaine. Moreover, teen gamblers have been found to be more likely to do poorly academically and to be involved in petty crime such as stealing.

Male teens gamble more and are more likely to become involved in problem gambling than female teens (Stinchfield, Cassuto, Winters, & Latimer, 1997). In addition, gender differences have been identified in the types of games in which males and females become involved. While females are more likely to participate in bingo, scratch cards, lotteries, and other games of chance, males are more likely to engage in games of skill, such as poker and black jack (National Research Council, 1999;

Volberg, 2003). Males also appear to make larger bets and, in general, take more risks when they gamble than females. This, of course, increases their chances of getting into the financial difficulties associated with gambling.

SUPPORTING THE BINGO HABIT

While bingo may seem a particularly innocuous form of gambling, partly due to its frequent connection with church fund-raising activities, a recent story demonstrates the power bingo may exercise over a person's life. The story describes a grandmother who was arrested and convicted for possessing a trunk load of marijuana. It seems that she transported the drugs in order to obtain funds so that she could continue her addiction to bingo.

Some have argued that there may be a common pathway or cause of these various problems (Chambers & Potenza, 2003), but that the commonality may differ for males and females. For example, for males the common path between gambling and drug use has been linked to excitability or sensation seeking; for females, to depression (Gupta & Deverensky, 1998). What this suggests is that males who enjoy becoming involved in exciting activities are at increased risk of gambling and other teen risk behaviors, while females who are depressed are at risk of involvement in such behaviors.

It also seems that family factors are involved in the origins of teen gambling, because there is a clear link between parent and teen gambling (Wood & Griffiths, 1998). Statistics reveal that between 40 and 68 percent of teens gamble with family members. This could take the form of sports betting, in which a father and son wager when their favorite teams compete in football or baseball. According to the 1999 National Research Council report, gambling runs in families. Perhaps there is some form of indirect genetic link to gambling or to involvement in exciting behaviors. It might also be that teens become interested in gambling when they observe their parents engaging in gambling-related activities, including making bets online, hosting poker parties, or spending leisure time going to the racetrack or to Las Vegas.

Friends' gambling activities have also been associated with teen gambling rates. If a teen's friends are involved in gambling, the teens themselves are also likely to be involved (Griffiths, 1990, 1995). Consequently, however, when teens become heavily involved in gambling and focus more and more of their attention on acquiring funds to allow them to continue gambling, they may lose their friends. According to Deverensky and Gupta (2000), when friends are lost because of gambling, teens then substitute gambling associates for friends. With their increasing preoccupation with gambling, teens will spend increasing amounts of time planning their gambling activities, including lying and stealing to obtain funds to support these activities (Gupta & Deverensky, 2000).

While gender and peer factors have been associated with teen gambling, opportunity and motivation or interest in gambling may be equally, if not more, important. Not surprisingly, individuals who gamble in adolescence generally continue to do so into adulthood (Gupta & Deverensky, 1998). As previously indicated, family factors have an impact both on gambling opportunities and interest. Children growing up with parents who play cards and gamble at home may develop a greater interest in these activities than do children who never or rarely see such activities. Then, too, children in homes where parents gamble also have far greater access to cards, dice, and other elements of gambling.

Still other factors have been related to teenage gambling. For example, racial- and ethnic-minority teens and teens from poorer backgrounds have been found to be more involved in gambling (Stinchfield & Winters, 1998; Gupta & Deverensky, 1998). A study conducted by the Illinois state lottery commission found that individuals who earned less than $10,000 a year gamble six times more often than individuals who earn over $50,000 a year.

Consequences of Teen Gambling

While the negative consequences of some risk behaviors such as sexual intercourse may be obvious, for other behaviors including teen gambling, they are less so. According to a number of sources, however, teen gambling can inflict a great deal of damage well beyond the huge debt frequently incurred. Because it generates immense social, occupational, and personal health problems, adolescent gambling has been viewed as a public health problem. While family and peer disruptions are included among its greatest social costs, adolescent gambling can also lead to job loss and physical and mental health difficulties, including depression, physical disability associated with poor diet, and exhaustion, as an individual focuses exclusively on his or her gambling.

For example, in warning of the dangers associated with internet gambling, the Federal Trade Commission states that teen gambling has been associated with depression and disrupted social relations. Teen gamblers may lose their friends and develop strained relationships with their parents and siblings. Moreover, because gambling is often associated with criminal elements in society, teens who gamble may come in contact with organized crime and loan sharks only too willing to advance funds for gambling at astronomically-high interest rates. To procure the funds needed to continue gambling, teens may also engage in stealing, drug dealing, or prostitution.

A Note of Caution

Gambling is neither a simple nor a unitary disorder, but rather it is multifaceted. Because of this complexity, it is difficult to distinguish between social or normal gambling and pathological or abnormal gambling. Moreover, definitions may vary from adolescents to adults, which only adds to the complexity. While there may be a continuum from normal to abnormal gambling, it is difficult to determine the point at which the first kind stops and the other starts—where one actually steps over that obscure line.

Somewhat surprisingly, despite the dramatic growth in availability of and opportunity for gambling, there has been relatively little research conducted on adult or adolescent gambling. What work has been carried out has generally focused only on lottery scratch cards and slot machines.

In addition to the relative lack of research on adolescent gambling, a number of problems have also been identified in how gambling studies have been designed and conducted (Shaffer & Korn, 2002; Potenza, 2003). In fact, the main conclusion of the National Research Council's groundbreaking report on gambling was that after 20 years of research on gambling, "In all aspects of pathological gambling considered by the Committee, we found much of the extant research to be of limited value."

One example of these limitations can be found in the fact that different measures have been used to assess adolescent and adult gambling. Consequently, although the research indicates that a greater proportion of adolescents than adults gamble excessively or engage in pathological gambling that adversely affects their lives, the meaning of these differences are hard to interpret because the proportions were not generated by the same measures of gambling.

Then too, relatively little attention has been given to developing theories to explain the origins and progression of gambling among adolescents. In the absence of relevant theory, the research in the area has been largely descriptive in nature. In addition, studies of adolescent gambling can be characterized as snapshots of behavior rather than extended and ongoing pictures of it. To overcome this problem many researchers have called for longitudinal studies in which groups of adolescents would be studied over extended periods of time. Such studies are required to generate trend data that can inform us regarding ongoing changes in gambling behavior within the same adolescents (Volberg, 2003). Unfortunately, this type of research is extremely expensive which explains, in part, why such studies have not yet been systematically undertaken.

There has been some research that has investigated the association between personality traits, which are stable over time, and addiction. Specific research examining drug abuse and personality characteristics has concluded that the addictive personality precedes the addiction (Sharma, 1995). Also, research out of the International Center for Youth Gambling Problems and High-Risk Behavior has found that personality differences were able to distinguish teens with gambling problems from those without (Gupta, Deverensky, & Ellenbogen, 2006). Problem teen gamblers were found to score higher on scales that measure Excitability and Cheerfulness and lower on scales that measure Conformity, Self-Discipline, Intelligence, and Emotional Stability. The researchers concluded from this that teens with gambling problems exhibit fewer self-regulatory behaviors and instead exhibit behaviors such as impulsivity, distractibility, over-activity, self-indulgence, and difficulty conforming to group norms. Although much of the research in this area is tentative, it offers an appealing theory that many researchers and clinicians take seriously. It has been argued that a explanatory model of pathological gambling would need to include biological, personality, developmental, cognitive, and environmental factors (Blaszczynski, 2000), because each of these components has been frequently associated with the most extreme forms of gambling.

Prevention of Teen Gambling

According to Potenza (2003), adolescents simply do not understand the risks associated with gambling. This position is supported by an interview in which a teen suggested that, "Compared to what kids could be doing, it's [that is, gambling] relatively safe." In one sense, this may be true; it may be less dangerous to bet on sports than to shoot cocaine or snort heroin. On the other hand, gambling carries some serious consequences that teens need to recognize.

Potenza has argued that one way to combat teen ignorance about these consequences is to provide necessary knowledge about them, which may help to prevent teen gambling. Unfortunately, considerable research from the field of teen substance abuse prevention suggests that knowledge is not an effective prevention strategy—at least on its own. Generalizing from this work, it is highly unlikely that the mere presentation of information about the dangers of gambling will do much to keep teens from becoming involved with a behavior so frequently glamorized in the media.

Adolescents' attitudes toward gambling-related activities may be most strongly shaped by media advertising that highlights fun, glamour, excitement, and quick payoffs. To some, these activities share much in common with other popular teen activities including watching television, playing video games, and surfing the internet. In fact, television programs have recently given a great deal of attention to such poker games as Texas hold 'em and have enlisted movie and television celebrities to participate in games broadcast on network and/or cable television.

Moreover, much of the advertising for gambling can be found in contexts that are quite appealing to teens, such as clubs, bars, and casinos. In recent years, Las Vegas has sought to establish itself as a family vacation spot, and it is quite common for casinos to include arcades for children or other activities that appeal to children and teens including roller coasters, along with the gaming tables and slot machines (Stinchfield & Winters, 1998).

Some researchers have called for greater restriction on adolescent gambling because it has been argued that, similar to teen alcohol consumption, little can be done to change this illegal and dangerous behavior until greater restrictions and consequences are set in place. Unfortunately, for alcohol these calls have gone largely unheeded and little progress has been made in this direction (DeJong & Langford, 2002).

It is worth noting that the general lack of attention or concerted effort to control both teen gambling and drinking may arise, at least in part, from the fact that both are behaviors that adults engage in legally. It is also important to understand that both activities have extremely powerful lobbying forces and corporate sponsors in Washington that shower a great deal of money on U.S. Representatives and Senators. Because of this, it is often difficult to get both houses of Congress to pass strong legislation that would actually make an impact on the numbers of teens that become involved with alcohol and gambling.

While some would like to eliminate or restrict all gambling in the country, this seems a wildly unrealistic solution. At the same time, there is suggestive evidence that where serious safeguards are in place to restrict underage gambling, even in contexts where a great deal of gambling occurs, the restrictions may have a limiting function (Volberg, 2002). For example, while it would be reasonable to assume that more teen gambling would be found in Nevada, given the far greater opportunity there than in other states, actually, fewer Nevada teens report engaging in such activities (49 percent) than teens from other states (66 percent). Fewer Nevada teens report having gambled in casinos as well.

One possible explanation for this is the perception of harm created by the widely publicized sanctions that are present and enforced in Nevada. Then, too, Nevada also has made services widely available to its teenagers struggling with gambling, and this may be helpful in intervening in problem gambling once it starts.

It has been suggested, however, given the high proportion of teens that report having gambled and the relatively high rate of teen problem gamblers, that physicians should ask questions of teens during annual checkups to determine the likely presence of problem gambling (Grant, Kim, & Potenza, 2002). This type of thinking is in line with the view that gambling is an addiction and should be considered as such. Although pathological gambling is classified in the *DSM-IV* as a disorder of impulse-control, some clinicians and researchers question this thinking and believe that it belongs to the category of addictive disorders (Kim, Grant, Eckert, Faris, & Hartman, 2006).

Findings support a common neurobiological pathway in pathological gambling and other addictive disorders, indicating that pathological gambling is a chronic relapsing brain disease. Specific evidence comes from an investigation that found that 50 percent of pathological gamblers carried a gene receptor variant common in other addictions (Comings, Gade-Andavolu, Gonzalez, Wu, et. al., 2001). While attempts to identify biological forces underlying various addictions have been around for some time, the reader should be careful not to assume that simply because some biological marker has been found to be associated with gambling or any other addiction, that therefore it must be the cause of this behavior. Such thinking is often referred to as biological reductionism because it attempts to explain extremely complicated human behaviors by using simple, single causes.

Intervention for Teen Gambling

There are several prevailing strategies that clinicians and educators use to intervene in cases of pathological gambling. Although research into the effectiveness of these treatments is sparse and pertains to adult populations, mounting evidence indicates that there are viable options for those seeking help. Two of the most prevalent options include pharmacotherapy and cognitive-behavioral treatments.

One set of pharmacological or medication-based treatments has largely focused on the use of a class of antidepressants known as Selective Serotonin Reuptake Inhibitors (SSRI). Research studies that have investigated the use of antidepressants in the treatment of pathological gambling have excluded subjects who also exhibited a mood disorder (either depression or bipolar symptoms). Thus conducted, the investigations were able to isolate the effects of the antidepressants on gambling, without relation to mood, suggesting that improvement in pathological gambling symptoms was not due to the improvement of a mood disorder (Kim & Grant, 2001). Additionally, as mood disorders frequently exist concurrently with gambling problems, other investigations have looked at the use of mood stabilizers for treatment. Findings indicate improvement in symptoms in short-term efficacy investigations with adults (Hollander, Sood, Pallanti, Baldini-Rossi, & Baker, 2005).

Another avenue of pharmacological treatment involves the use of a class of medications known as opiate antagonists, two of which go by the names naltrexone and nalmefene. This class of medications has been approved to treat other addictive disorders such as alcoholism and drug dependency. Investigations found that this class of drugs gave superior results over a placebo in controlling gambling symptoms (Kim & Grant, 2001; Grant & Potenza, 2005). The basis for this avenue of treatment is that pathological gambling is an addiction disorder, and those drugs known to counter other addiction disorders may also effectively fight this disorder.

Although there is mounting evidence to suggest a neurobiological basis for the most severe gambling problems and some individuals are helped with opiate antagonists (Perkinson, 2007), it is unwise to ignore the host of social and contextual variables that are often associated with teen gambling. It also is premature to assume that all problems can be solved through biochemical intervention, without any personal effort or motivation. As such, there are cognitive-behavioral interventions for the treatment of pathological gambling. Interventions based on a cognitive-behavioral perspective operate from the position that gamblers hold erroneous beliefs in regard to the outcome of the game. In other words, they fail to understand the random or uncontrollable aspect of games of chance. Research has shown that pathological gamblers verbalize and believe gambling-related misperceptions more than do gamblers who do not have a pathological problem (Ladouceur, 2004); following are provided some examples of such beliefs and perceptions. Thus cognitive-behavioral interventions that attempt to change the erroneous beliefs of problem gamblers may be particularly helpful with such individuals.

1. The gambler's fallacy—the belief that completely random events, such as the outcome of flipping a coin, are influenced by recent events: "I first flipped heads so I believe that I am less likely to get heads on the next flip." Because each flip of the coin is an independent event unaffected by previous events, this type of belief is referred to as the gambler's fallacy. "I keep losing money in the slot machine so my chances of winning should be increasing." Unfortunately, each outcome on a slot machine is wholly random and independent, so one does not influence the next.

2. According to Sundali (2006), the hot outcome is the opposite of the gambler's fallacy, in which people believe that "since the color red keeps winning in roulette, it is likely to keep appearing"—they think that the outcome is somehow hot and consequently likely to continuing appearing. Notice, in both of the distorted beliefs, how supposedly random and independent events are supposed to operate.

3. In contrast, there are also distortions in which positive and negative gambling outcomes are attributed to the player, rather than to the workings of chance. For example, the frequently-seen hot hand belief dictates that good outcomes are somehow the result of the individual player—the person throwing the dice in craps who obtains multiple passes somehow has the "hot hand." Opposed to this belief is the "stock of luck" belief, in which individuals are believed to possess only a certain amount of luck so that "if you have won repeatedly, you're likely to run out of luck pretty soon."

4. In addition, research has shown that people who gamble are likely to overestimate their "skill" level. Although the outcomes are

largely governed by chance, when people bet and win, they are likely to have an increased feeling that they are skilled at this particular game. People also overestimate their abilities to predict the outcomes of sporting events, according to research (Sundali, 2006).

Cognitive-behavioral treatments generally take one of two approaches—either they follow a policy of total abstinence, or they work from a perspective known as harm reduction, which aims at controlled gambling. The abstinence-only philosophy can be traced to such movements as Gamblers Anonymous, which is based on the 12-step program of Alcoholics Anonymous. For many, the abstinence-only model is the only viable treatment outcome goal because the individuals who embrace this perspective are working from a disease model of illness. For these individuals, pathological gambling is a disease residing within the individual that can only be controlled by refraining from all forms of gambling. For some individuals with severe gambling disorders, this may be the best course of treatment. However, as only 10 percent of pathological gamblers seek treatment and 30 percent of those who seek treatment drop out (Ladouceur, Gosselin, Laberge, & Blaszczynski, 2001), it may be wise to consider a harm reduction model.

There is some research from the addiction field indicating there is merit to a harm reduction perspective (Ladouceur, 2005). Programs that promote the reduction of a socially-sanctioned behavior rather than its elimination offer an alternative to individuals who do not believe in their ability to totally quit. Research that derives from work on controlled drinking indicates that there are four conditions associated with successful controlled drinking—less-severe drinking symptoms, younger age, regular employment, and less contact with Alcoholics Anonymous, an abstinence-only organization (Heather & Robertson, 1986). Although there have been no empirical investigations on a harm reduction perspective for problem gambling, clinical case studies of adults suggest that this may be a viable alternative. In addition, as three of the four conditions suggested for controlled drinking would also be present in teen gamblers—younger age, less-severe symptoms, and less contact with an association that promoted an abstinence-only approach (e.g., Gamblers Anonymous)—a harm reduction model might be well suited for teen gamblers.

Little is known about the effectiveness of school-based gambling-prevention or intervention programs. This is probably because the vast majority of addiction-focused school programs that have been developed relate to drug (including alcohol and tobacco) abuse, or to violence prevention. In fact, many books on school-based prevention of risk behaviors fail to even mention teen gambling. However, due to increased awareness in the research and clinical communities, some states have developed or are considering developing gambling-prevention programs. Indiana is one state that has implemented a gambling-prevention course into its already established after-school programs on drug and alcohol abuse. Indiana's programs enroll approximately 14,000 students aged 10–14 each year. In this new course on gambling prevention, topics such as recognizing addiction and the odds of winning will hopefully help combat the growing national problem (Leinwand, 2006).

Other states, such as Oregon, are investigating the integration of gambling-prevention curriculum into already extensive programs for drug and alcohol prevention (Student Affairs Leader, 2006). In addition, college campuses throughout Oregon are being offered a variety of prevention options to combat the growing problem of gambling in college settings. Surveys of colleges across the country suggest that while almost all colleges have drug and alcohol policies, only 25 percent of colleges have a policy on gambling. It is noted that a harm reduction perspective is most appealing in regard to educational curriculum developed for gambling. One effort in place to raise awareness of the problem across the country is a campaign called National Problem Gambling Awareness Week (http://www.npgaw.org/). This campaign hopes to raise awareness, provide resources for where to get help, and educate individuals on responsible gambling.

As with so many other risk behaviors, including drug and sexual experimentation, it is important to keep in mind that teen gambling is normative in that the majority of teens have been involved with it in one form or another. As a result, it is probably unrealistic to believe that we will ever be able to prevent it from occurring. What we may need to do instead is to try to help teens avoid the most serious consequences associated with problem or pathological gambling.

Problem Gambling Resources

The Addiction Technology Transfer Center (ATTC) Network—Dedicated to identifying and advancing opportunities for improving addiction treatment, including gambling addiction
http://www.nattc.org/index.html

The California Council on Problem Gambling—A nonprofit organization dedicated to assisting problem gamblers and their families
http://www.calproblemgambling.org/

Compulsive Gambling Treatment Program—Connecticut Valley Hospital, Middletown, CT
860–344–2244

Gam-Anon.org—Support for family and friends
http://www.gam-anon.org/

Gamblers Anonymous
800–266–1908
http://www.gamblersanonymous.org

The Gambling Clinic at the University of Memphis
http://thegamblingclinic.memphis.edu

The Gambling Disorders Clinic—New York, New York
212–543–6690 OR 212–543–5367

The National Council on Problem Gambling—Information on state affili-
ates and information for treatment
http://www.ncpgambling.org

National Problem Gambling Awareness—24-hour confidential national
helpline
800–322–4700

National Problem Gambling Awareness Week
http://www.npgaw.org/

The New York Council on Problem Gambling—A not-for-profit independent corporation
http://www.nyproblemgambling.org/

Problem Gambling Helpline—24 hours a day for gamblers and their
families in Connecticut, Massachusetts, and Rhode Island
800–346–6238

The Problem Gambling Prevention Program of Saratoga County, NY
http://www.preventioncouncil.org/

Safe Harbor Compulsive Gambling Hub—A site for conversation with
peers about gambling addiction
http://www.sfcghub.com

Want to Stop Gambling—Service for problem gamblers
http://www.wanttostopgambling.com/

Works Cited

American Psychiatric Association. (1994). *Diagnostic and statistical manual of mental
    disorders* (4th ed.). Washington, DC: Author.
Blaszczynski, A. (2000). Pathways to pathological gambling: Identifying typolo-
    gies. *E-Gambling: The Electronic Journal of Gambling Issues, 1*, 1–11.

Chambers, R. A. & Potenza, M. N. (2003). Neurodevelopment, impulsivity and adolescent gambling. *Journal of Gambling Studies, 19*, 55–89.

Chevalier, S., Gupta, R., Martin, I., & Deverensky, J. (2005). Jeux de hazard et d'argent. In G. Dube (Ed.), *Enquete quebecoise sur le tabagisme chez les eleves du secondaire* (pp. 131–146). Quebec, Canada: Institut de la Statistique du Quebec.

Comings, D. E., Gade-Andavolu, R., Gonzalez, N., Wu, S., et al. (2001). The additive effect of neurotransmitter genes in pathological gambling. *Clinical Genetics, 60*, 107–116.

Cox, S., Lesieur, H. R., Rosenthal, R. J, & Volberg, R. A. (1997). *Problem and pathological gambling in America: The national picture.* Columbia, MD: National Council on Problem Gambling.

Dalla, N. & Alson, P. (2006). *One of a kind: The rise and fall of Stuey "The Kid" Ungar, the world's greatest poker player.* New York: Atria Books.

DeJong, W. & Langford, L. M. (2002). A typology for campus-based alcohol prevention: Moving toward environmental management strategies.*Journal of Studies on Alcohol, S14*, 140–147.

Deverensky, J. L. & Gupta, R. (2000). Youth gambling: A clinical and research perspective. *E-Gambling: The Electronic Journal of Gambling Issues, 2*, 1–11.

Deverensky, J. L., Gupta, R., Dickson, L., Kardoon, K., & Deguire, A. (2003). Understanding youth gambling problems: A conceptual framework. In D. Romer (Ed.), *Reducing adolescent risk: An integrated approach* (pp. 239–246). Thousand Oaks, CA: Sage Publications.

Grant, J. E., Kim W. W., & Potenza, M. N. (2003). Advances in the pharmacological treatment of pathological gambling disorder. *Journal of Gambling Studies, 19*, 85–109.

Grant, J. E. & Potenza, M. N. (2005). Tobacco use and pathological gambling. *Annals of Clinical Psychiatry, 17*, 237–241.

Griffiths, M. D. (1990). The acquisition, development, and maintenance of fruit machine gambling in adolescents. *Journal of Gambling Studies, 6*, 193–204.

Griffiths, M. (1995). *Adolescent gambling.* London: Routledge.

Griffiths, M. (2003). Adolescent gambling: Risk factors and implications for prevention, intervention, and treatment. In D. Romer (Ed.), *Reducing adolescent risk: An integrated approach* (pp. 223–238). Thousand Oaks, CA: Sage Publications.

Gupta, R. & Deverensky, J. (1996). The relationship between video game playing and gambling behavior in children and adolescents. *Journal of Gambling Studies, 12*, 375–394.

Gupta, R. & Deverensky, J. (1998). Familial and social influences on juvenile gambling. *Journal of Gambling Studies, 13*, 179–192.

Gupta, R. & Deverensky, J. (2000). Adolescents with gambling problems: From research to treatment. *Journal of Gambling Studies, 16*, 315–342.

Gupta, R., Deverensky, J. L., & Ellenbogen, S. (2006). Personality characteristics and risk-taking tendencies among adolescent gamblers [Electronic Version]. *Canadian Journal of Behavioural Science, 38*, 201–213.

Heather, N. & Robertson, I. (1986). Why is abstinence necessary for the recovery of some problem drinkers? *British Journal of Addictions, 25*, 19–34.

Hollander, E., Sood, E., Pallanti, S., Baldini-Rossi, N., & Baker, B. (2005). Pharmacological treatments of pathological gambling. *Journal of Gambling Studies, 21,* 99–108.

Kim, S.W. & Grant, J.E. (2001). Psychopharmacology of pathological gambling. *Seminar on Clinical Neuropsychiatry, 6,* 184–194.

Kim, S.W., Grant, J.E., Eckert, E.D., Faris, P.L., & Hartman, B.K. (2006). Pathological gambling and mood disorders: Clinical associations and treatment implications. *Journal of Affective Disorders, 92,* 109–116.

Ladouceur, R. (2004). Perceptions among pathological and non-pathological gamblers. *Addictive Behaviors, 29,* 555–565.

Ladouceur, R. (2005). Controlled gambling for pathological gamblers. *Journal of Gambling Studies, 21,* 51–59.

Ladouceur, R., Gosselin, P., Laberge, M., & Blaszczynski, A. (2001). Dropouts in clinical research: Do results reported in the field of addiction reflect clinical reality? *The Behavior Therapist, 24,* 44–46.

Lazoritz, M. (2002, October). *Teen gambling: Evidence from the University of Florida's statewide epidemiological study.* Paper presented at the American Academy of Child and Adolescent Psychiatry's 49th Annual Meeting, San Francisco, CA.

Leinwand, D. (2006, September 7). Indiana moves to fight youth gambling addictions. *USA Today.* Retrieved November 8, 2006, from Academic Search Premier.

National Council on Problem Gambling. Retrieved from http://www.ncpgambling.org

National Research Council. (1999). *Pathological gambling: A critical review.* Washington, DC: National Academy Press.

Perkinson, R. (2007). *Teenage Gambling* by Robert R. Perkinson, Ph.D. Retrieved January 4, 2007, from http://www.robertperkinson.com/teen_gambling.htm

Potenza, M.N. (2003). A perspective on adolescent gambling: Relationship to other risk behaviors and implications for prevention strategies. In D. Romer (Ed.), *Reducing adolescent risk: An integrated approach* (pp. 247–255). Thousand Oaks, CA: Sage Publications.

Shaffer, H.J. & Korn, D. (2002). Gambling and related mental disorders: A public health analysis. *Annual Review of Public Health, 23,* 171–212.

Sharma, O.P. (1995). The dilemma of addictive personality and resolvability of drug dependence. *Journal of Indian Psychology, 13,* 47–50.

Stinchfield, R., Cassuto, N., Winters, K., & Latimer, W. (1997). Prevalence of gambling among Minnesota public school students in 1992 and 1995. *Journal of Gambling Studies, 13,* 25–48.

Stinchfield, R.E. & Winters, K.C. (1998). Gambling and problem gambling among youths. *Annals of the American Academy of Political and Social Science, 556,* 172–185.

Student Affairs Leader. (2006). *Key elements of problem gambling prevention programs,* 34(11) [Brochure]. Retrieved from http://www.studentaffairs.com

Sundali, J. (2006). Biases in casino betting: The hot hand and the gambler's fallacy. *Judgment and Decision Making, 1,* 1–12.

Two charged in payments from wagers on internet. (2007, January 12).*New York Times.*

Volberg, R.A. (2002). *Gambling and problem gambling among adolescents in Nevada.* Carson City, NV: Department of Human Resources. Retrieved May 18, 2007, from http://hr.stat.nv.us/directions/gamblingamongadolescents-Nevada.pdf

Volberg, R.A. (2003). Why pay attention to adolescent gambling? In D. Romer (Ed.), *Reducing adolescent risk: An integrated approach* (pp. 256–261). Thousand Oaks, CA: Sage Publications.

Wagner, F.A. & Anthony, J.C. (2002). From first drug use to drug dependence: Developmental periods of risk for dependence upon marijuana, cocaine, and alcohol. *Neuropsycholopharmacology, 26,* 479–488.

Wood, R.T.A. & Griffiths, M. (1998). The acquisition, development, and maintenance of lottery and scratchcard gambling in adolescence. *Journal of Adolescence, 21,* 265–272.

Wynne, H., Smith, G., & Jacobs, D.F. (1996). *Adolescent gambling and problem gambling in Alberta.* Edmonton, Alberta, Canada: Alberta Drug and Alcohol Commission.

CHAPTER 4

Adolescent Sex

Oral sex has become an extension of what teens call "making out" or "hooking up" as for most teens it is not considered sex. Adolescents do not talk about the progression of sexual acts in the way most adults are accustomed to, with the analogy of baseball bases. While traditionally kissing may have been first base, and feeling a girl's breasts indicated a move to second base, currently kissing, touching, and a girl performing fellatio on a guy are all parts of what is normally called hooking up. In fact, in many instances a hook-up may forgo kissing altogether, as kissing for many is considered too intimate.

Along with hunger, thirst, and pain avoidance, sex is a basic human drive. Without it, humans would not reproduce themselves and we'd become extinct. Consequently, it is hardly surprising that members of our species, including young people, possess an innate curiosity about sexual reproduction and sexual activity and the body parts associated with both. In adolescence this curiosity increases tremendously, at least in part because of the maturing of male and female sexual organs with the onset of puberty. Today, this increase may also occur because of exposure to mass media messages emphasizing the importance of sex and frequently equating sex with having a good time.

In earlier times, this interest and the sexual exploration associated with it were often considered normal, though dangerous. Females were considered more in danger than males because of the possibility of unwanted pregnancy and also because of the negative social consequences associated with a female who engaged in such exploration too frequently, with too many partners, or with an inappropriate partner—the "Scarlet Letter" phenomenon. More recently, however, concern with adolescent sexual exploration and experimentation has increased in many parts of American society because of far more dangerous consequences than pregnancy and social condemnation. Adolescent sexual behavior today is associated with a host of risks that range from contracting sexually transmitted diseases through death.

While sexually transmitted diseases such as herpes, gonorrhea, and syphilis have contributed to this concern, the emergence of HIV-AIDS in the 1990s and its links to various forms of sexual activity greatly increased the danger of teenage sex. This is both because HIV-AIDS is a deadly disease transmitted through sexual intercourse and other sexual acts, including various types of oral and anal sexual activity, and also because there is still no known cure for the deadly virus.

Consequently, prohibitions against teen sexual activity have grown many times over the past 15 years. The remainder of this chapter highlights some recent findings regarding the nature and extent of teen sexual behavior and the likelihood that that behavior will lead to various unwanted and sometimes dangerous consequences. The chapter also covers the programs that have been developed to prevent teen sex or to stop it once it starts.

A Note of Caution

Before summarizing some of the findings on teen sexual activity, it is extremely important to emphasize the difficulties involved in obtaining accurate information on this highly sensitive human behavior. While it would be comforting to believe that teens answer study questions honestly when asked whether they have previously engaged in sexual intercourse and if so, how often, a more realistic assessment would force us to assume that many teens are not honest when they respond to these types of questions.

It is hardly surprising that the validity or truthfulness of such self-report measures has been widely debated for many years by researchers in the field (e.g., Babor & Del Boca, 1992; Ericcson & Simon, 1980; Nisbett & Wilson, 1977). Of course, this issue was dealt with at some length in the previous chapter on adolescent substance abuse. As a result, we only address it briefly here.

Even when properly assured that their responses will be protected and not shared, young respondents may not fully believe that their responses will remain completely anonymous or confidential. If adolescents believe that their responses may be seen by others and identified as their own, the accuracy of the responses is called into question.

Systematic response distortion can arise from individual characteristics, primarily self-presentation concerns. For example, in studies of sexual behavior, there is typically a large gender discrepancy in respondents' reports of the number of sexual partners they have had (Centers for Disease Control and Prevention, 2002; Corwyn, 1999; Smith, 1992) with males reporting having had more sexual partners than females. The gender discrepancy may very well be due to male over-reporting and female under-reporting the nature of their sexual encounters rather than due to actual differences in numbers of partners. That is, self-presentation concerns may contribute to this response pattern, such that males over-report to avoid appearing sexually inadequate while females under-report to avoid appearing promiscuous. Indeed, Tourangeau and Smith (1996) found that when sensitive behaviors, such as those related to numbers of sexual partners, were assessed using an audio computer-assisted self-interview (ACASI), a more anonymous method of obtaining self-reports of behavior than paper and pencil self-interviews or face-to-face interviews, the gender discrepancy was sharply reduced. That is, use of ACASI appeared to reduce the number of female partners that males self-reported and increase the number of male partners that females self-reported, probably tapping into more accurate responses than participants were willing to give using traditional self-report methods.

A study by Rosenbaum (2006) also highlighted the problems associated with self-report studies of adolescent sexual activity. In this study, teens were asked on two separate occasions, a year apart, about their sexual activity and whether or not they had ever taken a virginity pledge. In the second survey, over half of the students who had reported in the first survey that they had taken a virginity pledge now denied ever having done so. Those who reported having sex for the first time on the second survey were more than three times as likely to deny ever having taken a virginity pledge. A *New York Times* article summarizing this research suggested that "the study raises questions about how much reliance should be placed on surveys about sexual activity among teenagers, and how accurately experts can measure the results of programs that encourage them to abstain from sex to avoid pregnancy and sexually transmitted disease" (Nagourney, 2006, p. 10).

In addition, we must confront the dual issues of how researchers interpret adolescent responses and how adolescents, in turn, interpret the questions put to them. Since condoms need to be used 100 percent of the time to prevent pregnancy and disease transmission, researchers often only include in the condom-use category those teens who report that they always use condoms during sexual intercourse (DiClemente, Lodico, et al., 1996). Not surprisingly, however, other researchers have observed that the term "always" is variously interpreted by different teens to mean never, sometimes, or every-time use of condoms. Such interpretive problems certainly make it still more difficult to understand what teens mean when they respond to sensitive questions about their sexual activity on self-reported questionnaires. With these cautions in mind, we now summarize some of the major findings on teen sexual activity.

Teen Sexual Practices

Many obstacles exist in regard to obtaining information about the sexual practices of adolescents. The primary difficulty lies with the inability to define what constitutes sexual behavior. For many individuals who have come of age during or after the Bill Clinton presidency and the Monica Lewinsky scandal, oral sex does not necessarily represent a form of sexual relations. As a result it is no wonder that many of today's youth possess far less clear guidelines regarding what does and does not constitute sexual behavior. The ambiguity surrounding sexual practices amongst teens can be seen in the growing numbers of teens who engage in oral sex (Remez, 2000). Oral sex has become a popular way for teens to engage in what is often considered safe sex because there is no fear of pregnancy.

A Kaiser Family Foundation report published in 2003 indicated that 46 percent of the respondents felt that oral sex was not as intimate as sexual intercourse. With that belief it is no wonder that results from the same study found that 38 percent of 15- to 17-year-olds reported having engaged in oral sex. The commonality of this practice is especially risky for this group since 19 percent of those 15- to 17-year-olds also did not know that sexually transmitted diseases, or STDs, could be spread through oral sex.

In addition, although anecdotal evidence from teenage girls may suggest that there is mutual gratification in oral sex, other research indicates that for the most part it is girls who are performing oral sex on guys. The emotional cost of oral sex for girls notwithstanding, the health costs can be great. Most teenagers report that they do not use condoms for oral sex; that condoms are only utilized for "sex," which traditionally means intercourse. However, figures from the Centers for Disease Control state that in 2000, 48 percent of new cases of sexually transmitted diseases occurred within the age group of 15- to 24-year-olds. Additionally, girls 15–19 have the highest reported incidence of both gonorrhea and chlamydia.

Furthermore, oral sex has become an extension of what teens call "making out" or "hooking up" as for most teens it is not considered sex. Adolescents do not talk about the progression of sexual acts in the way most adults are accustomed to, with the analogy of baseball bases. While traditionally kissing may have been first base, and feeling a girl's breasts indicated a move to second base, currently kissing, touching, and a girl performing fellatio on a guy are all parts of what is normally called hooking up. In fact, in many instances a hook-up may forgo kissing altogether, as kissing for many is considered too intimate. A hook-up for a teenager is a one-time encounter, between two individuals who may know each other casually or who have just met. The act of hooking up is unemotional and there is no expectation of developing a relationship. Teenagers may hook up at parties or at mutual friends' homes, and frequently there is alcohol involved (Paul, 2002).

Another aspect of hooking up that has recently gathered attention in the popular media is the emergence of "friends with benefits" (Denizet-Lewis, 2004). As more adolescents spend time hanging out in mixed-gender groups, either in person or on the internet, some of these friendships naturally become charged with sexual tension. However, for many teenagers the notion of a romantic relationship seems old-fashioned. Although most adolescents believe that one day in 10 or 15 years they will meet someone special and settle into marriage, for the present they want to engage in intimate relationships with people they feel close to but to whom they are not tied down. Thus, a friend with benefits is someone that a teen may repeatedly hook up with.

Even within this type of relationship there are many variations. For some adolescents, the person they repeatedly hook up with is also a person that they hang out with regularly—someone whose company they enjoy—while for others the friend with benefits may be someone that they just get together with for sexual purposes. However, despite the open approach to sex that adolescents seem to convey, there is still the potential for hurt. Most experts on adolescent sexuality insist that not all individuals can compartmentalize their feelings as required for a hook-up or a friend-with-benefits situation to work. In addition, girls will sometimes use a hook-up as a way to get more serious with a guy, although this route often backfires today as it did for the previous generations (Hughes, Morrison, & Asada, 2005).

In addition to the lack of guidelines as to what constitutes sexual activity, there is also growing acceptance amongst teens regarding alternative sexual orientations. In 1999 the Kaiser Family Foundation reported that 54 percent of adolescents indicated that they had no problem with homosexuality. The depiction of gay characters in the media has added to the acceptance of gay, lesbian, bisexual, and transgender individuals in popular culture (Hoff & Greene, 2000). In 2003 the United States Supreme Court made the sexual encounters of this group of alternative-lifestyle individuals legal with the eradication of anti-sodomy laws that had prohibited sexual acts associated with anal penetration. Increasingly teens accept that the exploration of sexuality will include encounters with individuals of the same sex. In fact, the 2001 Kaiser Family Foundation report indicated that 15 percent of teens had had a same-sex sexual encounter (Hoff, Greene, & Davis, 2003).

These and other changes in teen sexual behavior clearly demonstrate that teens today hold very different attitudes about the nature and appropriateness of specific sexual behaviors than their parents—and because of this, it is important for parents and teachers to be aware of these differences. Without such knowledge a parent might interpret a child's sexual attitudes and behaviors as evidence of pathology and deviance, when in fact the child is actually comfortable within current, mainstream teen thinking and actions about sex. While parents may not like or support a child's beliefs or behaviors, it is essential that they understand that the child may not be statistically aberrant, but normal for this generation and the child's peer group.

Rates of Teen Sexual Intercourse

In 2001, 46 percent of high school students reported having engaged in sexual intercourse in the past year. The rates increased with grade level, with 34 percent of ninth graders and 61 percent of twelfth graders reporting having sex (Grunbaum et al., 2002). Research also suggests that most teens who report having sex during a specific time frame indicate having done so with only one partner (Moore, Driscoll, & Lindberg, 1998).

Recently-released findings from the annual Youth Risk Behavior Survey, or YRBS, conducted by the Centers for Disease Control and Prevention (CDC) indicated that 46.8 percent of American students reported having engaged in sexual intercourse at some time in their lives (National Center for Chronic Disease Prevention and Health Promotion, 2007). The findings from this study are important because of the extensiveness of the data collected in these annual surveys and the trends that can be observed by comparing findings from one year to the next.

Although comparative findings from 1991 to 2005 revealed reductions in the percentage of students reporting ever having had sexual intercourse, from 54.1 percent to 46.8 percent, data reported in the *New York Times* in December 2007 indicates that teenage sex is on the rise. Rates of sexual intercourse rose three percent per thousand for adolescents 15–17 years old, four percent for 18- to 19-year-olds, and declined slightly in adolescents 14 and younger. This is particularly disturbing as the same article reported that condom use has declined since 2003. Not surprisingly, with the increase in sexual intercourse and the decrease in condom usage, rates of sexually transmitted diseases and teenage pregnancy rates are on the rise.

A number of other findings were presented in the 2006 CDC report. For example, results revealed clear racial/ethnic differences in lifetime rates of sexual intercourse, with self-reported rates higher from African American youth (67.6 percent) than Hispanic (51 percent) or White youth (43.0 percent). The reported group differences were even more exaggerated among males, as 74.6 percent of African American males reported that they had engaged in sexual intercourse, compared with 57.6 percent of Hispanic males and 42.2 percent of White males.

The same survey also examined other behaviors that would place adolescents at greater risk for becoming infected with various sexually transmitted diseases. Included among these behaviors were engaging in sexual intercourse before 13 years of age and having engaged in sexual intercourse with four or more partners. Across the nation, 6.2 percent of students reported having had sex before they were 13 years old. Males were more likely than females to report such early sexual behavior (8.8 percent versus 3.7 percent). Again, racial/ethnic differences were apparent, as 16.5 percent of African Americans, 7.3 percent of Hispanics, and 4.0 percent of Whites reported early sexual intercourse.

With respect to multiple partners, YRBS findings indicated that 14.3 percent of American students reported having had sexual intercourse with four or more partners in their lives. Once again, this was more likely to be the case among male (16.5 percent) than female (12.0 percent) students and more likely among African American (28.2 percent) than Hispanic (15.9 percent) and White (11.4 percent) students.

In considering these racial/ethnic group differences, we believe that it is important to bear in mind that these findings are based upon self-reported behavior. As discussed above, previous studies have emphasized that systematic distortions may produce group differences in sensitive behaviors, including sexual activity, where one group (males, for example) wants to exaggerate a particular behavior and another group (females) wants to minimize it. Such distortions may have something to do with the above-mentioned gender and racial/ethnic group differences as some groups may wish to appear less involved with sexual activity while others wish to appear more involved.

There is also the commonly-held belief that urban adolescents engage in promiscuous sex more frequently than suburban teens. A report conducted by the National Institute of Child Health and Human Development (2004) found this belief to be false. Findings from this study showed that twelfth graders from the suburbs engaged in sex outside of a romantic relationship 43 percent of the time as compared to urban teens who engaged in uncommitted sex 39 percent of the time. Another study conducted by Longmore, Manning, and Giordana (2006) reported that 55 percent of local eleventh graders had reported having intercourse and that 60 percent of those respondents reported having intercourse with an individual who was no more than a friend.

Rates of Teen Pregnancy

Regarding rates of teen pregnancy, research from the 1990s indicated that among women between 14 and 19 years of age there was a 9.4 percent chance of becoming pregnant (Ventura, Mosher, Curtin, Abma, & Henshaw, 2001). It is interesting to note that this rate far exceeds that found in industrialized European nations, where France had a rate of 2.3 percent, Germany a rate of 1.9 percent, and Italy, Spain, and the Netherlands rates of 1.4 percent (Singh & Darroch, 2000).

In summarizing research on factors associated with teen sexual activity, Kirby (2001) noted factors that were apparently associated with lesser likelihood of sexual activity and later initiation. Included among these were attachment to faith-based communities, exposure and attachment to peer groups with protective values, and behaviors antagonistic to teen sex. These factors seem to suggest that teens who conduct their daily lives in contexts that do not support sexual exploration or activity are less likely to engage in either.

Following is a summary of some of the key findings on teen sex based on results from the CDC's YRBS 2005.

- 46.8 percent of teens report having engaged in sexual intercourse at some time.

- 14.3 percent of teens report having engaged in sexual intercourse with four or more partners.

- 6.2 percent of teens had sexual intercourse before they were 13 years old.

- 55 percent of males and 54 percent of females reported engaging in oral sex in 2002.

- Adolescents 15–24 years old account for 19 million new cases of sexually transmitted diseases each year.

- 62.8 percent of adolescents used a condom during sexual intercourse.

- 17.6 percent of adolescents used birth control to prevent pregnancy.

- 87.9 percent of adolescents were taught about HIV-AIDS in school.

Teen Condom Use and Factors Associated with the Use of Condoms

Some of the national pregnancy differences may result from national differences in teens' use of condoms. In the United States, the majority of teens who report being sexually active also report that they use condoms most of the time (Albert, Brown, & Flanigan, 2003). While this may be encouraging in terms of preventing disease transmission, it leads to the question of why these teens do not consistently employ condoms. According to Kirby and his colleagues (Kirby et al., 1999), the answer may be found in the sporadic nature of teen sexual activity. When asked why they don't always use condoms during sexual intercourse, teens reported that, on those occasions when they did not use condoms, they had not expected to be having sex and as a result did not have one available to use.

Research suggests that there have been sharp increases in the number of teens using a condom at the time of their first intercourse (Manlove et al., 2000). Summarizing data on contraceptive use by American teens, researchers reported an increase from 48 percent in 1982 to 76 percent in 1995. While increases were noted in all groups, they were least among Hispanic females. Such findings are certainly encouraging in terms of preventing the transmission of sexual diseases.

A variety of factors have been related to teen contraceptive use and sexual behavior, including cultural background, cultural values, and age. For example, Hispanic and African American teenagers appear to begin sexual activity at earlier ages and are at greater risk of pregnancy than

White and Asian American teenagers (Kirby, 2001). This suggests that His-panic and African American teens may be less likely to use contraception than these other groups. Along with this is the possibility that these groups may be more exposed to adult models in their lives that do not regularly use contraceptives. There is also an association between age and condom use, with older teens being more consistent in their condom use, as well as an association between poverty and earlier and less-protected sexual activity. Beyond these associations, research suggests that living in generally disorganized and dysfunctional surroundings may encourage early sexual exploration and discourage contraceptive use. Whether this occurs because of deficits in knowledge, differences in personality, or some other factors or interacting factors is not clear.

Not surprisingly, early romantic relationships are also associated with earlier sexual activity, and prior sexual experience is also associated with increasing likelihood of subsequent experiences. In terms of condom use and romantic or "serious" relationships, a report in the *Journal of Adolescent Health* (2006) found that teens were more likely to use condoms when involved in casual sexual relationships and less likely to do so when involved in a "committed" relationship (Lescano, Vazquez, Brown, Litvin, Pugatch, et al., 2006). Unfortunately, since adolescents do not always use condoms when involved with casual sex partners, when they do not use them with their serious partners they have increased the odds of transmit-ting any STD contracted during those unprotected sexual encounters!

Finally, teen sex is also associated with a host of other risk-taking prac-tices, including drug and alcohol involvement and juvenile delinquency.

Teen Sex Prevention and Intervention Programs

The most effective teen sex prevention programs focus both on sex and non-sex factors. Various types of teen pregnancy prevention programs have been developed over the past 15 years. Two general categories are abstinence-only, which focuses on helping teens to remain sexually abstinent, and abstinence-only in combination with sex or HIV education programs, referred to as abstinence-plus programs. A major concern about programs that include sex education is that they may inadvertently encourage teen sexual exploration and activity. While the research on the impact of prevention programs is often not particularly well-designed from a research perspective (Moore & Brooks-Gunn, 2003), making it difficult to draw any clear conclusions based on the findings, evidence demonstrates that abstinence-plus programs do not increase teens' sexual intercourse either by lowering the age of initiation or by increasing the numbers of teens' partners. Numerous studies support these conclusions (Aarons et al., 2000). Moreover, research suggests that such programs may be particularly effective with those teens at greater risk of pregnancy (Coyle et al., 1999; Jemmott et al., 1999).

Virginity pledges are an example of an abstinence-only type of program. Teens who participate in these programs pledge to remain sexually abstinent until marriage. The Southern Baptist Church began to sponsor such pledges in 1993. Since then, millions of teens have signed the pledge to abstain from sexual intercourse until married.

Research has found that, while those who sign such pledges are less likely to engage in sexual intercourse than those who do not sign, this effect only holds for early and middle teens and has no effect on older teens (Bearman & Bruckner, 2001). According to these authors, the delaying effects of taking such pledges can be substantial, but the effects depend upon the age of the pledger and the proportion of students pledging in a particular context. When the proportion of pledgers exceeds 40 percent, the impact of virginity pledges diminishes. According to the authors, this is because when too many teens pledge to remain abstinent that becomes the norm and, therefore, is less likely to prevent them from becoming sexually active. Why this is the case is not clear—at least to us.

Interestingly, research has also found that although virginity pledges can impact when and if teens engage in sex, they do not appear to reduce rates of STD transmission (Bruckner & Bearman, 2005). This is probably because while pledgers are less likely to be exposed to risk factors associated with STD transmission, they are probably also less likely to use condoms when they begin to have sex and are less likely to be tested and diagnosed for STDs if they are having sexual relations. This, of course, increases the spread of these diseases.

Supporters of abstinence-based programs were surprised and deeply disappointed by the results of the most extensive study to test their effectiveness, an $8 million, 9-year study conducted by Mathematic Policy Research (Beil, 2007). Students in abstinence programs were compared with those not receiving such programs—the control group. Because of their importance, the key findings are reproduced here:

> Findings indicate that youth in the program group were no more likely than control group youth to have abstained from sex and, among those who reported having had sex, they had similar numbers of sexual partners and had initiated sex at the same age. (Trenholm, Devaney, Fortson, Quay, Wheeler, & Clark, 2007, p. xvii)

Kirby (2003) highlights ten characteristics that appear to distinguish effective teen pregnancy prevention programs from ineffective programs. Included among these characteristics are that effective programs: are based upon some type of theoretical system, possess a clear message, provide positive modeling behavior for students, and include activities that help teens deal with anticipated peer pressure to engage in sex.

Research suggests that the most effective teen pregnancy prevention programs focus both on sexual and nonsexual risk behaviors (Flay, 2002). In fact, focusing on only one risk factor has been found to have little impact on teen pregnancy rates (Kirby, 2003). At the same time, sex education programs are more effective when they extend beyond the simple presentation of factual information about the spread of sexually transmitted disease and additionally highlight various ways of becoming pregnant and various ways of transmitting disease.

In light of this fact, a variety of multi-component prevention programs have become available in recent years. Such programs frequently combine media campaigns, sex education, and access to condoms and/or counseling (Kirby, 2000). Research findings suggest mixed success regarding the effectiveness of these multi-component programs.

Preliminary research has also suggested the effectiveness of social marketing strategies to prevent teen pregnancy (Polen & Freeborn, 1995). In such programs, messages are presented to teens through posters, public service announcements, and advertisements that attempt to correct their misconceptions that "all teens are doing it." It appears that to the extent that teens overestimate the proportion of their peers that are sexually active, they are that much more likely to become active as well.

The National Campaign to Prevent Teen and Unplanned Pregnancy has been the largest media campaign of this type. The goal of this program was to reduce teen pregnancy rates by a third from 1996 to 2005. Recently, increasing attention has been given to youth development programs which focus more on positive aspects of adolescent development rather than on preventing adolescent problem behaviors (Roth & Brooks-Gunn, 2000). Spurred by the move to develop a more positive approach to psychology and mental health generally, such programs seek to enhance adolescents' self-esteem and their sense of personal autonomy. At the same time, in their evaluation of pregnancy prevention programs, Moore and Brooks-Gunn (2003) stated that contraceptive-based programs "have the greatest success at reducing sexual activity and pregnancy" (p. 291).

Sex Education in the Schools

Providing information in public schools about sex and pregnancy and how to prevent the transmission of sexually transmitted diseases is a controversial topic in American society. Many opponents to providing such information in public schools argue that, instead, it should be provided by parents at home. However, with teen pregnancy rates far higher in the United States than in any other Western industrialized nation, it appears that many parents are not providing very effective sex education at home. Accordingly, it seems appropriate that our schools take on a more central role in the fight to prevent teen pregnancy. This is particularly true since public schools represent the American institution with the greatest access to the vast majority of American teens. In 2003, the courts supported the right of American schools to provide sex education (Fischer, Schimmel, & Kelly, 2003). It seems appropriate that teens learn about the transmission of sexual diseases and how to prevent such transmission. Recent research, for example, has shown that condom use effectively prevents the transmission of viruses that cause genital warts as well as other sexually transmitted diseases. While parents and school health officials should be providing teens with such information, unfortunately, often neither group does for a variety of reasons, including the assumption that doing so is not their responsibility or because of self-consciousness or personal embarrassment.

A 1999 survey indicated that 93 percent of the American public supports sex education in public schools (Sexuality Information and Education Council of the United States). In the same year researchers found that while only 19 percent of American schools provided comprehensive sex education programs, 51 percent provided abstinence-plus programs, and 35 percent abstinence-only programs (Landry, Kaeser, & Richards, 1999). As of the year ending 2007, the United States Congress only provides federal funds to support abstinence-only programs at an annual cost of $176 million a year (Harris, 2007). With personnel changes in both houses of Congress, it is possible that this situation may change and funds be made available for a broader array of school-based sex education programs.

Although prevention research has often found that the mere presentation of information is generally ineffective at preventing various risky behaviors including alcohol and drug use, given the importance of providing American youth information about the life-threatening risks associated with contracting HIV-AIDS, it is important that American students, at the very least, be exposed to some form of HIV-AIDS education as part of their health education school curricula.

The YRBS data included a question in which students were asked whether or not they had been taught either about AIDS or about HIV infection in school (National Center for Chronic Disease Prevention and Health Promotion, 2006). Across the nation, 87.9 percent reported that they had received instruction about one or the other topic. While this relatively high percentage may be gratifying from the perspective of public health in this country, there is at least one reason for concern. This percentage represented a drop from 91.5 percent in 1997. While the reason for this reported drop is not apparent, if accurate, it indicates the importance of redoubling our efforts in this regard. The AIDS crisis is hardly over and young people represent a particularly vulnerable segment of the population, given their frequent failure to use condoms and the relatively large number of American teens that report having engaged in sexual intercourse with four or more persons. Unfortunately, far too little information is available about HIV-AIDS and youth.

In closing this chapter, it is important to consider the developmental impact of equating adolescent sexual exploration with risk taking. While there can be no question that such exploration exposes adolescents to various unhealthy outcomes including pregnancy and disease transmission, and thus is inherently risky, adolescent sexual curiosity and exploration are not aberrant behaviors, but rather are developmentally normal. By setting up a situation where adolescents are afraid to do what previous generations have done since the days of our prehistoric ancestors, adults run the risk of pathologizing or making abnormal what is biologically normal and necessary for the survival of the species. How this will ultimately impact the adult sexuality of these new generations of adolescents is unclear. What should be clear, however, is that, given its biological origins, adolescent sex will eventually find some outlet or form of expressing itself for many, if not most, adolescents. Both Darwin and Freud understood this basic point; too many adults today unfortunately do not, and somehow foolishly believe that by simply pointing out the dangers associated with sex, we can deter the biological stirrings that give rise to this important form of human interaction.

Teen Pregnancy Resources

American Academy of Child and Adolescent Psychiatry—Facts for families—Sex #62
http://www.aacap.org/page.ww?section=Facts+for+Families&name=Facts+for+Families

The National Campaign to Prevent Teen and Unplanned Pregnancy
1776 Massachusetts Avenue. NW, Suite 200
Washington, DC 20036
202–478–8500
202–478–8588 (fax)
http://www.teenpregnancy.org

Works Cited

Aarons, S.J., Jenkins, R.R., Raine, T.R., El-Khorazaty, M.N., Woodward, K.M., Williams, R.L., et al. (2000). Postponing sexual intercourse among urban junior high school students: A randomized controlled evaluation. *Journal of Adolescent Health, 27,* 236–247.

Albert, B., Brown, S., & Flanigan, C. (Eds.). (2003). *14 and younger: The sexual behavior of young adolescents* [Summary]. Washington, DC: The National Campaign to Prevent Teen and Unplanned Pregnancy

Babor, T.F. & Del Boca, F.K. (1992). Just the facts: Enhancing measurement of alcohol consumption using self-report methods. In R. Litten & J. Allen (Eds.), *Measuring alcohol consumption* (pp. 3–19). Totowa, NJ: Humana Press.

Bearman, P. & Bruckner, H. (2001). Promising the future: Virginity pledges and first intercourse. *American Journal of Sociology, 106,* 859–912.

Beil, L. (2007, July 18). Abstinence education faces uncertain future. *New York Times,* p. A1.

Bruckner, H. & Bearman, P. (2005). After the promise: The STD consequences of adolescent virginity pledges. *Journal of Adolescent Health, 36,* 271–278.

Centers for Disease Control [CDC]. (2002). CDC Wonder. Compressed Mortality File. Office of Statistics and Programming. Retrieved February 8, 2008, from http://wonder.cdc.gov/mortSQL.html

Centers for Disease Control [CDC]. (2006). Youth Risk Behavior Surveillance—United States 2005. *Morbidity & Mortality Weekly Report, 55* (SS-5), 1–108.

Corwyn, R.F. (1999). Multiple contingency table analyses of the deviance syndrome: How much overlap is there? *Journal of Child and Adolescent Substance Abuse, 9,* 39–56.

Coyle, K.K., Basen-Enquist, K.M., Kirby, D.B., Parcel, G.S., Banspach, S.W., Collins, J.L., et al. (1999). Short-term impact of safer choices: A multicomponent school-based HIV, other STD, and pregnancy prevention program. *Journal of School Health, 69,* 181–188.

Denizet-Lewis, B. (2004, May 30). Friends, friends with benefits and the benefits of the local mall. *New York Times.* Retrieved February 10, 2007, from http://nytimes.com

DiClemente, R.J., Lodico, M., Grinstead, O.A., Harper, G., Richman, R.L., Evans, P.E., et al. (1996). African-American adolescents residing in high-risk urban environments do use condoms: Correlates and predictors of condom use among adolescents in public housing developments. *Pediatrics, 98,* 269–278.

Ericcson, A. & Simon, H.A. (1980). Verbal reports as data. *Psychological Review, 87,* 215–251.

Fischer, L., Schimmel, D., & Kelly, C. (2003). *Teachers and the Law.* New York: Longman.

Flay, B.R. (2002). Positive youth development requires comprehensive health promotion programs. *American Journal of Health Behavior, 26,* 407–424.

Grunbaum, J.A., Kann, L., Kinchen, S.A., Williams, B., Ross, J.G., Lowry, R., & Kolbe, L. (2002). Youth risk behavior surveillance—United States, 2001. *MMWR Surveillance Summaries, 51,* 1–62.

Harris, G. (2007, December 6). Teenage birth rate rises for first time since '91. *New York Times.* Retrieved from http://www.nytimes.com/2007/12/06/health/06birth.html

Hoff, T. & Greene, L. (2000). *Sex education in America: A view from inside the nation's classrooms.* Menlo Park, CA: Kaiser Family Foundation. Retrieved January 15, 2007, from http://www.kff.org

Hoff, T., Greene, L., & Davis, J. (2003). *National survey of adolescents and young adults: Sexual health knowledge, attitudes and experiences.* Menlo Park, CA: Kaiser Family Foundation. Retrieved from http://www.kff.org

Hughes, M., Morrison, K., & Asada, K.J.K. (2005). What's love got to do with it? Exploring the impact of maintenance rules, love attitudes, and network support on friends with benefits relationships [Electronic Version]. *Western Journal of Communication, 69*, 49–66.

Jemmott, III, J.B., Jemmott, L.S., Fong, G.T., & McCaffree, K. (1999). Reducing HIV risk-associated sexual behavior among African American adolescents: Testing the generality of intervention effects. *American Journal of Community Psychology, 27*, 167–187.

Kirby, D. (2000). What does the research say about sexuality education? *Educational Leadership, 58*, 72–76.

Kirby, D. (2001). *Emerging answers: New research findings on programs to reduce teen pregnancy.* Washington, DC: The National Campaign to Prevent Teen and Unplanned Pregnancy. Retrieved from http://www.teenpregnancy.org/resources/research/reports.asp

Kirby, D. (2003). Risk and protective factors affecting teen pregnancy and the effectiveness of programs designed to address them. In D. Romer (Ed.), *Reducing adolescent risk: An integrated approach* (pp. 265–284). Thousand Oaks, CA: Sage Publications.

Kirby, D., Brener, N.D., Brown, N.L., Peterfreund, N., Hillard, P., & Harrist, R. (1999). The impact of condom distribution in Seattle schools on sexual behavior and condom use. *American Journal of Public Health, 89*, 182–187.

Landry, D., Kaeser, L., & Richards, C. (1999). Abstinence promotion and the provision of information about public school district sexuality education policies. *Family Planning Perspectives, 31*, 280–286.

Lescano, C.M., Vazquez, E.A., Brown, L.K., Litvin, E.B., Pugatch, D., et al. (2006). Condom use with "casual" and "main" partners: What's in a name? *Journal of Adolescent Health, 39*, 1–7.

Longmore, M.A., Manning, W.D., & Giordana, P.C. (2006). Identity exploration and adolescents' high risk sexual behaviors: A longitudinal analysis. *Working Paper Series 06–16.* Bowling Green State University, Bowling Green, OH: Center for Family and Demographic Research.

Manlove, J., Terry, E., Gitelson, L., Romano, A., Papillo, A., & Russell, S. (2000). Explaining demographic trends in teenage fertility: 1980–1995.*Family Planning Perspectives, 32*, 166–175.

Moore, K.A., Driscoll, A.K., & Lindberg, L.D. (1998). *A statistical portrait of adolescent sex, contraception and childbearing.* Washington, DC: The National Campaign to Prevent Teen and Unplanned Pregnancy.

Moore, M.R. & Brooks-Gunn, J. (2003). Healthy sexual development: Notes on programs that reduce the risk of early sexual initiation and adolescent pregnancy. In D. Romer (Ed.),*Reducing adolescent risk: An integrated approach* (pp. 284–292). Thousand Oaks, CA: Sage Publications.

Nagourney, E. (2006, May 9). Patterns of deceit raise concerns about teenage sex surveys. *New York Times.* Retrieved from http://www.nytimes.com/2006/05/09/health/09virg.html

National Center for Chronic Disease Prevention and Health Promotion. (2006). *Fewer high school students engage in health risk behaviors; racial and ethnic differences persist.* Retrieved from http://www.cdc.gov/HealthyYouth/yrbs/press-release.htm

National Center for Chronic Disease Prevention and Health Promotion, Division of Adolescent and School Health. (2007). *Healthy youth! Sexual risk behaviors.*

Retrieved from http://www.cdc.gov/HealthyYouth/Sexualbehaviors/index.htm

National Institute of Child Health and Human Development, NIH, DHHS. (2004). *Growing up healthy: An overview of the National Children's Study* (04–5414). Washington, DC: U.S. Government Printing Office.

Nisbett, R.E. & Wilson, T.D. (1977). Telling more than we can know: Verbal reports on mental process. *Psychological Review, 84,* 231–259.

Paul, E.L. (2002). The casualties of 'casual' sex: A qualitative exploration of the phenomenology of college students' hookups [Electronic Version]. *Journal of Social and Personal relationships, 19,* 639–661.

Polen, M.R. & Freeborn, D.K. (1995). *Outcome evaluation of Project ACTION.* Portland, OR: Center for Health Research, Kaiser Permanente.

Remez, L. (2000). Oral sex among adolescents: Is it sex or is it abstinence? *Family Planning Perspectives, 32,* 298–304.

Rosenbaum, J. (2006). Reborn a virgin: Adolescents retracting virginity pledges and sexual histories. *American Journal of Public Health, 96,* 1090–1103.

Roth, J.L. & Brooks-Gunn, J. (2000). What do adolescents need for healthy development: Implications for youth policy. *Society for Research In Child Development Social Policy Report, XIV*(1), 14. Retrieved from http://www.srcd.org/spr.html#

Sexuality Information and Education Council of the United States and Advocates for Youth. (1999). *SIECUS/Advocates for Youth survey of Americans' views on sexuality education.* Washington, DC: Sage.

Singh, S. & Darroch, J. (2000). Adolescent pregnancy and childbearing: Levels and trends in developed countries. *Family Planning Perspectives, 32,* 14–23.

Smith, T. (1992). Discrepancies between men and women in reporting number of sexual partners: A summary from four countries. *Social Biology, 39,* 203–211.

Tourangeau, R. & Smith, T.W. (1996). Asking sensitive questions: The impact of data collection mode, question format, and question context. *Public Opinion Quarterly, 60,* 275–304.

Trenholm, C., Devaney, B., Fortson, K., Quay, L., Wheeler, J., & Clark, M. (2007). *Impacts of four Title V, Section 510 abstinence education programs.* Princeton, NJ: Mathematica Policy Research Inc. Document No. PR07–07.

Ventura, S.J., Mosher, W.D., Curtin, S.C., Abma, J.C., & Henshaw, S. (2001). Trends in pregnancy rates for the United States, 1976–1997: An update. In *National vital statistics reports 49*(4). Hyattsville, MD: National Center for Health Statistics.

CHAPTER 5

Adolescent Violence

Though bullying represents a far less dangerous form of interpersonal violence than [some], it exacts a terrible toll on numerous children and may signal an underlying pathology for extreme future violence. While some bullies may be social outcasts, others are quite socially adept and obtain considerable social praise for their bullying behaviors. Research has shown that a common reason given for bullying is the prestige associated with it and the desire to "look cool."

Freud believed that both sex and aggression play central roles in human society and are key motivators of our interactions. It seems somewhat fitting, therefore, to follow our discussion on sexual risk taking with a brief overview of youth violence or aggression. In our previous discussions of specific risk behaviors, we stressed the links repeatedly observed between them. For example, teens who smoke often drink and also often engage in early sexual exploration. Then, too, those who experience family problems or psychological disorders are more likely to attempt suicide and to engage in each of these other risky behaviors as well. It is hardly surprising, therefore, to find that youth violence is frequently linked to other adolescent risk taking. Studies have found that youth violence is associated with drug and alcohol involvement, emotional distress, and early sexual activity.

According to a recent editorial by Bob Herbert, "Americans are addicted to violence" (2007, p. A25). While we are repeatedly shocked by the horrific toll that violent acts take on our lives, we seem unwilling to do anything about them or to force our leaders to seriously address the problem. The presidential candidate Barack Obama addressed the same issue when speaking in Chicago about the 32 school children killed in the district in 2006 and our seeming inability to do much to curb the epidemic of violence in the land.

It is also not surprising that violence in youth has been associated with such family factors as family structure, authoritarian child-rearing practices, low levels of parental monitoring, and parental substance use and criminality. In particular, an increased level of delinquent behavior is found in youth residing in single-parent homes (Demuth & Brown, 2004). This is an especially alarming finding, as the divorce rate in the United States hovers around the 50 percent mark. Although the single-parent family structure is problematic regardless of who heads the household, as there is still only one parent to supervise children, more delinquent transgressions have been associated with single-father households. This is probably due to the lower levels of supervision, involvement, and emotional closeness that have frequently been found in father-only families. Demuth and Brown (2004) have indicated that parental closeness along with strong controls and monitoring practices can remedy the difficulties inherent in this family structure.

Youth violence has also been associated with such peer/school factors as involvement with delinquent youth and gangs, and low school bonding (National Center for Injury Prevention and Control, 2007). Dishion and colleagues (1999) have coined the term "deviancy training" to indicate the process through which association with deviant peers leads to more problem behaviors in youth. Deviant talk and behaviors are inherent in groups of youth that exhibit antisocial behavior and are met by the same individuals with positive social reactions such as laughter, attention, and interest, thereby reinforcing the behaviors. Additionally, group support provides the motivation to continue committing delinquent acts, setting youth up for problems throughout adulthood.

At the same time, a number of myths related to youth violence have also been identified in the literature. Some of these myths are presented here and were discussed in the surgeon general's groundbreaking report on youth violence (U. S. Department of Health and Human Services, 1999):

1. Most future offenders can be identified in early childhood.
2. A new, violent breed of super predators threatens the United States.
3. Most violent youths will end up being arrested for a violent crime.
4. Nothing works with respect to treating or preventing violent behavior.

Rates of Teen Violence

The general statistics on youth violence can be startling as they reveal the pervasiveness of such behavior. Approximately a third of all injury-related deaths in the United States are related to intentional violence. In national surveys of high school students, 33 percent reported being in one or more physical fights in the past 12 months while 17 percent reported carrying a weapon at least once in the past month. In 2004, over 750,000 youth between 10 and 24 years of age were treated in emergency rooms because of interpersonal violence. In 2003, approximately 15 youth in the same age range were murdered each day in this country. The costs of youth violence, including medical costs and lost productivity, have been estimated beyond $158 billion annually.

While these statistics demonstrate the extent of the problem, they fail to indicate how disproportionately violence impacts different groups throughout the nation. For example, of the 5,570 youth murdered in 2003, 86 percent were males. Moreover, homicide was the leading cause of death for African American youth and the second leading cause of death for Hispanic youth. The juvenile justice system also indicates that minority youth are disproportionately incarcerated. Furthermore, youth of color are more likely to receive harsher punishment within the system for the equivalent crimes of Caucasian youth. The reason for this disproportionate representation is unclear as researchers cannot determine if it is due to bias in the system or to the fact that minority youth are actually committing more crimes or to some combination of these factors.

With respect to trends in youth violence, the surgeon general's report concluded:

> Over the past two decades, the number of violence acts by high school seniors increased nearly 50%, a trend similar to that found in arrests for violent crimes. But neither this incident rate nor the proportion of high school seniors involved in violence has declined in the years since 1993— they remain at peak levels. (p. 6)

It is important to keep in mind, however, that this report was completed in 1999.

The surgeon general's report concluded that youth violence was a problem that could be solved. It also emphasized that there appeared to be two distinct patterns of youth violence: one in which youth were violent before entering their teens and generally committed more crimes and more serious crimes, and another pattern which began in the teenage years and stopped during the transition to adulthood. The former group often exhibited a pattern of increasing violence throughout childhood, and sometimes continued this pattern into their adult years. However, predicting which youth will become and remain violent is not possible.

Youth violence has been associated with several environmental factors. These include poverty, child abuse, bullying, neglect, and availability of weapons. The surgeon general's report also revealed that the commission of serious violence is part of a general pattern of behaviors or lifestyle. Often it is a product of lack of career opportunities or socialization and the pattern often includes drug use, gun possession, and early sexual activity.

Table 5.1   Risk and Protective Factors Associated with Youth Violence

Individual Factors

Risk	Protective
1. Attention deficit/hyperactivity	1. Intolerant attitude toward deviance
2. Poor behavioral control	2. High grade point average
3. Exposure to family violence and conflict	3. Religiosity

Family Factors

Risk	Protective
1. Harsh or inconsistent punishment	1. Family bonding/attachment
2. Parental substance abuse/criminality	2. Frequent shared activities
3. Poor parental monitoring	3. Discussion of problems with parents

Peer/School Factors

Risk	Protective
1. Involvement in gangs	1. School bonding
2. Social rejection by peers	2. Involvement in social activities
3. Poor academic performance	

With regard to risk and protective factors, the National Center for Injury Prevention and Control summarized research that has identified risk factors within the individual, the family, the peer groups, and schools. Table 5.1 summarizes selected risk and protective factors in each of these domains.

Because of terribly violent school tragedies such as those at Virginia Tech, Columbine, and similar events in Kentucky, Minnesota, and Pennsylvania, there is a public perception that schools are particularly violent places for children to be. Despite this public perception, the U.S. Department of Education indicates that the odds of being shot at a school are approximately one in a million (Reddy, Borum, Berglund, Bossekuil, Fein, & Modzeleski, 2001). Furthermore, according to the surgeon general's report, schools are generally safe havens for children. In fact, research has shown that although school homicides have increased, children are safest in schools (Leone, Mayer, Malmgren, & Misel, 2000). Compared to homes and local neighborhoods, there are fewer injuries and deaths in schools. Others have drawn a similar conclusion and even reported that school homicides accounted for less than one percent of homicides among school-aged youth. If and when school-related deaths do occur, they generally are perpetrated on racial/ethnic minorities, in high schools, and within urban schools.

In regard to other acts of violence, since 1992 incidents of serious crimes on or near school property have declined. These crimes include rape, sexual assault, theft, and simple assault. Additionally this downward trend holds for all age ranges, includes both genders, and covers both rural and suburban settings. Additionally, high school students are less likely to carry a weapon to school. In 1991, 26 percent of high school students indicated they carried a weapon to school while in 1999 only 17 percent said they did.

Although the statistics indicate that schools are safe places, the public perception of them as dangerous persists. Even the 2002 educational legislation known as No Child Left Behind has called for safer schools. Policy adopted by President George W. Bush seeks to reward schools that adopt a zero-tolerance agenda against students who are chronically disruptive. Although this stance seems like sound policy on first glance and represents the position that parents and administrators alike want to hear, the result is that students are suspended, expelled, and arrested at increasing rates. This removes the problem from view, instead of addressing the underlying causes and developing real strategies for prevention or intervention.

Research points out that one way to keep students out of trouble is to provide schools of high quality. Thus instead of rewarding a zero-tolerance agenda, the federal government might serve students, families, and communities by rewarding schools that meet the standards of quality, as expressed by families of attending students. In this research, high quality schools as measured by the mother's perceptions included variables such as the teacher's skill, communication between teachers and parents, the safety of the school, and the level to which the school helped students understand right from wrong (Kowaleski-Jones, 2000).

Teen Gang Involvement

Another topic of considerable interest in the field of youth violence concerns gangs and gang-related violence. One reason for this has to do with reports on gang violence in the media (Perrone & Chesney-Lind, 1997). The frequent representation of youth gang violence in the media is particularly evident in Los Angeles, where a young African American female was recently killed in a drive-by shooting by a Hispanic gang member. The mayor of Los Angeles recently spoke on National Public Radio about the dramatic rise in gang-related violence in his community and requested federal assistance to address the growing problem (NPR, 2007).

According to a fact sheet released by the Violence Prevention Coalition of Greater Los Angeles, while gang violence started to decline in the city in the early 1990s, from 1995 to 2002 there was a steady and accelerating increase. In 2002, there were 256 gang homicides in Los Angeles from January to August. This represented a 22 percent increase from the same period in the previous year. It also represented a 47 percent increase from the 5-year average for those months. The statements by the mayor of

Los Angeles indicate that the trend of increasing gang violence continues today.

According to the same fact sheet, most gang violence is neither random shootings nor is it related to drug disputes, but instead reflects conflicts over turf, over status, and acts of revenge. In addition, while many people believe that youth gangs are very cohesive and tightly organized, the facts suggest otherwise. Most gangs are loosely knit with fluctuating membership and varying member commitment to the gang. The media often promotes the image that refusal to join a gang results in harm to individuals or their families. This may occur in rare circumstances if the youth expresses disrespect to the members or the invitation, but it is more likely that an assault will occur as an initiation ritual to the youth who agrees to join (Kittredge & McCarthy, 2000).

According to the Report on the State of Los Angeles Street Gangs, there were more than 1,300 street gangs that included over 150,000 members in Los Angeles County in 2002. These gangs accounted for over half of all the homicides committed in the County during that period. Most were carried out with handguns.

This later fact relates directly to a recent report summarized by Nagourney (2007) that found that states that have the largest number of guns in the home also have the highest rates of homicide. While it is possible that people in violent states are more likely to purchase guns than those in less-violent states for self-protection, the authors of the report did not feel that such an explanation was supported by their data. An alternative suggestion, obviously, is that the presence and availability of guns makes them more likely to be used, with deadly consequences. Recently a group of mayors across the United States came together to call for greater gun control as one way of reducing violent crime and curbing escalating gang violence in their cities.

Summarizing a report on teen gangs, Greene and Pranis (2007) concluded that: "Youth crime in the United States remains near the lowest levels seen in the past three decades" (p. 5). Following are some of the major conclusions of this important report:

- There are fewer gang members in the U.S. today than a decade ago and there is no evidence that gang activity is increasing.
- Gang members account for a relatively small proportion of crime in most locales.
- Gangs do not dominate the drug trade.
- Most gang members join when young and then quickly outgrow their gang involvement with little help from law enforcement or gang intervention programs.
- Heavy-handed approaches to suppressing gang activity can increase gang cohesion and have a poor record of reducing crime and violence.

- Resources should be redirected from failed gang enforcement attempts to more proven public safety strategies.

Teen Bullying

Though bullying represents a far less dangerous form of interpersonal violence than those previously considered, it exacts a terrible toll on numerous children and may signal an underlying pathology for extreme future violence. While some bullies may be social outcasts, others are quite socially adept and obtain considerable social praise for their bullying behaviors. Research has shown that a common reason given for bullying is the prestige associated with it and the desire to "look cool."

Research has estimated that somewhere between 15 percent and 20 percent of school-age children are bullied in any given year. Victims of bullying may experience somatic symptoms, school phobia, low self-esteem, and, in extreme instances, suicidal thoughts and behaviors. It is important to understand that in this age of information and instant communication, bullying doesn't just occur in school or on the playground, but also occurs quite frequently over the internet, with far-ranging emotional consequences for its victims.

Cruel bullies, those who carefully and systematically taunt and psychologically torture other children, may have psychopathic or antisocial personalities. They experience little or no guilt about their actions, are often quite bright, and frequently escape detection. Treating such individuals is often considered quite unproductive.

Prevention/Intervention for Teen Violence

Policy makers and educators have instituted programs in order to facilitate pro-social development in youth to prevent or counteract youth violence. Instead of waiting for youth to engage in violent behaviors, prevention programs stress the teaching and modeling of academic and social skills needed for success. Effective prevention programs are thought to: be inclusive to all youth, provide a range of educational and social opportunities, reinforce behaviors that are appropriate across all settings, and establish partnerships to facilitate shared responsibility (Christle, Jolivette, & Nelson, 2001). These programs center around two models of delivery—those offered in community settings and those offered in schools. Those offered in community settings include programs such as Big Brothers Big Sisters and leadership training sponsored by YMCAs. At best, the difficulty with this type of program is that it is voluntary in nature and sometimes there is a cost to enroll. This type of program attracts motivated individuals looking to change their current life situations. However, at their worst, research has shown that these types of mentoring programs are just not effective unless there is an intense level of contact, which most mentoring programs don't provide (Keating, Tomishima, Foster, & Alessandri, 2002).

A number of school-based programs have been developed. The benefit of these programs is that they are embedded in the school's curriculum and therefore all students are exposed to them. One example of a school program used to counteract the typical bully and bullying behavior in general is called Names, and it was recently profiled in the *New York Times,* (Hirshey, 2007). This program has been used widely in Connecticut. The program is directed by teachers and trained student volunteers who help the students discuss important but frequently difficult-to-discuss topics like gossip, rumor, physical harassment, drugs, depression, and suicide. By opening up the lines of communication and providing alternative forms of behavior, this and other programs hope to reduce bullying behavior in our schools.

With respect to violence prevention generally, the surgeon general's report pointed out that scant information is available regarding the scientific effectiveness of hundreds of youth violence prevention programs in use throughout the country. This is a matter of considerable concern as previous evaluation work has found that many such programs were ineffective or even counterproductive as they increased rather than reduced the levels of youth violence.

However, the surgeon general's report found that those programs that address both individual and contextual risk factors associated with youth violence have the greatest chance of successfully combating it. Programs that focused on enhancing school climate, youth-school bonding, and parent effectiveness, and, at the same time, that worked to build interpersonal skills in individual youth were particularly effective.

On the other hand, it was emphasized in the same report that over 50 percent of the prevention programs currently in use have never been evaluated and that little is known about how to prevent involvement with delinquent peers and gangs, two of the most "powerful predictors of youth violence." Finally, the surgeon general's report concluded that program implementation was as important for success as program type. Failure to properly put in place an otherwise successful youth violence prevention program will almost ensure that the program will fail.

Youth Violence Resources

American Academy of Pediatrics
http://www.aap.org/healthtopics/violprev.cfm

Delinquency Prevention Council
http://www.helpingkidsnow.com/teen_court.html

Family First Aid—Help for troubled teens
http://www.familyfirstaid.org/youth-violence.html

National Youth Violence Prevention Resource Center
http://www.safeyouth.org/

Office of Juvenile Justice and Delinquency Prevention
http://www.ojjdp.ncjrs.org/pubs/delinq.html

Works Cited

Bush, G.W. (2001, January 29). *No child left behind* [Online]. Retrieved March 25, 2005, from http://www.ed.gov/inits/nclb/

Christle, C.A., Jolivette, K., & Nelson, C.M. (2001). Youth aggression and violence: Risk, resilience, and prevention. *Eric Digests,* Retrieved November 30, 2006, from http://www.ericdigests.org/2001-4/youth.html

Demuth, S. & Brown, S. (2004). Family structure, family processes, and adolescent delinquency: The significance of parental absence versus parental gender. *Journal of Research in Crime and Delinquency, 41,* 58–81.

Dishion, T.J., McCord, J., & Poulin, F. (1999). When interventions harm: Peer groups and problem behavior. *American Psychologist, 54,* 755–764.

Greene, J. & Pranis, K. (2007, July). *Gang wars: The failure of enforcement tactics and the need for effective public safety strategies* [Report]. Justice Policy Institute.

Herbert, R. (2007, April 26). Hooked on violence. *New York Times,* p. A25.

Hirshey, G. (2007, January 28). Pushing back at bullying. *New York Times,* p. 10.

Keating, L.M., Tomishima, M.A., Foster, S., & Alessandri, M. (2002). The effects of a mentoring program on at-risk youth [Electronic Version]. *Adolescence, 37,* 717–735.

Kittredge, K., & McCarthy, A.R. (2000). Today's youth face pressures from many unprecedented factors, not only peers [Electronic Version]. *The Brown University Child and Adolescent Behavior Letter, 16,* 1–4.

Kowaleski-Jones, L. (2000). Staying out of trouble: Community resources and problem behavior among high-risk adolescents. *Journal of Marriage and the Family, 62,* 449–464.

Leone, P.E., Mayer, M.J., Malmgren, K., & Misel, S.M. (2000). School violence and disruption: Rhetoric, reality, and reasonable balance. *Focus on Exceptional Children, 33,* 1–20.

Nagourney, E. (2007, January 23). Consequences: Gun ownership linked to high homicide rates. *New York Times,* p. 23.

National Center for Injury Prevention and Control (2007). *Youth violence: Fact sheet.* Retrieved from http://www.cdc.gov/ncipc/factsheets/yvfacts.htm

National Public Radio. (2007). Interview with the mayor of Los Angeles.

Perrone, P. & Chesney-Lind, M. (1997). Representations of gangs and delinquency: Wild in the streets? *Social Justice, 24,* 96–116.

Reddy, M., Borum, R., Berglund, J., Bossekuil, B., Fein, R., & Modzeleski, W. (2001). Evaluating risk for targeted violence in schools: Comparing risk

assessment, threat assessment, and other approaches. *Psychology in the schools,*
   38, 157–172.
United States Department of Health and Human Services [USDHHS]. (1999).*Youth
   violence: A report of the surgeon general.* Rockville, MD: Author. Retrieved from
   http://www.surgeongeneral.gov/library/youthviolence/toc.html
Violence Prevention Coalition of Greater Los Angeles. (2002). *Gang violence in Los
   Angeles County: Fact sheet.*

CHAPTER 6

Adolescent Suicide

> The suffering of the suicidal is private and inexpressible, leaving family members, friends, and colleagues to deal with an almost unfathomable kind of loss, as well as guilt. Suicide carries in its aftermath a level of confusion and devastation that is, for the most part, beyond description. (Centers for Disease Control and Prevention web site)

While violence is generally carried out against others, there are instances in which it is turned inward, as in the case of self-mutilation and, of course, suicide. It may seem strange to include a chapter on suicide in a book covering adolescent risk taking, since a completed suicide is not really a risky behavior, but a behavior that ends life. There are, however, good reasons for grouping the general topic of suicidal thoughts and behaviors along with other adolescent risk taking. One reason is that while a particular action may appear to the outside observer as suicidal in nature—ingesting a variety of unknown substances, for example—for the teenager engaging in this behavior, it may simply signify thrill seeking or a desire to alter one's current mental state. Moreover, while some adolescent behaviors including drag racing and unprotected sexual intercourse may appear to some as risky choices, to others, depending on the circumstances—such as their partner's HIV risk status—and the motivations involved, such actions may seem suicidal.

It is important to bear in mind that there are vast differences between the number of teens reporting that they have attempted suicide during any specified time period and the number who successfully commit suicide. This suggests that for many of those "attempting" suicide, the goal may not have actually been to end their lives. For some, a suicide attempt may represent a dramatic call for attention from important significant others including family members and friends. For others, it may represent the frustrations associated with a seeming inability to cope with the increasing complexities and stresses as one transitions through adolescence to adulthood. Then, too, it could represent a wish to stop the psychic pain associated with the disintegration of a first love or failure to gain admittance to the college of one's choice. It may even be an accompaniment to some specific form of sexual gratification, such as occurs in autoerotic asphyxia. See the following textbox for more about this unusual connection. In these and other instances, a seeming suicide attempt may not reflect that the adolescent actually wanted to die, but rather that he or she wanted to dramatically alter current life circumstances.

AUTOEROTIC ASPHYXIA

Autoerotic asphyxia is a dangerous sexual activity in which the pleasure of masturbation is enhanced by near-asphyxiation. In many cases, the near strangulation is achieved by tying a noose around one's neck. While the goal is to increase self-induced sexual pleasure, in some instances, the individual loses consciousness too quickly and is unable to remove the noose before strangling to death. Many of these deaths may be mislabeled as suicide, as guilt- and grief-stricken parents remove all evidence of sexual activity before authorities are called, only increasing the mislabeling process.

Certain distinctions are made in discussions of suicide. For example, experts in the area distinguish between suicidal ideation, suicide attempts, and completed suicide. Suicidal ideation refers to whether or not an individual has considered taking his or her own life and the nature and completeness of such thoughts. Many have fleeting thoughts of ending it all, or momentarily wonder if life is worth continuing. But most adolescents do not go beyond such isolated ideas or thoughts. For others, however, these thoughts reoccur and, in some instances, the adolescent develops a plan about the circumstances and method he or she would employ to take his or her own life. Obviously, these individuals are quite distinct and of far greater concern to health professionals than the first group.

Next, we have individuals who indicate that they have actually attempted suicide. Once again, distinctions can be made within this group between those who have attempted suicide, based upon the nature of the methods employed and subsequent consequences, including serious injuries and hospitalizations. For practical purposes, all of these individuals are labeled "attempters."

From the risk-taking perspective, some attempts are far more risky than others, if only because some methods are more difficult or impossible to undo. If you jump off a chair with a rope around your neck, it is too late to reverse the process or undo what you've started. In contrast, someone ingesting sleeping pills, before losing consciousness, can make a call to friends or a help line and be revived.

As in many types of high-risk behavior, there is a gender difference in suicidal behavior. As we will soon see, males once again tend to engage in far more risk taking when it comes to the methods employed in planning and attempting suicide.

A Note of Caution

From the above discussion it should be clear that accurately determining the seriousness or threat level of adolescent suicidal behavior is no simple matter. For one, many attempts may never be categorized as suicidal behavior because they do not result in serious injury, or in medical or psychological intervention. Then too, researchers must confront the issue that studies of suicidal ideation and attempts must rely, to a large extent, on adolescent self-reports that have already been shown to be suspect at best.

There are many reasons to question the validity or truthfulness of self-report in regard to attempted suicides. Some adolescents seriously considering suicide are not likely to discuss their feelings with significant others involved in their lives for fear that these individuals will attempt to dissuade them or, worse still, have them institutionalized for their own protection.

Moreover, some adolescents may report having thought about suicide as a way of garnering attention from their parents, siblings, teachers, or friends. This of course does not mean that one should ignore self-reported statements about suicidal thoughts or plans, but rather that their meaning may be extremely complicated and difficult to decipher.

Additionally, when warning signs are not found following successful adolescent suicides, researchers have no information about an individual's motivations or thinking at the time. And, as is so often the case when we interpret events after the fact, specific behaviors are sometimes inaccurately fitted to the outcome even if they had little to do with it.

It is difficult to determine what constitutes a "serious" or real attempt versus a "non-serious" attempt, other than the extent of the subsequent injuries. This is problematic because these injuries may have more to do with the method selected by a teen than with the seriousness of their desire to die.

Finally, it is undoubtedly the case that there are instances in which an adolescent suicide is labeled an accident or, conversely, instances in which an accident is labeled a suicide. An example of the first instance could occur when an adolescent traffic fatality is judged an accidental death that occurred when the teen lost control of his/her car, crossing the double line and plowing into oncoming traffic. In some cases, this "accident" may actually reflect a conscious decision on the teen's part to cross the double line and crash into the oncoming traffic. In the absence of a note or of signs of depression, an accident designation may seem more accurate than suicide. At the same time, an accident designation may save family members additional emotional hardship and burden at a time of already unbearable suffering, thus leading to an accident designation when in fact a death was known to be a suicide.

There may also be instances in which a suicide designation actually was an accidental death. An example of this could occur in instances of autoerotic suicide, in which an individual, generally an adolescent male, employs asphyxia to enhance the intensity of a masturbatory orgasm. According to Brody (1984), "In many cases, researchers believe these deaths are mislabeled suicide, sometimes after horrified parents have removed all evidence of the sexual nature of their child's death." A distraught mother has argued, at the same time, that it is essential to break the almost-universal silence associated with such deaths. She went on to argue, "Adolescents and others should be warned of the dangers of this practice and parents should know how to detect the warning signs before more young lives are needlessly lost." Others have argued for the need to educate emergency room physicians and nurses who may lack adequate knowledge of the phenomenon (Kirksey, Holt-Ashley, Williamson, & Garza, 1995).

Types of Teen Suicide

Adolescent suicides and suicide attempts can take many forms. Ingesting various toxic substances is a common method, as is the use of firearms. Teens may take their own lives by hanging, jumping from bridges or buildings, slashing their wrists, or driving into oncoming traffic. Males are more likely to employ violent and fatal methods including hanging and firearms than are females, who are more likely to ingest toxic substances or cut themselves.

Although the use of firearms appears to be a particularly violent means to an end, statistics indicate that more than half of all deaths attributed to suicide involve a gun. In studies of the 34 wealthiest nations, 34 percent of reported adolescent suicides resulted from firearms (Johnson, Krug, & Potter, 2000). For the United States alone this percentage was 68 percent of adolescent suicides, and the U.S. accounted for 62 percent of all firearm-related suicides.

Rates of Teen Suicide

Although the overall rate of suicide among teens has been on the decline since 1992, it is estimated that an adolescent or young adult commits suicide every 100 minutes, while each year approximately

1,900 adolescents take their own lives (Anderson & Smith 2003). According to the National Center for Health Statistics (1999), suicide was the fourth leading cause of adolescent death for teens between the ages of 10 and 13 and the third leading cause for teens between the ages of 15 and 19.

In terms of suicidal ideation, research has found that 19 percent of high school students "seriously considered" killing themselves in the previous year, while 15 percent developed a specific plan for carrying out the suicide, and about 9 percent indicated that they had made an attempt in the past year; of these, 2.2 percent were considered medically serious attempts (Grunbaum et al., 2002).

Suicide is not at all common in childhood, and most suicides that occur in the group between 10 and 14 years of age occur among those aged 12 to 14. Incidents of successful suicide increase sharply in older teens and continue at relatively high rates into the early twenties.

With regard to suicide trends over time, from the 1960s until 1988, general rates of adolescent suicide increased among those 15 to 19 years of age but then leveled off. Since that time, however, there has been a steady decline in the rates of suicide among this group of teens as well as among those 20 to 24 years of age.

In contrast to the decreasing trend found among older adolescents and young adults, during the past two decades the rate of suicide among those 10 to 14 years of age has steadily increased. Although the rate is rising in this group, successfully completed suicides are less likely to be found in the younger than in the older group of adolescents. This finding appears to be universally true, across cultures and societies, and it has led some to suggest that this occurs because depression and/or drug use are more likely to co-occur with suicide attempts among older adolescents and increase the seriousness of the attempt.

In the United States, males are more likely to successfully complete a suicide attempt, although females appear more likely to experience suicidal ideation, to plan a suicide, and to attempt suicide (Centers for Disease Control and Prevention, 2004; Grunbaum et al., 2002). In fact, males in the United States are four times as likely to succeed in killing themselves than females (Centers for Disease Control and Prevention, 2004). Interestingly, this pattern of gender difference appears to be culturally determined. For example, in some Asian countries there is no gender difference in attempts and successfully completed suicides, while in China specifically, female teens are more likely to successfully complete suicide.

In terms of racial/ethnic differences, suicide is generally more common among White than among African American adolescents, although there has been a relatively sharp rise in suicides among African American adolescent males. In general suicide has been less prevalent among African American than White or Hispanic adolescents, although recently a rather sharp and disturbing increase has been noted among

Hispanic female adolescents, frequently those who have experienced familial stress attending their own acculturation to American culture. Nonetheless, the highest overall rates of adolescent suicide have been observed among Native Americans, where the rates for 15- to 19-year-olds have been reported as high as 27.7 per 100,000, with Native American males constituting the majority of suicides in this group. This rate is well over twice the rate observed for adolescent suicides in general (Gould, 2003).

There is also a recognized difference in geographic distribution of suicide. Adolescent suicide rates in the United States have been found to be highest in the western states and Alaska and lowest in northeastern and midwestern states. These differences may be due either to differences in racial/ethnic dispersion and/or firearm availability.

Finally, little data are available regarding the socioeconomic dispersion of adolescent suicide. That is, we do not currently know whether rates of adolescent suicide are relatively higher or lower among upper, middle, or lower class adolescents.

Other Factors Associated with Adolescent Suicide

In addition to age, gender, race/ethnicity, and geographical location, a host of other factors have been identified as risk factors linked to attempted and completed teen suicides (Portner, 2000). Some factors have also been identified as protective factors that appear to reduce the chances that a teen will engage in suicidal behaviors. The following list summarizes some influential factors:

- Teens with a family history of suicide are at increased risk.
- Teen suicide has been linked to depression, bipolar disorder, and substance abuse.
- Not surprisingly, adverse life circumstances such as a death in the family and romantic break-up have been linked to adolescent suicide.
- There is evidence of a contagion effect with adolescent suicide, where a widely publicized suicide is followed by a spike in adolescent suicides and attempted suicides.
- Adolescent suicide has been frequently linked to other problem behaviors including delinquency and early sexual promiscuity.

Family Characteristics

As is the case with many adolescent risk behaviors, suicidal behavior appears to run in families. Teens with a family history of suicide are far more likely to successfully complete their suicides than those with no family history. The reasons for this difference are not clear. One possible explanation is that depression runs in families and is also clearly linked to suicide, so that may produce the increasing odds of a completed suicide associated with family history.

Studies have found a link as well between adolescent suicide attempts and completions and mental illness in parents (Gould, 2003). Research has found a particularly strong link between parental depression and substance abuse and suicidal behavior in their teenage children.

Adolescents involved in suicidal actions are also more likely to come from divorced than from intact families. Interestingly, however, this connection is reduced substantially when one takes into account the mental health of the parents. That is, if the parents of a teen from a broken home manifest little or no mental health disturbance, then the teen is not more likely to attempt suicide. This of course suggests that it is the parental mental illness and not the divorce that increases the likelihood that teens from divorced families will engage in suicidal actions (Gould, Greenberg, Velting, & Shaffer, 2003).

In a similar vein, poor parent-child relationships have also been linked to suicide actions. Teen suicide victims have also been found generally to have less contact and less- satisfying relationships with their parents compared with other teens.

Personal Characteristics

A teen's personal characteristics have also been associated with his or her suicidal actions. The most salient of these characteristics has been found to be the mental health status of the teen. Findings have indicated that teen suicide is strongly related to previous suicide attempts, depression, bipolar disorder, substance abuse, and conduct disorder. In fact, research has demonstrated that approximately 90 percent of teens committing suicide had at least one major psychiatric disorder, with depression being the most common. This might be because teens suffering from a depressive illness may see suicide as an escape from their emotional pain and chronic unhappiness. Any individual who experiences mood disorders will find daily living a challenge of utilizing good judgment while keeping difficulties in perspective.

Substance abuse is not as important a risk factor for the young as for older adolescents. It appears to be a major risk factor for older adolescents, who are also more likely to be more heavily involved in various forms of drug and alcohol abuse than younger teens. Drugs and alcohol impair the ability to assess risk and to think through a situation. These substances frequently have a depressive effect on the brain, and misuse of them can further complicate a risky situation by altering judgment.

Personality and cognitive factors have also been linked to adolescent suicide. For example, feelings of hopelessness have often been strongly linked to adolescent suicide. However, when researchers have statistically controlled for level of depression in hopeless teens, hopelessness on its own is not strongly associated with teen suicide.

Then, too, many teens that have attempted or completed suicide possessed relatively poor interpersonal skills, and some have been found to be aggressive and/or impulsive in their dealings with others. It may be the case that poor interpersonal skills make it difficult for these teens to get along with others and this, in turn, may ultimately lead to feelings of low self-esteem and depression.

Finally, two possible links have been found between biological factors and adolescent suicide. One connection is with a brain enzyme, Protein Kinase C (PKC). A comparison of teens who died from suicide and those who died of other causes found lower levels of PKC in the brains of those who died as a result of suicide. Furthermore, PKC has been related to mood disorders. Researchers suggest that if further studies confirm this connection, a PKC blood test could potentially be developed that would screen adolescents for risk of suicidal behavior and medications could then be developed and administered to correct the PKC deficiency (Caruso, 2007).

Another biological connection found in some adolescents following suicide has been with abnormal levels of serotonin, a neurochemical, or, brain chemical, required for normal mental activity. Imbalances in serotonin levels have been indicated as one of the causes of mood disorders, and as we have already indicated, mood disorders have a strong association with suicide because suicidal adolescents often display depressive symptoms. As depressed adolescents are particularly at risk for suicidal behavior, it is crucial for them to be seen immediately by a physician who has expertise in this area. Pediatricians, general practitioners, and psychiatrists are the first line of treatment for depressed and suicidal children. Frequently these children are prescribed antidepressants to combat their illness. Concerns over this practice specifically relate to lack of research on the use of antidepressants in children and adolescents. With research and investigations pending, in March 2004, the FDA required pharmaceutical companies to re-label ten of the most commonly used antidepressants (e.g. Selective Serotonin Reuptake Inhibitors, also known as SSRIs) to add strong warnings indicating that patients under the age of 18 should be watched for suicidal behavior and increased anxiety.

The reason for these black box warnings, the most serious warnings listed on medications, is because preliminary research findings indicate that 2 to 3 percent of individuals under the age of 18 who take antidepressants will experience an increase in suicidal thoughts and/or behaviors. Although the slight increase in suicidal ideation for adolescents taking SSRI medication has been noted, the American Medical Association adopted a resolution in 2005 stating that children and adolescents should not be denied potentially lifesaving care because of the slight increase in risk. They caution that clinical judgment should guide the decision to prescribe antidepressants to those less than 18 years of age. Moreover, in May 2007, an advisory committee suggested that the black box warnings be taken a step further by recommending to the FDA that the caution be extended up until the age of 25. However, the advisory committee also made an unusual recommendation, suggesting that the warning highlight the danger of suicide risk for untreated mental illness. Clearly, the jury is out on this issue, as each case must be viewed on an individual basis with caution guiding the decision to treat individuals under 25 with antidepressants ("Antidepressants and Suicide," 2007).

Before concluding this section, it is important to point out that the results of two recently published research studies brought into question the earlier-established link between drug treatment for depression and adolescent suicide. In both studies, it was found that treating depression with medication, especially in the early stages, was associated with reduced incidence of suicidal behavior (Bakalar, 2007).

Current Life Circumstances

While specific attention has been given to divorce as a potential cause of adolescent suicide, other adverse life circumstances have also been identified. For example, the death of significant others, including parents, siblings, and friends, may increase the likelihood of suicide for some adolescents. Moreover, a connection between self-reported sexual abuse and adolescent suicide has also been noted in the literature (Fergusson & Lynskey, 1997). Other researchers have uncovered a relatively strong link between being bullied or being a bully and thoughts of suicide in adolescents (Kaltiala-Heino et al., 1999).

Societal and Contextual Factors Including Contagion

In addition to family and personal factors and adverse life events, other circumstances in teenagers' lives may predispose them to suicide. Some research (Gould et al., 1996) has found that school difficulties can pose significant risks for teens whereas Shaffer and his colleagues (1996) found that teens who were disconnected from their school or work environments were at elevated risk of suicide.

One of the most interesting aspects of teen suicide is that it appears to be contagious, as teens may imitate the suicides of others in their immediate social context. Researchers have found that outbreaks or clusters of suicide are often observed among teens or young adults (Gould, Wallenstein, & Kleinman, 1990). This is an interesting phenomenon and demonstrates not only the suggestibility of teens but also the important influence that information can have in shaping adolescent as well as adult choices.

Suicide contagion also highlights the important and sometimes pervasive impact that mass media can have on human behavior (Annenberg Public Policy Center of the University of Pennsylvania). There is evidence to indicate that mass media reports of suicide are often followed by sharp increases in the number of reported suicides (Gould & Shaffer, 1986). Sometimes such contagion occurs only in circumscribed geographic areas, and at other times it is found across the nation. One example of this phenomenon was how the number of adolescent suicides increased immediately after the widely-publicized suicide of the teen music idol Kurt Cobain. Another example was the increase in the number of suicides by playing the game Russian roulette after the movie *Deer Hunter* was released (Collins, 1982).

Finally, studies have also shown the linking or clustering of adolescent suicide and a host of other adolescent risk behaviors. Suicide among adolescents has been linked with alcohol and drug use, delinquency, and sexual promiscuity. Research has also demonstrated links between suicide and physical fighting, cigarette use, and failure to wear seat belts. When looking at such clustering, it is important to keep in mind that many of these behaviors may be related to some other, unidentified cause such as depression or thrill-seeking motivation.

Protective Factors

As is the case with most adolescent risk behaviors, protective factors have been identified that appear to buffer adolescents or reduce their involvement in suicidal behavior. However, it is important to reiterate at this point that protective factors should not be simply characterized as the opposite of risk factors, because they don't simply balance negative forces, but rather, they promote positive actions and mitigate the impact of risky actions. Parental substance abuse has been identified as one risk factor for adolescent suicide. If opposite actions were necessarily protective factors, then having parents that abstained from using alcohol could be classified as a protective factor. But, in fact, the absence of drinking in parents does not bestow any particular advantage or protection against adolescent suicide, so that it cannot be considered protective.

Having said this, a number of protective factors have been identified in the research on adolescent suicide, including family cohesion and religiosity. More specifically, research has found that residing in a close-knit family is associated with a reduced risk of adolescent suicide. Being religious, as defined by church attendance and beliefs, has been found to reduce ideas and thoughts about suicide, suicide attempts, and completed suicides (Hilton, Fellingham, & Lyon, 2002).

Another protective mechanism may be to reduce the availability of preferred methods of suicide—for example, restricting the availability of

Table 6.1 Factors Associated with Suicide

Family	

Risk	*Protective*
1. Parental substance abuse	1. Cohesion/support
2. History of psychiatric disorders	2. Religiosity
3. Disruption/stress/conflict	

Personal	

Risk	*Protective*
1. History of psychiatric disorders	1. Problem-solving skills
2. Drug/alcohol abuse	2. Life goals/future plans
3. Previous suicide attempt	3. Academic achievement
4. Impulsive behavior	4. Limited self-blame
5. Feelings of hopelessness	5. Social/peer connections
6. Social isolation/rejection	
7. Physical/sexual/emotional abuse	
8. Chronic illness	
9. Preoccupation with death	

Life Circumstance/Context	

Risk	*Protective*
1. Access to lethal means, e.g., guns, drugs, etc.	1. No access to lethal means
2. Stressful life event/loss	2. Limited stressful events
3. Minority/immigrant/gay/lesbian/ transgender youth without support	3. Community/school connection
	4. Health care support

firearms may reduce the likelihood of adolescent suicide, especially in the United States where firearms are a commonly-used method. Some have suggested that eliminating firearms from the home would reduce the likelihood of many adolescent suicides (Brent, Perper, Moritz, et al., 1993). In line with this, some have suggested that changing trends in the rates of adolescent suicide can be related to the changing availability of firearms to American youth (Grunbaum et al., 2002). Table 6.1 summarizes some of the risk and protective factors associated with adolescent suicide.

Preventing Adolescent Suicide

The Centers for Disease Control and Prevention (2001) developed the following list, which provides an overview of some methods currently used to assist in the prevention of adolescent suicide:

- Build support for families, communities, and neighborhoods
- Ensure accessible and effective clinical care for mental, physical, and substance abuse disorders

- Expand suicide prevention efforts for youth, emphasizing non-violent handling of disputes, conflict resolution, and skill building in problem solving
- Promote awareness of suicide intervention resources such as mental health centers, counseling centers, and hotlines
- Restrict inappropriate access to firearms

It should come as no surprise that many of these approaches are referred to as "school-based" because they are embedded within the school curriculum, most frequently as part of health education. Although preventive approaches may be embedded in health curricula, few schools and communities have in place comprehensive prevention programs that screen for problems, refer help, and provide crisis intervention as needed.

A major reason for this emphasis on school-based prevention is because it has the greatest potential to deliver cost-efficient, broad-based prevention to primary and secondary school students from diverse socio-economic and ethnic backgrounds. Not only are schools the venue with the broadest access to diverse youth, but they also represent a logical environment in which to provide information and strategies that might assist youth to more effectively cope with various stresses and more responsibly solve their problems. Quite simply, school is the only institutional context in which the full array of children and adolescents can be reached easily and, therefore, school is where effective prevention efforts can be most widespread and cost efficient.

Unfortunately, evidence to support the effectiveness of most adolescent suicide prevention programs is scant or nonexistent. More disturbing is the fact that there is at least some evidence to suggest that some programs may have counterproductive effects on teens at risk for suicide because they lead to less help-seeking; in fact, they may actually provide models for suicide that could produce the type of contagion phenomenon described previously in this section.

In some prevention programs, selected teens are trained as peer counselors to help peers deal with emotional difficulties. To date, however, there is no evidence to support the effectiveness of such programs. Skills-training programs in which trainers seek to enhance teens' self-esteem or to provide more effective stress-coping skills have yielded some positive findings, however.

Rather than focusing directly on suicide prevention, some programs seek to address its underlying causes such as depression. In these depression prevention programs, emphasis is placed upon training adolescents to cope more effectively with the types of problems that typically arise in their lives or to restructure their negative thoughts and to think more rationally about their current circumstances. So rather than allowing a teen to repeatedly state that he or she cannot go on any longer, a trainer might work with the teen to begin saying instead that things are difficult at times, but with time and patience difficulties can be overcome. Some research found that teens exposed to these programs were less depressed than control teens with no exposure to the programs.

Recently, teen screening programs have been developed in which teens are assessed at various times to determine their risk status for suicide. The effectiveness of such screening, however, rests to a very large extent upon whether or not the necessary services are available for a teen that has been assessed and then identified as being "at risk." During the screening there are many warning signs that would alert the individual performing the screening to the possibility of a suicide attempt. The warning signs listed below are adapted from the Teens Health Answers and Advice on Suicide web site (http://www.kidshealth.org/teen/your_mind/feeling_sad/suicide.html). For those aware of warning signs for depression, the similarity is evident.

- Talking about suicide, death, or "going away"
- Talking about feelings of guilt or hopelessness
- Giving away possessions and referring to things that "won't be needed"
- Losing interest in favorite activities such as being with friends and family
- Having trouble concentrating
- Changes in eating and sleeping habits
- Engaging in self-destructive behaviors such as self-mutilation, use of drugs and alcohol

Other elements of contemporary adolescent suicide prevention may include community crisis centers and suicide hotlines, or restricting firearm availability in particular communities. Efforts have even gone into the training of media personalities in how best to report adolescent suicide to prevent contagion, as well as the training of primary health care workers in identifying teens at risk for suicide, because these workers may have critical contact with teens at particularly vulnerable times, such as just before starting school in the fall.

Finally, attempts have also been made to intervene following an adolescent suicide, in order to prevent contagion, to reduce the associated trauma, and to provide grief counseling to assist teens through the crisis. Particular attention is also given to working with teens following a suicide attempt, since attempts themselves represent an important risk factor and oftentimes reflect a cry for help on the part of the teen.

If you are concerned that you or someone you know displays these warning signs, contact the National Suicide Prevention Hotline at 1–800–SUICIDE.

Suicide Prevention Resources

American Foundation for Suicide Prevention
http://www.afsp.org

National Center for Injury Prevention and Control (NCIPC)
800–232–4636

National Institute of Mental Health
http://www.nimh.nih.gov

SAVE—Suicide Awareness Voices of Education
800–273–8255
http://www.save.org/

Teens Health Answers and Advice on Suicide
http://kidshealth.org/teen/your_mind/mental_health/suicide.html

Youth Suicide Prevention Programs—A Resource Guide
http://wonder.cdc.gov/wonder/prevguid/p0000024/p0000024.asp

Works Cited

Annenberg Public Policy Center of the University of Pennsylvania. *Suicide and the media.* Retrieved from http://www.annenbergpublicpolicycenter.org/07_adolescent_risk/suicide/dec14%20suicide%20report.htm

Antidepressants and suicide. (2007, July). *Harvard Mental Health Letter, 24,* 1–3.

Bakalar, N. (2007, July 10). Suicide findings question link to antidepressants. *New York Times,* p. F7.

Brent, D.A., Perper, J.A., Moritz, G., Allman, C., Friend, A., Rother B.S.W., et al. (1993). Stressful life events, psychopathology and adolescent suicide: A case control study. *Suicide and Life-Threatening Behavior, 23,* 179–187.

Brody, J. (1984, March 27). 'Autoerotic death' of youths causes widening concern. *New York Times.*

Caruso, K. Brain enzymes linked to teen suicide. Retrieved January 26, 2007, from http://www.suicide.org/brain-enzyme-linked-to-teen-suicide.html

Centers for Disease Control and Prevention. (2001). *Safe USA: Preventing suicide.* Available from http://www.cdc.gov/

Centers for Disease Control and Prevention, National Center for Injury Prevention and Control. (2004). *Web-based injury statistics query and reporting system.* Retrieved June 21, 2004, from http://www.cdc.gov/ncipc/wisqars/default.htm

Collins, J.M. (1982, July/August). Can movies kill? Twenty-eight people died by playing Russian roulette—apparently after watching The Deer Hunter. *American Film, 4,* 32–41.

Fergusson, D.M. & Lynskey, M.T. (1997). Childhood circumstances, adolescent adjustment, and suicide attempts in a New Zealand birth cohort. *Journal of the American Academy of Child and Adolescent Psychiatry, 34*, 612–622.

Gould, M.S. (2003). Suicide risk among adolescents. In D. Romer (Ed.), *Reducing adolescent risk: An integrated approach* (pp. 303–320). Thousand Oaks, CA: Sage Publications.

Gould, M.S., Fisher, P., Parides, M., Flory, M., & Shaffer, D. (1996). Psychosocial risk factors of child and adolescent completed suicide. *Archives of General Psychiatry, 3*, 1155–1162.

Gould, M.S., Greenberg, T., Velting, D.M., & Shaffer, D. (2003). Youth suicide risk and preventive interventions: A review of the past 10 years. *Journal of the American Academy of Child and Adolescent Psychiatry, 42*, 386–405.

Gould, M.S. & Shaffer, D. (1986). The impact of suicide in television movies: Evidence of imitation. *New England Journal of Medicine, 315*, 690–694.

Gould, M.S., Wallenstein, S., & Kleinman, M. (1990). Time-space clustering of teenage suicide. *American Journal of Epidemiology, 131*, 71–78.

Grunbaum, J.A., Kann, L., Kinchen, S.A., Williams, B., Ross, J.G., Lowry, R., & Kolbe, L. (2002). Youth risk behavior surveillance—United States, 2001. *MMWR Surveillance Summaries, 51*, 1–62.

Hilton, S.C., Fellingham, G.W., & Lyon, J.L. (2002). Suicide rates and religious commitment in young adult males in Utah. *American Journal of Epidemiology, 155*, 412–419.

Johnson, G.R., Krug, E.G., & Potter, L.B. (2000). Suicide among adolescents and young adults: A cross-national comparison of 34 countries. *Suicide and Life Threatening Behaviors, 30*, 74–82.

Kaltiala-Heino, R., Rimpela, M., Marttunen, M., Rimpela, A., & Rantanen, P. (1999). Bullying, depression, and suicidal ideation in Finnish adolescents: School survey. *British Medical Journal, 319*, 348–351.

Kirksey, K.M., Holt-Ashley, M., Williamson, K.L., Garza, R.O. (1995). Autoerotic asphyxia in adolescents. *Journal of Emergency Nursing, 21*, 81–83.

National Center for Health Statistics. (1999). *Death rates for 358 selected causes, by 5-year age groups, race, and sex: Unites States* (Worktable 292a, Worktable GM292A_1,2001). Retrieved April 5, 2007, from http://www.cdc.gov/nchs/data/statab/VS00199.TABLE292A.pl1.pdf

Portner, J. (2000). Complex set of ills spurs rising teen suicide rate. *Education Week, 19*, 23.

Shaffer, D., Gould, M.S., Fisher, P., Trautman, P., Moreau, D., Kleinman, M., et al. (1996). Psychiatric diagnosis in child and adolescent suicide. *Archives of General Psychiatry, 53*, 339–348.

Teens health answers and advice on suicide. Retrieved from http://www.kid shealth.org/teen/your_mind/feeling_sad/suicide.html

CHAPTER 7

Beyond Risk: Adolescent Mental Disorders

The causes of many mental health disorders are unclear and probably quite complex. Experts agree that such disorders develop out of an intersecting set of risk factors that include genetic predisposition, brain chemistry, personality and temperament, and parent and family interactions, as well as life experiences. Not surprisingly, these are the same factors that have been most frequently highlighted as possible causes of adolescent risk taking.

There are a number of good reasons for including a chapter on adolescent mental disorders in a book on adolescent risk taking. For one, there are strong and consistent connections between a number of specific adolescent risk behaviors, such as drug use and violence, and specific mental health conditions during adolescence (Wicks-Nelson & Israel, 2000). These connections or comorbidities indicate the existence of related causal mechanisms or other similarities. Then, too, sometimes it is difficult to distinguish sequences between risk behaviors such as drug use and specific adolescent psychological disorders including depression and anxiety. For example, do depressed adolescents consume excessive amounts of alcohol to counteract their feelings of depression or anxiety, or does this consumption produce these feelings for an adolescent? It is often difficult to determine cause and effect—which is the chicken and which is the egg?—when risk behaviors and mental disorders co-occur during adolescence. It is also possible that both sequences occur, depending on the particular individual involved.

While this may seem a largely academic issue, it is extremely important, because in diagnosing mental disorders, it is essential to know whether the mental disorder is the primary problem confronting the individual or whether the disorder is secondary to some other problem such as substance abuse. The importance of getting an accurate diagnosis is sharply increased by the fact that for many psychiatric diagnoses, medication is the treatment of choice. This is important to understand because many of the medications prescribed for teens may have serious side effects and, in some instances, their effects may be changed and their impact increased substantially when taken in conjunction with drugs such as alcohol or prescription painkillers.

Recent estimates indicate that three to four million American young people under the age of 18 are prescribed and take psychiatric drugs. This number has doubled in the past decade, partially because children at increasingly younger ages are being identified as having mental health issues and are prescribed psychiatric drugs. The problem with this trend is that most of the psychiatric drugs prescribed were not developed for or safety-tested in young patients. Concerns about method of action, side effects, and long-term consequences of using these substances abound, yet the medications are being prescribed at ever-increasing rates.

How is this possible? Drug companies tend to pursue the simplest route to market for their medications, and this generally means obtaining approval from the Food and Drug Administration (FDA) for the adult use of medications only. Back in 1970 the FDA declared that the medications doctors prescribed for children must be tested in children. However, the FDA's limited power and influence make it impossible for the agency to monitor prescription practices of physicians. Currently, the FDA estimates that between 70 percent and 80 percent of all drugs prescribed to children have not been approved for use by children. Although the use of what is called "off-label" treatment is a common medical practice, the FDA and the U.S. Department of Health and Human Services continue to push for studies on pediatric patients. Slowly, things are changing. Organizations such as the National Institute of Mental Health are leading the way by funding investigations into basic drug biology and clinical trials that look into how these drugs affect children's brains.

The complexities associated with the co-occurrence of risk taking and psychological disorders during adolescence are compounded by the limited amount of time physicians generally spend observing and interacting with the children they are charged with serving. Then, too, many of these physicians are not psychiatrists trained in such areas, but are family physicians or pediatricians who are diagnosing outside of their specialties.

Therefore the judgments and observations of parents and teachers become crucial in the diagnostic process. This is important for both groups to understand because their descriptions of problematic risk behaviors or apparent aberrant psychological functioning often carry considerable weight in the diagnostic process. Thus it is absolutely essential that the informants in regard to an adolescent's mental health accurately describe what they have observed, and also that they are certain that the behavior under discussion is both frequent and unusual in its occurrence for individuals in this life stage and particular circumstances

An incorrect diagnosis could lead the physician to prescribe medication appropriate for the disorder but not for this particular instance of the disorder, because the diagnosis is in error. One unfortunate and long-standing negative consequence of such a mistake is that once the medication has been taken, it may dramatically alter the adolescent's behavior and, thereby, make it increasingly unlikely that an accurate diagnosis of the original problem will be made. The following textbox presents a case study in which such a mistake may have led to long series of misdiagnoses and incorrect prescriptions that ultimately may have created permanent problems for an individual child. For these and other reasons, it is extremely important for parents and those professionals who work with adolescents to better understand the linkages between adolescent risk taking and adolescent psychiatric disorders. In the previous chapters, we sought to provide information about the most common risk-taking activities adolescents are involved with. In the current chapter, we highlight the psychiatric disorders frequently associated with these risky activities.

BRIAN—A CAUTIONARY TALE OF MULTIPLE DIAGNOSES AND MEDICATIONS

When I first met Brian he seemed like a fairly normal five-year-old boy who loved trains and everything associated with them. He had already been diagnosed with Tourette's Syndrome and was on medication to control its symptoms. By the time Brian turned eight he had also been diagnosed with learning disabilities, spatial integrative problems, and obsessive-compulsive disorder. New medications had been added and some old ones discontinued. While his father often felt he needed more medication, his mother wished he were on less or fewer medications. As a young teen, Brian was diagnosed with manic-depression and attention deficit hyperactivity. Additional and sometimes dangerous medications had also been introduced, which required constant monitoring and blood testing. Brian was lonely, depressed, and without friends. He threatened suicide and sometimes burst into violent outrages. He is now 18 and still carries multiple diagnoses and ingests multiple medications on a daily basis. He attends a school for the emotionally disabled where his parents visit frequently. He is the mother's only child. Whether an early and accurate diagnosis and treatment would have prevented many of the unfortunate circumstances of Brian's early life and adolescent years is unclear. What is clear is that inconsistent diagnoses and frequent medication changes did alleviate his early behavior problems but, in some degree, may have actually made them more problematic and difficult to deal with for Brian and his family than they would have been otherwise.

Adolescent Mental Health Background

The number of youth diagnosed with mental health disorders is soaring as debate rages over the trend to diagnose and treat children and adolescents who may deviate from behavioral expectations. But are children truly over-diagnosed and medicated so that parents and teachers can manage them better, or, are parents and clinicians becoming more aware of normal development and behavior, enabling them to identify early symptoms of problems?

In the identification process of a mental health problem, all medical professionals utilize the criteria of symptoms and exclusions listed in the *Diagnostic and Statistical Manual of Mental Disorders, Fourth Edition (DSM-IV)* to diagnose children and adolescents. As the *DSM-IV* is a medical system of classification, most educators and parents are not familiar with the behaviors, symptoms, and exclusions listed as indicators of the various disorders. Moreover, adults who are well informed as to the distinction between typical behaviors and exceptional behaviors in children are in a better position to know when to seek professional help and how to participate actively in the diagnostic process.

The causes of many mental health disorders are unclear and probably quite complex. Experts agree that such disorders develop out of an intersecting set of risk factors that include genetic predisposition, brain chemistry, personality and temperament, and parent and family interactions, as well as life experiences. Not surprisingly, these are the same factors that have been most frequently highlighted as possible causes of adolescent risk taking.

While professionals concur that the earlier a condition is recognized, the sooner an appropriate course of treatment can begin and the better the long-term prognosis or outcome, this does not make the sometimes-difficult job of making an accurate diagnosis any easier. If an incorrect diagnosis is made, inappropriate treatment might seriously complicate the diagnostic process and inhibit the ability to determine the "most-appropriate treatment" plan.

With these cautionary remarks in mind, we briefly introduce the reader to four mental health disorders commonly and increasingly diagnosed in our children and adolescents. With all four disorders, the treatment plan generally consists of medications such as stimulants or antidepressants and psychotherapy. In this way both the biological and the environmental contexts of the disorder can be addressed. With a comprehensive treatment plan in place, the subsequent risk-taking behaviors that go along with these mental health difficulties, such as substance use, gambling, sexual misconduct, delinquency, and suicide, may be eliminated or reduced to levels of normal experimentation.

Attention Deficit Hyperactivity Disorder

Attention deficit hyperactivity disorder (ADHD) is one contributor to the current increase in the diagnosis of mental health disorders. ADHD has become the most common neuropsychiatric syndrome diagnosed in children. According to the U.S. Department of Education, ADHD is reported to affect between two percent and five percent of school-aged children, a figure that represents approximately two million children nationwide. Despite the growing numbers of children who are diagnosed with this disorder, ADHD continues to evade efforts to pinpoint a universally accepted definition (National Institutes of Health, 1998). The *DSM-IV* states that the atypical behavior observed in the individual must be present for at least six months, that the child must display six or more symptoms from the inattention (attention deficit disorder) or the hyperactivity/impulsivity (attention deficit hyperactivity disorder) categories prior to the age of seven, and that the behavior must be present in two or more settings (i.e. home, school, and work). Complicating these guidelines is the fact that ADHD is a multifaceted disorder, encompassing a variety of behavioral symptoms that manifest differently in individual children. Children with ADHD include those with symptoms of difficulty sustaining attention, distractibility, lack of task persistence, and disorganization. However, children can also be included who have excessive motor activity and impulsive-responding behavior. Russell Barkley, one of the primary and leading researchers in the area, provided one of the most helpful definitions of ADHD in 1990, indicating that it is a "developmental disorder characterized by inappropriate degrees of inattention, over activity and impulsivity. These often arise in early childhood; are relatively chronic in nature; and are not readily accounted for on the basis of gross neurological, sensory, language, motor impairment, mental retardation, or severe emotional disturbance" (p. 47). Despite the rise in research investigating this disorder over the last two decades, ADHD still remains a challenge to diagnose as there are frequently comorbid—co-occurring—conditions complicating the diagnosis. These conditions include anxiety disorders, mood disorders, learning disabilities, conduct disorder, and oppositional defiant disorder.

Mood Disorders: Depression and Bipolar Disorder

Mood disorders have been called the "common cold" of psychiatric illnesses. While everyone experiences shifts in moods from time to time, most of us do not understand the depths of depression or the highs and lows of bipolar disorder. It is estimated that more than 20 million Americans will suffer a mood disorder episode during their lifetime; however, only one in three people who experience this debilitating disorder will seek treatment. Although it was once commonly thought that children did not experience mood disorders, clinical opinion has turned and it is now believed that individuals throughout the lifespan can and do experience the helplessness that accompanies mood disorders. As with all psychiatric disorders, mood disorders are diagnosed with the use of the *DSM-IV*, which divides them into depressive disorders and bipolar disorders. Not surprisingly, such mood disorders have frequently been associated with adolescent risk taking in the following domains: substance abuse, gambling, sex, and suicide.

Depression is a mood disorder characterized by changes in emotion, motivation, physical well-being, and thoughts (Papolos & Papolos, 1997). The emotional state of adolescents experiencing depression can be characterized as overwhelming feelings of sadness or worthlessness. Changes in motivational states are recognized as changes in an individual's desires and behavior, perhaps including changes in friendships or stopping associations with friends altogether, changes in recreational activities or stopping participation in these activities, and changes in schoolwork, most often resulting in a decline in grades. Changes in physical well-being are also observed through exhibition of behaviors in the individual that are recognized as different from his or her normal patterns of behavior. These can include alterations such as eating and sleeping too much or too little, disregarding personal hygiene and appearance, and having vague physical complaints such as aches and pains that have no origin. Thought and cognition changes also occur which help to sustain the disorder in the individual as he or she believes him or herself to be worthless, ugly, and unable to do anything right, along with believing that life is hopeless.

Research has found that symptoms of depression manifest differently in children, adolescents, and adults, fueling the debate over whether children actually experience depression. In children, depression is mixed with a larger array of behavioral characteristics that are often misunderstood, leading to the difficulty in diagnosis. Depressed children often display aggression, irritability, undifferentiated anxiety, antisocial behavior, and school failure. In addition, depression often occurs in conjunction with other disorders such as conduct disorder, substance abuse, eating disorders, and anxiety disorders. According to the American Academy of Child and Adolescent Psychiatry, approximately 3.4 million children and adolescents in the United States have been diagnosed with depression.

Bipolar disorder, known throughout most of the twentieth century as manic-depressive illness, is experiencing rising rates of diagnosis in children and adolescents. Just as it was thought that children do not experience depression, it was also believed that bipolar illness does not occur in individuals until late adolescence or early adulthood (Papolos & Papolos, 1999). Although it is estimated that between one and two percent of adults worldwide may experience bipolar disorder, due to the appearance of several different types of difficulties occurring together, known as comorbid conditions, estimates of children afflicted with the disorder are presumed to be inaccurate. These comorbid conditions include the high-risk behaviors previously considered such as substance abuse, sexual contact, gambling, and suicide, as well as academic and social difficulties.

Current diagnosis of bipolar disorder indicates that approximately one million children and adolescents in the United States are affected. However, according to the American Academy of Child and Adolescent Psychiatry, up to one third of the children and adolescents currently diagnosed with depression may actually be experiencing early-onset bipolar disorder. In addition, it is suspected that many of the children currently diagnosed with ADHD may also have early-onset bipolar disorder. It is important to note here that there is considerable controversy today among clinicians regarding the use of the bipolar diagnosis with children.

While depression is characterized by mood states that are low, individuals who suffer from bipolar disorder experience exaggerated mood states. An individual with bipolar disorder is depressed at times and then swings to the other end of the mood spectrum and has heightened levels of activity, ideas, and energy known as mania. Bipolar disorder presents itself differently in adults and children, which initially led to the belief that children and adolescents did not experience it. The *DSM-IV* criteria for the classification of bipolar disorder requires that the manic and depressive episodes that the individual experiences go on for a prescribed duration—days or weeks. However, this is not the pattern that is generally found in children, who appear to experience a more chronic and erratic course, frequently with many shifts in mood throughout a day. Thus, many children and adolescents do not meet the diagnostic criteria specified in the *DSM-IV*. Additionally, as there is a great deal of overlap in the demonstration of symptoms in children and adolescents, frequently these individuals are diagnosed with other psychiatric labels such as ADHD, depression, oppositional defiant disorder, obsessive-compulsive disorder, or separation anxiety disorder.

Anxiety Disorders

All of us experience anxiety at some time and to some degree. Low levels of anxiety can be beneficial in helping a person to remain alert in situations that require focus and can also improve performance in some areas. In fact, anxiety is considered normal at specific points in development. One example of this is the anxieties that infants exhibit starting at about eight months of age upon separation from individuals they are attached to. However, high levels of anxiety can be debilitating and can cause interference with the daily routines experienced at different points in development such as separating from parents, going to school or work, and making friends in new social situations.

Anxiety disorders are characterized by excessive amounts of fear, worry, and uneasiness, and cause significant impairment in academic, social, and familial functioning. The anxiety experienced by some individuals can be debilitating and become so distressing that depression results from it. As anxiety disorders often coexist with depression, suicidal behavior is a concern that must be monitored closely in such instances. This can cause an additional worry as a class of antidepressant drugs known as SSRIs, or Selective Serotonin Reuptake Inhibitors, are frequently used in the medical treatment of anxiety disorders and have been thought to lead to heightened levels of suicidal ideation in adolescent patients.

There are many types of anxiety disorders. Table 7.1 presents a brief description of some of the more common anxiety disorders. Children and adolescents can develop any of these subtypes; however, some are more common in childhood than others (Langley, Bergman, & Piacentini, 2002; Saavedra & Silverman, 2002). Younger children tend to experience separation anxiety, specific phobias, and early symptoms of

Table 7.1 Anxiety Disorder Subtypes with Brief Descriptions

Separation Anxiety Disorder	Persistent thoughts and fears about safety for self and parents, school refusal, physical complaints, extreme worry over sleeping away from home, trouble sleeping, and nightmares.
Specific Phobia	Irrational fear reaction to a specific object or situation such as spiders or heights. Can lead to the avoidance of everyday situations.
General Anxiety Disorder	Characterized by excessive, chronic, and unrealistic worry that lasts six months or more. Symptoms may include trembling, physical complaints, insomnia, and irritability.
Social Anxiety Disorder	Extreme anxiety at the thought of being judged by others. Irrational fear of behaving in a way that will cause embarrassment. Physical symptoms may include heart palpitations, faintness, trembling, and profuse sweating.
Panic Disorder	Severe attacks of panic that can occur in a variety of situations and result in physical symptoms such as heart palpitations, chest pain, sweating, fear of dying, fear of losing control, and fear of unreality.
Obsessive-Compulsive Disorder	Persistent recurring thoughts (obsessions) that reflect fears or anxiety. Obsessions lead the individual to perform a routine behavior (compulsions). Examples of compulsions include washing hands, repeating phrases, and turning lights on and off a certain number of times.
Post-Traumatic Stress Disorder	Follows exposure to a traumatic event such as assault, death, and natural or man-made disasters. Symptoms include reliving the event through flashbacks or nightmares, avoidance behaviors and emotional numbing, and physiological arousal such as irritability and poor concentration.

obsessive-compulsive disorder, while generalized anxiety disorder and social anxiety disorder are more common to middle childhood and adolescence, and panic disorder usually develops during adolescence. Another subtype of anxiety disorder, post-traumatic stress disorder, can occur at any point that a trauma is experienced. The *DSM-IV* is used to diagnose anxiety disorders based on the clinical judgment of presenting symptoms, while utilizing specific diagnostic criteria to determine the subtype of the anxiety disorder and to rule out other comorbid disorders.

High levels of untreated anxiety can lead adolescents to engage in other high-risk behaviors in an effort to calm these fears. For example, substance abuse accompanies many of the profiled anxiety disorders as individuals take various substances to cope with their difficulties. This is seen in instances of social anxiety disorder when an individual employs cigarettes, alcohol, or drugs to help them to interact socially, or in post-traumatic stress disorder when drugs or alcohol are used to avoid reexperiencing the traumatic event. Additionally, an anxiety disorder can be experienced in connection with the use of a variety of legal and illegal substances, as well as during the withdrawal from the use of these substances. The substances known to evoke anxiety reactions include alcohol, cocaine, caffeine, and marijuana, among others.

Another high-risk behavior adolescents engage in to reduce feelings of anxiety, stress, and tension is self-mutilation. Although media attention on "cutting," as it is familiarly known, has increased, this behavior is not new. Part of self-mutilation's higher profile has come about in part due to celebrity confessions of engaging in the behavior during stressful times. For example, the public figure Princess Diana, prior to her untimely death, and the movie idol Johnny Depp had confessed to cutting themselves to relieve inner pain. Previously clinicians had focused on self-mutilating behaviors as a symptom of other psychiatric disorders, such as borderline personality disorder. However, more recently, the mental health community has looked at the behavior as a problem in and of itself. Self-mutilation can be defined as the deliberate destruction of one's body tissue, although there is no thought about suicide. It includes such behaviors as cutting, burning, pulling hairs, and skin scratching. These behaviors occur in approximately one in one thousand individuals and appear at first to be a viable coping mechanism to the adolescent. However, as the cutting continues, it becomes almost an addiction, an act that is needed in order to reduce anxiety (Egan, 1997).

Eating Disorders

Over the past 20 years, there has been a significant increase in cases of eating disorders (Neumark-Sztainer, Story, Hannan, & Croll, 2002). These disorders are defined in terms of: 1) maladaptive attempts to control body weight, 2) serious disruptions in eating behavior, and 3) abnormal attitudes about body shape and weight. Although it would seem more understand-able if these behaviors were to occur in a morbidly obese individual, in reality, eating disorders may occur in people who are overweight, normal weight, or underweight. Individuals with eating disorders seek to control their weight either through binging, restricting food intake, or employing inappropriate compensatory mechanisms to help eliminate or purge the food they have consumed (Neumark-Sztainer, Story, Dixon, & Murray, 1998). Although there are two main categories considered when most peo-ple think of eating disorders—anorexia nervosa and bulimia nervosa—a third category, binge-eating disorder, is starting to garner attention also. Eating disorders generally begin in adolescence, and occur most frequently in white females from middle- to upper-income households; however, they also occur in males and in lower-income households.

Anorexia nervosa is a life-threatening disorder that is characterized by an intense fear of gaining weight, by having a body weight less than 85 percent of the individual's expected weight, and by having distorted body images that lack recognition of the low body weight. Female anorexics experience disruption of the menstrual cycle and can place themselves at risk of death from the extreme restrictions on caloric intake that they impose; however, they do not perceive their low body weight as posing a health risk. Anorexic individuals are classified as falling into one of two categories—they either are a restrictive subtype or a binge-eating/purging subtype. The restrictive type accomplishes weight loss through dieting, fasting, or excessive exercise. The binge-eating/purging type accomplishes weight loss through the purging of food after eating. This can take the form of self-induced vomiting, or the misuse of laxatives and diuretics. Although a frequency has not been established, individuals usually engage in this behavior at least once a week.

Individuals with anorexia nervosa exhibit symptoms of emotional dis-turbance (Bruch, 1979). These symptoms may manifest themselves in behaviors that resemble depression and obsessive-compulsive disorder. Those with the binge-eating/purging subtype also exhibit impulse-control difficulties frequently related to adolescent risk taking such as substance abuse and sexual activity.

Whereas anorexics restrict their intake, similar to the anorexic binge-eating/purging subtype, those exhibiting bulimia nervosa engage in binge eating and then utilize inappropriate compensatory means—self-induced vomiting—to prevent weight gain. In addition, these individuals are excessively influenced by body shape and weight and their self-evaluations in this regard often affect their feelings of self-esteem. To be diagnosed with this eating disorder, the binging—compensatory cycle has to have occurred at least twice a week for a period of three months. There are two subtypes of bulimics which indicate the method used to compensate for the binge eating—purging and non-purging. The individual that employs purging relies on self-induced vomiting or the misuse of laxatives or diuretics to prevent weight gain, while those that fall into the non-purging subtype will employ methods such as fasting or excessive exercise to control weight gain.

As with anorexia nervosa, individuals with bulimia also exhibit depressive symptoms. Additionally, anxiety disorders are frequently present and approximately one third of bulimics turn to alcohol or stimulants in an attempt to control their appetite.

The third category of eating disorder—the one increasingly recognized—is called binge-eating disorder. This disorder has not been officially sanctioned as a disorder by the medical community and thus is included in the *DSM-IV* as an area in need of further study. Despite this, many experts in the field of eating disorders acknowledge the validity of the classification. Binge eating is a disorder in which the individual consumes an unusually large amount of food in a limited time period and feels a lack of control and significant distress over the eating. In addition, the binge eater expresses concern over the long-term effects of the binge eating on body weight and shape. This behavior must occur at least twice a week for a period of six months. The disorder is different from bulimia nervosa in that there is an absence of the inappropriate compensatory mechanisms such as fasting, purging, use of laxatives or excessive exercise.

In comparison to anorexia with an incidence rate of 0.6 percent and bulimia with a rate of 1.0 percent, the incidence rate for binge eating was 2.8 percent. Discussing the limitations of the study, the lead author pointed out that it relied on self-reported behavior so that it was not really possible to state the true prevalence of the various eating disorders in adolescents or adults (Bakalar, 2007).

Binge-eating disorder is associated with psychological disturbances as were anorexia nervosa and bulimia nervosa. Specifically, overeating was associated with body dissatisfaction, depressed mood, low self-esteem, anxiety, and high levels of interpersonal sensitivity (Ackard, Neumark-Sztainer, Story, & Perry, 2003). Additionally, these individuals also engage in substance abuse and express suicidal ideation and suicidal behaviors.

The profile of health issues facing American children changed significantly in the twentieth century. The broad availability of immunizations and antibiotics has drastically reduced, and in some cases eliminated, contagious diseases that once posed serious threats to children's survival. At the present time, the most pervasive and rapidly growing challenges to children's health have strong environmental components that interact with genetic predispositions and vulnerabilities; these challenges include the mental health disorders briefly discussed. The complexities of these disorders require comprehensive approaches to prevention and intervention. The fact that many of these mental health disorders appear during a developmental life stage that is characterized by increased stress and pressure is not a coincidence. The environmental stressors adolescents experience interact with biological predispositions to contribute to the surge in incidence. These same stressors also contribute to an increase in adolescent risk-taking behavior. Although it is not always possible to know which came first, adolescent risk taking or mental health difficulties, the combination of the two can create a deadly duo for any adolescent. As with all high-risk behaviors, careful attention to prevent and treat these problems is important.

Mental Health Resources

American Academy of Child and Adolescent Psychiatry—Facts for families
http://www.aacap.org/page.ww?section=Facts+for+Families&name=Facts+for+Families

American Psychiatric Association
1000 Wilson Boulevard, Suite 1825
Arlington, VA 22209–390
888–35–PSYCH (357–7924)
703–907–7300
http://www.psych.org

American Psychological Association
750 First Street, NE
Washington, DC 20002–4242
800–374–2721
202–336–5500
http://www.apa.org

Center for Mental Health Services (CMHS)
Knowledge Exchange Network (KEN)
P.O. Box 42490
Washington, DC 20015
800–789–2647
http://www.mentalhealth.org

Depression and Bipolar Support Alliance (DBSA)
730 North Franklin Street, Suite 501
Chicago, IL 60601–7204
800–826–3632
http://www.dbsalliance.org

Depression and Related Affected Disorders Association
Meyer 3–181
600 North Wolfe Street
Baltimore, MD 21287–7381
410–955–4647

Depression Resources at WebMD
http://www.webmd.com/depression/guide/depression-resources

Juvenile Bipolar Research Foundation
http://www.bpchildresearch.org/juv_bipolar/index.html

National Alliance for Research on Schizophrenia and Depression
60 Cutter Mill Road, Suite 404
Great Neck, NY 11021
800–829–8289
http://www.narsad.org

National Alliance for the Mentally Ill
Colonial Place Three
2107 Wilson Boulevard, Suite 300
Arlington, VA 22201–3042
800–950–NAMI (950–6264)
703–524–7600
http://www.nami.org

National Eating Disorders Association
http://www.edap.org

National Foundation for Depressive Illness, Inc.
P.O. Box 2257
New York, NY 10116
800–239–1265
http://www.depression.org

National Institute of Mental Health (NIMH)
Public Inquiries
6001 Executive Boulevard, Suite 8184, MSC 9663
Bethesda, MD 20892–9663
301–443–4513
http://www.nimh.nih.gov

National Mental Health Association
2001 North Beauregard Street, 12th Floor
Alexandria, VA 22311
800–969–NMHA (969–6642)
http://www.nmha.org

Something Fishy—Website on eating disorders
http://www.something-fishy.org

Works Cited

Ackard, D., Neumark-Sztainer, D., Story, M., & Perry, C. (2003). Overeating among adolescents: Prevalence and associations with weight related characteristics and psychological health. *Pediatrics, 111,* 67–74.

American Academy of Child and Adolescent Psychiatry. ADHD #6. *Facts for families.* Retrieved from http://www.aacap.org/page.ww?section=Facts+for+Families&name=Facts+for+Families

American Academy of Child and Adolescent Psychiatry. Anxiety #47. *Facts for families.* Retrieved from http://www.aacap.org/page.ww?section=Facts+for+Families&name=Facts+for+Families

American Academy of Child and Adolescent Psychiatry. Bipolar disorder # 38. *Facts for families.* Retrieved from http://www.aacap.org/page.ww?section=Facts+for+Families&name=Facts+for+Families

American Academy of Child and Adolescent Psychiatry. Depression #4. *Facts for families.* Retrieved from http://www.aacap.org/page.ww?section=Facts+for+Families&name=Facts+for+Families

American Academy of Child and Adolescent Psychiatry. Eating disorders # 2. *Facts for families.* Retrieved from http://www.aacap.org/page.ww?section=Facts+for+Families&name=Facts+for+Families

American Psychiatric Association. *Diagnostic and statistical manual of mental disorders* (4th ed.). Washington, DC: Author.

Bakalar, N. (2007, February 13). Survey puts new focus on binge eating as a diagnosis. *New York Times.* Retrieved from http://www.nytimes.com/2007/02/13/health/psychology/13eat.html

Barkley, R.A. (1990). *Attention-deficit/hyperactivity disorder: A handbook for diagnosis and treatment.* New York: Guilford.

Bruch, H. (1979). *The golden cage: The enigma of anorexia nervosa.* New York: Vintage.

Egan, J. (1997, July 27). The thin red line. *The New York Times Magazine.* Retrieved from http://www.jenniferegan.com/articles/1997_07_27_nyt_line.html

Langley, A., Bergman, L., & Piacentini, J. (2002). Assessment of childhood anxiety. *International Review of Psychiatry, 14,* 102–113.

National Institutes of Health. (1998). Diagnosis and treatment of attention deficit hyperactivity disorder. *Consensus development conference statement, 16,* 1–37.

Neumark-Sztainer, D., Story, M., Dixon, L.B., & Murray, D.M. (1998). Adolescents engaging in unhealthy weight control behaviors: Are they at risk for other health-compromising behaviors? *American Journal of Public Health, 88,* 952–955.

Neumark-Sztainer, D., Story, M., Hannan, P.J., & Croll, J. (2002). Overweight status and eating patterns among adolescents: Where do youths stand in comparison with the Healthy People 2010 objectives? *American Journal of Public Health, 92,* 844–851.

Papolos, D. & Papolos, J. (1997). *Overcoming depression* (3rd ed.). New York: Harper Collins.

Papolos, D. & Papolos, J. (1999). *The bipolar child.* New York: Broadway Books.

Saavedra, L. & Silverman, W. (2002). Classification of anxiety disorders in children: What a difference two decades make. *International Review of Psychiatry, 14*, 87–101.

Wicks-Nelson, R. & Israel, A.C. (2000). *Behavior disorders of childhood.* Upper Saddle River, NJ: Prentice Hall.

CHAPTER 8

Possible Causes of Adolescent Risk Taking

How events such as parental drug use, incarceration, divorce, and moving from one community to another affect children and impact their own risk taking may depend on the timing of these events. At the same time, how drug use, gambling, or violence impacts the child's later development also depends upon their own timing. According to Johnson, Hoffman, and Gerstein (1996), "there is widespread agreement among researchers that substance use during adolescence, especially more serious patterns of use, may interrupt the normal course of development and thus engender lower educational attainment, troubled interpersonal relations, poor mental health, physical health problems, and arrested achievement of adult social roles and milestones" (p. 8).

The introductory chapter of this book included a brief summary on theories or explanation of why adolescents are so prone to risk taking. The current chapter provides a more in-depth discussion of this question while detailing some of the specific factors such as genes and family dynamics that have been proposed in an attempting to make sense of adolescent risk taking.

Genetics

To what extent could risk taking in adolescence result from genetic predispositions operating during this period of life when a whole host of risk-taking behaviors become more available? While terms such as "born criminal" or "wild by nature" suggest that people sometimes believe that biological forces lead people, almost involuntarily, to engage in risky or inappropriate behavior, what real evidence is there to suggest that genes, rather than environmental forces, produce such behavior? We begin our examination of the possible biological origins of adolescent risk taking with the concept of child temperament.

Child Temperament

Temperament has been defined as constitutionally-based, characteristic ways of responding to the world (Thomas, Chess, & Birch, 1968). While many adults have noticed that infants differ in the characteristic ways in which they behave and respond to the world around them, systematic investigations of child temperament did not begin until the 1950s with the work of Chess and Thomas. Working in New York City, these developmental researchers conducted longitudinal research in which they followed children from shortly after birth through adulthood. To accomplish this, they conducted a series of interviews with parent at strategic points in development, asking them to describe their children and their characteristic ways of responding in and to the world. After analyzing the results of questionnaires on an initial sample of 141 children, Chess and Thomas identified nine basic dimensions of infant temperament (see the following textbox).

NINE DIMENSIONS OF TEMPERAMENT: CHESS & THOMAS

- Activity level
- Regularity (eating and sleeping patterns)
- Adaptability to change
- Approach or withdrawal (new experiences)
- Sensitivity
- Intensity of reaction
- Distractibility
- Persistence
- Mood (positive or negative)

Following this identification process, they rated each child on these dimensions and were able to classify the majority of them as one of three basic temperamental styles—easy, difficult, and slow-to-warm. Easy babies were described as playful and regular with regard to their biological functions of eating, sleeping, and elimination. They also adapted quickly to new environments and circumstances. Difficult babies were described as irregular in biological functions. They did not adapt quickly and instead responded intensely and negatively to new environments. Finally, slow-to-warm babies were described as low in activity level. These babies tended to withdraw rather than approach new environments. They required additional time to adapt to new circumstances.

While there is considerable research to support the idea of temperamental differences between infants, debate continues today regarding the persistence of these differences over time and the source of any observed continuity. Of greater importance for our discussion is whether or not such temperament differences between individuals might be associated with later differences in adolescent risk taking. We focus here on one of the nine dimensions of temperament originally identified by Chess and Thomas, approach-withdrawal.

According to their research, by 10 years of age a child characterized by positive approach enjoys engaging in new experiences—loves going to camp and learning to ski. The child characterized by negative withdrawal immediately becomes homesick or refuses to even get on the chair lift or put on his or her skis. While the "approach" child enjoys new experiences, the "avoidance" child does not. These descriptions indicate that, as a result of these basic temperamental differences, while the "approach" child might be curious and interested in experimenting with drugs or taking other risks, the "avoidant" child would not be. Interestingly, in this scenario a trait that might be generally viewed positively—positive approach—might predispose an adolescent to engage in risk activities while a trait generally viewed negatively—negative avoidance—might protect an adolescent from such engagement. In the next section, we discuss sensation seeking, a personality trait thought to influence a great deal of adolescent risk taking that may have its origin in genetically-determined temperament.

Sensation Seeking

Sensation seeking has been defined as "the need for varied, novel, and complex sensation and experiences and the willingness to take physical and social risks for the sake of such experiences" (Zuckerman, 1979, p. 10). Sensation seeking clearly goes well beyond the approach dimension of temperament to include a host of other dimensions that might predispose an adolescent to risk taking behavior. According to Zuckerman, sensation seeking is prevalent in some adolescents as a result of brain chemistry and hormonal differences. At the same time, sensation seeking during adolescence may partly result because of the general maturation process in conjunction with the process of separation from the family.

A number of research studies have linked sensation seeking to a number of risky practices including failure to use seat belts as well as drinking and driving. Importantly, critics point out that many adolescent risky practices, such as smoking cigarettes, do not easily fit into the characterization of thrill seeking so frequently associated with sensation seeking. On the other hand, the nicotine rush that occurs when one smokes could be considered some support for the idea that adolescents are seeking to change their levels of stimulation by smoking. The illegality of this behavior among underage adolescents may further appeal to those characterized by sensation seeking.

For many developmental researchers, however, an exclusive or overly-determined focus on genetic causes of adolescent risk taking seems unwarranted, since there are so many environmental factors that contribute to risky adolescent actions. From these researchers' point of view there is little reason to place such extreme emphasis on genetic, predetermined behavior patterns in our attempts to explain adolescent risk taking.

Environmental Influences

In this section we consider some of those environmental influences and their impact on adolescent risk taking. We illustrate environmental influences by highlighting specific theories of development that have impacted our own thinking regarding such influences and the multiple ways they may affect adolescent risk taking.

Transactional Model of Development

Because of the central role accorded mothers in Freud's psychoanalytic theory of child development, some have concluded that mothers are to blame for children's negative behaviors, including their risk taking. That is, because the theory places mothers at the center of children's early developmental course, if a child develops abnormal need for drugs or shows overt signs of antisocial behavior, it must be because the mother did something wrong or failed to provide the correct environment for "normal" development. From this perspective, adolescents take risks either because of something the mother did to them or because of something she failed to do. For most contemporary developmental researchers, this is not only an extremely biased view, but, more importantly from our current understanding, an overly simplistic one, as it ignores so many other family influences, including those exerted by fathers, siblings, and grandparents, as well as the influences of significant others outside the family, such as teachers and peers.

Even when the influences of both parents on behavior are acknowledged, however, most of us still tend to advocate overly-simplistic views of children's behavior such as those depicted in the following textbox.

SIMPLISTIC EXPLANATIONS OF ADOLESCENT RISK TAKING

He's always been a bad kid.

His parents never loved him.

She runs around with a bad crowd; what do you expect?

She's a slut.

Gambling's in his blood; he can't help himself.

He's been feeling bad; that's why he turned to drugs.

It's her mother's fault; she never set a good example.

In each example, children's actions are depicted as if they result solely from the impact of parents' behaviors upon them. For most of human history, this is the way people have thought about the socialization process in which children are shaped by parents over time to move from being helpless newborns to well-adjusted members of society. From this point of view, the lines of influence are unidirectional, flowing from parents and their actions directly to children.

Parents>>>>>>>>>>>>>>>>>Children's Actions

In 1968 an alternative, revolutionary, yet still relatively simplistic view of socialization was put forth by Bell. In it he suggested that rather than being unidirectional, socialization was a bi-directional process that operated from children to parents as well as from parents to children. From Bell's perspective, while parental actions clearly impacted their children, the actions and reactions of children to these actions, in turn, influenced parents. One obvious implication of this more-complex perspective is that during socialization parents are also learning about what works and what does not in raising children and modifying their behavior. One consequence of such learning is the frequently observed fact that parents are more relaxed with later-born children and frequently react differently to them than their older children. The point here is that children as well as parents have an impact on the socialization process that occurs within the family unit.

Parents>>>>Children's Actions>>>>Parents' Actions>>>>Children's Actions, Etc.

The ultimate choices a child makes, whether risky or not, do not result simply from what parents have done to him or her but come as a result of how that child responds to his or her parents, as well. Children are not simply reactive organisms; they too initiate actions, and these may have important impacts on their long-term development and willingness to take risks. From this bi-directional view of socialization, a risk-taking adolescent may have become a risk taker not only because of his or her parents' treatment, but also because of the characteristic ways in which the child responded to the parents and because of his or her genetic make up or temperamental style.

While this bi-directional view of socialization was a major advance over the view that parents influence children but are not influenced in return, it hardly provides a realistic view of the complexities involved in parent-child relationships. Not surprisingly, therefore, developmental researchers eventually moved to the more complex transactional model to depict the forces that influence child development within a family. According to the transactional theory of development, it is not only the parents or the temperamental characteristics of a child that determine whether he or she will engage in adolescent risk taking; instead, the ultimate outcome of parent-child interactions depends on the transactions that occur between parents and children over years together, as well as on the fit or correspondence between the behaviors of the parents and those of their children.

Chess and Thomas (1987) emphasized a similar point when they demonstrated that a child's particular characteristics are not what determine developmental outcomes, including the use of illicit drugs or early sexual exploration, so much as it is the goodness of fit between the child's endowments and the environment—the fit between the child and key individuals in the child's environment, including parents, siblings, and teachers.

According to Patterson and his colleagues in the Oregon Research Group, both innate and environmental forces are at play in producing aggressive children and adolescents (Patterson, 1982; Patterson, Cohn, & Kao, 1989). While the child's temperament may predispose him or her to angry outbursts and low tolerance for frustration, how a parent responds to such behaviors may be critical in determining whether such negative behaviors become habitual patterns or isolated occurrences. This suggests that parents who respond to such behaviors by becoming angry themselves simply provide models of the very behavior they are trying to eliminate. Similarly, a parent who gives in to a child's tantrum to quiet an unpleasant outburst in a public space unwittingly rewards that precise behavior, ensuring its occurrence in similar situations in the future. Unfortunately, these types of negative behavior also frequently lead to peer rejection in childhood and adolescence and may move such children toward antisocial peer groups that support such negative behaviors. From this perspective, the fit between the child's temperament and attendant actions and the parents' reactions to them is critical in determining whether the negative behaviors become isolated incidents or become established, long-standing, and frequent behavioral patterns. Patterson and colleagues have developed family intervention strategies to assist parents to avoid producing or maintaining negative behavior patterns in their children.

Another type of poor parent-child fit that may ultimately lead to inappropriate child or adolescent behavior can be seen in the following example of a drug-abusing parent and child. There are many reasons to assume that the fit is often not particularly good between drug-abusing mothers and their drug-exposed infants. The profiles of addicted mothers include higher levels of depression and stress and lower levels of self-esteem than those of mothers who have been matched on various characteristics but are non-drug-abusing (Fiks, Johnson, & Rosen, 1985; Luthar, D'Avanzo, & Hites, 2003). Furthermore, cocaine-abusing mothers have been found to be less attentive and responsive to their infants (Mayes et al., 1996), and addicted mothers hold more negative perceptions of their children (Bernstein & Hans, 1994). At the same time, research suggests that the drug-exposed infant is more likely to be characterized as a "difficult baby" using the classic description of Chess and Thomas (1987). The infant often presents a distinctly intense cry and is irritable and difficult to comfort and console (Lester et al., 2001). Some of the characteristics may actually represent symptoms of neonatal narcotics abstinence syndrome (Finnegan, 1976). In any event, these characteristics make the task of providing love and responsive care particularly demanding.

Together, these two groups of characteristics, those of the substance-abusing mother and those of the drug-exposed infant, produce a potentially destructive mismatch between the drug-addicted mother's limited emotional resources and the infant's intense caregiving needs and demands (Johnson, Bejarano, Nusbaum, & Rosen, 1996). The tension within the dyad created by this mismatch is likely to limit the mother's emotional responsiveness to her infant. The resulting mother-child transactions often produce negative rather than positive child behaviors, including various types of risk-taking behaviors in the child.

From another perspective, drug-exposed children are sometimes characterized as "damaged goods" and considered abnormal in their interactions with the environment. To a great extent, however, many of the characteristics these children exhibit make sense as reactions or adaptations to their experience. Thus a child whose caregiver is erratic or abusive, as would be the case with many drug-addicted mothers, may well learn not to engage in extended social interactions with the mother. There are no models for these interactions in the child's experience, and the interaction carries with it the possibility of negative consequences (Johnson, Bejarano, Nusbaum, & Rosen, 1996). For many drug-exposed children, remaining unengaged and non-communicative is an adaptive skill of survival. So in this case, normal adaptive processes can result in deviant outcomes (Sameroff, 1994), and the disorders reported in drug-exposed children may in fact reflect the operation of normal developmental processes in response to atypical infant-mother transactions.

At the same time, it is important to understand that the same parenting style may have a widely different impact, depending on the circumstances surrounding its use and on the temperament of the child receiving it. For example, while authoritarian parenting characterized by harsh discipline has frequently been associated with alcohol abuse and antisocial behaviors in Caucasian youth (Kandel & Yamaguchi, 2002), the same parental behavior may exert a positive influence on the substance use of non-Caucasian children living in environments typical for their sociocultural background (Baumrind, 1972; Johnson & Johnson, 1999).

The Interactionist Perspective and Other Complexities

Having highlighted genetic and environmental approaches to understanding adolescent risk taking, we now turn to the interactionist model. In this model, the combination or interactions of biological and

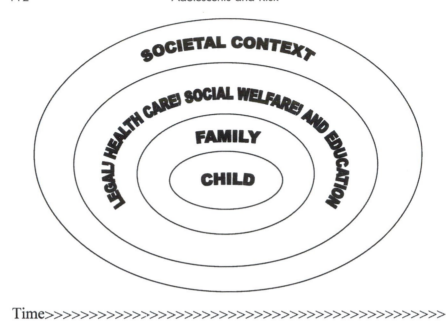

Time>>>

Figure 1   Ecological Theory of Development

environmental factors cause behavior. While placing particular emphasis on combinations of biological and environmental forces, the interactionist model also emphasizes that behavior does not generally result from a single source or cause, but rather is the result of multiple factors. This is important to understand, because so often when asked to explain why an adolescent engages in a specific risk behavior like smoking cigarettes, we point to a single cause or factor such as peer pressure or parental modeling. A more realistic view of adolescent risk taking is to consider it as multi-determined and complex in its origins.

The ecological model of Bronfenbrenner (1979) is perhaps the best example of such a complex interactionist theory of child development. Recently renamed the bio-ecological systems theory of development, the model highlights the multiple layers of environment that, together with the individual's own biological predispositions, interact to ultimately explain individual behaviors. At the innermost layer of environmental influences we find the microsystem that includes peers, family, and classroom. Outside of this we have the exosystem that includes school, community, and the mass media. At the outermost environmental layer we have the macrosystem that is composed of culture and society. Not only does each of these systems interact in multiple ways with one another, but they do so over time as well. The resulting theory of development is highly detailed and complex, which may make sense to provide an accurate portrait of the complex forces that ultimately produce adolescent risk-taking activities. From the perspective of providing a clear and easily understandable theory of behavior, however, the ecological model may be overly cumbersome. One of the theory's strengths, it should be noted, is the importance it attaches to the timing of specific events in a child's life and to the ways in which that timing can impact a child's development for years to come. Figure 1 provides a simplified schematic of this rich theory of development and its multiple layers of interacting influences.

The time dimension indicates that these influences are ongoing and repetitive throughout development.

We now turn to the issue of timing and the ways in which it can impact adolescent development and risk taking.

Timing and Developmental Outcomes

Developmental psychologists including Bronfenbrenner (1979) have reframed the nature-nurture or genetics-environment debate on the interplay between organic and environmental influences in determining developmental outcomes. In some instances the impact of particular influences, such as illicit drug use, varies with its timing, as illustrated in the case of maternal substance abuse during pregnancy. The effects are most harmful to the child's development during the first trimester, and this initial early exposure may have a direct and specific impact on development (Bernstein & Hans, 1994). The significance of maternal drug use in the life of a child, however, is realized through the response of the environment over time to the endowments, capacities, and inclinations of the particular child, as well as through the influence of the child's changing needs and behavior on the environment. The significance of maternal drug use is also realized through the impact of this use on health care, social welfare, criminal justice consequences, and educational outcomes for the child.

How events such as parental drug use, incarceration, divorce, and moving from one community to another affect children and impact their own risk taking may depend on the timing of these events. At the same time, how drug use, gambling, or violence impacts the child's later development also depends upon their own timing. According to Johnson, Hoffman, and Gerstein (1996), "there is widespread agreement among researchers that substance use during adolescence, especially more serious patterns of use, may interrupt the normal course of development and thus engender lower educational attainment, troubled interpersonal relations, poor mental health, physical health problems, and arrested achievement of adult social roles and milestones" (p. 8).

One reason that early drug use has such widespread effects is that early adolescence, the period when a great deal of drug experimentation and use occur, is a unique period of life when children begin the complex process of making the transition to adulthood. The rapid pace of physical and cognitive development during this period influences all aspects of life and propels children to contend with new social, emotional, and intellectual challenges. The volatility of this period places children at heightened risk for the development of maladaptive coping strategies, including use and abuse of drugs and alcohol and engagement in violence and other antisocial behaviors.

During early adolescence, the majority of students have their first encounter with substance use in social settings. Although in many American communities some experimentation with drugs is "normative" for adolescents, there is strong evidence of links between early onset of drug and alcohol abuse and involvement in violence. There is also strong evidence that this "early onset" population is particularly vulnerable to extended involvement in problem behavior.

Developmental researchers such as Schulenberg and Maggs (2002) have emphasized the importance of timing with respect to youth drug experimentation. The same cautions could be applied to other forms of adolescent risk taking including sexual exploration, gambling, and violence. There are some times when students are particularly vulnerable to becoming involved with drugs. While drug use at some points in an adolescent's life may have relatively little impact on future development, drug use at critical time points may forever alter an individual adolescent's life trajectory, thereby limiting future life success.

For example, an adolescent who becomes heavily involved with drugs in high school, when most students are setting educational and long-range occupational goals, may decide to drop out, increasing the potential for disastrous, lifelong consequences. In fact, a child who becomes involved with drugs during times of critical brain development may actually permanently alter the trajectory of his or her brain development (Spear, 2002).

Clustering of Risk-Taking Behaviors

At various points throughout this book we have written as if individual risk behaviors like gambling and drug use occur alone; the reality is that this is rarely the case. For the most part, research studies have demonstrated the opposite over and over again. The classic work of psychologists Jessor and Jessor (1977) on problem behavior theory demonstrated that behaviors including drug abuse, delinquency, and early sexual activity tend to occur in clusters within individuals; thus, adolescents are likely to engage in more than one type of risky behavior if they engage in any. The initiation and maintenance of problem behaviors in early adolescence are significant predictors of the educational and occupational trajectories of individuals, influencing whether adolescents follow successful educational and occupational paths or not, thereby restricting their future life success. Schulenberg and Maggs (2002) have summarized work demonstrating the importance of early involvement in problem behaviors to these life paths. As a result even when you are talking about the impact of individual risk behaviors and their long-term effects, you are actually talking about multiple behaviors because they so frequently co-occur. It may be this combination of risky behaviors that actually produces such long-range devastating impacts.

Works Cited

Baumrind, D. (1972). An exploratory study of socialization effects on black children: Some black-white comparisons. *Child Development, 42,* 261–267.

Bell, R.Q. (1968). A reinterpretation of the direction of effects in studies of socialization. *Psychological Review, 75,* 81–95.

Bernstein, V.J. & Hans, S.L. (1994). Predicting the developmental outcome of two-year-old children born exposed to methadone: The impact of social-environmental risk factors. *Journal of Clinical Child Psychology, 23,* 349–359.

Bronfenbrenner, U. (1979). *The ecology of human development.* Cambridge, MA: Harvard University Press.

Chess, S. & Thomas, A. (1987). *Origins and evolution of behavior disorders: From infancy to early adult life.* Cambridge, MA: Harvard University Press.

Fiks, K., Johnson, H., & Rosen, T. (1985). Methadone maintained mothers: Three-year follow-up of parental functioning. *International Journal of Addictions, 20,* 651–660.

Finnegan, L.P. (1976). Clinical effects of pharmacological agents on pregnancy and the fetus and the neonate. *Annals of the New York Academy of Science, 281,* 74–89.

Jessor, R. & Jessor, S.L. (1977). *Problem behavior and psychosocial development: A longitudinal study of youth.* New York: Academic Press.

Johnson, H.L., Bejarano, A., Nusbaum, B., & Rosen, T. (1996). An ecological approach to development in children with prenatal drug exposure. *American Journal of Orthopsychiatry, 69,* 448–455.

Johnson, H.L. & Johnson, P.B. (1999). Teens and alcohol. *The Professional Counselor, 14,* 1–3.

Johnson, R.A., Hoffman, J.P., & Gerstein, D.R. (1996). *The relationship between family structure and adolescent substance use.* Rockville, MD: Office of Applied Studies.

Kandel, D.B. & Yamaguchi, K. (2002). Stages of drug involvement in the U.S. population. In D.B. Kandel (Ed.), *Stages and pathways of drug involvement: Examining the gateway hypothesis* (pp. 65–89). New York: Cambridge University Press.

Lester, B., ElSohly, M., Wright, L.L., Smeriglio, V., Verter, J., & Bauer, C.R., et al. (2001). The maternal lifestyle study: Drug use by meconium toxicology and maternal self report. *Pediatrics, 107,* 309–317.

Luthar, S.S., D'Avanzo, K., & Hites, S. (2003). Maternal drug abuse versus other psychological disturbances: Risks and resilience among children. In S.S. Luthar (Ed.), *Resilience and vulnerability: Adaptation in the context of childhood adversity* (pp. 104–129). Cambridge, United Kingdom: Cambridge University Press.

Mayes, L.C., Bornstein, M.H., Chawarska, K., Haynes, O.M., & Granger, R.H. (1996). Impaired regulation of arousal in 3-month-old infants exposed prenatally to cocaine and other drugs. *Development and Psychopathology, 8,* 29–42.

Patterson, G.R. (1982). *Coercive family process.* Eugene, OR: Castalia.

Patterson, G.R., Cohn, D.A., & Kao, B.T. (1989). Maternal warmth as a protective factor against risks associated with peer rejection among children. *Development and Psychopathology, 1,* 21–38.

Sameroff, A. (1994). Models of development and developmental risk. In C.H. Zeanah (Ed.), *Handbook of infant mental development* (pp. 3–13). New York: Guilford.

Schulenberg, J. & Maggs, J. (2002). A developmental perspective on alcohol use and heavy drinking during adolescence and the transition to young adulthood. *Journal of Studies on Alcohol, 14,* 54–70

Spear, L.P. (2002). The adolescent brain and the college drinker: Biological basis of propensity to use and misuse alcohol. *Journal of Studies on Alcohol, Supplement 14,* 71–81.

Thomas, A., Chess, S., & Birch, H. (1968). *Temperament and behavior disorders in children.* New York: University Press.

Zuckerman, M. (1979). *Sensation seeking: Beyond the optimal level of arousal.* Hillsdale, NJ: Lawrence Erlbaum.

CHAPTER 9

Preventing Adolescent Risk Taking

Authoritative parenting has been shown to be the most effective parenting style in reducing adolescent risk and promoting psychological adjustment for several reasons. First, it allows for the parent to adopt a balance between autonomy and control. Children are given opportunities to develop independence within a framework of standards, limits, and guidance. Also, authoritative parenting allows children to engage in verbal interaction with parents. Within this type of atmosphere children learn to express their views, realizing that their opinions are welcomed and considered. Finally, the parental involvement that is characteristic of this style of parenting renders the child more receptive to parental influence. The links between authoritative parenting and child competence and mental health have been found across ethnic groups, social strata, and family structure.

As we have highlighted throughout this book, adolescent risk taking is often considered a normal part of development and is caused by genetic as well as environmental factors, such as family, peers, and school/community. It is particularly important to understand these environmental factors in order to develop more effective prevention programs. Individuals who work with adolescents recognize that one-shot interventions are not adequate to prevent most adolescent risk taking. Prevention must be ongoing, should involve all the important areas of an adolescent's life, must be sensitively timed to an adolescent's developmental stage, and needs to be tailored to the adolescent's needs including the current family, peer, and school pressures.

While we previously considered prevention as it related to specific domains of adolescent risk taking, such as drug use or gambling, in this chapter we will consider it more broadly. In doing so, we will highlight the types of factors that frequently influence adolescents to become involved in various risky practices or develop specific mental health problems. We will also emphasize family, peer, and school/community factors frequently highlighted by developmental experts as risk or protective factors for adolescent risk taking. That is, wherever possible, we pinpoint factors experts contend place adolescents at heightened risk as well as factors that appear to moderate or reduce their risk status.

Family Factors Influencing Adolescent Risk Status

In this section we discuss the various ways in which the family may increase or decrease adolescent risk. By their nature, factors associated with reduced risk taking may be considered preventive in that they buffer adolescents from involvement in various risk-taking practices or from the development of specific forms of psychological disturbance.

The configuration of the American family has changed drastically over the last several decades, for many reasons—increasing divorce rates, the rise of single-parent families, mothers working outside of the home, blended families, extended families, and culturally and racially diverse families. As a result, there is no typical American family and today the American family is a conglomerate of attitudes and behaviors as diverse as the cultures that make up the people in those families. In fact, most children will experience transitions in their living arrangement multiple times throughout their young lives (Wu, 1996). The following list summarizes the range of family structures.

- Two Parents and Children
  - Mother–Father—Traditional nuclear family
  - Father–Father
  - Mother–Mother
- Single Parent and Children —Due to divorce, death, or single parenting by choice
  - Father
  - Mother
- Blended Families—Also known as stepfamilies; single parents (due to divorce, death, or single parenting) with children choose to remarry or live with another person with or without children
- Extended Families—Any configuration of family structure with additional members living in the same household; typically may consist of one or both grandparents, aunts, uncles, or cousins; may also include non-blood relatives considered family by the members of the household

Some of these conditions have been found to increase adolescent risk taking or vulnerability to mental health disorders. Divorce is one of these. Divorce is estimated to affect 40 percent of children born to married parents in the United States. Research indicates that approximately 25 percent of the children of divorce will have greater adjustment difficulties than their non-divorce-affected counterparts (Heatherington & Stanley-Hagan, 2002). These adjustment difficulties include academic problems, externalizing behaviors (such as stealing), internalizing behaviors (such as self-mutilation, i.e., cutting), substance abuse problems, and a variety of social problems (such as bullying). With high levels of divorce come increasing rates of remarriage. The rate of remarriage has steadily grown, producing a variety of blended families or families comprised of members from previous family units. As in divorced families, children in such stepfamilies experience more adjustment problems than their counterparts in non-divorced families (Heatherington & Stanley-Hagan, 2002). Again, not all children confronted with these circumstances experience difficulties. In fact the majority will not; only 25 percent of the children in blended families experience adjustment difficulties like those associated with divorce.

Another result of the increased divorce rate is the rise in single-parent families. Mothers with custody of their children experience the most difficult transition during a divorce. The loss of the husband's full income, previously used to support the family, results in a significant change in lifestyle for both mother and children. In addition, custodial mothers typically experience increased workloads, high rates of job instability, and residential moves to less desirable neighborhoods. Researchers emphasize the need for continuation of a positive relationship between the divorced spouses in order to help children adjust during this stressful time. The following textbox provides an extreme example of how parental conflict associated with divorce proceedings can negatively impact the children involved. It is important for parents in these circumstances to understand the long-term negative effects that their actions may produce in the children they love and whom they should want to protect from such consequences.

DIVORCE AND THE DEVELOPMENT OF ADOLESCENT RISK TAKING—AN EXTREME EXAMPLE

Four years ago at this writing, an acquaintance of the author told her husband that she wanted a divorce and requested that he leave the house to avoid exposing their son and daughter to the conflict that would inevitably ensue should he stay as the divorce proceeded. The husband refused and fought the divorce every step of the way and has remained in the house. Initially, the son, who was entering his teenage years, began to have a series of academic problems. He then began to act out in more overt ways by drinking and smoking with a new group of friends. He was arrested for vandalism and now has a criminal record, and he has announced his intention of dropping out of school when old enough.

While there are undoubtedly many reasons for the development of the son's negative behavior pattern, it is likely that among these is the incessant and long-standing exposure to parental conflict while the divorce was proceeding, which could have been greatly reduced if the father had agreed to separate living arrangements. While conflict would certainly have continued between the parents, its immediate and repeated impacts on the teenage boy would likely have been lessened with the physical separation of the parents.

Although divorce impacts almost fifty percent of all marriages in the United States and more than half of the children will spend some time in a single-parent household ("Divorce Rate," 2007), there is another group of single parents who have not experienced a divorce but who are raising children on their own. These are the mothers and fathers who either cohabit or have chosen to continue their pregnancy and raise the child on their own. Approximately one third of all children are born to unwed mothers (Demuth & Brown, 2004). Research has consistently shown that children in single-parent households experience poorer outcomes than their counterparts in two-parent families. One reason for the poor outcomes is the finding that parental absence is related to adolescent delinquency (Demuth & Brown, 2004). Eighty percent of single-parent households are headed by women; however, father-headed single-parent households are the fastest growing family structure in the United States (Heatherington, 1999). Higher levels of delinquency have been found in single-father-headed households; this has been attributed to lower levels of supervision and closeness in single-father households.

Although children growing up in broken or single-parent homes experience higher rates of delinquency than those in intact two-parent families, it is important to remember that family processes such as cohesion and monitoring act as protective factors in all family structures.

Maternal employment is another component of contemporary American life. Women may choose to work outside of the home for a variety of reasons. For some women, working may be a necessity of life in order to provide sufficient income for their families, perhaps due to the employment instability of their spouses, divorce, or single-parent responsibilities. However, for an increasing majority of women, working outside of the home is a choice made to fulfill their own personal needs and career goals. Overall, research has found that maternal employment in and of itself does not negatively impact child development (Hoffman & Youngblade, 1999). However, in specific circumstances research has detected effects that relate to maternal employment. Jeanne Brooks-Gunn and colleagues reported detrimental cognitive effects for three-year-old children whose mothers went back to work full-time prior to the infant turning nine months of age, compared to mothers who stayed at home during the first nine months. These effects were less-pronounced when the mothers worked less than 30 hours a week, were sensitive in their caregiving, and had high quality child care outside of the home (Brooks-Gunn, Han, & Waldfogel, 2002). This suggests that the impact of maternal employment on child development is complex, depending upon the age of the child and the circumstances of the employment, as well as the mother's continuing relationship with the child.

Another area of concern related to the increasing number of working mothers is the increasing number and risk status of "latchkey children." Latchkey is the term used to describe the population of children who are home alone after school or when school is not in session. Latchkey children may be at risk for specific behaviors because they receive considerably less adult supervision and guidance than other children (Belle, 1999). Children left alone can engage in unsupervised peer contact, delinquency, and other externalizing behaviors. However, just as the experience of children who have working mothers varies, the experience of latchkey children varies.

As research has demonstrated, working mothers who effectively monitor their children's behavior even while working, by calling them regularly and by requesting that neighbors keep a watch, can have children who are at no greater risk of engaging in problem behaviors than non-latchkey children. Parental monitoring can help children cope more effectively with their latchkey experience (Pettit, Bates, Dodge, & Meece, 1999; Steinberg & Silk, 2002). In addition to parental monitoring, involvement in community after-school programs can improve outcomes for latchkey children. After-school programs run by warm, supportive staff provide flexible schedules and multiple activities, offering children opportunities for positive interaction. Such after-school programs have been associated with greater academic achievement and social adjustment for latchkey children.

Parenting practices are a mix of behaviors acquired by parents in interaction with the environment, culture, and individuals. A leading expert on parenting, Diana Baumrind (1972), formulated a classification of parenting styles that has been widely used and validated in research on parenting. The classification system posits that there are four main styles of parenting—authoritarian, authoritative, neglectful, and indulgent. Refer to the following textbox for an overview of these four parenting styles.

PARENTING STYLES

- The authoritarian parent is strict and punitive, placing firm limits and controls on the child while allowing for little verbal exchange. Authoritarian parents may use physical punishment and coercion techniques with their children, often relying on negative interactions. Research has found that children of authoritarian parents frequently engage in more aggressive interactions.

- The authoritative parent encourages the mature, independent, and age-appropriate behavior of the child, while maintaining rules but allowing for verbal exchange. Baumrind asserts that an authoritative parenting style is the best as it encourages parents to behave in a supportive, affectionate manner with their children while developing rules that govern their functioning.

- The neglectful parent is uninvolved in the child's life, not knowing where the child is or what he or she is doing. Children of neglectful parents tend to be socially incompetent and display low self-esteem.

- The indulgent parent is very involved in the child's life, yet places few demands or restrictions on the child. These children may have difficulty regulating their own behavior, display traits of egocentrism and noncompliance, and often struggle in peer relations.

Authoritative parenting has been shown to be the most effective parenting style in reducing adolescent risk and promoting psychological adjustment for several reasons. First, it allows for the parent to adopt a balance between autonomy and control. Children are given opportunities to develop independence within a framework of standards, limits, and guidance. Also, authoritative parenting allows children to engage in verbal interaction with parents. Within this type of atmosphere children learn to express their views, realizing that their opinions are welcomed and considered. Finally, the parental involvement that is characteristic of this style of parenting renders the child more receptive to parental influence. The links between authoritative parenting and child competence and mental health have been found across ethnic groups, social strata, and family structure.

Discipline

While parental demands and controls have been indicated as part of the most effective parenting style, it is also important to consider the methods parents use to enforce those limits: forms of parental discipline. Different methods have been associated with different levels of risk taking and psychological adjustment. Martin Hoffman, an early researcher into parental discipline, identified three methods of discipline: love withdrawal, power assertion, and induction (Hoffman, 1988). Love withdrawal and power assertion are the methods associated with poor child outcomes. Love withdrawal is a technique in which the parent either refuses to interact with the child or verbally expresses dislike for the child. It often incorporates an emphasis on losing a parent's love: "If you don't do what I say, I won't like you anymore!" Hoffman contends that this style of discipline fosters considerable anxiety in the child. The discipline style of power assertion is an attempt to gain control over the child.

It is frequently associated with corporal (physical) punishment such as spanking. Due to the negative child outcomes associated with both of these discipline methods, researchers sometimes combine them into a spectrum of behaviors known as over-reactive discipline, which includes yelling, physical aggression, name-calling, criticism, threats, and setting unreasonable expectations. Such techniques often produce aggressive acting out and antisocial behaviors that can lead to school difficulties, delinquency, substance abuse, and adult antisocial behavior.

The use of corporal punishment by parents is legal in every state in the United States; however, many countries throughout the world have laws forbidding parents to physically punish their children. Sweden was the first country to pass such a law in 1979, but it has since been joined by Finland, Denmark, Norway, Austria, Cyprus, Latvia, Croatia, Germany, and Israel. Since the enactment of the anti-spanking law in Sweden, rates of juvenile delinquency, alcohol abuse, rape, and suicide have declined, although these trends may also be representative of changing social attitudes throughout Sweden (Durrant, 2000). The message that this sends to the United States and like-minded countries is that corporal punishment may not improve the well-being of children and may, in fact, increase their risk status in various ways.

Corporal punishment has been associated with higher rates of immediate compliance in children but is also associated over time with higher levels of aggression and problem behavior and lower levels of behavioral control, less concern for the welfare of others, and less conformity to social rules (Gershoff, 2002; Baumrind, Larzelere, & Cowan, 2002). Despite research that indicates that physical punishment may cause more harm than good, parents from the Caribbean, the United States, Canada, and many other parts of the world continue to engage in corporal punishment as a means to discipline and control their children (McLoyd & Smith 2002; Smith & Mosby, 2003; Wilson, Wilson, & Fox, 2002). Physical punishment does not teach appropriate behavior; however, it may provide a parent model of out-of-control, aggressive, or abusive behavior. Thus, educating parents in culturally-sensitive ways to alternative methods of discipline is good, not only for the well-being of the child, but also for the well-being of society.

The last discipline method is one endorsed by psychologists, other mental health professionals, and informed individuals around the world: induction. Induction promotes the use of reason and explanation when disciplining children and utilizes the warm, supportive relationship that should exist between child and parent. The idea is to explain to the child the effect that his or her action had on others. Induction does not focus attention on the child's shortcomings and misbehavior but instead teaches him or her alternative, appropriate behavior, thoughts, and emotions. This helps the child develop a sense of empathy for other people.

Induction is the discipline method taught by parenting education programs. These programs teach interested parents more-adaptive ways of interacting with children at various developmental stages to promote their healthy functioning. Although parenting programs vary in their specific details, they generally give parents the opportunity to learn skills for parental monitoring, techniques to engage in age-appropriate interactions with their children, and techniques for providing positive feedback to children to promote desired and appropriate behavior. Additionally, these programs teach parents how to give clear, reasonable instructions to their children and they also provide a variety of techniques for brief, nonphysical discipline. Changing parental discipline styles may be effective in reducing behavioral problems in children. Parental education is the key to helping parents find discipline styles that work to facilitate healthy growth and development in children at every age. See the following textbox for an overview of the parenting skills that research shows are effective with adolescents (Simpson, 2001).

EFFECTIVE PARENTING SKILLS

1. Provide Love and Connection
   a. Praise when deserving
   b. Listen, acknowledge, and appreciate
   c. Spend time individually and as a family
2. Monitor and Observe Behavior
   a. Know where they are and who they're with
   b. Get involved in their school and activities
   c. Watch for warning signs of trouble
   d. Connect to other adults in their lives
3. Set up Boundaries and Limits
   a. Set high standards
   b. Set safety rules that can't be negotiated
   c. Choose your battles and negotiate smaller issues
   d. Provide opportunities for responsibility and choice
   e. Be flexible but firm when necessary
4. Teach by Example
   a. Behave how you want your teens to behave
   b. Talk openly and honestly
   c. Demonstrate the importance of family traditions
   d. Help teens explore options for their futures

5. Provide for their Needs and Advocate for their Success
   a. Choose to live in a safe environment
   b. Find schools and activities that foster growth
   c. Provide for health and mental health care

Peer Factors Influencing Adolescent Risk Status

The transition from childhood to adolescence has been conceptualized in theory and documented in research as a gradual shift away from parental influence to peer influence. As children enter and advance through adolescence the peer group becomes an increasingly important force influencing their social maturation. During adolescence, the peer group satisfies needs of acceptance and intimacy that were previously sought from family members. In this way, the peer group becomes a significant agent in promoting independence from the family, making peer group affiliations an important part of healthy identity development in adolescents (Classen & Brown, 1985).

As peers become increasingly important in an adolescent's life, the formation of friendships becomes the focal point of social interactions. Individuals with similar interests and attributes are drawn together to form friendship pairs, cliques, and crowds (Dunphy, 1963), and groups of friends with similar interests and attributes combine to form cliques and crowds. Cliques are small, cohesive groups, generally consisting of three to nine members. The small number in a clique provides for intimacy, similar to the family, and facilitates a transfer of security and allegiance from the family to the clique. Research on cliques has found that talking is a primary activity; in this way, information is disseminated, and members are prepared for social activities that then are discussed and evaluated. Cliques move from unisexual in preadolescence to heterosexual in late adolescence.

Crowds are homogeneous social groups larger than cliques that consist of about 15 to 30 members. There may be several cliques that make up a crowd, although not all cliques are associated with a crowd. The crowd is heterosexual in nature and is the center of organized social activities that facilitate interaction between boys and girls within the crowd. A crowd label is put on students who act the same way even if they do not spend a lot of time together. Crowds are generally homogeneous in the types of activities that are preferred both at school and at home. In addition, members of crowds generally report having most of their friends within the same crowd. A name is given informally to a crowd, an adolescent accepts this label, and then this label associates the individual with different lifestyle characteristics. Labels for some crowds are positive and promote the development of a constructive social identity. These labels indicate intellectual skills, status in the schools, or the normality of the individuals in these groups. Other crowd labels can be seen as negative by outsiders and may contribute to the formation of a destructive social identity. In this case, the label may call attention to a low status position in the school or participation in drug use or delinquent activities. Research has identified four of the most prominent crowds identified and labeled variously by adolescents as: brains/smart ones, jocks/popular/preps, average/normal kids, and druggies/toughs/burnouts/heads/losers/rejects (Downs & Rose, 1991).

Homogeneity of Peer Groups

The peer system and the social environment that cliques and crowds function within have a profound effect on the development of risk-taking behavior in adolescents. In particular, research has shown that association with drug-using peers is among the strongest predictors of adolescent substance use (Stanton, Lowe, & Silva, 1995; Morgan & Grube, 1991). Research investigations found that those adolescents who reported themselves as smokers or users of alcohol and drugs also reported almost twice as much time spent with friends than non-using adolescents (Shilts, 1991). This indicates that these adolescents spend their free time in non-structured alcohol/drug-related activities, as opposed to participating in extracurricular activities and/or having strong family involvement. Consequently, those adolescents who used drugs tended to associate with peers who did the same.

In one investigation of adolescent smoking habits (Stanton, Lowe, & Silva, 1995), the best predictor of continued smoking status was maintaining friends who smoked. Those adolescents that continued to smoke over a two-year period had friends who smoked, and those that stopped smoking had no friends that smoked. The researchers concluded that once adolescents tried smoking, their choice of friends was a function of their smoking status. Research in this area has found similar results for other activities: having friends that engage in delinquent behaviors maintains such behavior in the adolescent. In addition, having a best friend that engaged in smoking and drinking was even more strongly predictive of the maintenance of those behaviors in the adolescent.

Researchers have determined that there are two processes that account for the similarity among peers: peer selection and peer influence (Ennett & Bauman, 1994). The first process, peer selection, implies that similar or initially dissimilar adolescents choose each other as friends based on lifestyle characteristics and personality variables. The second process, peer influence, plays a role when those who are already in a group are socialized via direct and indirect pressure to become and remain more similar. Peer influence can incorporate verbal pressure and modeling as well as perceptions of peer approval; in this way, it can lead to stability in the attitude and behavior of friends who were originally similar, or it can lead to change in the attitude or behavior of friends who were originally dissimilar.

It is important to note that peer selection and influence are not mutually exclusive processes; they may both contribute to a peer group's homogeneity, since peer group relationships are fluid. Research conducted by Barbara Schneider and David Stevenson found that over the course of high school, the majority of students changed their peer group affiliations. What is indicated by this finding is that an adolescent's individual autonomy in choosing a relationship is as important as the peer influences that he or she is exposed to. Adolescents therefore move into or out of peer groups based on interests, goals, or conflicts experienced (Schneider & Stevenson, 2000).

Peer Pressure Versus Peer Selection

Pressure from other people to behave in a certain manner is something that everyone has experienced at one time or another in life. Initially, pressure to behave in a certain way comes from parents and other adults who are in positions of authority over a child. As the child matures these pressures begin to come from members of his or her peer group and are experienced either directly or indirectly by the child. Peer pressure exerts influence on adolescents through aspects of modeling, direct verbal pressure, the dispensing of social reinforcers, and the perception of peer approval (Urberg, Shyu, & Liang, 1990). Such pressure can lead to a change in the adolescent's attitude and behavior. For example, an adolescent who does not smoke cigarettes or drink alcohol may attend a party where many people he or she is friendly with are smoking and/or drinking. Although there may be no verbal pressure to participate, the teen may begin to feel that all of his or her friends are engaging in these behaviors. The modeling of this type of behavior will lead the teen to assume that it is accepted and is a way to gain approval. The next time the teen is at a party, he or she may accept a cigarette or drink offered by a friend, and after trying the substance, the teen now has to reconcile previous feelings with her or her own behavior. In this subtle way, the adolescent's attitudes and behaviors are modified.

Research has found that the influence of peer pressure does affect an adolescent's intention to engage in risk-taking behaviors such as substance use. The normative group influence determines what behaviors are acceptable within the group, and if the adolescent wants to stay included, he or she is susceptible to these group norms. Since behaviors such as the use of illegal substances are learned and reinforced through interactions with people who engage in those behaviors, having best friends, parents, or siblings who smoke, drink, or use drugs will increase the likelihood that the adolescent will also engage in the behaviors. Thus through the pathways of peer pressure an adolescent is influenced to conform to the behavior of the group.

Results from a classic study of peer pressure within adolescent crowds (Classen & Brown, 1985) indicated that peers are capable of discouraging as well as encouraging risk-taking behavior. Results of this investigation revealed that individuals perceived as friends were seen more often as discouraging rather than encouraging cigarette smoking, alcohol use and sexual experimentation. However, an important finding from this investigation was the shift in pressures across grade levels. Although adolescents in this investigation reported that pressure to conform to peer norms diminished in late high school, they also reported that pressure to engage in misconduct increased in late high school. Peer pressures to engage in misconduct moved from a point of discouraging participation in the lower grades to a neutral or encouraging position with increasing age. The researchers thought that perhaps for some adolescents the engagement in some types of risk-taking behaviors was an effort to take on adult norms.

Throughout this book the idea has been discussed that adolescents engage in risk-taking behavior as an exploration of adult norm. After all, things like smoking cigarettes, drinking alcohol, sexual engagement, and gambling are all risk-taking behaviors that are legal for adults to pursue. One investigation (Harton & Latane, 1997) found that early adolescents who are popular with the opposite sex held more "mature" attitudes. The "mature" attitudes in this investigation included positive views toward activities that would be considered normative, such as kissing, wearing makeup, and dating. However, "mature" early adolescents also held positive attitudes toward other less-normative behaviors such as smoking and drinking.

The complex web of peer systems in which adolescents engage is a powerful resource for families, communities, and schools to utilize in the prevention of adolescent risk-taking behavior. As previously indicated, peers can have a positive as well as a negative influence over an adolescent. Parents and other influential adults can make an impact in this area by monitoring adolescents' friends, whereabouts, and behavior. Parental restrictions, control, and influence are possible if an adolescent knows that he or she is being monitored and will be held accountable for behavior. Research on parental monitoring has shown positive outcomes for adolescents when their parents and other significant adults are involved in their lives. Teens do want adult participation in their lives, and yet research compiled by Nichols and Good (2004) concludes that the careless indifference of adults creates a variety of dangerous situations for youth. These situations range from the adverse effects of poverty to abuse and neglect in teens' own homes. The variety of dangerous situations can be mediated, however, if parents take more responsibility for their children through knowing and regulating their children's activities, friends, and media usage.

School/Community Systems

Although control of adolescent risk taking has been attempted through the employment of federal age restrictions, this tactic frequently does not work. Teens have not only set up their own gambling pools, but they now have access to a wider range of gambling options through the internet. Laws are in place that restrict sexual engagement between an adult and an adolescent under the age of 18, but there is no such legal prohibition restricting activity between two adolescents. Tobacco sales have always been restricted to individuals 18 years and older, but younger adolescents have always found ways to procure cigarettes, either through vending machines or through stores that do not ask for identification. Additionally, although the legal age requirement to purchase alcohol is 21 years of age, most individuals younger than that are able to find ways to purchase alcohol themselves or else to have someone else purchase it for them. It is apparent for these normative behaviors that age restrictions may work to some degree, but they cannot be the only prevention approach.

In the United States, prevention programs for adolescent risk taking take both informal and formal routes to gain teens' attention and raise the awareness of the problem being targeted. One avenue that is pursued frequently is the public service announcement. These announcements occur on television and radio programs that teenagers frequently tune in to and may employ a celebrity thought to be held in high esteem by teens. These brief spots are used to inform adolescents about a risky behavior and discourage them from engagement in it. Although these public service announcements are well-intended, there is no evidence of their effectiveness in discouraging adolescents from engaging in risk-taking behavior.

In addition, the contrast between the brief messages that many public service announcements convey and the content depicted on the longer and more-developed television programs, movies, video games, and music that teens are exposed to is a clear indication of the entertainment industries' marketing priorities. The subject matter addressed by entertainment media often includes adult themes such as premarital sex, drug use, and violence. Adolescents are exposed to this subject matter without understanding how these depictions may alter their perceptions of what the societal norms are. For example, *The O.C.*, a weekly television program popular with teenagers, follows the exploits of four adolescents and their friends as they navigate high school. Story lines for this program have included alcohol and drug abuse, premarital sex, homosexuality, violent encounters, and suicide attempts, as well as abusive interactions with adults including sex with the parent of a friend. After viewing this hour-long teen drama, adolescents are likely to walk away believing that this is what the average teen encounters and that this is how average teens behave when confronted with such situations.

Just as the public service messages are too brief to counteract other media messages, research has found that prevention programs are frequently too short in duration and their effectiveness is not backed by research (Swisher, 2000). Additionally, there is a problem of issue "burn-out." As a topic becomes popular, the media and public will rally behind it. Public disinterest quickly takes over, however, when the problem does not improve with the focused attention. Although those organizations formed to educate the public about the particular problem still remain, they often are left to operate without the necessary support of research and funding (Lilja, Wilhelmsen, Larsson, & Hamilton, 2003). The following textbox presents an overview of factors that influence the effects of prevention programs, adapted from the research of Lilja and colleagues.

FACTORS THAT INFLUENCE THE EFFECTIVENESS OF PREVENTION PROGRAMS

- Is the aim of the program to alarm or educate?
- Is a problem-solving approach used or is the program lecture based?
- Is the program voluntary or compulsory?
- What do the participants expect to get out of the program?
- Are the participants motivated to participate and do they attend the sessions?
- Have the instructors been trained to lead the program?
- Do the program participants provide support to each other?
- Is there community support for the program?
- How long will the program continue to be offered?

Two examples of organizations whose well-meaning programs continue without support by research are Mothers Against Drunk Driving (MADD) and the Drug Abuse Resistance Program (D.A.R.E.). MADD, formed to deter individuals from drinking and driving, is an organization with an important message as automobile accidents are a primary cause of death among individuals aged 10 to 24 and alcohol is involved in many of these accidents. Not only do teens commonly get behind the wheel and drive after having had several drinks, but they are also often willing to get in a car with an individual who has been drinking. A typical anti-drinking program for MADD and its sister organization, Students Against Drunk Driving (SADD), is to tour high schools with displays of wrecked cars and pictures of fatal car accidents. This one-shot, consequence-based scare approach has proved to be ineffective in prevention research on cigarette use and has also not persuaded young drivers to change their drinking and driving habits.

The D.A.R.E. program has been highly visible in schools with the "just say no" approach. This program conveys the message that drugs are bad, and when offered drugs by anyone, you should "just say no" or else your life will be ruined. However, research evidence indicates that this approach is ineffective. To promote this message, police officers trained in this program go into elementary school classrooms around the country to speak with children before they have experimented with cigarettes, alcohol, and drugs. This hard-line approach makes sense to people who do not want to address the reality that adults frequently use cigarettes, alcohol, and sometimes drugs without ruining their own lives. In fact, it became public knowledge during the 2004 presidential election that both candidates had used drugs in the past; Al Gore admitted to smoking marijuana, and George Bush admitted to having used cocaine and struggling with problems of alcohol abuse. Thus two very public, very successful men have provided the example that drugs will not destroy your life.

Although these prevention approaches have not proved effective, research into effective prevention programs for adolescent risk taking has continued, and different approaches are being developed. Previously in this book, other areas of risk taking have been presented that have come to the same conclusion about risk-taking behavior—it is impossible to tell adolescents that they must employ total abstinence when a behavior is normative for adults. This is the conclusion drawn in research on gambling, sex, and substance use. As such, the D.A.R.E. program and others are revamping their approaches to prevention. The new type of program will be delivered to adolescents instead of children and will be flexible, emphasizing knowledge and decision-making skills. These newly developed programs will take a developmental approach that recognizes teens' need to have autonomy over their own behaviors.

Many prevention programs attempt to change the adolescent's risk assessment of a particular behavior; this is a difficult task. A teen's own risk assessment of a behavior is embedded in his or her thinking and has been built up over years of watching others, hearing others talk about a particular behavior, and perhaps experimenting with such behavior him or herself. Therefore, a prevention program that focuses on changing an adolescent's thoughts about a particular behavior, when youth are only exposed to that program for a few hours, is likely to fail from the start.

However, research from various areas of adolescent risk taking has determined several things about the most successful prevention programs. These programs seek to treat adolescents as informed decision makers. They provide accurate knowledge about the topic. Successful programs present the information in an interactive format with plenty of opportunity for discussion, shared ideas, and role playing; also, cultural differences in the community are respected and addressed. Finally, these programs emphasize the autonomy of the individual, that is, the ability of the teen to make a smart decision when placed in the various circumstances.

As the emphasis moves toward more-comprehensive, long-range prevention programs, the most logical placement for the delivery of these programs is in the school. Students are in the school setting for six to eight hours a day, and many of these programs can be embedded into the curriculum of the courses that students already take. Proponents of this approach suggest, for example, that students in social science classes investigate substance use and its impact on society, that students in biology classes investigate substance use and its impact on the body, and that students in geography classes investigate the production, distribution and consumption of drugs in different parts of the world. Of course this would require not only the revamping of curriculum but also training teachers to take on another aspect of the socialization of our nation's children. Although this approach may seem to be the most rewarding in regard to the long-term reduction of adolescent risk behavior, the fact remains that teachers in the United States are currently overburdened with tasks levied by the implementation of the federal legislation commonly known as No Child Left Behind.

School districts and teachers under the burden of No Child Left Behind have all but given up on the individuation of the curriculum, as they have been forced to teach a structured curriculum for a set amount of time, without deviation, throughout the school day (Bush, 2001). In this way, schools and districts hope to better prepare their students for the barrage of mandated federal and state tests that children take in every area of the curriculum. Thus any special class that a child takes, such as art, music, or gym, has either been reduced to a very small number of contact hours or has been delegated to after-school opportunities. Many prevention programs have also suffered this fate. Some school districts do offer prevention programs as an after-school optional class, but as may be expected, these programs' enrollment is reduced, and they may not be attended by the students who might benefit the most. As stated at the beginning of this chapter, prevention of adolescent risk taking cannot utilize a one-shot approach. Researchers who investigate adolescent risk taking have learned this lesson; now it is time for the community to also recognize this fact and lobby for the integration of these programs into adolescents' regular school curriculum.

Biological Considerations

Although biological factors have been highlighted in discussions of gambling and violence and were discussed at some length in the chapter on mental disorders, the general emphasis to our discussions of prevention or intervention strategies with adolescent risk-taking behaviors has been environmental. For many researchers, practitioners, and policy makers, biological forces are the ultimate cause of all human behavior, including adolescent risk taking. It is not surprising, therefore, to increasingly find studies emphasizing biological factors and calling for more-biologically-oriented treatment, as has been in vogue with adolescent mental health disorders.

Illustrating this point, recent research reported to have found the "quit switch" for those addicted to cigarettes (Naqvi, Rudrauf, Damasio, & Bechara, 2007). Inspired by studies of brain-damaged smokers and ex-smokers, the study pinpointed the insula as the brain structure involved smoking addiction. Some have suggested that we immediately begin research to develop medications that would impact the insula and thereby shut off a patient's urge to smoke. In a similar vein, other researchers have been working on developing a vaccine to reduce nicotine cravings (Bunce, Loudon, Akers, Dobson, & Wood, 2003). Again, such research starts with the basic belief that human cravings, addictions, and risk taking ultimately stems from our bodies and their reactions to specific stimuli in the environment.

While these types of results are fascinating and important to follow up on, it is important for readers to not fall too quickly into the biological reductionism mode, whereby every aspect of life is reduced to cell firings and chemical reactions. Human behavior is incredibly complex and, as such, is probably dependent on biological, psychological, and environmental forces. For this reason we have emphasized the ecological model of development, because it highlights that accounting for both internal and external forces is essential to developing a clear and accurate understanding of human behavior in general and adolescent risk taking in particular.

It is also important to bear in mind that drug or other biological treatments to minimize adolescent risk taking often trigger unforeseen and quite damaging side effects. In the psychiatric annals lobotomy remains a most chilling, cautionary tale in this regard. The surgery, in which specific brain areas are purposely damaged or removed, was developed during the mid-twentieth century to improve the symptoms of those with severe mental disorders; however, its too-often unpredictable and sometimes devastating consequences for the patients have caused its discontinued use. When we alter our bodies biologically, we run the risk of not only solving some specific problems but of creating new and sometimes more-serious problems in the process. Numerous examples of such negative effects have been observed with child and adolescent use of psychiatric medications. So while biological treatments may be promising, they can also be perilous. It is essential that we understand both possibilities and proceed with deliberate caution, not overstating early claims or dismissing potential negative consequences.

Works Cited

Baumrind, D. (1972). An exploratory study of socialization effects on black children: Some black-white comparisons. *Child Development, 42,* 261–267.

Baumrind, D., Larzelere, R.E., & Cowan, P.A. (2002). Ordinary physical punishment: Is it harmful? Comment on Gershoff. *Psychological Bulletin, 128,* 590–595.

Belle, D. (1999). *The after school lives of children: Alone and with others while parents work.* Mahwah, NJ: Erlbaum.

Brooks-Gunn, J., Han, W.J., & Waldfogel, J. (2002). Maternal employment and child cognitive outcomes in the first three years of life: The NICHD Study of Early Child Care. *Child Development 73,* 1052–1072.

Bunce, C.J., Loudon, P.T., Akers, C., Dobson, J., & Wood, D.M. (2003). Development of vaccines to help treat drug dependence. *Current Opinion in Molecular Therapy, 5,* 58–63.

Bush, G.W. (2001, January 29). *No child left behind* [Online]. Retrieved from http://www.ed.gov/policy/elsec/leg/esea02/index.html

Classen, D.R. & Brown, B. (1985). The multidimensionality of peer pressure in adolescence. *Journal of Youth and Adolescence, 14,* 451–468.

Demuth, S. & Brown, S. (2004). Family structure, family processes and adolescent delinquency: The significance of parental absence versus parental gender. *Journal of Research in Crime and Delinquency, 41,* 58–81

Divorce Rate. Retrieved December 20, 2007, from http://www.divorcerate.org/

Downs, W.R. & Rose, S.R. (1991). The relationship of adolescent peer groups to the incidence of psychosocial problems. *Adolescence, 26,* 473–492.

Drug Abuse Resistance Program [D.A.R.E.]. *About D.A.R.E.* Retrieved January 24, 2007, from http://www.dare.com/home/about_dare.asp

Dunphy, D.C. (1963). The social structure of urban adolescent peer groups. *Sociometry, 26,* 230–246.

Durrant, J.E. (2000). Trends in youth crime and well-being since the abolition of corporal punishment in Sweden. *Youth and Society, 31,* 437–455.

Ennett, S.T. & Bauman, K.E. (1994). The contribution of influence and selection to adolescent peer group homogeneity: The case of adolescent cigarette smoking. *Journal of Personality and Social Psychology, 67,* 653–663.

Gershoff, E.T. (2002). Corporal punishment by parents and associated child behaviors and experiences: A meta-analysis and theoretical review. *Psychological Bulletin, 128,* 539–579.

Harton, H.C. & Latane, B. (1997). Social influence and adolescent lifestyle attitudes. *Journal of Research on Adolescence, 7,* 197–220.

Heatherington, E.M. (1999). Family functioning and the adjustment of adolescent siblings in diverse types of families. *Monographs of the Society for Child Development, 64,* 1–25.

Heatherington, E.M. & Stanley-Hagan, M. (2002). Parenting in divorced and remarried families. In M.H. Bornstein (Ed.), *Handbook of parenting: Vol. 3. Being and becoming a parent* (2nd ed.). Mahwah, NJ: Erlbaum.

Hoffman, M.L. (1988). Moral development. In M.H. Bornstein & E. Lamb (Eds.), *Developmental psychology: An advanced textbook* (2nd ed.). Hillsdale, NJ: Erlbaum.

Hoffman, L.W. & Youngblade, L.M. (1999). *Mothers at work: Effects on children's well-being.* New York: Cambridge.

Lilja, J., Wilhelmsen, B., Larsson, S., & Hamilton, D. (2003). Evaluation of drug use prevention programs directed at adolescents. *Substance Use & Misuse, 38,* 1831–1863.

McLoyd, V.C. & Smith, J. (2002). Physical discipline and behavior problems in African American, European American, and Hispanic children: Emotional support as a moderator. *Journal of Marriage and Family, 64,* 40–53.

Morgan, M. & Grube, J.W. (1991). Closeness and peer group influence. *The British Journal of Social Psychology, 30,* 159–169.

Mothers Against Drunk Driving [MADD]. *Overview of MADD's youth programs.* Retrieved January 24, 2007, from http://madd.org/madd_programs

Naqvi, N.H., Rudrauf, D., Damasio, H., & Bechara, A. (2007). Damage to the insula disrupts addiction to cigarette smoking. *Science, 315,*531–534.

Nichols, S. & Good, T. (2004). *America's teenagers—Myths and realities.* Mahwah, NJ: Lawrence Erlbaum Associates.

Pettit, G.S., Bates, J.E., Dodge, K.A., & Meece, D.W. (1999). The impact of after school peer contact on early adolescent externalizing problems is moderated by parental monitoring, perceived neighborhood safety, and prior adjustment. *Child Development, 70,* 768–778.

Schneider, B. & Stevenson, D. (2000). The ambitious generation: America's teenagers, motivated but directionless. New Haven, CT: Yale University Press.

Shilts, L. (1991). The relationship of early adolescent substance use to extracurricular activities, peer influence, and personal attitudes. *Adolescence, 26,*613–617.

Simpson, A.R. (2001). *Raising teens: A synthesis of research and a foundation for action.* Boston, MA: Center for Health Communication, Harvard School of Public Health.

Smith, D.E. & Mosby, G. (2003). Jamaican child rearing practices: The role of corporal punishment. *Adolescence, 38,* 369–381.

Stanton, W.R., Lowe, J.B., & Silva, P.A. (1995). Antecedents of vulnerability and resilience to smoking among adolescents. *Journal of Adolescent Health, 16,* 71–77.

Steinberg, L. & Silk, J.S. (2002). Parenting adolescents. In M. Bornstein (Ed.), *Handbook of parenting: Vol. 1. Children and parenting* (2nd ed.). Mahwah, NJ: Erlbaum.

Students Against Drunk Driving [SADD]. *About SADD.* Retrieved July 10, 2007, from http://www.sadd.org/mission.htm

Swisher, J.D. (2000). Sustainability of prevention. *Addictive Behaviors, 25,* 965–973.

Urberg, K.A., Shyu, S., & Liang, J. (1990). Peer influence in adolescent cigarette smoking. *Addictive Behaviors, 15,* 247–255.

Wilson, C.M., Wilson, L.C., & Fox, C.A. (2002). Structural and personal contexts of discipline orientations of Guyanese parents: Theoretic and empirical considerations. *Journal of Comparative Family Studies,* 1–13.

Wu, L.L. (1996). Effects of family instability, income, and income instability on the risk of premarital birth. *American Sociological Review, 61,* 386–406.

CHAPTER 10

Conclusion

One way in which parents may deter their children's risk taking is through the explicit messages they transmit to their children in their discussions and admonitions regarding these behaviors. When parents talk with their children about the dangers of alcohol, tobacco, gambling, and aggression, they not only provide information about the dangers associated with such risk taking, but they also go on record as opposed to their children's involvement with such behaviors. Conversely, when parents fail to talk with their children, the failure to do so can be interpreted by the child to mean that they are not necessarily opposed to an activity, or that the issue is just not that important to them. This interpretation may also follow from the fact that parents generally talk with their children about activities and behaviors that they do consider important, like doing well in school and excelling in sports. Parents also talk about personal cleanliness and neatness for the same reason. As a result, when parents do not discuss a behavior like gambling or substance use, a child may interpret this failure to mean that his or her parents are not concerned about that behavior.

After reading about the most common adolescent risk-taking behaviors and the psychological disorders frequently associated with them, the reader may wonder: "What is a concerned parent or educator to do?" This question takes on added urgency when one realizes that only selected risky behaviors and mental disorders were described here.

In addressing the question it must first be understood that, despite the plethora of potential risks confronting adolescents and their mental health today, the vast majority of teens not only survive their adolescent years but go on to become fully functioning, autonomous adults. One reason for this is that, as a species, human beings are extremely adaptable, able to roll with life's punches and survive despite the many risks attending development generally and adolescence particularly. As Piaget, the noted child theorist, emphasized some time ago, intelligence is the ability to adapt to changing circumstances that one necessarily confronts in life. From this perspective, children and adolescents are remarkably intelligent!

But what about the inordinate power of peers to influence adolescents and push and pressure them into risk taking; doesn't this pressure inevitably lead American youth to participate in dangerous and sometimes lethal behaviors? While recognizing that peers do gain influence as children make the transition to adolescence, we contend that parents and teachers still possess considerable influence to impact and direct adolescents' decisions and behavioral choices, often more than they recognize. Furthermore, we suggest that by overestimating the power of peers, both parents and teachers have unwittingly ceded or undercut their own ability to direct adolescents away from risky and health-harmful activities and move them toward healthier pursuits.

One of the most widely used school-based, anti-drug programs emphasizes the need to train children and adolescents to use "refusal skills" to counter the destructive power of peer pressure to push students to experiment with drugs. Such training reflects the underlying assumption that peer influence or pressure is the most important determinant of adolescent experimentation with alcohol, tobacco, and illicit substances. From the perspective of this particular prevention/intervention program, in the absence of teaching young people to resist and refuse this pressure, parental influence is inadequate to counter the overwhelming influence that a peer group exerts over adolescent substance use.

With few exceptions, this position has become the accepted wisdom in the prevention field. It is interesting to note the hold that this position regarding the power of peer pressure has taken on our national beliefs, despite a growing literature that consistently demonstrates strong, positive associations between parental behaviors such as alcohol and tobacco use and interpersonal violence and these same behaviors in their children. In support of these findings, Glynn (1981) long ago concluded a review of research on drug-use transitions by emphasizing that parental substance use was the most powerful influence on a child's use of substances. He made this statement at the same time that school-based prevention programs were just beginning to emphasize refusal skills counteracting peer pressure as the best way to help children and adolescents remain drug free. While the prevention field generally has moved to accept the preeminent influence of peers over parents, this move may be both premature and unwarranted.

For although there is an extensive body of literature demonstrating that peer risk taking is strongly associated with adolescent risk taking generally, there is reason to believe that the prevention field has overstated peer influence and understated parental influence with regard to adolescent risk taking. For example, when smoking studies distinguish between parents who have never smoked and those that previously smoked, rather than collapsing the two groups into one "nonsmoking" category, they demonstrate that parental smoking status is at least as powerful a predictor of current adolescent smoking as peer smoking status. Similarly, when studies comparing the differential influences of parent and peer alcohol use employ the same measure to assess both parent and peer alcohol use patterns, findings reveal that parental alcohol use is at least as powerful a predictor as peer use.[1]

From this, it should be obvious that one way parents foster or deter their children's involvement in risky activities is by the extent to which they themselves engage in and model specific risk-taking behaviors, including drug abuse, gambling, and violence. Children of heavy drinkers, heavy smokers, frequent gamblers, and those who engage in interpersonal aggression are exposed to many repetitions of behaviors such as pouring, sipping, lighting, puffing, shuffling cards, betting, yelling, and hitting. Unfortunately, some children are exposed to many of these acts simultaneously, over and over again, with predictable consequences. Engaging in these behaviors may follow almost automatically from these children's repeated observation.

Another point to bear in mind is that while some peers undoubtedly pressure friends to engage in various risky behaviors, evidence suggests that adolescents seek out peer groups compatible with their own backgrounds and interests. In this way, adolescent children of parents who drink, smoke, and engage in violent interactions are familiar and even comfortable in the presence of such behaviors and may also be more comfortable with peers who are also involved with them. These peers engage in familiar behaviors while providing support and validation for the teen's earlier experiences with his or her parents.

According to some research and theory, substance use becomes largely automatic after repeated involvement. Moreover, adolescents frequently exposed to adult risk-taking activities by members of their families or other adults in their lives may begin to view those risky behaviors not only as normal and appropriate, but also in a generally positive light. This is partly because repeated exposure to a behavior produces generally positive attitudes towards it—the "mere exposure" hypothesis (Zajonc, 1968). Moreover, adolescents exposed to frequent incidents of risk-taking behavior within the family appear to possess more positive expectancies of these behaviors than those not exposed in that context. These adolescents possess more positive beliefs about risk-taking activity in addition to considering these behaviors a fundamental element of everyday life.

A second way in which parents may deter their children's risk taking is through the explicit messages they transmit to their children in their discussions and admonitions regarding these behaviors. When parents talk with their children about the dangers of alcohol, tobacco, gambling, and aggression, they not only provide information about the dangers associated with such risk taking, but they also go on record as opposed to their children's involvement with them. Conversely, when parents fail to talk with their children, the failure to do so can be interpreted by the child to mean that they are not necessarily opposed to the activity, or that the issue is just not that important to them. This interpretation may also follow from the fact that parents generally talk with their children about activities and behaviors they do consider important, like doing well in school and excelling in sports. Parents also talk about personal cleanliness and neatness for the same reason. As a result, when parents do not discuss a behavior like gambling or substance use, a child may interpret this failure to mean that his or her parents are not concerned about that behavior.

Furthermore, failure both to discuss the dangers of specific risk-taking behaviors and to admonish children to avoid them could be interpreted as tacit approval of involvement, especially in families where the parents themselves engage in such behaviors. Jackson and Henrikson (1997) found that children of parents who smoked but whose parents discussed the dangers of use were less likely to smoke. This demonstrates that discussions about the dangers of risky behaviors may be valuable even when initiated by parents who themselves engage in them. The same should apply to the use of other substances, to gambling, and to involvement with interpersonal aggression.

At various points throughout this book we have pointed out that just presenting information to kids is not an effective way of preventing adolescent risk taking. Brooks (2007) made a similar point in stating: "American schools are awash in moral instruction. . . .and basically none of it works. Sex ed doesn't change behavior. Birth control education doesn't produce measurable results" (p. A21).

So why should it make any difference if we talk to our kids about what we want and do not want them to do? For one thing, parents are not teachers, and their discussions should be more important to their children than those discussions coming from a health education or gym teacher. Brooks may be right when he says, "The fact is, schools are ineffective when it comes to values education." But because of their centrality in the lives of their children, parents should be far more influential than teachers and should want to make sure that their children know where they stand when it comes to drug use, gambling, violence, and sex!

A final way parents may foster or deter their children's involvement in risky behaviors is by the message transmitted through the use of sanctions when they find out that their children have engaged in them. When children do poorly in school or behave badly at home, parents often invoke various sanctions to modify their behavior—cutting off allowances, grounding, etc. By sanctioning a child's behavior, parents send the message to their children that there will be negative consequences when they do something they have been taught to avoid. Negative consequences or sanctions are one method parents use to teach their children that a specific behavior is unacceptable.

So what message(s) do parents convey to a child when they become aware that the child has experimented with alcohol or tobacco, having been told not to do so and that punishment will follow such behavior, but no consequences follow his or her experimentation? For some children, the lack of consequences may mean that the behavior is actually acceptable. This is a likely interpretation among adolescent experimenters who live with parents who engage in these behaviors.

The important deterrent power of parental admonitions and sanctions is clear from a growing literature on the use of alcohol and tobacco in African American adolescents, a group with generally low rates of drinking and smoking. One explanation for these low rates is that African American families often employ a "no-nonsense" style of parenting in which the parent clearly states and enforces specific behavioral rules including the prohibition of youthful substance use. Such parenting also emphasizes the negative consequences that follow violation of norms, including the restrictive drinking norms found in African American families (Johnson & Johnson, 1999).

While such sanctions may seem inconsistent with the previously described authoritative child-rearing style favored in the mental health chapter, there is actually no inconsistency. In fact, authoritative practices include discussing with children and specifying precisely what behaviors parents approve and do not approve in conjunction with explanations for that approval or disapproval. At the same time, while authoritative parents do not employ physical punishment or withdrawal-of-love techniques to sanction their children, they do sanction them by withholding privileges and by clearly indicating their disapproval of unwanted behaviors. This would be particularly true with regard to specific behaviors that parents have told their children they do not want them to become involved with, including substance abuse, gambling, and early sexual exploration. It is important to understand that while authoritative parents discuss their values and the behaviors consistent or inconsistent with these values, they do not disregard these values when children disagree with them or violate them. In fact, authoritative parents are consistent in their discussions with their children as well as in their actions related to these discussions, thus making it easier for children to understand the rules that govern parent-child interactions and the consequences that will follow should the child clearly and/or consistently violate the rules.

Obviously, for this interactive process to work in practice, it becomes essential for parents to monitor the behavior of their children as well as the circumstances in which their teenagers are likely to be found, in order to gauge the likelihood of risk in the situation. While it may seem intrusive, such practices as asking teens where they are going and who they are going with or calling them on their cell phones to check up on them are important. These practices are important not only because a parent should want to know, but also because doing so sends teens the message that you're watching out for them, and even that you now have information about who they're with and their whereabouts that you will use to hold them accountable. It is also appropriate to stay up and talk with your teens after they come in following a night out—not necessarily every night, but certainly some nights. This allows you to determine their mood and support them if they have had a bad interpersonal experience. It also allows you to determine both by behavior and cues (smell, coordination, etc.) whether they have been drinking or smoking or involved with illicit substances.

With young teens, it is also not unreasonable to call the parents of the friend who is having a party to determine how they plan to monitor the affair, or if there actually is going to be a party. A friend recently phoned another parent to ask about this regarding a party her teenage daughter had been invited to. She was stunned when, in response to her question about supervision and substance use, the parent stated: "Absolutely not; no drugs will be allowed; we'll only be serving beer and wine. No drugs, no hard liquor!"

This not only illustrates the importance of monitoring, but the multiple forms that it may take. Again, such parental behavior is important not only because it provides valuable information you need to determine whether a child is in harm's way, but also because it sends an important message that you care and, as a result, will be watching and following up. Often, although teens complain about such parental "intrusion," it makes them feel more secure while offering them a ready-made excuse for why they cannot go certain places or engage in certain activities.

To summarize, parents communicate to children about the appropriateness or inappropriateness of risk-taking activities in various ways. For one, they do this through their own involvement in these activities. But parents also transmit messages through their willingness to discuss with children the inappropriateness of specific behaviors. These discussions should include both admonishments to abstain from involvement as well as clearly specified sanctions to be imposed if involvement should occur. Such discussions specify the rules regarding teens' involvement with various risk-taking activities. Parents emphasize the importance of these rules and their desire for teens to avoid involvement in risk-taking by monitoring their children's whereabouts (place, companions, and activities). In the absence of parental monitoring, parental rules about risk-taking and the admonitions associated with them have little meaning and less personal significance for the child. When parents are really worried about children and life-threatening risks—a toddler running into the street or falling into a swimming pool—they engage in a whole series of monitoring activities to ensure that the behavior will not occur. Because of the very real dangers associated with underage drinking, gambling, early sexual experimentation, suicide attempts, and interpersonal aggression, the vigilance associated with such monitoring is no less critical.

The last way in which parents transmit messages to their children about the inappropriateness of risk-taking activities is through their consistent use of predetermined sanctions when rule violations occur. If parents really feel strongly that their teens should not engage in specific behaviors, it is not enough to just talk about consequences; it is absolutely essential to enforce the sanctions that were discussed when the teens were told that they should not engage in this or that type of activity. Failure to follow through sends counter messages including that the parents do not feel that an activity is really that dangerous, or, if it is dangerous, it suggests that parents must not care so much about the child since they are willing to let him or her engage in that activity without consequence. Parents who constantly warn a child that there will be negative consequences should he or she engage in some unwanted action but who fail to respond when the child does so are saying that they really do not care about the action that much and/or that they do not care whether the child puts him or herself at risk. The following textbox summarizes the three ways parents transmit their feelings about risk-taking behavior to their children.

THREE WAYS IN WHICH PARENTS INFLUENCE THEIR CHILDREN'S RISK TAKING

- Through the parents' own involvement in risk-taking behaviors—smoking, drinking, fighting
- Through parents' discussions with their children about what is and is not acceptable behavior
- Through consistent parental use of sanctions when children engage in behaviors the parents have said are unacceptable

---

In discussing ways of preventing adolescent involvement in specific risk-taking behavior, we have sought to provide parents, teachers, and others involved with teens with the knowledge we believe will best assist them to help young people avoid such involvement. This emphasis on knowledge is somewhat paradoxical, because there is considerable literature in the field of school-based prevention that shows that knowledge by itself is not enough to deter teens from becoming involved with drugs, gambling, or other risky practices. We contend, however, that this is because so little of this knowledge or information is processed by teens or seen as particularly relevant to them. In the current instance, you have actively chosen to read this book, probably because you want more information, and surely because you believe that the knowledge obtained will help you reduce teen risk-taking. Accordingly, the knowledge gained should have a far greater influence on your subsequent behavior than that traditionally transmitted to teens in their health education classes.

In a similar vein, we conclude by reemphasizing another piece of information that should provide you with a positive perspective on the process of steering teens toward healthy rather than stunted and troubled futures. In their classic work on children born at high risk of developing all sorts of physical and psychological disorders, Werner and Smith (1992) pointed out that children can be amazingly resilient despite the incredible challenges and obstacles they are forced to confront. They concluded by pointing out that the single most significant predictor of whether an at-risk child went on to thrive or to wither was whether or not the child had a close, positive relationship with a caring and supportive adult. It did not matter whether the adult was a parent, grandparent, or teacher. Those children who possessed such relationships were far more resilient, regardless of their circumstances, than those who did not. In reading and thinking about the issues raised in this book, you have shown your concern and desire to help make adolescents' lives less dangerous. Many of you will hopefully come to represent a significant adult figure for one or more at-risk adolescents or for your own children or students.

Note

1. As Andrews, Hops, and Duncan (1997) have emphasized, most researchers assess the impact of parental alcohol use by dichotomizing the behavior into yes/no categories. When these same researchers used a continuous measure of parental alcohol use that required parents to describe their use more specifically—from "never use" into a range of current use categories including "use daily" when assessing peer alcohol use—parents' use was as predictive as peers' use.

Works Cited

Andrews, J.A., Hops, H., & Duncan, S.C. (1997). Adolescent modeling of parent substance use: The moderating effect of the relationship with the parent. *Journal of Family Psychology, 11,* 259–270.

Brooks, D. (2007, June 22). When preaching flops. *New York Times,* p. A21.

Glynn, T.J. (1981). From family to peer: A review of transitions of influence among drug-using youth. *Journal of Youth and Adolescence, 10,* 363–383.

Jackson, C. & Henrikson, L. (1997). Do as I say: Parent smoking, antismoking socialization, and smoking onset among children. *Addictive Behaviors, 22,* 107–114.

Johnson, H.L. & Johnson, P.B. (1999). Teens and alcohol. *The Professional Counselor, 14,* 1–3.

Werner, E. & Smith, R.S. (1992). *Overcoming the odds.* Ithaca, NY: Cornell University Press.

Zajonc, R.B. (1968). The attitudinal effects of mere exposure. *Journal of Personality and Social Psychology, 9,* 1–27.

Index

abstinence: gambling, 41; sex, 55
adolescence, defined, 3
Alcoholics Anonymous, 41
American Psychiatric Association,
    Diagnostic and Statistical Manual of
    Mental Disorders, Fourth Edition
    (DSM-IV). See *Diagnostic and Statis-*
    tical Manual of Mental Disorders,
    Fourth Edition (DSM-IV)

Barkley, Russell, 93
Bell, Richard, 109
biological factors, 106–8, 132–33
Bronfenbrenner, Uri, 6, 112–13

Center for Substance Abuse Prevention
    (CSAP), 21
Centers for Disease Control and
    Prevention (CDC), 10, 15, 50, 52
Chess and Thomas. *See* child
    temperament; goodness of fit
child temperament (Chess and
    Thomas), 106–111. *See also* goodness
    of fit
clustering of risk-taking behaviors,
    114–15
Combat Methamphetamine Epidemic
    Act, 17

community systems. *See* school and
    community systems

Diagnostic and Statistical Manual of
    Mental Disorders, Fourth Edition
    (DSM-IV), 29–30, 38, 92–95, 97, 99
divorce, 118–20
Drug Abuse Resistance Program
    (D.A.R.E.), 130–31
drug-exposed children, 111
drug use, 9–25; Center for Substance
    Abuse Prevention (CSAP), 21;
    Centers for Disease Control and
    Prevention (CDC), 10, 15; Combat
    Methamphetamine Epidemic Act,
    17; geography, 18–19; illicit drug use,
    9–13, 16, 18; indicated prevention,
    20; Monitoring the Future (MTF)
    study, 11, 14–16, 18–20; National
    Center on Addiction and Substance
    Abuse (CASA), 18; National
    Household Survey (NHSDA), 15,
    18–19; National Institute on Drug
    Abuse (NIDA), 9–10; Office of
    National Drug Control Policy
    (ONDCP), 21; Partnership for a
    Drug-Free America, 12–15, 21;
    performance-enhancing drugs, 17;

ROUTES TO READING SUCCESS
AND FAILURE

Macquarie Monographs in Cognitive Science

General Editor: MAX COLTHEART

The newly launched Macquarie Monographs in Cognitive Science series will publish original monographs dealing with any aspect of cognitive science. Each volume in the series will cover a circumscribed topic and will provide readers with a summary of the current state-of-the-art in that field. A primary aim of the volumes is also to advance research and knowledge in the field through discussion of new theoretical and experimental advances.

The first volume in the series is *Routes to Reading Success and Failure* by Nancy Ewald Jackson and Max Coltheart. Subsequent volumes are planned on various topics in cognitive science including visual cognition, evolutionary psychology, masked priming, computational modeling of visual word recognition, and theory of mind and social behavior

Macquarie Monographs in Cognitive Science

ROUTES TO READING SUCCESS AND FAILURE

Toward an Integrated Cognitive Psychology of Atypical Reading

Nancy Ewald Jackson
The University of Iowa

Max Coltheart
Macquarie University

PSYCHOLOGY PRESS
ALERE FLAMMAM
Taylor & Francis Group

USA	Publishing Office:	PSYCHOLOGY PRESS
		A member of the Taylor & Francis Group
		29 West 35th Street
		New York, NY 10001
		Tel: (212) 216-7800
		Fax: (212) 564-7854
	Distribution Center:	PSYCHOLOGY PRESS
		A member of the Taylor & Francis Group
		7625 Empire Drive
		Florence, KY 41042
		Tel: 1 (800) 634-7064
		Fax: 1 (800) 248-4724
UK		PSYCHOLOGY PRESS
		A member of the Taylor & Francis Group
		27 Church Road
		Hove
		E. Sussex, BN3 2FA
		Tel.: +44 (0) 1273 207411
		Fax: +44 (0) 1273 205612

ROUTES TO READING SUCCESS AND FAILURE: Toward an Integrated Cognitive Psychology of Atypical Reading

1 2 3 4 5 6 7 8 9 0

Printed by Sheridan Books, Ann Arbor, MI, 2001.
Cover design by Ellen Seguin.

A CIP catalog record for this book is available from the British Library.
∞ The paper in this publication meets the requirements of the ANSI Standard Z39.48-1984 (Permanence of Paper).

Library of Congress Cataloging-in-Publication Data
Jackson, Nancy Ewald.
    Routes to reading success and failure : toward an integrated cognitive psychology of atypical reading / Nancy Ewald Jackson and Max Coltheart.
        p. cm.—(Macquarie monographs in cognitive science)
    Includes bibliographical references and index.
    ISBN 1-84169-011-2 (alk. paper)
    1. Reading.   2. Word recognition.   3. Cognition.   I. Coltheart, Max.
II. Title.   III. Series.

LB1050.44. .J33 2001
372.4—dc21

                                                                            2001019214

ISBN 1-84169-011-2 (case)

For David and Anne Jackson
and
Alice and Veronika Coltheart

Contents

About the Authors

Nancy Ewald Jackson is Professor of Educational Psychology at The University of Iowa. She earned her Ph.D. in Psychology from the University of Washington in 1975 and was a member of that university's faculty until 1989, when she moved to Iowa. Her research in cognitive development has included studies of precocious reading acquisition, individual differences among successful readers, reading in nonalphabetic orthographies, and the development of intellectual giftedness.

Max Coltheart is Director of the Macquarie Centre for Cognitive Science, having previously held academic positions at Macquarie University, the University of London (Birkbeck College), Reading University, Waterloo University, Monash University, and the University of Sydney. He is also a Research Affiliate in the Philosophy Program at the Australian National University. His research interests are in cognitive neuropsychology (particularly acquired and developmental disorders of cognition, especially disorders of reading), in cognitive neuropsychiatry (particularly delusions and hallucinations) and in the computational modeling of cognitive processes. He is a Fellow of the Academy of the Social Sciences of Australia and a Fellow of the Australian Academy of Science.

Acknowledgments

*T*he authors thank Virginia Berninger, John Morton, and G. Brian Thompson for the many penetrating comments and criticisms they made about an earlier draft of this work.

Nancy Ewald Jackson also thanks Patricia Martin for her skilled assistance in editing the manuscript and drafting the figures; The University of Iowa for the leave that made it possible for her to begin working with Max Coltheart in Australia in 1995; the faculty, administration, and staff of Macquarie University for their hospitality during that visit; the members of her Spring 2000 Cognitive Psychology of Reading class who read and made constructive suggestions for several chapters of a preliminary version of the manuscript; and Claire Fletcher-Flinn for many conversations about precocious reading.

Max Coltheart also thanks John Morton, John Marshall, Kathy Rastle, and Anne Castles for intellectual inspiration of various kinds.

1

Introduction

Only connect. . . .
E. M. Forster, *Howards End* (c. 1910/1985)

Good fences make good neighbors.
Robert Frost, "Mending Wall" (c. 1967)

This book is about making connections and about preserving the distinctions that make sound connections possible. It is the product of an interpersonal connection we have made across hemispheres of the globe and very different backgrounds. Throughout our careers, the two of us have pursued the study of individual differences in reading and reading acquisition from different perspectives. One of us (Jackson) is an American developmental psychologist who has studied the full range of individual differences in how children learn to read, and who has been concerned with the educational implications of those differences. The other (Coltheart) is an Australian cognitive neuropsychologist whose research has focused on previously competent impaired readers, and who has used knowledge about the varieties of these impairments to inform a cognitive psychological model of reading. Together, we represent at least a few of the disparate communities of researchers who have been concerned with understanding the nature of skilled reading and reading acquisition.

MAKING CONNECTIONS ACROSS STUDIES OF TYPICAL AND ATYPICAL READERS

Our purpose in writing this book has been to use our different backgrounds as a foundation for broader consideration of individual and developmental differences than is usual in work on atypical reading. We have considered the cognitive psychological literatures in which models of skilled reading have been proposed and tested and the disruption of skilled reading in acquired dyslexia has been described and interpreted. We also have considered theories of normal reading acquisition and the literatures in which both extremely poor and ex-

tremely good variants of reading development have been described. Synthesizing all of these literatures creates opportunities for strong tests of any theory of reading. We have tried to make these tests or at least suggest how they might be framed.

The study of individual differences in reading and reading acquisition has been conducted by separate groups concerned about different populations and often dismissive of one another's work. Those who study reading acquisition often have been skeptical about the relevance of cognitive neuropsychology to their concerns. For example, Bishop (1997a, b) argued that studies of acquired dyslexia are not applicable to the study of developmental dyslexia and other language disorders in children. Snowling, Bryant, and Hulme (1996) also have been skeptical about the value of such connections. Similarly, Vellutino, Scanlon, and Tanzman (1991) dismissed much of what might be called precognitive neuropsychology as immaterial to understanding the reading processes and educational needs of children who are failing to learn to read.

Some of the lack of communication among communities of reading researchers probably has been more a function of information overload, subdisciplinary chauvinism, and methodological biases than of anything else. Each group of researchers has tended to publish in a different set of journals and attend different conferences. As we began to work together, we often realized that we knew, and were ignorant of, different subsets of the reading literature. Therefore, we have made one of our goals for this book the drawing together of references to studies published in journals ranging from *Cognitive Neuropsychology* to *Psychological Review* to the *Journal of Educational Psychology*.

Making broad connections is a tricky exercise. Some cognitive psychologists who have developed models of skilled reading have made what we think are unrealistic assumptions, or have generated implausible conclusions, about children's reading acquisition (e.g., Harm & Seidenberg, 1999; Seidenberg & McClelland, 1989). Other scholars, including one of us, have focused on how the skilled reading system functions in its intact or various damaged states (e.g., Coltheart, 1985; Coltheart, Rastle, Perry, Langdon, & Ziegler, 2001) without considering beginning reading or reading acquisition. In this book, we propose standards for making what seem to us to be sound connections across studies of different levels of reading skill and different forms of atypical reading.

There are some traditional boundaries we have not crossed. Throughout this book, we have used the term *reading* to indicate pronouncing or recognizing the meaning of individual words, or of wordlike strings of letters. We have not considered theories of text comprehension. We wholeheartedly acknowledge that comprehension is the goal of reading, but theories of text and discourse comprehension constitute a domain of their own in which we are not expert. Furthermore, our concern throughout this book has been with reading in English, in its American, British, and Australian dialects. When we have digressed to consider other writing systems—Chinese, Hebrew, and Dutch—this has been done only to draw analogies, in chapters 5 and 6, about points concerning how English might be learned and read.

MAKING CONNECTIONS ACROSS METHODOLOGICAL ORIENTATIONS

The communities of reading researchers who have studied different populations have each developed certain methodological biases. Each of the literatures we have reviewed in chapters 3 through 7 has been shaped by its own intrinsic constraints and the resources to which researchers working in that area have had access. In this book, we have drawn on many different kinds of research, pointing out the strengths and limitations of each approach and emphasizing their complementarity.

Single *N* experimental designs have characterized the study of acquired dyslexia that we have reviewed in chapter 4 (for reasons see, e.g., Caramazza, 1984). Previously skilled readers whose reading has been disrupted in theoretically interesting ways cannot be assembled simultaneously in groups of 30 or 100. Therefore, the kinds of direct comparative studies that have characterized the study of normal skilled readers (such as the ubiquitous college sophomores), or of urban first graders at risk for reading failure, do not exist in the literature on acquired dyslexia. Within this literature, comparisons across richly described cases have accrued across time in programmatic studies by a community of researchers who have used similar methods and within-subject experimental contrasts.

In contrast, researchers studying reading acquisition failures in children have had access to larger populations and frequently to generous financial support from government agencies concerned about the social costs of illiteracy. This rapidly accumulating and often methodologically sophisticated literature, which we have considered in chapter 6, merits the attention of anyone who is interested in the nature of reading. However, its influence on some broader research questions may have been excessive. In the United States, much attention recently has been given to large-scale educational interventions for poor readers. Conclusions about how all children should learn to read have been drawn by extrapolation from findings about what works best for children who are most at risk for reading failure (Allington & Woodside-Jiron, 1999). We have considered this issue in chapter 5, proposing a model of reading acquisition that has been derived from a more balanced knowledge of the broader literature on typical and atypical readers.

Studies of reading acquisition and its failures have been plagued by their own sampling problems (see, especially, chapters 2 and 6). However, the enormous volume of these studies, many with sample sizes in the hundreds, may have led researchers in this community to conclude that there is nothing new they can learn from studies of single cases. We disagree. It is appropriate for those who are concerned about poor reading in children to be alert to substantive differences between previously skilled readers and those who have never learned to read well, but it is not appropriate to ignore a literature because its research designs are unfamiliar.

The cognitive neuropsychological literature on acquired dyslexia is not the

only reading literature dominated by single case or small *N* designs. With some dramatic large sample exceptions (e.g., Jackson, Donaldson, & Mills, 1993), these designs also have characterized studies of precocious readers. Here, too, we think it is appropriate for those who have studied poor readers to consider how a single case (in this instance, of precocious reading) might qualify the generalizations drawn about the nature of individual differences in reading acquisition. Furthermore, the large *N* studies of precocious reading that also are available provide an important point of comparison for interpreting the kinds of individual differences in skill patterns found among poor readers.

Some of the newest methods for studying reading may be especially appropriate for making connections across different types of readers. The most influential of these methods, computer simulation or computational modeling of reading, is discussed at length in chapter 3. In the past few years, major research initiatives (e.g., Berninger & Corina, 1998; S. E. Shaywitz et al., 1998) also have been directed toward establishing parallels between reading behaviors and brain functions. Powerful new methods such as brain imaging techniques have been added to the cognitive neuropsychologist's repertoire of techniques for drawing inferences about how various parts of the brain might be involved in aspects of reading. These new imaging techniques are noninvasive and can be used with children as well as adults. Therefore, they are equally applicable to studying skilled or beginning readers, very poor or very good readers. At present, results of these neuroscientific investigations should be interpreted with great caution (Berninger & Corina, 1998; Byrnes & Fox, 1998). We review some of these results briefly in chapter 6. At present, these findings may not add much to our ability to choose among theories of individual differences in reading, but their potential is exciting (Stanovich, 1998).

MAINTAINING GOOD FENCES

A central theme of *Howards End*, the novel for which "only connect" is the epigram, is the importance of seeing things clearly (i.e., with analytical precision) at the same time as one sees them whole (E. M. Forster, c. 1910/1985). Too much of either propensity, unbalanced by the other, leads to disaster in the lives of the novel's characters. The same is true in thinking about psychological issues, as Meehl once observed (1972).

Those of us who have taught for many years know how eagerly some of our brightest students draw connections among disparate ideas. They make intuitive leaps from neurological to behavioral, or from individual to societal, levels of analysis. They may assume that similar terms mean the same thing in different theoretical contexts. On very rare occasions, these connections are brilliant, but they often are just muddleheaded. Part of our job as teachers is to help students learn to make needed distinctions while, at the same time, encouraging their desire to construct new understandings by making broad connections.

We have tried to do the same for readers of this book. Understanding distinctions is as important as making connections, and the broader the connections one wants to make, the more critical the right distinctions become.

We recognize that there are fundamental differences between a child struggling to learn to read, a previously literate adult who has lost some reading skills because of a stroke, and a very young child who has learned to read in a few months, long before being exposed to instruction in school. However, we have tried to think carefully about when and how these differences matter. Throughout this book, we have adopted a convention that has helped us to do this.

A fundamental set of distinctions we have drawn separates the behavioral description of current reading performance, cognitive models proposed to account for that performance, and reasons why that performance and its cognitive model have come to be the way they are. Thus, we have identified *proximal* causes of reading performance failure (or success) as causes that can be identified within the parameters of a particular model of reading. In other words, proximal causes of reading failure refer to what might be going wrong in a reader's mind at the moment when he or she is trying to read a particular word. This is the realm in which most cognitive neuropsychological models of reading have been designed to operate.

We place what we have called *distal* causes of reading failure (or success) within another realm. When we ask why an individual's current reading system has come to operate the way it does, we may invoke such disparate variables as genetic predispositions, brain lesions, exposure to print, or familiarity with nursery rhymes.

Distinguishing among causes that fall along a continuum from proximal to distal has been fairly commonplace among developmental theorists (e.g., Morton & Frith, 1995; Scarr, 1985). Nonetheless, these distinctions often have not been observed in the reading literature. Indeed, accounts of reading development (e.g., Ehri, 1999) typically have not distinguished between the nature of a child's reading system at the moment he or she is reading a particular text, the only entity for which we have used the term proximal cause, and the learning processes that led to the current state of this system. We have called the latter distal causes even if they have taken place within the past hour or week.

Many missed connections, or misconnections, across studies of acquired dyslexia, reading acquisition failure, and precocious reading are the results of researchers' failures to consider reading system influences on reading behavior (proximal causes of success or failure) separately from distal experiential and organic influences on the system's current form. An adult with brain damage and a child who has received poor reading instruction may read in similar ways, and their reading failure may be interpretable in terms of the same kind of proximal cause at the level of the reading system, even though their problems have different distal origins. We elaborate this distinction in chapter 2, and it structures the way we make connections throughout this book.

THEORETICAL AND HISTORICAL CONTEXT

We favor a particular theory, the dual-route cascaded (DRC) model of reading. This theory was designed to account for normal skilled reading and for the atypical skill patterns shown by formerly skilled readers who have acquired specific reading difficulties (e.g., Coltheart, 1978, 1985; Coltheart, Langdon, & Haller, 1996; Coltheart et al., 2001; Morton & Patterson, 1980). We have extended this theory to create a context for understanding both typical and atypical beginning reading. Therefore, our book is unified by a particular theoretical perspective.

Our use of dual-route theory to understand beginning reading reflects a long tradition. From the late 1970s through the 1980s, an early version (Coltheart, 1978) of what eventually became the DRC computational model of reading dominated research on beginning reading and its failures, but the connections made were rather loose. At that time, the level of theorizing about both skilled and beginning reading was relatively unsophisticated. Theories of reading acquisition were descriptions of successive stages in skill development that did not include specifications for mechanisms of change (e.g., Chall, 1983), and differences among poor readers were conceptualized as a set of discrete subtypes. Neuropsychologists focused on organic causes of reading problems, while cognitive psychologists modeled reading failures in terms of cognitive systems (Vellutino et al., 1991).

Recently, as we demonstrate in chapter 3, models of skilled reading have become much more powerful and falsifiable, setting a standard for how beginning reading also could be modeled (e.g., Coltheart, Curtis, Atkins, & Haller, 1993; 2001; Plaut, McClelland, Seidenberg, & Patterson, 1996). Developmental and educational theorists also have begun to propose and test dynamic theories about the process of reading acquisition; that is, about how children learn to read (e.g., Share & Stanovich, 1995b; Thompson, 1999). All of these theoretical advances have created a context in which it is reasonable to start drawing diverse literatures together. Reducing one phenomenon to another can be misguided, especially when one or both are poorly understood, and this is not our goal. However, we have determined that current theories of skilled reading and of both acquired and developmental reading failure and success have reached a point at which they can facilitate the bidirectional connections that will be able to generate strong, inclusive theories (Stanovich, 1998).

Our organization and interpretation of the literature has been guided by the particular theory of skilled reading that we favor. However, many of our arguments are conceptual and methodological rather than theoretical. Therefore, they also are relevant to other theories. We hope that our disciplined consideration of the kinds of logical links that can and cannot be drawn across populations of readers will encourage others to propose alternative models of the phenomena we have reviewed.

SOME QUESTIONS ABOUT READING

We have raised questions more often than we have found answers. This balance seems appropriate to us because our goal is to change the way researchers think about reading and reading acquisition. Our hope is that, after finishing this book, the developmental and educational psychologists among our readers will ask themselves questions such as these:

- Are children who are having difficulty learning to read by sounding out new words similar in some ways to adults who have lost the ability to pronounce unfamiliar letter strings after suffering a stroke?
- Are other children who are having difficulty learning to read more like adults whose greatest difficulty is with reading words that have exceptional, irregular spelling patterns?
- Do all of these struggling readers have superficial variants of the same fundamental reading problem, or do they have different problems?

We also hope that our readers will understand how findings about exceptionally good reading acquisition of precocious readers might increase understanding of the conditions that are necessary for reading success. For instance, those who have devoted their attention to reading failure might ask themselves questions such as these:

- Do some children learn to read words well by the age of 3 years without showing any awareness of the sounds of individual letters in words?
- Do some very young beginning readers make very rapid progress without being particularly good at sounding out words?
- If these phenomena exist, what do they mean for the argument that awareness of sounds within words and ability to sound out new words are necessary for successful reading acquisition?

Finally, we hope that those of our readers who have studied skilled reading from a cognitive or cognitive neuropsychological perspective will finish this book with a new concern for questions about beginning reading and reading acquisition. Researchers whose theories have been tested primarily with studies of college sophomores or adult clinical cases might consider how the reading skills typical of an average first grader, a fourth grader who has failed to learn to read, or a 3 year old who is reading fluently all might be modeled in ways that are consistent with what we know about the nature of skilled reading. All of these variants of reading pose potential "individual differences tests" (Underwood, 1975) for theories of reading that could clarify advantages and disadvantages of competing models.

A NOTE ABOUT NOTATION

A book about reading requires some conventions about how to designate the printed words being read, how readers pronounce words, and the mental representations that are hypothesized to underlie readers' responses. We introduce these conventions here so that our readers can refer back to a single place to remind themselves of what means what.

For written real words that are read correctly, we have used a standard notation. The written word presented to the reader is given in italics. The reader's oral response is given in regular type, enclosed in quotation marks. For example, the word read might be *flew* and the reader's correct response would be "flew."

When the written text presented is not a real word but a nonword letter string or single letter, we still designate it using italics. However, in order to indicate how such a letter string was or should be pronounced, we need a special notation. This phonetic transcription system is indicated in Table 1.1. The pronunciation distinctions made in this system are similar to those in more standard notation systems, but we chose this one because it is sufficient for our

TABLE 1.1. Phonetic transcription conventions with examples for American English

Consonants							
Consonant pairs					**Other voiced consonants**		
Voiceless		**Voiced**					
p	"pat"	b	"bat"		m	"meat"	
f	"fat"	v	"vat"		n	"neat"	
th	"thin"	TH	"then"		w	"win"	
t	"tip"	d	"dip"		y	"yellow"	
s	"sewn"	z	"zone"		r	"read"	
sh	"bush"	zh	"beige"		l	"lead"	
ch	"chin"	j	"gin"		h	"hat"	
k	"curl"	g	"girl"		ng	"sing"	

Vowels						
Short vowels		**Vowel + "r" options**[a]		**Long vowels and diphthongs**		
a	"apple, sad"	Ar	"air"	A	"ate"	oy	"boy, soil"
e	"elephant"	Er	"ear"	E	"eagle"	ow	"cow, sound"
i	"in, chip"	Ir	"ire"	I	"ice"	
o	"cod"	Or	"oar"	O	"open"	
aw	"yawn"				
u	"up, hull"	ar	"car"	U	"pew"	
oo	"good, could, full"	er	"fern, bird, burn"	OO	"shoot"	

Schwa (reduced vowel)	°

[a]These conventions do not apply to Australian English.
Note. (Adapted from B. Wise and H. Datta, personal communication, November 1, 1999)

purposes and easy to learn. Using this system, we would indicate that a reader who read the nonword letter string *cade* correctly would pronounce it /kAd/. We also have used this phonetic transcription system to indicate readers' incorrect pronunciations of real words. For example, if a reader pronounced the word *flew* as if it were written *few*, without the sound of letter *l*, we would indicate the response as /fU/.

We have used additional forms of notation to indicate abstract letter and word forms hypothesized to be in the reader's mind. We have indicated these in capital letters when we are referring to the reader's abstract mental representation of a single letter form as an abstract letter unit or a full word's written form in what we call the orthographic lexicon. Thus, the reader might recognize *f* as the abstract letter unit F or *flew* as corresponding to the orthographic lexicon entry FLEW.

We also have hypothesized that readers have pronunciations of words that are in their oral vocabularies represented mentally in what we have called a phonological lexicon. These mental representations are indicated by capital letters enclosed in brackets, as in [FLEW].

Different dialects of English with somewhat different pronunciation systems are standard in different English-speaking countries. We have tried to avoid examples in which the phonetic transcription is required and the transcription of, say, an American and an Australian reader's pronunciation would differ. We have used American pronunciation as our standard in Table 1.1 and elsewhere.

2

Proximal and Distal Causes of Individual Differences in Reading

*T*he purpose of this chapter is to create a logical framework for our subsequent consideration of the disparate literatures about three groups of atypical readers. Because many problems in the study of individual differences in reading are rooted in lack of precision in the way such individual differences have been defined and studied, we begin by setting forth a definition that we think is widely accepted, but has implications that have not always been considered. Throughout this volume, we make certain fundamental assumptions about what reading is.

DEFINITIONS

Reading

We take reading to be a cognitive activity that is accomplished by a mental information-processing system that is made up of a number of distinct processing subsystems. The input to this system is print. The processes applied by the system to this input yield, as output, such things as word meanings, syntactic representations of sequences of words, and pronunciations. We will use the term *reading system* to describe the cognitive system that derives such semantic, syntactic or phonological representations from printed input. The nature and functioning of this mental information-processing system is expected to change as a reader becomes more practiced and skilled and acquires new knowledge. It also can change as a result of brain damage in people who had become fully literate, and, perhaps, as a result of the impact of physical maturation on cognition.

We acknowledge that the purpose of reading is usually to comprehend extended text. However, we choose to focus on reading at the individual-word level for several reasons. First we agree with Gough (e.g., Gough, Hoover, & Peterson, 1996) and many others that it is useful to decompose text reading ability into two constructs. One concerns abilities to operate at the level of single words or wordlike letter strings (e.g., to recognize as known, to understand, or to translate to phonology single printed words); the other concerns listening comprehension. The literature on discourse comprehension is largely distinct from that on word reading, and we do not consider it here. Second, we feel comfortable with our relatively narrow focus because we conclude that individual differences in the ability to operate at the single-word level words are a major source of individual differences in ability to read text (e.g., National Reading Panel, 2000a; Perfetti, 1985; Shankweiler et al., 1999). This statement is true for readers who are children or adults, beginning or skilled, progressing well or poorly, brain damaged or not.

Skilled reading requires much more than the basic building blocks of reading that can be defined at the single-word level. Skilled reading is much more than basic reading skills such as ability to translate print to pronunciation, to recognize whether a letter string represents a known word, and to access the meanings of single words. However, we are willing to assume that (a) learning to read requires adequate acquisition of all three of these basic reading skills (of course, learning to read requires much more than this, too) and (b) that skilled reading requires a high level of skill in all three of these basic reading skills (of course, skilled reading requires much more than this, too).

We acknowledge the argument that some readers may comprehend text poorly because of deficiencies beyond any difficulty they may have in processing at the level of individual words (e.g., Pressley, 1998). However, understanding individual differences at the basic level of word reading takes one a fair distance toward understanding differences in reading as more broadly defined. Our goal is to go that distance.

Acquired Versus Developmental Disorders of Reading

This is a straightforward but essential distinction on which we will rely in much of this book. Someone who has achieved a normal level of skill in some cognitive domain and subsequently loses some or all of that skill exhibits an acquired disorder of cognition—acquired in the sense that prior to some point in that person's life no disorder of that particular cognitive skill was present. In contrast, someone who has never been able to perform at a normal level in this cognitive domain exhibits a developmental disorder of cognition. This distinction is crucial because how one goes about seeking to discover the causes of any disorder of cognition—abnormally poor reading, for example—is very different in these two situations.

CAUSAL MODELING OF INDIVIDUAL DIFFERENCES IN READING AND READING DEVELOPMENT

Our general approach to explaining individual differences in reading development has much in common with Morton and Frith's structural approach to developmental psychopathology, which they have expounded in relation to developmental dyslexia as well as other conditions such as autism (Morton & Frith, 1995). Like them, we distinguish between three levels of analysis:

1. a behavioral level that refers to observed performance on reading tasks;
2. a cognitive level where characteristics of such observed reading performance are explained in terms of hypothesized properties of the reading system; and
3. a biological level where we may seek explanations in terms of brain structure or function for the current nature of the reading system and may also seek biological explanations for why, over the course of development, the reader's biology and cognitive reading system came to have the properties they currently possess.

We also provide for environmental influences on the cognitive and biological levels. These environmental influences may themselves be biological (e.g., malnutrition) or experiential (e.g., a particular method of reading instruction). We will illustrate this approach with a hypothetical example. Suppose a boy revealed on reading assessment a specific difficulty in "sounding out" or "phonic knowledge"; that is, in reading aloud pronounceable pseudowords such as those used in the Word Attack subtest of the Woodcock tests (e.g., Woodcock & Johnson, 1989). This is an observation at the behavioral level that we wish to explain. In our terms, there must be something abnormal about this child's reading system (if there were not, reading aloud of pseudowords would be normal).

We therefore carry out further reading tests designed to provide data that will allow us to infer in exactly what way his reading system is abnormal. Let us say we find that the boy's ability to recognize and name letters is normal for his age but he makes many errors when asked to give the appropriate individual sounds in response to single letters. So we propose that what is wrong with his reading system is that knowledge of grapheme-phoneme correspondence (GPC) rules is inadequate.

That is one link in the causal chain: It is indeed the last link because it is a claim about the link from the cognitive level to the observational (behavioral) level. What about earlier links? Why is it that this child has inadequate knowledge of GPC rules? Suppose we find, on further investigation, that the boy was slow to learn to speak, still shows some difficulties in pronouncing words, and performs poorly on various tests of phonological awareness. Also suppose that we can rule out sensory and psychosocial problems. It would be reasonable then to conclude something at the biological level: that this child has a specific

abnormality of the brain systems on which the ability to process the sounds of speech depends—some abnormality of left temporal lobe structures in the brain, for example. Suppose this led us to carry out a functional brain imaging study with this boy, which did indeed reveal regions of left temporal lobe which were not activated in the normal way as he carried out reading tasks.

Now, we have a causal model for this particular child's current reading problem—a statement that causally links the biological level to the cognitive level and causally links the cognitive level to the behavioral level, as depicted in Figure 2.1.

We might feel that we are now beginning to develop a good understanding of this boy's developmental reading difficulty—good, but far from complete. What, for example, caused the current abnormality of the left temporal lobe? Further investigations might reveal that a number of the boy's immediate relatives also had great difficulty in learning to read; perhaps, even the same specific difficulty with phonics that he has. We therefore might feel there are good grounds for elaborating Figure 2.1 as shown in Figure 2.2; and, indeed, genetic analysis might provide strong support for this.

Suppose, however, that it had turned out that all of this boy's relatives were excellent readers, the genetic analysis had shown nothing unusual, and that medical records indicated that his birth had been a stressful one with the likelihood that he had sustained a period of oxygen deprivation during the birth. That might lead us to conclude that perinatal anoxia was the cause of the temporal lobe abnormality.

Now, we have a link in the causal chain that is not internal. It instead is environmental. Figure 2.2 is a purely internal biological account: A genetic abnormality caused a specific abnormality of neural development (abnormality in

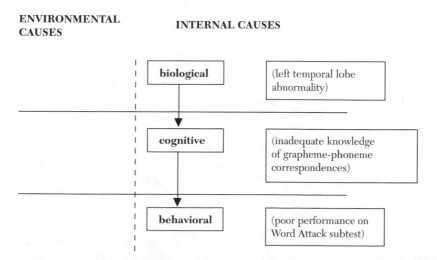

FIGURE 2.1. One possible causal model of a current developmental reading impairment.

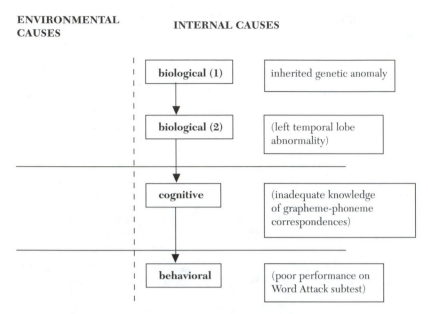

ENVIRONMENTAL CAUSES

INTERNAL CAUSES

| biological (1) | inherited genetic anomaly |

| biological (2) | (left temporal lobe abnormality) |

| cognitive | (inadequate knowledge of grapheme-phoneme correspondences) |

| behavioral | (poor performance on Word Attack subtest) |

FIGURE 2.2. A model of a current developmental reading impairment that postulates a prior genetic biological cause for the current state of the system.

some left temporal lobe structures) which, in turn, caused a specific abnormality of reading development (inadequate knowledge of GPC rules). But, Figure 2.3 includes a cause that is environmental, and that is an important difference, which needs to be represented in figures like these. We will follow Morton and Frith (1995) by representing environmental causes with open-bodied arrows, and locating them to the left of the dotted line, as in Figure 2.3.

As a final example, suppose the boy presenting with poor performance on the Word Attack subtest had no relatives with reading difficulties, a normal birth, and no history of any known neurological conditions or early oral language problems. Instead, what further investigations revealed was that he had been attending a school in which reading tuition involving phonics was barred and that all reading lessons involved instruction in whole-word recognition in the context of reading books. That might lead us to yet another different causal model, that shown in Figure 2.4.

Note that once again we have introduced an environmental cause, though this time the environmental cause is at the cognitive rather than the biological level. Also note that, in this particular causal model, there is no primary cause within the biological level. It is true that the brain of someone with inadequate knowledge of GPCs must differ from the brain of someone with a good knowledge of such correspondences, but that fact is not immediately helpful in understanding the causes of the poor Word Attack performance. In contrast, knowledge about the kind of reading instruction this boy received is directly helpful in understanding such causes.

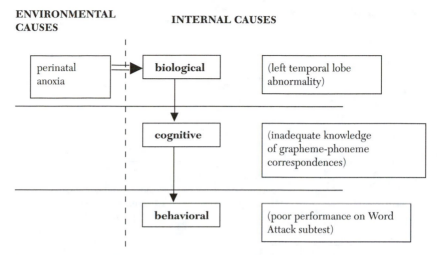

FIGURE 2.3. A model of a current developmental reading impairment that postulates a prior environmental biological cause for the current state of the system.

In an ideal scientific world, information about the instructional history of any reader would be available and a part of the distal explanation of current reading performance, even when other kinds of distal causes seem more salient, as in Figures 2.1, 2.2, or 2.3. This information is particularly relevant to developmental disorders of reading, and it also could bear on disorders acquired after formal reading instruction has ceased (V. Berninger, personal communication, August 24, 2000). However, because instructional history often is unknown,

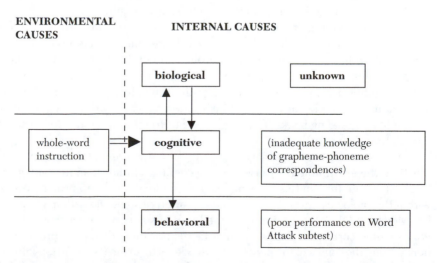

FIGURE 2.4. A model of a current developmental reading impairment that postulates a prior learning experience as the environmental cause for the current state of the system.

we have left it unspecified but implicit in the Environmental Causes section of most of our figures.

We depart from Morton and Frith's (1995) model a little in that we want to make a distinction among these links in the causal chains. The last link in any chain—the link that directly influences the behavior—we refer to as the *proximal cause* of the behavior, while all earlier links in the causal chain we refer to as *distal causes* of the behavior. We will argue for the view that the proximal cause of individual differences in reading behaviors is always at the cognitive level, whereas distal causes of such individual differences can be cognitive, biological (including genetic and environmental), or perceptual-cognitive experiences.

Yet another way in which our proposed scheme for understanding individual differences in reading performance departs a little from Morton and Frith's (1995) is that we believe both typical and atypical development require explanation. We consider acquisition of the ability to read written words as a culturally engendered "unnatural act" (Gough & Hillinger, 1980). Therefore, the presence of a reading system hypothesized to account for typical reading performance requires as much explanation as the disordered reading systems hypothesized to cause atypical performances. Furthermore, as we show in chapter 7, we also need to be able to explain exceptionally good reading performance as it is manifest in the phenomenon of precocious reading.

A sketch of how reading and influences on its development might be understood very generally within this framework is presented in Figure 2.5.

According to this framework, a complete explanation of any kind of individual difference in reading behavior requires three things, working from the bottom up in Figure 2.5:

1. a description of the reading performance that can be compared with performances of other readers;
2. at least one hypothesis as to its proximal cause, which must be at the cognitive level;
3. at least one hypothesis as to the distal cause or causes which brought about the cognitive condition, which then is the proximal cause. At least one such distal cause must be at the biological level (given that there can be no cognitive differences without brain differences).

Furthermore, given that neither reading nor reading failure develops in the absence of experience, all three of these levels of explanation ideally should be offered in the context of information about the individual's instructional history. The children described in Figures 2.2 and 2.3 might have developed normal reading ability with some kinds of instruction.

Of course, explanations do not have to be complete to be of value: if in relation to some particular aspect of reading, we had (1) and (2) above without (3), that would be worthwhile even though incomplete. Indeed, we will have relatively little to say about biological distal causes, because these are just be-

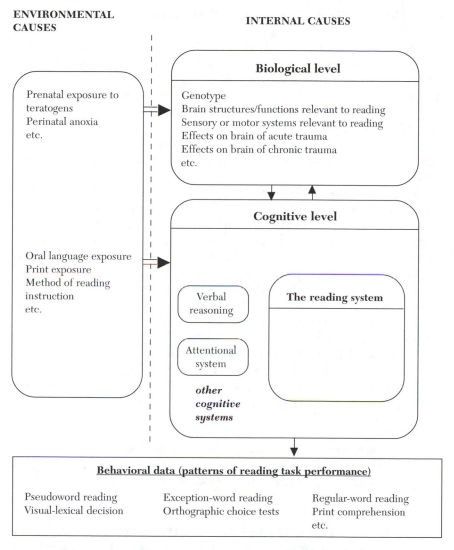

FIGURE 2.5. A general model of reading and influences on reading development.

ginning to be understood. We now consider, in turn, these three elements of explanation.

In Figure 2.5, the reading system is a blank, or black, box. In chapter 3, we fill in this box with a specified reading system; that is, with a specific proposal concerning what are the processing subcomponents within this system. However, some preliminary comments seem appropriate here. First, the processing subsystems listed within the reading system certainly are not components solely of that system: Many belong to other systems, too. For example, the system we use for speaking contains a semantic system and a phonological lexicon. The

evidence is very strong that these processing components are also parts of the reading system; that is, for example, the system of word meanings we use to understand spoken words is the system of word meanings we use to understand printed words. Second, when children come to the task of learning to read— the task of acquiring the reading system—they already possess some of the components of that system. At the time when they are beginning to learn to read, they already have acquired a semantic system and a phonological lexicon.

DESCRIBING INDIVIDUAL DIFFERENCES IN READING BEHAVIOR

Reading Performances

The tasks listed at the bottom level of Figure 2.5 are some that are used frequently by cognitive psychologists interested in reading. For example, many cognitive psychologists study the accuracy or speed with which a reader reads aloud pseudowords. These are nonword letter strings, such as *craid,* that have legitimate, pronounceable spellings. The nature of the other kinds of tasks we have listed will become evident in later chapters.

No matter how bland a list of tasks such as that in Figure 2.5 might appear to be, no description of reading performance is theoretically neutral. One's theoretical and metatheoretical views determine the constructs and the measures one chooses. Researchers would differ on exactly what should be included in a master list of word-reading tasks. For example, as we explain in chapter 3, some would want lists of words having more or less consistent, rather than regular or exceptional, spelling-to-sound relationships (Coltheart & Leahy, 1992). Behavioral descriptions are informed by theory, but it is possible and useful to differentiate performance descriptions from more theoretically specific inferences about the reading system underlying those performances.

Descriptions of individual differences in reading are summaries of overt, observable performances on reading tasks such those listed in Figure 2,5. A descriptive statement might be: "When reading a list of 20 four-letter pseudowords, she was correct on only 7 items." We consider such statements solely descriptive because they describe only a performance pattern and not any properties of the reader's reading system. Furthermore, they provide no information about any causes of a person's pattern of reading performance. Nevertheless, such descriptions are an essential starting point for any attempt to understand patterns of individual differences in reading ability, such as patterns of acquired dyslexia, precocious reading, or difficulties in learning to read.

Prevalence of Performance Patterns

Descriptions of individual differences in reading behavior should, but often do not, include information about how common a pattern of performance is within an explicitly defined population of interest. Pronouncing only 7 of 20

pseudowords correctly sounds like poor performance, but is it? Such a question can be answered only if one knows how a particular performance, such as pseudoword reading this low in accuracy, relates to performances of other individuals from an appropriate comparison group. If the reader is a college-educated adult, is pronouncing only 7 pseudowords correctly 2 *SD*s below the mean for this group, or is it within the average range? If the pseudoword reader is a fourth grader, is his or her performance below or above average relative to all children in that grade? How might this score rank relative to some more selected group of children who have been identified in terms of their reading ability, some background variable, or instructional history? Age, grade, and other relevant norms for specific skills facilitate these comparisons.

Norms for standard tests can provide useful descriptive information about the prevalence of some reading skill patterns. Individually or group administered reading tests may include subtests consisting of lists of real words or pseudowords that are read aloud and scored for accuracy or speed (Torgesen, Wagner, & Rashotte, 1999; Woodcock & Johnson, 1989). These tests yield good estimates of the prevalence of each total score in their standardization populations, and they often are incorporated into studies of individual differences in reading, particularly among children. However, commercially available standard tests tend to be constructed to maximize reliable discrimination among individuals on relatively broad constructs that have substantial predictive validity. For example, a word-reading list on a standard test is likely to include words that vary in their spelling-to-sound regularity and consistency, length, and frequency of occurrence in reading materials. Similarly, a standard test pseudoword list may contain some items that are identical to common real words except for a single letter (e.g., *slive*), other items in which the letter strings are more novel (e.g., *sliem*), and yet others whose pronunciation is identical to the pronunciation of a real word (e.g., *slite*). Therefore, our knowledge of the prevalence of component reading skills in particular populations, such as fourth graders or college-educated adults, often is limited to knowledge about performances that cannot be neatly tied to particular hypothesized cognitive processes. As researchers approach consensus about the structure of some reading skills, more theoretically informed standardized tasks are becoming available (e.g., Coltheart & Leahy, 1996; Edwards & Hogben, 1999; Torgesen et al., 1999).

Reading Better or Worse Than Expected? Age and Reading-Level Match Comparisons

One cannot even begin to consider whether a reader's performance on any reading test is atypical unless one begins with a description of what typical performance on this test is; and here there is more than one useful way to define typicality. One approach is in terms of chronological age (CA). This is the most obvious standard for evaluating the reading of children. Imagine a girl named Jennifer who is 8 years old and in the third grade. She seems to be reading poorly, relative to classmates of the same age. Perhaps, like many poor readers,

she seems to have a fairly substantial, although below average, sight vocabulary. Her teacher also noticed that Jennifer seems to be completely stumped whenever she encounters a new word in her reading. The child is referred for an assessment that involves tests of her ability to read both real words that might be familiar and pseudowords that certainly are novel.

Suppose the mean number correct on a pseudoword reading task by a group of 8-year-olds who are making normal progress in learning to read was known to be, say, 9/20, with an *SD* of 3.0. If 8-year-old Jennifer scores only 2/20, she is atypical. (An 8-year-old who scored 16/20 also would be atypical, but better than expected.) Furthermore, Jennifer's individual assessment confirmed that she was moderately below average for her age group on ability to read real words (perhaps earning a raw score of 7 on a test for this with a CA-matched mean of 10 and an *SD* of 3). For individuals or groups, CA-match comparisons such as these have the advantage of representing a straightforward and plausible causal model in which time (age) is a predictor variable. A child of a particular age (or grade level) is expected to perform within certain ranges of competence on tests of a variety of reading skills. Thus, we interpret these scores as showing that the child tested is a poor word reader and an exceptionally poor reader of pseudowords.

There is nothing unusual here. Although CA may be only a proxy for a complex of maturational and experiential variables, at least it is a proxy that is standard throughout the developmental literature. Indeed, this standard of evaluating children's performance is so automatic that we usually are not even conscious of using age as an explanation or cause for expected performance. However, an individual's or a group's current reading performance can be interpreted in contexts other than their prevalence relative to CA peers. There are other ways to provide a frame of reference for interpreting a reader's performance on various tasks.

An alternative that has been popular in the literatures on poor and precocious reading in children has been the reading level (RL)- or reading age (RA)-match design. We prefer the former term because "reading age" has a more absolute ring to it, as if it were a variable on the same order as chronological age. As we shall see, it is not.

In RL-match designs, groups of younger and older children are matched, case by case or as groups, on some reading task. An RL comparison involves logic similar to describing a child's standard test subscores in terms of the age levels at which those raw scores would be average. In this case, however, one picks an appropriate RL comparison group, usually of average readers, whose mean score on some fairly broad measure of reading ability is equivalent to the mean score of the target group of unusually good or poor readers.

Why would one bother to do this? At the descriptive level that concerns us at present, the value of an RL match can be increased precision. Let us return to the 8-year-old third grader we introduced earlier. We know that Jennifer's reading has been generally poor. Indeed, her teacher probably referred her for an individual assessment because her reading was below the level typical for

her classmates on a variety of everyday reading tasks. We know from CA norms that her pseudoword reading is several *SD*s below the age norm and her real word reading is 1 *SD* below that norm. However, we want to have an additional way of evaluating how poor her performance was on each task. We might want to know whether these two performances are comparable, individually and as a set, to those of beginning or late first graders, or perhaps even kindergartners.

For this rather typical poor reader, we might find that her real-word reading level is at the late first-grade level, but that her pseudoword reading level is well below the norm even for these younger children. Therefore, we know that Jennifer's pseudoword reading level not only is extremely poor relative to her age group, but it also does not seem to be keeping pace with her real-word reading level. Her pattern of reading skills does not look like that of younger average readers of any age. She may be only 18 months behind her age peers in her real word reading, but she is even further behind in pseudoword reading.

In the example we have given, the relative deficits in Jennifer's real-word and pseudoword reading scores are similar whether one uses CA-based deviation scores or RL-based comparisons to evaluate her scores. However, that need not be the case. Within-age distributions and developmental trends do not always line up neatly. It is possible that a child might have a CA-referenced deficit in pseudoword reading that is more extreme than his or her real-word reading deficit, but nonetheless may be performing on both measures at about the same RL, perhaps that of a beginning first grader. Therefore, an RL match gives us the option of investigating different ways to describe a child's atypical pattern of reading performances. Is this overall pattern similar to that of average younger (or, for exceptionally good readers, older) children? Alternatively, does the score pattern show something other than an even developmental lag?

No single score captures everything about a child's reading ability level. An RL match is a match on a single dimension of reading ability, not on reading ability as a whole. However, some test scores reflect core aspects of reading better than do others. A word-reading accuracy score, often from a standardized test, typically is used to match an exceptional group of readers with their RL mates. These scores are good choices because the ability to read a list of words accurately is correlated with most other aspects of reading.

In RL-match designs, "good" and "poor" reading are defined in terms of rate of development. The groups are similar in current performance level, but the older, slower progressing readers have taken more years to reach this point than the younger, faster progressing readers. At the descriptive level, the purpose of these designs is to compare the skill profiles of groups whose current reading performances are at the same level on at least one measure (the matching criterion). Investigators want to know whether a group of, say, third-grade poor readers that has a mean word recognition accuracy score at the same level as a group of average first graders is more or less delayed in other reading skills. Are these slower progressing older readers better than average first graders in text comprehension? Are there any reading tasks on which the struggling third graders are even poorer than first graders? RL-match comparisons provide a

second baseline, in addition to that provided by chronological peers, against which the relative strengths and weaknesses of an atypical group can be evaluated.

The value of these designs has been disputed. One of us has scorned them (Castles & Coltheart, 1993), and the other has used them repeatedly (e.g., Jackson & Biemiller, 1985; Jackson & Donaldson, 1989a; Jackson, Donaldson, & Mills, 1993). Critics cite the arbitrary nature of using any single reading test, or set of tests, to match children from separate age and grade populations (Castles & Coltheart, 1993). Even advocates for the designs acknowledge their limitations (Jackson & Butterfield, 1989; Stanovich & Siegel, 1994), and the two of us agree that the results of any RL-match design can vary with the matching criterion chosen.

Despite their limitations, RL-match designs have been popular in the reading acquisition literature, and they have played an important part in the studies we review in chapter 6. These designs have been widely used, in part, because they circumvent a problem that occurs when one tries to compare the performances of CA-matched (same age, grade, or both) groups of good and poor readers. There may be only small amounts of overlap in the distributions of CA-matched good and poor readers' scores on a battery of reading tasks, particularly if only a narrow age range is studied. In such a study, one or both groups easily can be at the floor or ceiling of some measures; groups may appear to differ more on some measures than on others simply because the former have greater sensitivity or reliability (Chapman & Chapman, 1985; Jackson & Butterfield, 1989; Manis, Seidenberg, Doi, McBride-Chang, & Petersen, 1996). These issues are a pervasive problem in the interpretation of statistical interactions (Loftus, 1978), but they are exacerbated when groups being compared are performing at widely spaced levels on two or more scales (Jackson & Butterfield, 1989).

Returning to struggling 8-year-old Jennifer, imagine that both her real word and pseudoword reading scores were more than two *SD*s below age norms, as might be the case for an extremely poor reader. It might then be especially useful to use RL standards to know whether her real word or pseudoword reading was more retarded.

Those who dislike RL-match comparisons may object to the necessarily arbitrary choice of one matching measure rather than others. No individual's or group's current RL is fully described by any single measure. A reading level is a test score, and it lacks the face validity of chronological age or grade level as a matching criterion. Fans of RL-match designs may counter that even age and grade level are imperfect markers of developmental constructs such as biological maturity or educational experience. However, RL-match designs do have a serious, fundamental flaw that stems from trying to equate samples from different populations on an arbitrary and imperfectly reliable measure. Unfortunately, matching different age groups on an observed test score RL criterion does not imply that the groups are matched on the underlying variable of interest.

Imagine that a group of poor readers is defined as those third graders with the lowest scores on a standard test of word-reading accuracy. To some extent, those extremely low scores must be the result of measurement error. If this

extreme group were tested again, their scores would be expected to be, on the average, somewhat higher. Furthermore, the poor word readers' performance on any other kind of reading test would be expected, by chance alone, to be somewhat less depressed than their word reading scores.

The extreme groups that are the targets of most RL-match designs are likely to have true scores on the matching variable that are closer to their chronological age and grade means than their observed scores. In contrast, comparison groups chosen for their averageness are likely to have true scores close to their observed scores. Therefore, by the fundamental statistical law of regression toward the mean, the target group, by chance alone, should perform at less extreme levels on any measure of reading performance other than the one by which they have been chosen as extreme (Jackson & Butterfield, 1989). An RL match is not a level playing field.

A related problem, although one not specific to RL match designs, is that investigators using these designs often go to great lengths to create what appears to be a perfect RL match between older slower progressing and younger average readers by selecting only the matchable cases from available groups. Thus, the "average" readers in an RL-match design may not be representative of average readers at all, but only of average readers who could be matched with a particular group of older poor readers. For example, they might be all males or restricted in range of IQ. Such biased sampling often limits the external validity of RL-match designs (Jackson & Butterfield, 1989).

Regression toward the mean also operates in CA-match comparisons of extreme and average groups, but the issue in those comparisons is simplified because the matching criterion itself (CA or grade level) is perfectly reliable and, in a sense, external to the comparisons of interest. In these designs, there is no illusion of a level playing field like that created by a fundamentally imperfect RL match. There are fewer things to think about, and researchers are more likely to be aware that children selected as the poorest in their class on one reading test are likely, by chance alone, to be less extremely poor on another.

In the 1990s, researchers began to acknowledge the limitations of both CA- and RL-match comparisons and to adopt sampling and analytical strategies designed to minimize the limits of the designs' ability to provide appropriate contexts for describing readers' performances (e.g., Jackson et al., 1993; Stanovich & Siegel, 1994). However, most studies in the literature present potentially biased estimates of the extent to which a particular group's performance on a given task is better or worse than expected, given what else we know about their reading. This is especially likely to be true when the expectation has been generated from an RL-match design.

Summary

By now, we should have made our point that even describing a person's component reading skills at the behavioral level is no simple task. There are three aspects to the task's complexity. First, what one chooses to describe is influ-

enced by theory. Second, the standard test scores that give the best information about the extent to which a performance is typical or atypical often are not theoretically interpretable. Third, at least two different kinds of standards, CA and RL matches, have been used for evaluating whether an individual score or pattern of performance is typical or not. As we move to the level of proximal causes of observed reading behaviors, it is important to remember that the validity of inferences about these always rests in the validity of the observed performance descriptions from which they are drawn. That is why we have devoted so much attention to this first level.

PROXIMAL CAUSES OF INDIVIDUAL DIFFERENCES IN READING

As indicated above, we take the view that proximal causes of individual differences in reading behaviors are always at the cognitive level (we will neglect such cases as a boy who forgets to wear his eyeglasses). More specifically, our view is that, when seeking the proximal cause of any pattern of reading behavior that is atypical on the basis of either a CA or RL match, the first goal should always be the same. One should first attempt to describe this atypicality as some difference, or set of differences, between the reading system of the reader who is reading in an atypical way and the reading systems of those who are reading as expected.

Interpreting Task Performances as Caused by Properties of the Cognitive Reading System

A statement about the proximal cause of atypical reading is a hypothesis about the way in which a person's current reading system is atypical, or simply different from others' reading systems. Clearly, if there is something atypical about a person's reading behavior, we expect there to be something atypical about his or her reading system. If there were not, why is not the reading behavior usual rather than unusual?

We categorize statements about aspects of the reading system assumed to be responsible for observed patterns of individual differences in reading performances as referring to proximal causes of those differences. These proximal causes refer to structures or processes within some stated or implied model of the reading system as it is functioning at a particular time. That time frame is not precise, but it is meant to be limited to the period of minutes, hours, or perhaps days during which an assessment of an individual's reading skills is made. The time frame is assumed to be narrow enough to exclude any substantial change in behavior (or in the reading system) as a result of new learning or maturation. It is meant to provide a single snapshot of cognition, not a motion picture of cognitive development.

Specific hypotheses about proximal causes of atypical reading performances

will be presented in the next chapter, when we elaborate a model of the reading system which is a component of the cognitive level of Figure 2.5. For now, we want only to introduce the general idea of what such hypotheses might look like. A statement about a proximal cause emerges in a dialogue such as

"What is atypical about Jennifer's reading?"
"She reads pseudowords poorly."
"Why does she read pseudowords poorly?"
"Because she doesn't have good knowledge of GPC rules linking letters with sounds."

This statement about Jennifer's knowledge of GPC rules is an inference one step removed from our previous description. In particular, we stress that such a statement is a causal one, not just a redescription of the data. It is a causal statement because it might be false (even if the description of the performance pattern it is designed to explain is accurate), since there are other possible causes of poor pseudoword reading (e.g., inaccurate letter perception).

Expressing this scenario in this way makes it immediately obvious why we say that to attribute Jennifer's poor reading of pseudowords to poor knowledge of GPC rules is not a circularity but a falsifiable empirical hypothesis. Imagine that, instead of poor knowledge of GPC rules, she had some other knowledge or processing deficit. Among other things, this could be poor visual identification of letters or a difficulty in blending together the phonemes produced by application of the GPC rules. Either of these problems also could lead to poor pseudoword reading. So, there are at least three different possible proximal causes of the same behavioral datum, poor pseudoword reading.

As we have said, there are a number of ways in which an abnormality of the reading system can cause the behavior of poor pseudoword reading. Any proposal concerning what these ways might be is of course theory dependent. It depends on one's model of the reading system. For example, we assume that the procedure by which pseudowords are read is solely via GPC rule use, but we acknowledge that others (e.g., Taft, 1992; Treiman, Goswami, & Bruck, 1990) have a different view; that is, a somewhat different theory about the nature of the reading system. With a different theory, the elements depicted within the currently blank reading system of Figure 2.5 would differ. We consider this issue further in the next chapter.

Of course, there can be circumstances in which the proximal cause of atypical reading is at the cognitive level as we claim it always is, but does not specifically involve the reading system. Children might fail a reading test simply because they do not comprehend the instructions, or because of an attentional deficit that also prevents them from attending to nonreading tasks. Cognitive factors external to the reading system generally are not considered in cognitive models of reading and are likely to operate as confounding factors when such models are used to explain reading performance. However, they can be important nuisances. For example, the role of general cognitive factors in reading

becomes central when we discuss whether the reading systems of "garden variety" poor readers differ from those of children whose poor cognitive performance is specific to reading tasks. Similarly, general cognitive factors may enter into interpretation of reading performances of extremely young precocious readers whose task failures may reflect lack of ability to adapt to novel task demands.

Designs for Studying Proximal Causes of Atypical Reading

Establishing causal links between properties of a hypothesized reading system and specific reading behaviors falls within the ambit of experimental cognitive psychology. Cognitive models are proposed that yield specific predictions about how certain stimulus variables should influence performance. When the researcher's goal is to explain aspects of performance common across individuals, these proximal explanations can be, and often are, fully experimental. For example, other things being equal, people in general read words with regular spelling patterns (such as *wag*) more quickly and accurately than they read equally familiar words with exceptional spelling patterns (such as *sew*), at least when the words are relatively low in frequency (see, e.g., Paap & Noel, 1991; Rastle & Coltheart, 1999). This suggests that the reading system responds in different ways to regular and exception words. The nature of that difference can be debated among theorists, but cause and effect are neatly constrained by experimental design. The critical condition, "other things being equal," is established by experimental control and randomization.

Experimental or partly experimental studies of proximal causes. Even at the proximal level, explaining individual differences is inherently complicated. If, for example, good and poor readers differ in the extent of their regular word advantage, any explanation must draw, at the very least, on preexisting cognitive differences as well as on response to the task currently being presented. Explanations of individual differences, of what often is called organismic variation, can be made at the proximal level in terms of the current structure and function of the individual's reading system. However, individual or group differences in how that system operates at the moment of assessment represent the interaction of organismic and experimental variance. The organismic variance in the cognitive system has more distal causes somewhere in the readers' personal histories. This may be one reason why proximal and distal explanations of atypical reading seem prone to being muddled.

Computational modeling (i.e., computer simulation). Because the structure and function of cognitive systems is inferred from observed behavior rather than being observed directly, hypotheses about exactly how such systems operate can be hard to evaluate. However, in recent years, researchers have made increasingly successful attempts to define exactly how alternative systems could operate. They have done this by creating and testing computer simulations of human performance on several different word-reading tasks (e.g. Ans,

Carbonnel, & Valdois, 1999; Coltheart et al., 1993; Harm & Seidenberg, 1999; Grainger & Jacobs, 1996; Norris, 1994; Plaut et al., 1996; Seidenberg & McClelland, 1989; Zorzi, Houghton, & Butterworth, 1998). When such simulations yield predictable and precise accounts of human performance differences, they indicate that the cognitive theory they embody is sufficient to account for the observed human performance. The proximal cause of a pattern of reading performance generated by these simulations is some property of a computer program. Unlike a human reading system, a computer program is directly and fully observable. Simulations provide the best means available to date for distinguishing among alternative reading systems as explanations of reading behavior, and we will consider them in greater detail in chapter 3.

Correlational studies of proximal causes: CA and RL matches.   We have shown that CA-match and RL-match designs provide different, perhaps complementary, perspectives on the description of differences between good and poor readers. Both kinds of designs are, of course, correlational. Nonetheless, both have been used to draw inferences about proximal causes of reading failure (or unusual reading success).

Recall Jennifer, who we introduced earlier as a third grader whose ability to read real words (which could be familiar to her) was poor relative to her classmates, but whose ability to read novel pseudowords was even worse. Researchers studying poor reading in children often identify the poor readers at a particular CA or grade level by screening them on a measure of word reading, often a standard test. A comparison of these poor word readers with average word readers from the same CA group may reveal that most of the poor readers have skill patterns like Jennifer's. Indeed, a significantly greater mean deficit often is found in the poor readers' pseudoword reading (e.g., Rack, Snowling, & Olson, 1992) than in their real word reading. Interpretation of that performance difference (essentially a group-by-task interaction) is likely to be made in terms of proximal cause. The researcher will conclude, usually with the caveats appropriate to interpretation of correlational findings, that the poor readers read words rather poorly because their reading systems are deficient in some mechanism in the system that is essential for reading pseudowords.

Readers of this chapter may have noticed that there is little difference between the correlational CA-match design just described and the situation in which inferences about proximal cause of reading differences are drawn from a partly experimental design. In the latter design, the interaction of an experimental task variable (type of word list read) with an organismic variable (good or poor reader) is used to draw conclusions about proximal causes of reading failure. This is equivalent to showing that children selected because they are poor word readers are even more poor at reading pseudowords. How researchers describe these similar designs often has more to do with their own backgrounds than with the designs' critical features.

In a CA-match design, a problem of interpretation arises when one wants to draw causal inferences about reading system differences that might underlie

differences between good and poor readers' performances. Again, imagine Jennifer and her third-grade classmates all reading the same lists of words and pseudowords. Both groups are likely to recognize that the pseudowords are unfamiliar and find them harder to read than the real words. If Jennifer has extreme difficulty with the pseudoword reading task, what is the reason? Is it because (a) she has a deficiency in GPC processing, (b) doing an obviously novel task makes her too anxious to concentrate (a proximal cause outside the reading system), or (c) the few pseudowords she would be able to read were not on the list she was given (a measurement artifact operating at the performance level)? In other words, extraneous variables might arise because the experimental tasks have different meanings for Jennifer and her higher performing classmates.

The problem of drawing inferences about reading systems from groups for whom a set of reading tasks are of different difficulty levels can be ameliorated somewhat by choosing average and poor readers to study such that both groups vary widely in CA and in reading ability across the same range of CA. This variant of the CA-match design is called the regression-outlier design. It has become popular (Manis et al., 1996; Shankweiler, Lundquist, Katz, & Steubing, 1999) since it was introduced by Castles and Coltheart (1993). The performance-level question addressed by this design is similar to the one that we have already stated. To what extent do children identified as poor readers on the basis of one measure, such as a real-word reading test, have scores on another measure, such as a pseudoword reading test, that lie outside confidence limits generated for the pseudoword reading scores of average-ability readers? Results of such an analysis are shown in Figure 2.6.

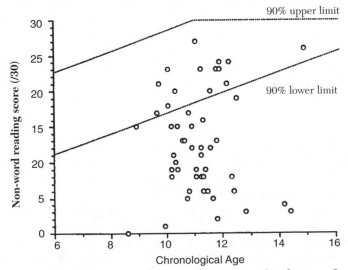

FIGURE 2.6. Example of a regression outlier plot showing distributions of poor readers' nonword reading scores relative to the regression confidence intervals in the same age range. From "Varieties of Developmental Dyslexia," by A. Castles and M. Coltheart, 1993, Cognition, 47, Figure 4, p. 167. Copyright 1993 by Elsevier Science Publishers B.V. Reprinted with permission.

The basic logic of this design as a test of hypotheses about proximal causes of differences in reading performance is the same as that for the other CA-match designs described above. However, this type of analysis includes good and poor readers whose ranges of performance are likely to overlap. For example, the particular list of pseudowords used might always be more difficult for poor than for good readers across the age range studied. However, some of the older poor readers will earn scores within the range of the youngest good readers. This makes measurement artifacts somewhat less likely.

The regression-outlier technique also sets a stringent standard for "worse than expected" performance on a comparison task and preserves useful information about individual performance patterns. For example, Figure 2.6 presents data for 53 boys who were all at least 18 months delayed in their word reading and who ranged in age from 8½ years to almost 15 years. Figure 2.6 shows that the nonword (i.e., pseudoword) scores of 38 of these boys fell below the 90% confidence interval established for the control group of boys in the same age range who were normal readers. In other words, the majority of the boys with dyslexia were reading as if the aspect of their reading system that is used in reading pseudowords was not functioning as adequately as it does in readers of average ability. As we shall show in chapter 6, Castles and Coltheart (1993) also identified poor readers with a different pattern of specific deficits in reading performance and, therefore, a different hypothesized reading system malfunction.

Although CA-match designs have often been used for this purpose, RL-match designs also have been used to suggest possible proximal (reading-system-level) causes of performance differences. Here, the performance data of interest are the various, often uneven, degrees of slowness in progress found across the reading skill profiles of poor readers. For example, a group of third-grade poor readers might have skill patterns like Jennifer's. They would be matched on real-word-reading level with a group of average first graders. If their pseudoword reading scores are even worse than those of the younger RL-match group, many investigators would conclude that the poor readers' reading systems had a problem in the mechanism needed to read pseudowords, which might be the GPC system (Bryant & Goswami, 1986; Jackson & Butterfield, 1989; Mamen, Ferguson, & Backman, 1986).

Some problems with this conclusion about proximal cause might lie in the descriptive-level complexities of these designs that we summarized earlier. Others might be third variable problems of a slightly different sort than one encounters in CA-match designs. For example, perhaps the older poor readers showed less slowness in progress in reading real words than in reading pseudowords, relative to first graders, because the part of their reading system on which they rely for reading real words is better developed. This could be true for a variety of reasons. Explanations at the distal level for this proximal alternative model include the possibility that several additional years of schooling (a distal cause) had given the older poor readers a chance to build up substantial reading vo-

cabularies (a proximal cause). Another possibility is that the older poor readers' additional years of living and listening had given them larger oral vocabularies to support their reading of real words. (This could be an alternative proximal cause because, as we explain in chapter 3, oral vocabulary knowledge can be considered both as part of and as distinct from the reading system.) In other words, RL-match designs do not resolve the fundamental ambiguities of correlational research.

However, a slight twist makes causal interpretations of findings from RL-match designs even more tricky. Good and poor readers in an RL match are defined in terms of rate of progress, and current reading levels of older poor readers and younger good readers (or younger excellent readers and older average readers) are set to the same level. Therefore, the below-matched-group performance of the poor readers on a task such as pseudoword reading is likely to be interpreted as a possible cause of their slow progress rather than, or in addition to, a possible cause of their current performance. In other words, an investigator might conclude that Jennifer has been making slow progress in learning to read because her GPC component has not been working properly. Within our system, any such hypothesis about rate of change is a hypothesis about distal, not proximal, cause, and it is likely to be even harder to defend. We will return to this issue when we consider designs for studying distal causes of differences in reading.

Yet another variant on correlational approaches to identifying possible proximal causes of reading failure is the continuous regression-based design introduced by Stanovich and Siegel (1994) as an improvement over RL-match designs. Their approach shares the advantage of the regression-outlier CA-match design in its ability to utilize participants who vary widely in age and current reading level. The children in Stanovich and Siegel's large sample were selected to be members of a group of average readers and two groups of poor readers. (Some poor readers had, and others did not have, discrepancies between their reading achievement and their IQs.) The three groups were not matched with one another on reading level by subject selection, an awkward procedure whose limitations are discussed at length by Jackson and Butterfield (1989). Instead, Stanovich and Siegel used an approach with greater external validity. Children in each of the three groups ranged from Grade 1 to Grade 5 reading levels on a standard test of word reading. Ages also overlapped. In this kind of analysis, matching for RL is done statistically, by regressing each criterion variable first on the word-reading measure and then looking at the variance that remains. This analysis uses regression equations to set levels of performance on alternative tasks that are expected for children whose word reading is at a certain level and to determine whether these expectations vary across groups. Stanovich and Siegel wisely interpreted their results at the level of proximal cause. However, their prudence does not obviate the fact that their continuous regression approach, like other RL-match designs, is prone to interpretations that blur the line between proximal and distal cause.

Summary

In going beyond the description of reading performances to proximal-cause descriptions of reading systems, the investigator faces several challenges.

1. The investigator must have a good performance description from which to work. If this is not the case, any causal explanation will account for performance that is of no importance.
2. The investigator must be aware that any reading system hypothesized as a basis for human behavior is an inferred system. Computer simulations can provide proximal accounts of how different patterns of reading performance might arise, but these simulations are at best only sufficient, not necessary, accounts of human behavior.
3. The various designs used to describe differences in reading performance all can be used to draw inferences about reading systems. However, most of those designs are at least partly correlational, with all that implies about third-variable and directionality problems.

DISTAL CAUSES OF INDIVIDUAL DIFFERENCES IN READING

Identifying cognitive models that account well for observed reading behavior is a fine activity, one that has engaged one of us (Coltheart) for many years. However, in the study of reading, as in so many other realms of psychology, we also want to answer practical questions, and these tend to be about distal causes. What can we do to change a child's experience so that he or she will be able to read better? Will children become better readers in first grade if their preschool curriculum includes instruction designed to facilitate their awareness of individual letter sounds (e.g., Byrne & Fielding-Barnsley, 1995; Byrne, Fielding-Barnsley, & Ashley, 2000)? Should they be taught to read using a "phonics" or "whole language" approach, or some combination of the two (e.g., Pressley, 1998)? If we give a child certain prerequisite skills at Time 1, will this guarantee that he or she will be a better reader at Time 2, increase the odds of his or her success, or have no detectable long-term effect?

Answering questions like these requires us to move up to the third level of our model. We already have introduced the following dialogue about proximal cause:

"What is atypical about Jennifer's reading?"
"She reads pseudowords poorly."
"Why does she read pseudowords poorly?"
"Because she doesn't have good knowledge of GPC rules."

This dialogue invites the further question:

"Why doesn't Jennifer have good knowledge of GPC rules?"

Since this is a question about why the proximal cause has arisen, it is a question about a distal cause of the unusual reading. As we have already mentioned, a full understanding of a currently observed atypical pattern of reading behavior requires knowledge of both the proximal cause and the distal cause or causes.

Dimensions of Distal Cause

In considering distal causes of atypical reading, we are by definition further from observed task performance, and that conceptual distance extends in at least two different directions. First, although the proximal cause must always be at the cognitive level, distal causes can be internal cognitive or biological causes, or they can be biological and psychosocial events and conditions. Second, although the proximal cause must always be a condition that is currently present, distal causes may be present conditions, or they may be conditions that occurred in the past and are not current.

For the neuropsychologist, the distal causes of atypical reading performance that are of most interest are likely to be at the biological level. The leap from proximal to distal can be a leap from mind to brain. In such a conceptualization, distal causes of atypical reading may be evident in images of damaged brain structures, or functional magnetic resonance imagery (fMRI) indicators of how active various brain structures become when a person does particular reading tasks.

Biological distal causes, as in Figure 2.1, are traditional in the explanation of acquired dyslexia, but they recently have become prominent in the study of poor reading in children or of adults who have always been poor readers, that is, have developmental disorders of reading (S. E. Shaywitz et al., 1998; Shaywitz et al., 2000). This may be the only aspect of distal cause in which potential links across the types of atypical reading we are considering are clear.

The condition representing this particular kind of neuropsychological distal cause—the imageable properties of the reader's brain—is, of course, current. In contrast, for developmentalists and educators, factors removed in time from an observed reading performance define important sets of potential distal causes. What aspects of a reader's prior history might explain the current state of his or her reading system and, hence, his or her current reading performance? History operates at multiple levels of discourse and is multi-faceted within each level. Depending on the preferences of a theorist for a particular level of discourse, distal causes may include a reader's own prior achievements in reading and related areas; the reading-related experiences and formal instruction that he or she has had at home and school (e.g., Figure 2.4); prenatal exposure to a teratogen that affected central nervous system or sensory function (Figure 2.3); or even the genotype he or she inherited at the moment of his or her conception (Figure 2.2).

For neuropsychologists studying acquired dyslexia, history also is significant, but in a more limited way that focuses on current biological cause. A stroke or some other trauma is likely to have caused a person's brain to be damaged in a way that explains his or her atypical reading. The complex personal history so central to developmentalists' attempts to understand atypical reading is a minor aspect of distal cause in the study of acquired dyslexia.

Because the proximal causes we consider must always be at the cognitive level, and because they must always be current conditions, we should consider whether all causes located at the cognitive level must be currently existing conditions, or whether there can be cognitive causes which are historical rather than current. Clearly, the latter is the case. For example, suppose there is a period early in childhood during which most children acquire key aspects of awareness of the sounds in their native language (e.g., Byrne, 1998). This knowledge is adequate for them to map sounds onto the letters of the written language they are beginning to learn. However, some children might not have that awareness when they begin reading instruction (Byrne, 1998; Metsala & Walley, 1998). If so, one cognitive cause for inadequate GPC knowledge would be poor awareness of sound patterns within words at the time of the relevant period of instruction. In this scenario, a person could currently have adequate awareness of letters' sounds, but have a current deficit in GPC knowledge because he or she did not have the prerequisite awareness at the time GPC correspondences were taught. By the time this unlucky person's knowledge of sound patterns within words could support instruction in GPCs, he or she might have been a fourth grader whose lessons no longer included this kind of instruction or who was too anxious about reading to attend to the instruction. Here, the cause of the poor GPC knowledge includes a condition that is cognitive but not current (poor awareness of sounds within words at some period in the past). Examples like this show that, even though the proximal cause must be a currently existing condition, other cognitive causes of currently atypical behavior can be conditions which once existed but no longer do.

Distinguishing Proximal and Distal Causes

Proposals about causes of poor reading may be unclear because one cannot tell whether the proposed cause is meant to be distal or proximal, historical or current. Confusion is especially likely when researchers who work from different perspectives try to communicate with one another. For example, Seidenberg and his colleagues have developed a series of highly influential computer simulations that can model proximal causes of reading failure (e.g., Harm & Seidenberg, 1999; Seidenberg & McClelland, 1989). In discussing his work at a meeting of reading researchers that included educators as well as cognitive psychologists, Seidenberg lamented the tendency of educators to draw parallels between how his computer model changes as it gains experience in "reading" and how children learn to read. He cautioned that his research should not be used to draw inferences about how reading should be taught in schools. To

bolster his argument, Seidenberg pointed out that the learning mechanism built into his computer simulation is not only highly artificial, but also gradual and implicit and limited to a vocabulary constrained by word length and number of syllables. Therefore, the way the simulation's performance changes with repeated exposure to words is radically different from the kind of learning children engage in when they are taught how to read in school (Seidenberg, 1999).

Seidenberg did not use our terms, but he also seemed to be pointing out the danger of drawing parallels between a cognitive model and human reading at the distal level, when the model was designed to account for human behavior at the proximal level. A model that was developed via some connectionist learning algorithm such as back propagation could be a correct description of the human reading system, even if learning via back propagation has no resemblance at all to any of the ways that people learn. How the skilled reading system is structured is a completely different issue from how it was learned.

Mixing up proximal and distal cause also can cause confusion when educators or developmentalists try to communicate with neuropsychologists about causes of poor reading. Consider a child who is poor at pseudoword reading because he or she has not mastered GPC rules and a previously literate adult who is poor at pseudoword reading because of having suffered a stroke which has impaired his or her prior mastery of GPC rules. Some developmentalists have argued that cognitive neuropsychology has nothing to say about the child's problems (Bishop, 1997a; 1997b). However, for both individuals, the answer to the question about the proximal cause of the poor pseudoword reading is the same in our model: The GPC rule system is functioning poorly. What differs are the distal causes of the individuals' current states, not the proximal causes. We acknowledge that a mature reading system that has become impaired may have proximal features distinct from a system that has never developed fully. However, determining the nature of such differences is an empirical question that can be addressed only if one acknowledges the potential similarities of the two proximal systems.

Examples of Dialogues about Distal Causes

The dialogue we introduced earlier about causes of poor pseudoword reading might continue in a variety of specific ways, depending on a researcher's disciplinary and specific theoretical orientation. We will consider three possible continuations. The first might go like this:

"Why doesn't Jennifer have good knowledge of GPC rules?"
"Because she has never become aware of how word sounds can be divided into smaller units of phonology, which has prevented her from learning about relationships between letters and their individual sounds."

This is not a complete account of distal cause because it is restricted to the cognitive level, and we have contended that a complete account must always

include at least one distal cause that is at the biological level. For a more complete account, we would want to know why some children have poor awareness of sound patterns within words and others do not. Therefore, we must persist, as follows:

"Why does Jennifer have poor awareness of individual letter sounds?"
"Because a region in the left temporal lobe of her brain, a region necessary for the development of this awareness, has never functioned normally. Therefore she has poor awareness of sound patterns within words, which prevents her from acquiring an adequate GPC system , and that prevents her from being able to read pseudowords normally."

The account of distal cause here has been extended to the biological level. Possible distal causes, both internal and environmental, should be part of a conceptual model of reading failure even if they cannot be fully specified. In subsequent dialogues, the biological condition of the individual's brain also might be attributed to a more distal biological cause, such as an anomaly on the short arm of chromosome 6 (Olson, Datta, Gayan, & DeFries, 1999).

A second and equally appropriate possible continuation of the same dialogue could be the following:

"Why doesn't Jennifer have good knowledge of GPC rules?"
"Because her reading education did not include direct instruction in such rules and she was (perhaps for genetic reasons or because of limited exposure to print) unable to infer them from instruction at the whole-word level."

In this example, there is an implication that Jennifer's reading system deficits are paralleled distally in the functioning of her brain, but that biological level is not of interest.

If Jennifer were not an 8-year-old with reading acquisition problems, but a person whose previously competent reading of pseudowords had suddenly become impaired, a third appropriate possible continuation of the same dialogue is:

"Why doesn't Jennifer have good knowledge of GPC rules?"
"She did once, but the stroke she suffered damaged a region of the brain that is important for operation of the GPC system that would permit her to read pseudowords."

Here the biological distal cause is of paramount interest.

The fact that these three accounts are appropriate distal extensions of a common proximal account of poor pseudoword reading makes plain the following fact: The fundamental distinction between developmental and acquired reading difficulties is a distinction that applies to distal causes, not to proximal

causes. The extent to which the biological step in a distal account of a particular atypical reading performance is the same or different in various cases is an area only recently opened to investigation (S. E. Shaywitz et al., 1998; Shaywitz et al., 2000). Therefore, we do not devote much attention to the biological level in this book. However, we have represented it in our figures and have noted its importance here because representation at the biological level is a logically necessary part of any full account of distal causes of reading behavior, whether we are dealing with developmental or acquired reading disorders or, indeed, with exceptionally precocious reading acquisition.

Summary

Questions whose answers lead most directly to strategies for helping poor readers are raised at the distal level. Distal explanations can take many forms. Although distal causes of atypical reading are best interpreted in the context of cognitive models of the reading system, they can and should be distinguished from this context; that is, from proximal, reading-system explanations of abnormal performance.

CONCLUSIONS

Considering an individual's current reading behavior in a broad context that includes both distal and proximal causes of that behavior is useful as a framework for seeking points of similarity and difference across various forms of atypical reading. Similarities among diverse phenomena such as poor reading in children, acquired dyslexia, and precocious reading are most likely to be found in patterns of current behavior and in proximal reading-system accounts of that behavior. Distal explanations of these phenomena are likely to differ. We also consider it essential to distinguish between historical distal causes and current distal causes.

Given our definition of proximal cause, hypotheses about proximal causes cannot even be formulated, let alone investigated, without first proposing a model of the cognitive information-processing system involved in reading. This is not the case with distal causes. One can study whether developmental dyslexia is caused by the presence of a particular gene, or by impaired awareness of sound patterns within words, or by inadequate instruction without having any model of the mental information-processing system by means of which we read. But, a complete account of atypical reading also will require specifications of proximal causes. To achieve this, we need a model of the reading system—and that is the subject of the next chapter.

3

Dual-Route Theories of Reading

As we said in the previous chapter, given our definition of proximal cause, hypotheses about proximal causes of atypical reading patterns cannot even be formulated, let alone investigated, without first proposing a theory of the cognitive information-processing system involved in reading. So we will describe such a theory in this chapter. Also, as we said in the previous chapter, we of course acknowledge that the purpose of reading is usually to comprehend extended text, but we will focus on reading at the individual-word level for two reasons. First, there is as yet no theory of the cognitive information-processing system involved in reading that deals with processes above the individual-word level and has been applied to the study of the kinds of atypical patterns of reading with which this book is concerned. Second, we believe that any such a general theory of reading, when formulated, will include a theory of what happens at the individual-word level. The latter type of theory is the subject of this chapter.

In the chapter, we will be adopting dual-route approaches to the explanation of both reading comprehension and reading aloud at the single-word level. Currently, according to Lukatela and Turvey (1998, pp. 1059–1060), "The most influential theory of visual word recognition is the dual-route theory." As well as currently being so influential, the dual-route theory of reading has a long history of support (Baron & Strawson, 1976; Bauer & Stanovich, 1980; Coltheart, 1978; Coltheart et al., in press; Ellis & Young, 1988; Forster & Chambers, 1973; Gough & Cosky, 1977; Marshall & Newcombe, 1973; Morton & Patterson, 1980; Paap & Noel, 1991; Patterson & Morton, 1985; Patterson & Shewell, 1987). Furthermore, as we will see, all of the current attempts at developing theories of skilled reading at the single-word level with which we are familiar adopt a dual route approach of some kind, even connectionist models such as those of Plaut et al. (1996) and Zorzi et al. (1998). These are the reasons for our adoption of this particular theoretical approach.

As we will explain below, a dual-route conceptualization has been applied to two different basic aspects of reading. There is a dual-route theory of reading

aloud, and there is a dual-route theory of (single-word) reading comprehension. Both are dual-route theories in the sense that both propose that the reading task in question can be accomplished in two distinct ways. But the two theories are logically separate: Accepting one does not entail accepting the other. As Frost (1998, p. 86) says,

> There are two versions of the dual-route model, and they should not be confused. The first one involves two possible routes for generating a phonological code, while the second involves two possible routes to accessing meaning. These issues are almost orthogonal.

Because we wish in this chapter to offer an account of a reading system that is capable of both reading aloud and of reading comprehension (at least at the single-word level), we will consider both of these dual-route theories; that is, the account of the reading system that we offer will incorporate a dual-route theory of reading aloud and also a dual-route theory of reading comprehension.

Our approach here will be to begin by describing the general properties of the dual-route approach to reading aloud—we will describe a generic dual-route theory of reading aloud. Then we will do the same thing for single-word reading comprehension, explaining how the dual-route conception applies in this case and describing a generic dual-route theory of single-word reading comprehension. We will then show that, both for reading aloud and reading comprehension, all existing theories are specific versions of the relevant generic dual-route theory. This is a useful preliminary exercise. However, specific rather than generic theories are needed if sufficiently precise explanations of phenomena in typical and atypical reading are being sought. Therefore, a choice needs to be made from among existing specific versions of the dual-route theories. We choose the dual-route cascaded (DRC) model of Coltheart et al. (2001) and explain our reasons for this choice. We then explain in a certain amount of detail how this model is applied to the explanation of how people read aloud and how they understand single printed words. This is our theory of the reading system—of what the child must acquire in the course of learning to read in order to become a skilled reader aloud and single-word comprehender. Throughout subsequent chapters, this is the theory we will use to describe proximal causes of atypical reading.

THE DUAL-ROUTE APPROACH TO THE EXPLANATION OF HOW SINGLE PRINTED WORDS ARE READ ALOUD

Any theory of reading aloud is a dual-route theory if it proposes that skilled readers simultaneously apply two different kinds of orthography-to-phonology conversion procedures when attempting to read aloud: One procedure involves retrieving a whole-word pronunciation from a body of knowledge of such pronunciations, and another procedure involves application of knowledge about

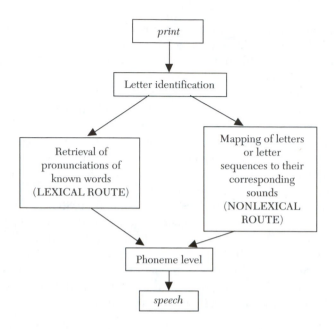

FIGURE 3.1. A generic dual-route theory of reading aloud.

relationships between letters and sounds at a subword level. For convenience, we will refer to these routes as the lexical and nonlexical reading routes without, for the time being, intending to commit ourselves to any particular views about how each route actually operates. (Something like "direct" and "indirect" routes would be less convenient but more neutral theoretically.) This type of theory is represented schematically in Figure 3.1.

In diagrams like this one and subsequent ones in this chapter, a box (often referred to as a "module"; Coltheart, 1999) stands for either a processor or a store of knowledge—a processing module or a knowledge module—and the arrows stand for pathways of communication between modules.

Understanding key terminology is central to understanding dual-route theory. Therefore, we begin our presentation of this generic theory of reading with a review of terms that are important and often misunderstood.

Lexical and Nonlexical Routes Are Not Visual and Phonological Routes

In accounts of dual-route theories, sometimes the lexical route is described as the "visual route" and the nonlexical route is described as the "phonological route." In both cases, the alternative terminology is inaccurate.

Consider the printed forms, *TREE, tree,* and *TrEe*. Each is visually different from the other two: There are three different visual representations here. If

the lexical route for reading were appropriately described as a "visual" route, then it would treat these three forms as different. But, in dual-route approaches, this is not so: The lexical route treats these three visually distinct stimuli as identical. At the initial stage of the lexical route, the letter identification stage, these three letter strings have identical representations. That is because the letter identification stage ignores the specific visual form of a letter. Such visual details as upper case or lowercase, serifed or sans serif, are discarded. All that matters is letter identity (not letterform, and not letter phonology). Thus, the lexical route ignores visual form, and so to refer to it as the "visual route" invites confusion and hence should be avoided. As for the evidence that word recognition involves a stage of abstract letter identification where specific visual form is discarded, much is reviewed in Harris and Coltheart (1986, chap. 6).

Why might the term "phonological route" be used as a synonym for "nonlexical route"? The only answer seems to be that the nonlexical route functions to derive phonology from print. But, so does the lexical route. Both routes are "phonological routes" in this sense, and hence to refer to the nonlexical route as "the phonological route" also invites confusion and should also be avoided. However, phonological assembly is indeed unique to the nonlexical route.

The two routes have a common initial stage (the letter identification stage) and a common final stage (the phoneme activation stage); for this reason it is not correct to say that, in dual-route theories of reading, there are two independent pathways from print to speech. Some processing components are common to both pathways; some are unique to a particular pathway.

This statement about independence applies to the way that the two routes operate on line during the process of reading aloud a word or a pseudoword, a process that takes less than a second. A completely different issue is the way that the two routes contribute to the process of reading acquisition, a process that takes several years. We consider this issue in chapters 5 and 6, where we will propose that there is a great deal of interdependence between the two routes during the course of normal reading acquisition, even though there is a great deal of independence between the two routes in the course of normal on-line reading aloud.

Phonemes and Graphemes

At this point, the terms *phoneme* and *grapheme* are necessary, so we need to explain what we mean by them.

A phoneme is an abstraction, the smallest unit of sound in a language that can be used to differentiate words (Ladefoged, 1993). Each phoneme is actually a set of similar sounds (allophones), such as the slightly different pronunciations of /p/ at the beginning and end of *pop*. The first /p/ must be pronounced with a puff of air, but the second often is pronounced without that puff. Phonemes are the sound categories that are linked with graphemes (defined below). Estimates of the number of phonemes in English vary depending on dia-

lect (e.g., American vs. Australian English) and exactly how one decides to draw distinctions, especially among similar vowel sounds. Table 1.1 lists a set of phonemes of English and the phonetic symbols we use in this book for representing these phonemes.

A *grapheme* is a letter or letter group that corresponds to a phoneme. So, for example, the word *thigh* must consist of two graphemes because it consists of two phonemes; its graphemes are *th* and *igh*.

Regular Words and Exception Words

The distinction between exception words (sometimes called irregular words), regular words, and pseudowords (i.e., pronounceable letter strings which are not real words) is of central importance to the dual-route approach. Exception words are those words of the language which disobey the predominant grapheme-to-phoneme mappings of a language's orthography, whereas regular words are those words of the language which obey these mappings. Languages such as Spanish, Italian, Hungarian, and Finnish have few if any exception words (since virtually all words of these languages obey the language's standard grapheme-to-phoneme mappings). French and German have some exception words (e.g., compare in French *Cassis*, in which the final s is pronounced, and *Chablis*, in which it is not). English has many exception words—perhaps as many as 25% of all English monosyllabic words contain at least one exceptional grapheme-phoneme correspondence (GPC).

The distinction between these three kinds of letter strings is central to the dual-route approach to reading aloud, because one of these kinds cannot be read correctly by the lexical route and another cannot be read correctly by the nonlexical route. The lexical route cannot correctly read aloud pseudowords, because pseudowords are not present in the mental lexicon, and so their pronunciations cannot be looked up in that lexicon. The nonlexical route cannot correctly read aloud exception words, because such words disobey the GPCs which that route uses.[1]

Only the lexical route is capable of correctly reading aloud all exception words, and only the nonlexical route is capable of correctly reading aloud all pseudowords. However, it does not follow that the lexical route does not process pseudowords, nor does it follow that the nonlexical route does not process exception words. To make these two claims would be to argue that whether a letter string were an exception word or a pseudoword could be detected in some way prior to the processing of that string by the model and that is clearly impossible. Thus, the two routes are applied to all letter strings when people

---

1. This is not to say that the translation of an exception word by the nonlexical route will always be completely wrong. All that will be translated incorrectly will be those graphemes whose phoneme correspondences are irregular. So, for example, two of the graphemes of the exception word *yacht* will be translated correctly, but its vowel grapheme will be translated incorrectly.

are reading aloud. What happens in the lexical route when the stimulus is a pseudoword (which that route cannot read correctly) and what happens in the nonlexical route when the stimulus is an exception word (which that route cannot read correctly) is discussed below.

The distinction between regular words and exception words is based on a conception of the nonlexical route as using a set of GPC rules that operate only at the level of graphemes and phonemes. That is why a word like *look* is classified as an exception word, even though in all of the words of English which end with *-ook*, except for one, the grapheme *oo* is pronounced /oo/ (as in *look*). That fact about *-ook* words is a fact that is beyond the grapheme-phoneme level, however. The relevant fact at the grapheme-phoneme level is that, given all of the words of English that contain the grapheme *oo*, in the vast majority of these words grapheme *oo* is pronounced /OO/ (as in *loot*).

Consider now the exception word *chef*. One might say that the correspondence *ch* → /sh/ is not exceptional, but regular, because in all English words of Romance origin which contain the grapheme *ch* that grapheme has the pronunciation /sh/. This is clearly a linguistic fact. However, it is not a fact which could be used by a nonlexical reading route: In order to use this route, the reader would have to identify a word as being of Romance origin before submitting it to the reading system, and there is no way that this could be achieved. There's nothing about the orthography of *chef* that identifies it as being of Romance origin rather than of Anglo-Saxon origin: compare *chef* (Romance) with *chest* (Old English). All that the nonlexical route knows about the grapheme *ch* is that its most common pronunciation at the beginning of a word is /ch/.

The Distinction Between Regularity and Consistency

For the past 20 years, the study of skilled reading aloud has been dominated by investigations of the effects on reading aloud of two psycholinguistic variables: regularity and consistency. Much work on learning to read has been influenced by this research, and so these two variables have also achieved some prominence in research on learning to read. So, we need to consider precisely what is meant by the distinction between regularity and consistency, and what implications this distinction has for theories of skilled reading and theories about learning to read.

Regular words are those which obey some specified set of GPC rules, and exception words are those which violate such rules. This distinction is not the same as the distinction between consistent words and inconsistent words. Consistency is defined (see, e.g., Glushko, 1979; Jared, 1997) in terms of a letter string's orthographic body;[2] so first, one needs to define what is meant by "or-

---

2. It is possible to define consistency in relation to orthographic segments other than the body (Rastle & Coltheart, 1999b) but all experimental work on the relationship between consistency and reading has used only the body definition of consistency, so that is the only form of consistency we will consider here.

thographic body" (or "body" for short). The rime of a monosyllable is that part of its pronunciation from the vowel onwards; the body of a monosyllable is the spelling of its rime. Thus, the rime of *sheep* or *fleep* is /-Ep/ and the body is *-eep*. A monosyllabic pronounceable letter string (word or pseudoword) is termed "consistent" if, in all the real words that have that string's orthographic body, there is only one pronunciation of that body (i.e., all these words have the same rime). Thus, the word *bean* and the pseudoword *fean* are consistent, since all words with the body *-ean* have the rime /-En/, whereas the word *bead* and the pseudoword *fead* are inconsistent, because of the existence of words such as *head*.

It is sometimes assumed implicitly—or even argued explicitly—that there is no real distinction between regularity and consistency; that regular words and exception words are not distinct categories, but are points on a continuum of consistency between spelling and sound (see, e.g., Plaut et al., 1996). This simply is incorrect. It might be empirically the case that what really affects human reading is not regularity but consistency, but that is not what is at issue here. What is at issue is whether one can define the terms "exception word" and "regular word" independently of the concept of consistency, and clearly one can do so.

If this were not true—if "exception" and "regular" merely labeled the end points of a continuum of consistency—there could be no regular words that are inconsistent, and no exception words that are consistent; but there are. Examples of words that are consistent but exceptional include *sold, walk, bolt, palm, would,* and *wealth*. Examples of words that are inconsistent but regular include *dome, lone, broth, couch,* and *gull*. The distinction between regularity and consistency was noted by Glushko (1979) in the first paper on spelling-to-sound inconsistency, but often subsequently has been overlooked.

Another way to demonstrate that regularity and consistency are quite distinct concepts is to point out that one can meaningfully refer to pseudowords as consistent (e.g., *fean*) or inconsistent (e.g., *fead*), but it is meaningless to refer to pseudowords as regular or exceptional. Whether a letter string is regular or exceptional depends on whether its rule-generated pronunciation is the same as or different from its dictionary pronunciation; and pseudowords do not have dictionary pronunciations.

The failure to appreciate the distinction between regularity and consistency has meant that, in almost all research on the effects of consistency on reading, consistency has been thoroughly confounded with regularity, so that any effects ascribed to the influence of consistency on reading could instead have been due to the influence of regularity on reading (see, e.g., the experiments by Treiman, Mullenix, Bijeljac-Babic, & Richmond-Welty, 1995). We know of no study of skilled reading in which these two variables have been completely unconfounded (though see the discussion of Jared, 1997, below). An inference can be drawn, however, from the results of Taraban and McClelland (1987). They found that reading-aloud latencies did not differ between regular-consistent and regular-inconsistent words, while exception-inconsistent words yielded longer reading-aloud latencies than regular-consistent words. By itself,

the latter result is ambiguous; it could be a regularity effect or a consistency effect. But, since no effect of consistency had been found with comparable sets of words, it is reasonable to conclude that these results taken as a whole show that there is a genuine effect of regularity on reading aloud.

Although Jared (1997) did not attempt to use exception words that were consistent in her studies, she nevertheless was able to study the variables of regularity and consistency independently in her Experiment 4. She defined the "friend" of a target word as a word which has the same body as that target word and has the same pronunciation of that body (so that *dive* is a friend of *five*), and the "enemy" of a target word as a word which has the same body as that target word but a different pronunciation of that body (so that *give* is an enemy of *five*). Inconsistent words for which the summed word frequency of the word's friends was higher than the summed word frequency of its enemies yielded naming latencies no different from the naming latencies for consistent words. But, exception words for which the summed word frequency of the word's friends was higher than the summed word frequency of its enemies yielded longer naming latencies than matched regular words. So, in these conditions, there was a regularity effect but no consistency effect.

However, Jared (1997) also obtained consistency effects: Regular inconsistent words for which the summed word frequency of the word's friends was lower than the summed word frequency of its enemies yielded longer naming latencies than regular consistent words. It therefore appears that reading aloud is affected by both regularity and consistency. However, Coltheart et al. (2001) reported that the DRC model, which is not sensitive to consistency, was also slower with Jared's (1997) inconsistent words than her consistent words. That was because more of her inconsistent words than her consistent words suffered from the "whammy effect" described later in this chapter: This is an effect to which the DRC model is sensitive. So, it still remains to be shown that consistency is a relevant variable for reading aloud.

ARE THERE ALTERNATIVES TO THE DUAL-ROUTE THEORY OF READING ALOUD?

Any theory of reading aloud which is described correctly by the general diagram given in Figure 3.1 is, in our parlance, a dual-route theory of reading aloud. There are a number of existing specific theories of reading aloud which Figure 3.1 fits. But, are there are any current theories of reading aloud which cannot be so described? That is, are there any such theories of reading aloud which are not dual-route theories?

One-Route Theories of Reading Aloud

It has sometimes been suggested that the reading aloud of pseudowords might be accomplished not by a nonlexical reading route, but by using the lexical

route to pronounce pseudowords by analogy to real words. If that were so, then one could claim, "One process, not two, in reading aloud: Lexical analogies do the work of non-lexical rules," which is the title of a paper by Kay and Marcel (1981). However, no reading theorist has ever specified what the processes are via which pseudowords could be read aloud by analogy to real words. For example, skilled readers can read aloud pseudowords such as *zuve* or *koce* for which there are no real-word analogies (note that there are no English words ending -*uve* or -*oce*). How could an analogy theory work here? And, we doubt that the pseudoword *zonge* would ever be read aloud with a pronunciation that rhymes with "lunge," even though that is the pronunciation which analogy (with *sponge*) dictates. No one has ever discussed how analogy theories of reading aloud could answer these questions. Thus, it is not even clear whether it is in principle possible for any such analogy procedure to yield a level of pseudoword reading accuracy comparable to that achieved by human readers. Hence, we will not consider the analogy theory of reading aloud further.

Another approach often cited as an example of one-route theorizing about reading aloud is that of Seidenberg and McClelland (1989). Their connectionist model, a neural net trained by back propagation, implemented just one route from print to speech (from letter level through hidden unit level to phoneme level). But, although only one route was computationally implemented by Seidenberg and McClelland, they were not proposing an alternative to dual-route theory, but just another form of dual-route theory: They said so themselves: "Ours is a dual-route model, but it is not an implementation of any previous model" (p. 559). Their reason for saying this was that, in addition to the computationally implemented route in their model that went directly from orthography to phonology, they contended that the reading system also contains a route that goes from orthography to semantics to phonology. (They did not seek to implement this route computationally.) Hence, they did propose that the human reading system possessed two different ways of converting print to speech; that is, they were proposing a dual-route model of reading aloud, not a single-route model.

Seidenberg and McClelland did argue, however, that the single implemented route of their dual-route theory of reading was capable of reading aloud all three kinds of letter string with which we are here concerned (exception words, regular words, and pseudowords):

> All items—regular and irregular, word and pseudoword—are pronounced using the knowledge encoded in the same sets of connections. . . . One of the main contributions of the model is that it demonstrates that pronunciation of exception words and pseudowords can be accomplished by a single mechanism. (Seidenberg & McClelland, 1989, p. 549)

This, however, turned out not to be so. Both Besner, Twilley, McCann, and Seergobin (1990) and Coltheart et al. (1993) pointed out that this one-route model, though it read words very well, was inadequate at the task of reading pseudowords.

Any computational model of skilled reading must be able to read both exception words and pseudowords as accurately as human readers can; this is one of the fundamental tests for such models. A second such test for these models is to be able to perform visual lexical decision: to classify letter strings as real words or pseudowords. A third fundamental test for such models is to be able to explain how various patterns of acquired dyslexia can arise when previously skilled readers receive brain damage. The two most important acquired dyslexias here, described in more detail in chapter 4, are *surface dyslexia* (in which the ability to read exception words aloud is selectively impaired relative to the ability to read pseudowords aloud; see, e.g., Patterson, Marshall, & Coltheart, 1985) and *phonological dyslexia* (in which the ability to read pseudowords words aloud is selectively impaired relative to the ability to read words aloud; see, e.g., Coltheart, 1996b). The Seidenberg-McClelland (1989) model was not successful on these second and third tests either.

Hence, as pointed out by Plaut (1997, p. 769):

> The theoretical impact of the Seidenberg and McClelland model is . . . undermined by certain inadequacies in its match to human performance, particularly in three respects. First, the model was much worse than skilled readers were in pronouncing orthographically legal nonwords. Second, it was unable to perform lexical decisions accurately under many conditions. Third, it failed to exhibit central aspects of fluent surface dyslexia when damaged.

Consequently, the Seidenberg and McClelland model did not fare much better than the analogy theory in offering a one-route account of reading aloud, and its authors subsequently replaced it with a different model (see Plaut et al., 1996).

The PMSP Model (Plaut, McClelland, Seidenberg & Patterson, 1996)

The model proposed by Plaut and colleagues, which we will refer to as the PMSP model following its authors' initials, has in common with the Seidenberg and McClelland (1989) model a computationally implemented route from an orthographic level through a hidden unit level to a phonological level; this route is a neural net trained by back propagation. However, the structure of the orthographic and phonological levels is very different in the two models; the Seidenberg and McClelland model uses distributed representations of graphemes and phonemes, whereas the PMSP model uses local representations at both of these levels. This use of local representations at input and output levels allows the model, after being trained on a set of 2,998 words, to generalize very well to pseudowords, which the model reads with accuracy levels comparable to those of human skilled readers. Here, then, we do have a one-route procedure that can read both exception words and pseudowords very well (but, as will be discussed below, attempts to explain acquired dyslexia in terms of this model complicate this conclusion).

The PMSP model therefore meets the first of the three desiderata men-

tioned in the quotation above from Plaut (1997)—accurate reading of both exception words and pseudowords. It does not, however, meet the second desideratum, since the model cannot perform the visual lexical decision task (for some ideas about how it might be modified so as to approach this question, see Plaut, 1997). And a complication arises when one considers the third desideratum, that is, when one considers what account this model might offer of acquired dyslexias (specifically, surface and phonological dyslexia).

Here, Plaut and colleagues (1996) made use of the fact that, like Seidenberg and McClelland (1989), they proposed that there are two routes from orthography to phonology—a direct route from orthography to phonology, which they have implemented, and an indirect route that goes from orthography through semantics to phonology, which has not been implemented. This second route will not, of course, permit reading aloud for letter strings that have no semantic representations; that is, pseudowords. This route can read only words. Hence, one might imagine explaining phonological dyslexia (selective impairment of pseudoword reading relative to exception-word reading) as due to selective impairment of the direct orthography-to-phonology route, because that route is essential for pseudoword reading. But, what about surface dyslexia (selective impairment of exception-word reading relative to pseudoword reading)?

Plaut and colleagues (1996) simulated acquired surface dyslexia by a version of their model in which the training of the direct route was deliberately stopped before it had completely mastered the task of reading aloud low frequency exception words. Under these circumstances, the model could succeed with these exception words only if there were a contribution to their reading from the indirect semantic route. If so, brain damage which impaired that contribution from the semantic route while leaving the direct route intact would result in impaired reading of low-frequency exception words with intact reading of pseudowords; that is, surface dyslexia.

Note that in order to achieve the third of the theoretical desiderata being considered here—the explanation of acquired dyslexias—Plaut and colleagues (1996) have proposed a model in which the route needed for reading pseudowords is imperfect at reading exception words. We will return to this important point below. Here, we focus on a different point. In order to explain acquired dyslexias, Plaut and colleagues need both routes of their model, not just the implemented direct route. Hence, their model is not in fact an alternative to a dual-route theory any more than the Seidenberg and McClelland (1989) model was. The PMSP model is an implementation of a dual-route theory of the form diagrammed in Figure 3.1.

The ZHB Model (Zorzi, Houghton, & Butterworth, 1998)

The computational model of reading aloud proposed by Zorzi and colleagues, which we will refer to as the ZHB model following its authors' initials, also turns out to be a dual-route model. As the authors say,

we have presented a "dual-process" connectionist model in which the interactions between different sources of phonological information—assembled phonology and retrieved phonology—can account for the standard experimental effects in the oral reading of single words. . . . [O]ur findings reaffirm the basic assumption of any two-process theory—that is, that the pronunciations of nonwords and exception words are computed by different processes. (p. 1157)

As with the PMSP model, only one of the routes in the ZHB model has been fully implemented, the assembled phonology (sublexical, direct) route.

The Dual-Route Cascaded (DRC) Model (Coltheart et al, 2001)

The DRC model, described in more detail below, is explicitly a dual-route model, as its name proclaims. Like the Seidenberg and McClelland (1989), the PMSP (Plaut et al., 1996), and the ZHB models, it is a computational model; unlike them, both of its routes are computationally realized, rather than just one.

Conclusion: There Are No Alternatives to the Dual-Route Theory of Reading Aloud

We have discussed above all of the computational models of reading aloud thus far developed for English. When all of these models are considered, it is the case that "there is general agreement that (at least) two pathways contribute to reading words and nonwords aloud" (Plaut et al, 1996, p. 100) and that

> "Both the lexical procedure in the dual-route account [i.e., in the DRC model] and the semantic pathway in the connectionist account [i.e., in the Seidenberg and McClelland, the PMSP, and the ZHB models] can read words but not pseudowords, and both the sublexical procedure [i.e., in the DRC model] and the phonological pathway [i.e., in the Seidenberg and McClelland, the PMSP, and the ZHB models] are critical for pseudoword reading and work better for regular words than for exception words. (Plaut et al., 1996, p. 100)

Thus, at present, there is a gratifyingly complete unanimity in favor of *a generic dual-route theory of reading aloud*, a theory which can be defined thus: Skilled reading aloud is achieved by using a reading system in which there are two routes from print to speech, which are defined by the following properties. One of these routes succeeds only when the letter string to be read is a word; whether that word is regular or not makes no difference. The other route succeeds whenever the letter string is a pseudoword, and also whenever it is a regular word; it produces an incorrect response for at least some exception words. To be a skilled reader, one must acquire both of these routes.

Whatever view one takes of learning to read, then, it has to be the case that a child is learning two routes for print-to-speech conversion, since there is gen-

eral agreement that adult skilled readers possess two such routes. We therefore conclude that what a child acquires in the course of learning to read is a reading system that possesses dual routes from print to speech. This is a valuable conclusion, but it is a rather general one, since the definition of "dual-route theory" on which it is based is a rather general one. If one wishes to be rather more specific about what print processing procedures the child is acquiring in the course of learning to read, the only way to do that is to commit oneself to some particular dual-route theory. Here, there currently are four models from which to choose, the four we have discussed above. We plump for the DRC model, for the following reasons:

- It is the only model in which both routes have been computationally realized;
- it is the only model which explains not only how people read aloud but also how they recognize printed words (i.e., carry out the visual lexical decision task);
- it is the only model that has been successfully applied to the simulation of patterns of acquired dyslexia; and
- the range of results from experimental investigations of skilled reading which the DRC model successfully simulates is far greater than is the case for any of the other three models—detailed comparisons between the models by Coltheart et al. (2001) have demonstrated this.

Having explained our reasons for preferring this specific model of reading, we now offer a more detailed account of the model.

THE DUAL-ROUTE CASCADED MODEL OF READING ALOUD

The DRC model is shown in Figure 3.2. According to this model, the initial stage in reading consists of visual feature analysis of the letter string's individual components. The sets of features thus extracted from the printed stimulus each correspond to a letter, and they activate the appropriate letter representations in a system of abstract letter units; that is, the process of letter identification. Note that this has nothing to do with phonology. To name a letter, one would have to activate its representation in a system of letter names (not shown here) on the basis of the activation of its abstract identity in the abstract letter units. To sound out a letter, one would have to activate its representation in the system of phoneme units in Figure 3.2 via an appropriate GPC rule on the basis of the activation of its abstract identity in the abstract letter units.

The abstract letter unit component of the model is part of both the lexical and the nonlexical routes for reading aloud. It is after this component that the two routes diverge (only to converge later, at the phoneme unit component). Grapheme-to-phoneme correspondence rules are applied to the output of the

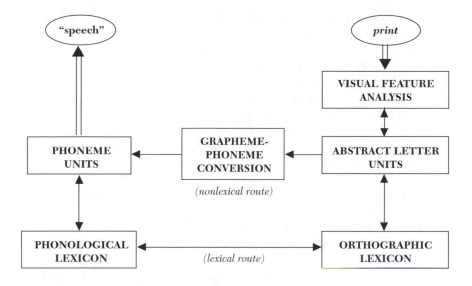

FIGURE 3.2. The dual-route cascaded (DRC) model of reading aloud.

abstract letter units component, resulting in activation of appropriate phonemes in the system of phoneme units. These rules are applied serially from left to right across the string of letters that is the output from the abstract letter units.[3] Because graphemes often consist of two or more letters, something which one might call "graphemic parsing" must be accomplished here: With a letter string such as *chooph*, which has only three graphemes despite having six letters; the six-letter string must be parsed into the three-grapheme string <*ch*> <*oo*> <*ph*> before grapheme-phoneme assignments can be correctly made. Since the process is operating left-to-right, the first GPC assignment will be the incorrect *c* → /k/. When the process gets to the second letter and so is dealing now with the letter string *ch*, this string will be identified as a grapheme, since it is present in the nonlexical route's dictionary of graphemes, and now a correct GPC asignment, *ch* → /ch/, will be made. That is how graphemic parsing is achieved

---

3. In this account, the nonlexical route operates serially, and makes no distinction between vowels and consonants. A very different conception of the nonlexical route was offered by Berent and Perfetti (1995): Their nonlexical route operates in parallel, and in two stages—first all consonants are translated, and then vowels are translated. Their conclusion came from reading experiments using visual masking and, as discussed by Coltheart (2000b), masks which they referred to as "consonant-preserving" in their work almost always contained the third phoneme of the to-be-read target; masks which they referred to as "vowel-preserving" almost always contained the second phoneme of the target. This confounding prevents their results from being evidence in favor of the two-cycle theory; indeed, these results instead actually support a serial left-to-right theory of the nonlexical route.

in this model. We discuss this further below in the section on the "whammy effect."

The full set of GPC rules used in the DRC model is listed in Rastle and Coltheart (1999). Some of these rules are position-specific; for example, at least for monosyllabic letter strings, the grapheme *y* is translated to the phoneme /Y/ when at the beginning of a letter string, to the phoneme /i/ when in the middle of a letter string, and to the phoneme /I/ when at the end of a letter string. Some of these rules are context sensitive; for example, the grapheme *c* is translated to the phoneme /k/ when followed by the graphemes *a*, *o*, or *u*, and otherwise translated to the phoneme /s/.

The system of phoneme units is something a child possesses before learning to read, because it is a component of the speech production system which children acquire as they acquire spoken language. We discuss phonological awareness—ability to consciously access and manipulate phonemic representations—in chapter 5. Here, we point out that the successful development of a system of phoneme representations used for speaking aloud (including reading aloud) does not guarantee that these can be used immediately in metalinguistic tasks such as phoneme deletion or phoneme addition that require a reader to answer questions such as, "What is 'part' without the /p/ sound?" We discuss these tasks in chapter 5.

The route from visual feature analysis through abstract letter units then to phoneme units via a process of grapheme-to-phoneme conversion is the nonlexical reading route. It will activate the correct phonemes when the input is a regular word or a pseudoword. It will activate at least one incorrect phoneme (i.e., will make a "regularization error") when the input is an exception word.

The abstract letter unit system not only feeds the GPC rules, but also sends input to an orthographic lexicon, which contains a distinct unit for each of the words in a reader's sight vocabulary. If the letter string being viewed is a real word, then the set of abstract letter units activated by the letter string will activate that word's representation in the orthographic lexicon. At that point, the word has been "recognized," and the response "word" in the lexical decision task could be made, even though nothing is yet known about the word's meaning or pronunciation.

The phonological lexicon contains a distinct unit for each of the words in a person's speech vocabulary. There are one-to-one connections from a word's unit in the orthographic lexicon to its unit in the phonological lexicon. The phonemes of a word are activated by connections from that word's unit in the phonological lexicon to the appropriate phonemes in the system of phoneme units.

The route from visual feature analysis through abstract letter units, then orthographic lexicon, then phonological lexicon, then phoneme units, is the lexical reading route. It will activate the correct phonemes when the input is a word (regular or exception), but not when it is a pseudoword (because there are no units for pseudowords in the orthographic or phonological lexicons).

When a letter string is submitted to the program, all the processes described above are executed by the program, culminating in activation of a specific set of phonemes in the program's set of phoneme units. That is the sense in which the model reads aloud.

Important general properties of this model include the following:

- It is a dual-route model because it possesses two routes from print to speech, a nonlexical route which uses GPC rules and a lexical route that uses the orthographic and phonological lexicons.
- The term *cascaded* refers to the fact that activations pass from one component of the model to the next in a continuous way rather than depending on thresholds being met within components. So, for example, as soon as letter units at the letter representation level receive any activation at all from a printed word, that word's representation in the orthographic lexicon also begins to be activated, and then its representation in the phonological lexicon.
- The pathways of the lexical route are represented as double-headed arrows because activation in that route flows in both directions, top-down as well as bottom-up; that is, this is an interactive-activation model.
- Within any set of units, every unit laterally inhibits every other; for example, within the orthographic lexicon, each word unit has an inhibitory connection to every other. Because at early stages of processing a word, the units for numerous words are partially active, these inhibitory connections are needed so that the incorrect units are eventually suppressed by the correct unit.
- Adjacent components of the model are fully interconnected. So, for example, the letter unit for T(1)—by which we mean T in the first position—not only has excitatory connections to all words in the orthographic lexicon that begin with a T and vice versa, but also the T(1) unit has inhibitory connections to every other word in the orthographic lexicon and vice versa.
- Letter and phoneme units have positional encoding. So that the model can discriminate between words which are made up of the same letters in different positions (anagrams such as *rat, art,* and *tar*), there is a separate full set of letter detectors for each possible position in the input string. So, the unit for the letter *t* that is activated is not the same for each of these words: It is T(3); that is, T in the third position, for *rat* and *art,* and T(1) for *tar* (and, of course, T(2) for *ate*). Since English monosyllables can be up to eight letters long, there are eight sets of letter units. The same kind of positional encoding occurs at the phoneme level.

At present, the DRC model deals only with monosyllabic words, because it is currently unknown how GPC works for polysyllabic words: Specifically, no one knows how readers decide to which syllables to give stress when reading aloud polysyllabic pseudowords such as *febol* (however, see Rastle and Coltheart

[2000] for some preliminary proposals regarding this). Apart from that, the model is realistic in size; its lexicons contain orthographic and phonological units for all the monosyllabic words of English (about 7,500 words).

SOME EXAMPLES OF THE DUAL-ROUTE CASCADED MODEL IN OPERATION

When the model is presented with a letter string, activations of phonemes at the phoneme level gradually rise over the course of a number of interactive processing cycles, this activation being jointly transmitted from the letter level by the lexical and the nonlexical routes. The model is considered to have successfully read the letter string when those phoneme activations reach some criterial level (this is described in more detail below). The number of cycles the model requires to reach this level is the model's reading-aloud latency. Words take between 59 and 116 cycles for this to occur, depending on variables such as frequency and regularity; pseudowords typically take between 100 and 240 cycles.

We noted above that, in dual-route models, both routes are applied to all types of letter strings, regardless of whether a particular route is capable of correctly translating a particular letter string from print to sound. This is true of the DRC model.

In the case of exception words, the lexical route will be activating the correct phonemes at the phoneme level while the nonlexical route will not: It will be activating those phonemes corresponding to the rule-based pronunciation of the exception word. Rastle and Coltheart (1999b) showed that the result is, in general, that the DRC model still pronounces the exception word correctly, but the time taken to generate the pronunciation is lengthened by the conflict at the phoneme level. Hence, in the model exception words have longer naming latencies than regular words. However, this happens (in the DRC model and in people) only when the words are low in frequency; when they are high in frequency, activation of the phoneme level by the lexical route is too rapid to allow any influence from the slower nonlexical route.

In the case of pseudowords, a pseudoword such as *sare* will partially excite the entries of its neighbor words such as *bare, sore, sane,* and so forth, in the DRC model's orthographic input lexicon, and this will feed back to the letter level, with each word unit giving activation to its constituent letters. Since by definition each of the neighbors of *sare* shares three of its four letters, the net effect of this feedback will be beneficial to the letter units excited by *sare,* and hence these letters will feed stronger activation to the nonlexical route than would be the case with a pseudoword like *zuve* which has no word neighbors. That is why there are lexical influences on pseudoword naming latency (Glushko, 1979): Pseudowords with many neighbors will profit from this property. So, the model will be faster at pseudoword reading when the pseudoword has many neighbors than when it has few; that is also true for skilled human readers (see, e.g., McCann & Besner, 1987).

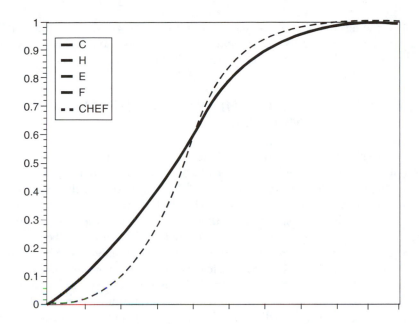

FIGURE 3.3. Activity in relevant letter units and the orthographic lexicon CHEF unit in response to the word *chef*. Each division of the X axis equals 10 processing cycles.

Visual aids are useful for giving the reader an idea of the ways in which this model operates. Figure 3.3 shows the activity in the relevant letter detectors— C(1), H(2), E(3), and F(4)—and the word detector for CHEF when the model is presented with the word chef for reading aloud; the model's naming latency for the word happens to be exactly 100 cycles.

Models of this kind typically limit possible values of unit activations to within the range 0.0 (no activation) to 1.0 (maximum possible activation), and activation rises over time in an S-shaped function. Note that activity in the four letter units rises essentially identically. That is because in the model all of its sets of letter units are activated in parallel from the visual feature level. Minor differences at the letter level occasionally arise through differential feedback to different letters from the word level (orthographic lexicon).

Figure 3.4 shows the activity in the orthographic and phonological lexical units for the word *chef*. One reason that the phonological activation lags behind the orthographic activation is that *chef* is an irregular word and so is receiving some inhibitory feedback from the phoneme unit for /ch/ in position 1, which is being activated by the GPC route.

It is not necessary for activation of a word's phonological lexical entry to reach the maximum possible value (1.00) for that word to be read aloud correctly by the model. Thus, on cycle 100, which is the cycle at which the model reads *chef* aloud, that word's activation in the phonological lexicon is a little over .90. However, all of its phonemes at the phoneme level have reached the critical

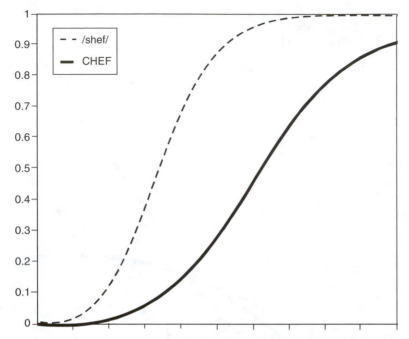

FIGURE 3.4. Activity in the orthographic lexicon CHEF unit and the phonological lexicon [CHEF] unit in response to the the word *chef.*

activation level[4] of .43 and so that is the trial at which reading aloud occurs. Having a relatively low activation criterion at the phoneme level corresponds to asking subjects to read aloud as quickly as they can without making too many errors. Asking subjects to read aloud at their leisure, with no time pressure, corresponds in the model to having a higher activation criterion at the phoneme level (which would, of course, increase the number of cycles the model needs to read a word).

Studying what goes on at the phoneme level when the DRC model is reading the word *chef* reveals much that is of interest; Figure 3.5 shows these results. Note that the earliest activation is of the phoneme /k/ in position 1, which begins to rise at cycle 10, peaks at cycle 27, then slowly declines. The next phoneme to begin to be active is the phoneme /ch/ in position 1; it begins to rise around cycle 27 and is still quite active at cycle 100, which is when the response

---

4. This value for the critical activation level that defines when the model is ready to read aloud is one of the parameters of the model that can be adjusted to maximize the model's explanatory power. Setting the parameter to a smaller value causes the model to regularize exception words more often than do human readers in reading-aloud experiments. Setting the parameter to a larger value makes the model less sensitive to whether a word is an exception word than are human readers. The value .43 optimizes the fit of the model to human data.

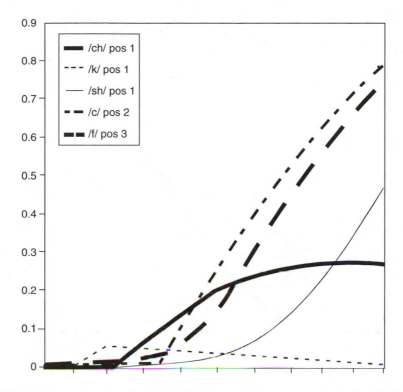

FIGURE 3.5. Activation of selected phoneme units in response to the the word *chef*.

"chef" is made. Since neither /k/ nor /ch/ is one of the phonemes in the pronunciation of the word *chef*, what is going on here? Several of the DRC model's properties are revealed by these results.

- It takes rather a large number of cycles before the DRC model's lexical route contributes any appreciable activation to the phoneme level. At early stages of processing, most of this activation comes from the nonlexical route.
- The nonlexical route operates serially left-to-right across the letter string. Parameters are set so that this route begins to contribute activation to the phoneme level after cycle 10, and from then on it moves on to an additional letter every 17 cycles. So on cycles 11–17, the nonlexical route is just translating the letter string *c*. The GPC for *c* is /k/. So, during this period, the incorrect phoneme /k/ in position 1 is being activated.
- At cycle 28, the nonlexical route now has the string *ch* to translate. The GPC for *ch* is /ch/. So, during cycles 28–45, the incorrect phoneme /ch/ in position 1 is being activated. Within the phoneme set for a given position every phoneme unit inhibits every other phoneme unit. So pho-

nemes /k/ and /ch/ in the first position will be inhibiting each other, and /ch/ will drive /k/ down during this period because /k/ is no longer getting any activation from the nonlexical route while /ch/ still is.

- Neither /k/ nor /ch/, however, is the correct first phoneme. The correct initial phoneme is /sh/, and it can be activated only by the lexical route because it involves an exceptional GPC. Activation of this correct first-position phoneme /sh/ is not seen until rather late: cycle 48. That lateness is a function of two things. First, the lexical route does not begin to activate the phoneme level appreciably until quite late, as mentioned above. Second, when the lexical route begins to activate the correct phoneme /sh/, this unit will be powerfully inhibited by the already strongly active /ch/. Over the next 36 cycles, these two phonemes battle it out, as depicted in Figure 3.5, and it is not until cycle 84 that the correct phoneme is more strongly activated than the incorrect one. This struggle between phonemes happens only for exception words, and its effect is to slow down the rate at which activation rises for any correct phoneme that involves an exceptional spelling-to-sound correspondence. That is the reason that the DRC model has longer naming latencies for exception words than for regular words (as, of course, skilled readers do).

- The DRC model considers that it has succeeded in reading a letter string aloud when each position-specific set of phonemes has a phoneme in it with an activation level greater than 0.43. Typically, because of the left-to-right contribution from the nonlexical route, it is the last phoneme in the letter string that is the last one to reach this level. But, with exception words, that often is not so. In the case of *chef,* notice that the correct second and third phonemes have passed .43 by cycle 74, but the system has to wait another 26 cycles before the first phoneme overcomes the resistance from /ch/ enough to reach this critical level.

The Whammy Effect

Noticing the DRC model's activation of spurious phonemes, such as the /k/ in initial position in response to *chef,* led to the discovery of the *whammy effect* (Rastle & Coltheart, 1998). Whenever a word or pseudoword (we will consider just pseudowords here) contains a grapheme which is spelled by a sequence of two letters, during the period when the nonlexical route has access to only the first of these letters, it will be activating an incorrect phoneme. When the second letter of the grapheme comes into the view of the nonlexical route, and so the correct phoneme begins to be activated, it will encounter inhibition from the incorrect phoneme, and the time needed to overcome that inhibition will increase reading-aloud latency. So, in a pseudoword like *cleth,* the incorrectly activated phoneme /t/ will interfere with the activation of the subsequently activated correct phoneme /th/ and thus slow reading aloud. No such interference effect will occur when every phoneme is spelled with a single letter (as in *clets*). Rastle and Coltheart (1998) called this interference the whammy effect (/th/ is

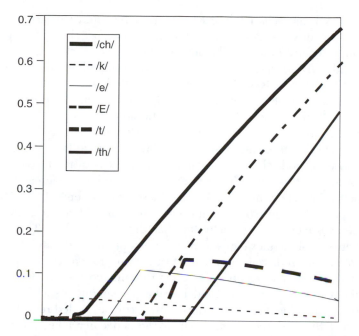

FIGURE 3.6. Activation of the correct phonemes /ch/ /E/ and /th/ and the spurious phonemes /k/ /e/ and /t/ for the triply whammied pseudoword *cheeth*.

whammied by /t/). There can be double whammies (as in the pseudoword *cheth*, where both the first and the third phonemes are whammied) and even triple whammies (*cheeth*). Both the DRC model and skilled human readers are slower at reading pseudowords when whammies are present than when they are not (Rastle & Coltheart, 1998).

Figure 3.6 shows the triple whammying of *cheeth*, which costs the DRC model 17 processing cycles; *cheeth* is read aloud by the model in 184 cycles, whereas an unwhammied stimulus of the same length (clenst) is read aloud in 167 cycles.

The whammy effect is a good example of a fact about reading that would not have been discovered if the DRC model had not been developed. So is the fact that how slow people are at reading aloud of irregular words depends on where in the word the irregular GPC is (Rastle & Coltheart, 1999b); the earlier the irregularity is, the worse the consequence for the reader. No other models of reading make these predictions, and no one had thought to investigate these particular effects until prompted to by studying the behavior of the DRC model.

Effects of a Pseudoword's Orthographic Neighbors

Studying the model's response to a pseudoword with many orthographic neighbors, such as *sare*, in comparison to a pseudoword with similar orthographic structure, such as *zuve*, is also instructive. When the stimulus is *sare*, a number

of word units in the orthographic lexicon become considerably activated—units for words that are neighbors of this pseudoword. Some of this is illustrated in Figure 3.7.

Various questions with instructive answers are suggested by study of these results, including the following:

- Why is SAME so much more active than the other neighbor words? Because SAME has a far higher word frequency than any of the others.
- Why is is SAKE a little more active than SALE? Because SAKE has a slightly higher word frequency than SALE.
- All right, then, why is SURE so much *less* active than SAKE, SAME, or SALE even though it is far higher in word frequency than any of them? Because among the 19 neighbors of *sare,* 17 of them have the letter A in the second position and only one has the letter U in the second position. So there is powerful excitatory feedback from the orthographic lexicon to A(2) and very little to U(2). Hence, lateral inhibition from A(2) will turn U(2) down, depriving SURE of some input; this weakness exposes SURE to the effects of lateral inhibition from the stronger words in the lexicon, those with an A in position 2, which are getting a lot of input from A(2). SORE suffers also from exactly this problem, and in addition

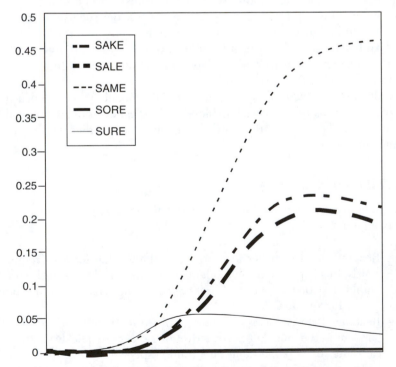

FIGURE 3.7. Activation levels of selected word units in the orthographic lexicon when the dual-route cascaded (DRC) model is reading the pseudoword *sare*.

it is a low freqency word: the combination of these two factors explains why the SORE unit is not activated at all. These intricate interactive-activation patterns provide a good way of explaining data from studies of word recognition using a forced-choice paradigm (McClelland & Rumelhart, 1981).

SOME DATA FROM STUDIES OF SKILLED ADULT READING THAT ARE SUCCESSFULLY SIMULATED BY THE DUAL-ROUTE CASCADED MODEL

The two most popular tasks among experimental psychologists for investigating reading are reading aloud and visual lexical decision (deciding whether a letter string is a real word or not). The DRC model is the only existing computational model that can perform both of these tasks. This opens up access to a rich database of empirical results that allow rigorous testing of the model. Whenever any variable is found to affect the speed or accuracy with which skilled human readers read words or pseudowords aloud or make lexical decisions, this provides a test of the model. Its performance of the task must be affected by this variable, and in the same way as the performance of skilled human readers. Since it is now typical for studies with human subjects to publish the actual items that were used, it is typically possible to carry out such simulations by submitting to the DRC model exactly the same items as submitted to the humans. And, since it is also typical to publish the mean human reaction time (RT) for each item, one can even calculate the correlation across items between human RT and the DRC model's RT.

Coltheart et al. (2001) describe extensive DRC model simulations of a great deal of data from studies of reading aloud and lexical decision, which will be briefly outlined here, first with regard to reading aloud and then with regard to lexical decision.

Simulations of Reading Aloud

For both human subjects and the DRC model, the following response patterns have been found:

- Reading-aloud latencies are shorter for high- than for low-frequency words; this happens in the model because the word units in the orthographic lexicon have resting levels of preexisting activation proportional to word frequency.
- Reading-aloud latencies are shorter for words than pseudowords; this happens in the model because activation rises more quickly via the lexical route than via the nonlexical route, especially for words with high frequency.

- Reading-aloud latencies are shorter for regular words than for exception words, but only when these are low in frequency; this happens in the model because, with exception words, there is conflict at the level of the phoneme system between phonemes activated by the lexical route and phonemes activated by the nonlexical route. This does not matter for high frequency exception words because lexical activation of the phoneme level is so much faster than nonlexical activation of that level when words are high in frequency.
- Reading-aloud latencies are shorter for pseudohomophones (pseudo-words such as *brane* which are pronounced exactly like some English word) than for non-pseudohomophones; this happens in the model because of facilitatory feedback from the phonological lexicon to the phoneme units when the pseudoword is a pseudohomophone.
- Reading-aloud latencies are subject to the whammy effect (described on pages 59 and 60).
- Reading-aloud latencies increase with the number of letters in the stimulus, with this effect being much larger for pseudowords than for words, and larger for low-frequency words than for high frequency words. This happens in the model because the longer a letter string is, the longer it takes to be translated by the serially operating nonlexical route; and so the more the nonlexical route is contributing to reading aloud (little for high-frequency words, more for low-frequency words, most for pseudowords), the greater the length effect on reading-aloud latencies will be.
- Reading-aloud latencies are subject to strategy effects: The relative balance between the lexical and nonlexical contributions to the reading-aloud response can be adjusted when this will improve performance; this is simulated in the model by varying a parameter that controls how rapidly the nonlexical route operates. Strategy effects are discussed in a following section.

Simulations of Lexical Decision

One virtue of the DRC model is that it is the only existing computational model that can both read aloud and carry out the lexical decision task. The model makes lexical decisions by monitoring what is going on in its orthographic lexicon. If, before a specific waiting time has elapsed, any unit in the orthographic lexicon has passed a critical activation level, the decision YES is made. Also, if, before a specific waiting time has elapsed, the summed activation of all the units in the orthographic lexicon has passed a critical activation level, the decision YES is made. If neither of these events has occurred by the time the specific waiting time has elapsed, the decision NO is made. For both human subjects and the DRC model, the following response patterns have been found in lexical decision tasks (see Coltheart et al., 2001, for explanations of why the model behaves in these ways):

- YES responses are faster for high-frequency than for low-frequency words;
- YES responses are faster for words with many orthographic neighbors than words with few, but only when these words are low in frequency;
- NO responses are slower for pseudowords with many orthographic neighbors; and
- NO responses are slower to pseudohomophones than non-pseudo-homophones.

Comparative Evaluation of Models of Reading

One way of comparing competing models of reading is to compare how well each can explain some basic set of results from studies of skilled human readers such as the 11 results described above. No other model of reading currently exists that can simulate even the majority of these effects, all of which are successfully simulated by the DRC model. Another method for comparative evaluation of models is to study, for particular sets of items, how high the correlations are between human naming latencies for these items and models' naming latencies. Coltheart et al. (2001) found that when this method for evaluation was used, the DRC model outperformed the other models overall; the most extreme case being with the pseudoword naming data of Weekes (1997). The DRC model accounted for 39.4% of the variance of the human naming latencies here; no other model accounted for more than 0.1% of this variance. When naming latencies just for words are investigated, there is little difference between the DRC and ZHB models in terms of the percentage of variance accounted for; both outperformed the PMSP model. Figure 3.8 illustrates these results.

Ultimately, facts about how children learn to read should provide yet another form of data that can be used for comparative evaluation of computational models of reading, but that is not the case at present. The structure of the DRC model is not developed via some kind of learning process; it is a computational model of what children eventually learn (if they learn to read normally), not a computational model of how they learn it. The other two models are developed via some form of learning process (some neural net learning algorithm such as back propagation) but the modelers do not claim any psychological reality for their learning algorithms, so would not expect any similarities between the model as it is learning and children as they are learning.

Strategic Effects in Reading

As we have seen, some of the processes in Figure 3.2 can actually be harmful for attempts at reading aloud. The nonlexical route gets in the way when the reader is attempting to read aloud an exception word. The lexical route is at best pointless when the reader is attempting to read aloud a pseudoword and in fact is probably harmful, since there will be partial activation by that route of various words that have many letters in common with the pseudoword, and all

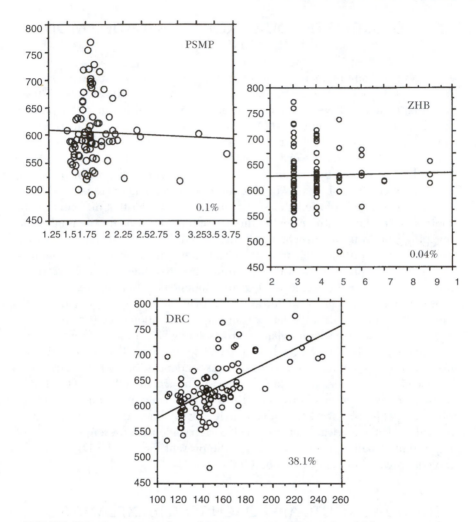

FIGURE 3.8. Regression plots of PSMP, ZHB, and DRC model latencies against latencies of human subjects for reading pseudowords, with percentages of variance explained (human data from Weekes, 1997).

of these are potential erroneous responses. If the reader could be sure that no pseudowords are to be presented, but there will be exception words, then it would pay the reader to turn down or even turn off the nonlexical route. If the reader could be sure that no exception words are to be presented, then it would pay the reader to turn down or even turn off the lexical route. Is the reading system such that readers can strategically adjust the relative strengths of the two routes? The answer appears to be affirmative (see, e.g., Job, Peressotti, & Cusinato, 1998; Rastle & Coltheart, 1999); Zevin and Balota (2000), Rastle and Coltheart (1999), and Coltheart (2000c) have shown that the DRC model can successfully simulate such strategic effects.

THE FUTURE OF THE DUAL-ROUTE CASCADED MODEL OF READING ALOUD

At present we know of no data from studies of reading aloud that are incompatible with this model. Such data may of course emerge in the future. These potential data are of two sorts. First, there are potential findings that would simply refute any version of the DRC model, such as showing that irregular words are no more difficult to read aloud than regular words and that existing conclusions that irregular words are harder are based on flawed experiments. Second, there are potential findings which would not refute all possible versions of the DRC model, but which would require the existing model to be modified.

For an example of the latter sort of findings, consider that different dual-route theories differ with respect to the size of the units used for the nonlexical mapping from print to speech. The DRC model, like the PMSP model, uses only one size of orthographic unit (the grapheme) and only one size of phonological unit (the phoneme). Other dual-route theorists such as Taft (1992) have proposed that an additional level of correspondence be used by the nonlexical route: correspondences between bodies and rimes. As we mentioned above, the rime of a monosyllable is that part of its pronunciation from the vowel onward, and the body of a monosyllable is the spelling of its rime, so that the rime of *sheep* or *fleep* is /Ep/ and the body is *-eep*. If it turns out that skilled readers use not only GPCs, but also body-rime correspondences for the nonlexical conversion of print to speech, that fact could easily be accommodated by the DRC model, simply by adding body-rime rules to its existing grapheme-phoneme rules. But, at present, we know of no convincing evidence for the view that this second level of nonlexical print-to-speech correspondence is present in the reading system of skilled readers. Hence, in the present form of the DRC model, the nonlexical route relies solely on GPCs.

THE DUAL-ROUTE APPROACH TO THE EXPLANATION OF HOW SINGLE PRINTED WORDS ARE UNDERSTOOD

There is a vital distinction between recognizing a printed word and comprehending it. Visual word recognition is typically assessed by the visual lexical decision task (deciding whether a letter string is a real word or a pseudoword), a task which does not require any knowledge of word meaning. Various tasks, all requiring knowledge of word meanings, can be used to assess single-word reading comprehension. For example, choosing from a set of pictures the one which matches a printed word, giving the definition of a printed word, or judging whether two printed words are synonyms are all tasks which, if performed normally, indicate that reading comprehension ability is intact. Such tasks contrast with the visual lexical decision task, which is not a test of reading comprehension, since it can be performed accurately by neuropsychologically impaired patients with severely impaired reading comprehension. For example, patient

E.M. of Blazely and Coltheart (2000), who had dementia, scored 103/106 on a forced-choice visual lexical decision task where, on each trial, she had to choose between a word and its pseudohomophone ("Which of *bread* and *bredd* is a word?"). But, when her comprehension of these 106 words was tested by picture-word matching, she scored only 67/106 correct. Thus, E.M. had very good visual word recognition but very poor reading comprehension. Any theory of reading comprehension which proposes that there are two routes from print to meaning, a direct route and an indirect route that is mediated by phonology, is a dual-route theory of reading comprehension. Figure 3.9 depicts the generic dual-route theory of reading comprehension.

There are some who have claimed that there is no direct route from print to meaning and that reading comprehension always depends on phonological mediation intervening between the printed word and the semantic system (e.g., Lukatela & Turvey, 1994; Van Orden, Johnston, & Hale, 1988). Here, a single-route theory of reading comprehension is being proposed. The dual-route theory represented in Figure 3.9 is, however, far more widely adopted, not only by those who have proposed the computational models of reading aloud described above (Coltheart et al., 2001; Plaut et al., 1996; Seidenberg & McClelland, 1989; Zorzi et al., 1998), but also by many others whose theories of reading are noncomputational (e.g., Ellis & Young, 1988; Folk, 1999; Luo, 1996; Patterson & Morton, 1985; Patterson & Shewell, 1987).

We showed earlier that the generic dual-route theory of reading aloud set out in Figure 3.1 has been developed into various different specific theories (including four different computationally realized models). The same is true for the generic dual-route theory of reading comprehension set out in Figure 3.9. One example is that different specific versions of the Figure 3.9 theory arise as a consequence of different specific ideas about how phonological representations are derived from the orthographic level. As mentioned above, we have chosen one particular account of how skilled readers convert orthography to phonology, the DRC model of reading aloud. Hence, our account of reading comprehension—our way of making a more specific theory from the general theory in Figure 3.9—will also be based on that choice.

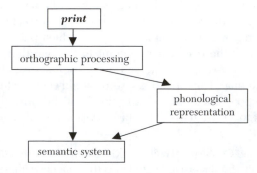

FIGURE 3.9. A generic dual-route theory of reading comprehension.

A DUAL-ROUTE THEORY OF READING ALOUD AND READING COMPREHENSION

Figure 3.9 described a generic dual-route theory of reading comprehension. We noted that, in order to make that theory more specific, commitment to a specific dual-route theory of reading aloud was required. Here we chose, for reasons explained earlier, to commit ourselves to the DRC model of reading aloud. That commitment leads us to the theory depicted in Figure 3.10, which is a specific theory that describes both reading aloud and reading comprehension and offers dual-route explanations of both of these activities. This theory is simply the theory given in Figure 3.2 with the addition of a semantic system and pathways to and from it. That semantic system, not yet implemented in the DRC model[5] is where word meanings are represented; word comprehension requires access to these semantic representations. Other tasks which use this system are spontaneous speech (the route is semantics to phonological lexicon to phoneme system) and spontaneous writing (the route is semantics to orthographic lexicon to abstract letter units to a system for writing not shown in the figure).

The reader will note that now there are three rather than two routes from print to speech, because the lexical route now contains a lexical-semantic pathway and a lexical-nonsemantic pathway. Both of these pathways are lexical, however, so the generic feature of dual-route theory (reading aloud can be lexical or nonlexical) still holds. An interesting question is, In skilled readers does the lexical-semantic pathway ever contribute to speeded reading aloud? This does appear to happen under very special circumstances. If the words to be read are exception words (so that the nonlexical route does not contribute to correct reading aloud) and of low frequency (which, arguably, slows the operation of the direct lexical-nonsemantic route), reading-aloud latencies are longer for those words whose meaning is some abstract concept than for those words whose meaning is some concrete concept (Strain, Patterson, & Seidenberg, 1995). This finding suggests that the semantic system can contribute to the translation of print to speech provided that the other two routes are operating slowly enough.

If the output modality in reading tasks is something other than speaking or writing, then there needs to be an executive system which, on the basis of what is happening in the reading system, decides the correct response. For example, imagine a reading comprehension task in which pairs of printed words were presented and the reader has to point to the one that is an animal. The two words would activate their semantic representations, one of which would be that of an animal. The executive system would coordinate that information with the instruction concerning what to do about the word that is an animal name (viz., point to it). Similarly, if the task is visual lexical decision and the response

---

5. Though see Coltheart, Woollams, Kinoshita, and Perry (1999) for a partial implementation of a dual-route cascaded (DRC) model with a semantic system, which successfully simulates a form of the Stroop effect.

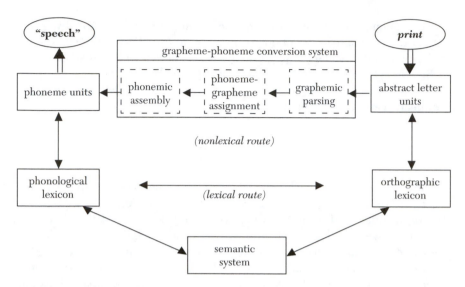

FIGURE 3.10. A theory of the reading system. The three subcomponents within the grapheme-phoneme conversion system that are indicated by dotted lines are hypothesized to exist, but their operations have not yet been validated empirically and they are not indicated in redrawings of the system in Figures 4.2 and 5.1.

mode is key pressing, this executive system would have to translate the detection of an above-threshold activation of one entry in the orthographic lexicon into the motor activity that would produce depression of the appropriate key. Such executive processing lies outside the system of Figure 3.10 but operates on the activities of that system.

In our earlier discussion concerning reading aloud, input to the phoneme level from the two routes would conflict and therefore compete, slowing processing. Such effects occur more generally throughout the system depicted in Figure 3.10. Consider the task where people are presented with single printed words and asked to decide, "Is this an animal?" The YES decision here might be made on the basis of the activation of the feature +ANIMAL in the semantic system being sufficiently strong. If so, suppose the word presented is *bare*. The route from abstract letter units to orthographic lexicon to semantic system will not activate the critical semantic feature because the unit for BARE in the orthographic lexicon is not connected directly to that semantic feature. But, two other routes will activate this feature: the route from abstract letter units to orthographic lexicon, to phonological lexicon, to semantic system and the route from abstract letter units to GPC, to phoneme units, to phonological lexicon, to semantic system. Both will activate a unit in the phonological lexicon that is directly connected to +ANIMAL in the semantic system. And if the input is *bair*, there will still be one route that will contribute activation to +ANIMAL in the semantic system: the route from abstract letter units to GPC, to phoneme

units, to phonological lexicon, to semantic system. This highly interactive property of the system would lead one to expect that pseudohomophones such as
bair would cause readers some difficulty here, and homophones such as *bare*
even more difficulty. Many studies have documented such difficulties in experiments on single-word reading comprehension with skilled readers (e.g.,
Coltheart, Patterson, & Leahy, 1994).

CONCLUSIONS

We argued in chapter 2 that hypotheses about proximal causes of atypical reading patterns cannot even be formulated, let alone investigated, without first
proposing a theory of the cognitive information-processing system involved in
reading. So we have devoted chapter 3 to reviewing such theories, to selecting
one which we will be using in the rest of this book (the theory depicted in
Figure 3.10), and to justifying this choice. Our first use of this theory is to offer
an account of the proximal causes of the different patterns of impaired reading
seen in previously literate people whose reading has been affected by damage
to the brain. That is the subject of our next chapter.

4

Acquired Dyslexia

Some people whose reading presents cause for concern are people who have never been good readers. They begin to learn to read and their reading abilities continue to improve, but their reading is never adequate. Other people's reading merits cause for concern for quite a different kind of reason: They are people who have achieved a perfectly adequate level of reading ability, but subsequently have lost some (or even all) of their reading skills. This chapter is about such losses.

The distinction here is between a developmental reading difficulty and an acquired reading difficulty, or what we will refer to for brevity's sake as *developmental dyslexia* and *acquired dyslexia*. Research on difficulties in learning to read—research of the kind discussed in chapter 6—traditionally has involved people who are young and who have no documented brain damage, whereas research of the kind discussed in this chapter generally has focused on people who are adults and who have documented brain damage. But, neither age nor brain damage is relevant to the distinction between developmental and acquired dyslexia.

Real cases have demonstrated that age is not relevant to this distinction. Suppose that we are studying a woman with a reading difficulty who is 80 years old and has some ability to read, but had great difficulty in learning to read. This person never became a fully competent reader; her reading at the age of 80 is no worse than it has ever been. Her reading difficulty is developmental, not acquired (see Howard & Best, 1996). Suppose instead that we are studying an 8-year-old boy. Before suddenly losing a great deal of his reading ability, he had been a normal reader for his age and had shown no difficulty in progressing in learning to read. His reading difficulty is acquired, not developmental (see Pitchford & Funnell, 1999). So, there is no necessary association between age and whether dyslexia is developmental or acquired.

Documented brain damage is not relevant to the distinction between developmental and acquired dyslexia for two reasons. First, as we discussed in chapter 2, there must be differences between the brains of children who are successfully learning to read and the brains of children who are struggling at

this task. Such differences are among the distal causes of poor reading in children, distal causes at the biological level. Developmental dyslexia, as we are using the term in this chapter, must be associated with some form of brain abnormality, whether that abnormality is a primary cause of the developmental reading problem (Figure 2-2) or a concomitant of reading failure (Figure 2.4). Hence, acquired dyslexia and developmental dyslexia cannot be distinguished on the ground that one is caused by brain damage and the other is not. Second, imagine a man who had been a normal reader and who woke up one morning to find that his reading ability had suddenly deteriorated; then suppose that, in this case, a full neurological investigation could find no trace of any brain abnormality. This would still count as a case of acquired dyslexia in our terms, despite the absence of any evidence of brain damage.

This is not at all to say that investigating the brains of people with developmental dyslexia is uninteresting or irrelevant. As we have said, children who are experiencing difficulty in learning to read must differ at the biological level from children who are not experiencing such difficulties, because there can be no differences at the cognitive level that are not accompanied by differences at the biological (brain) level. In children with developmental dyslexia, progress is beginning to be made in discovering relationships between particular abnormalities of the reading system (as we have used that term in our book) and particular abnormalities of the brain. This progress is illustrated by the work of the Shaywitz group (B. A. Shaywitz et al., 2000), which we discuss in Chapter 6.

As it happens, virtually all of the research we discuss in this chapter was done with people who were adults and for whom there was clearly documented brain damage. But, neither of those things qualified them for inclusion in the chapter. What qualified them was that, at some point in their lives, they experienced some form of major reduction in their reading abilities; that is, some form of acquired dyslexia.

Investigation of the brain impairments of people with acquired dyslexia is an important scientific enterprise. So is the search for neural correlates of developmental dyslexia, such as the work of Shaywitz and colleagues to which we have just referred. Such work, however, seeks an understanding of distal causes of reading difficulties, and our book is primarily concerned with a different issue—the understanding of the proximal causes of reading difficulties, whether these difficulties be developmental or acquired. So, the topic of this chapter must be understanding the proximal causes of acquired dyslexia.

As we argued in chapter 2, the proximal cause of any reading difficulty is always at the cognitive level. Furthermore, for us, the relevant component of the cognitive level is the reading system, as described in chapter 3 and depicted in Figure 3.10. In this chapter, we discuss the use of this particular dual-route theory of the reading system to understand different patterns of acquired dyslexia in terms of selective impairments of particular components of the theory. In chapter 6, we discuss different patterns of developmental dyslexia in terms of selective difficulties in acquiring particular components of the reading system in the course of learning to read.

We must not give the impression that this way of analyzing acquired im-

pairments of language in terms of their proximal causes is novel; it is not. On the contrary, neurologists in the second half of the nineteenth century analyzed all kinds of acquired impairments of language in just this way, and achieved much success (see, e.g., Lichtheim, 1885, or Wernicke, 1874; for a fascinating review, see Morton, 1984). Indeed, Lichtheim (1885) published a box-and-arrow diagram of the language-processing system that still has many adherents, such as Ellis and Young (1988) and Patterson and Shewell (1987). Despite its evident successes, this proximal cause approach to the understanding of acquired impairments of language (including reading) vanished early in the twentieth century, and did not return until the 1960s and the rebirth of cognitive psychology.

SIX SUBTYPES OF ACQUIRED DYSLEXIA

The theory of the reading system set out in Figure 3.10 proposes that this system has various quite distinct components responsible for different functions associated with reading—functions such as letter identification, visual word recognition, and the representation of meaning. So, this system has the property of functional modularity; that is, it consists of a set of processing modules, with each module having a separate function as far as the overall task of reading is concerned.

It is natural to wonder whether these functionally distinct processing modules are located in different brain regions; that is, to wonder whether there is anatomical modularity as well as functional modularity. Functional modularity does not necessarily imply anatomical modularity; for example, the set of neurons that constitutes the orthographic lexicon might be inextricably intermingled in the brain with the set that constitutes the phonological lexicon, even though these two lexicons are two quite distinct processing systems. But, there might be anatomical as well as functional modularity of the reading system, and if there were, then one might be able to interpret different ways in which formerly competent reading breaks down after brain damage in terms of different patterns of preservations and impairments of the processing components of the system described in Figure 3.10.

Phonological Dyslexia

Derouesné and Beauvois (1979) studied the reading abilities of their patient R.G., who had had a stroke that affected several of his language abilities, including reading and spelling. In tests of reading aloud, he did very well when the item to be read aloud was a word: When asked to read aloud 40 nouns of four to five letters length, he made no errors at all.

In contrast, his reading aloud of pronounceable pseudowords of the same length was very poor: He scored only 4/40 correct. Derouesné and Beauvois (1979) also reported studies of four other such patients. All of them read aloud all 40 of these real words correctly; all made errors in reading the 40 pseudowords, with their error rates ranging between 25% and 80%. Derouesné and Beauvois

(1979) gave the name *phonological dyslexia* to this pattern of good reading of words with impaired reading of pseudowords.

Since then, numerous other acquired dyslexic patients with a selective deficit of pseudoword reading relative to word reading have been reported (see Coltheart, 1996b, for a recent review). A particularly extreme case was reported by Funnell (1983). This patient's ability to read words aloud was close to normal: He scored between 87% and 93% correct on various tests of word reading that included long, low-frequency, abstract, and affixed words such as *satirical* and *preliminary*. But, when asked to read aloud 20 four- to five-letter pseudowords, he could not read a single one correctly. He could not even sound out any single letters, though he could name many of them correctly.

It is, of course, obvious what to say about patients with phonological dyslexia in relation to the dual-route theory shown in Figure 3.10: They have an impairment of the nonlexical route together with a relatively intact lexical route. That would be enough to produce bad reading of pseudowords accompanied by good reading of words. So, people with this form of acquired dyslexia provide strong reasons to believe that the modular system of Figure 3.10 is not only functionally modular but also anatomically modular. If that is true in general for the reading system, then a theory of that system should help us understand, and in turn be theoretically informed by, the forms of reading exhibited by people with different kinds of acquired dyslexia. Of course, a specific difficulty in reading aloud pseudowords also is seen in many children with developmental reading difficulties; we discuss this developmental phonological dyslexia further in chapter 6.

Encouraged by the fact that there are cases of acquired dyslexia in which it is the nonlexical reading route that is particularly affected by brain damage, and taking this result as suggestive of the possibility that the reading system is anatomically as well as functionally modular, we might then reflect on the fact that the nonlexical route is itself not just one module, but a set of several modules, all of which need to be intact if pseudoword reading is to be normal. If so, acquired phonological dyslexia, a form of acquired dyslexia, might itself come in several different forms, depending on which of the modules of the nonlexical reading route happened to have been impaired.

Graphemic complexity and phonological dyslexia.   We mentioned in chapter 3 that one procedure carried out by the nonlexical route is the parsing of letter strings into graphemes. In a pseudoword like *thob*, the letters *th* must be parsed into a single grapheme so that the appropriate grapheme-phoneme correspondence (GPC), *th* → /th/, could be applied. An impairment of the graphemic parsing component of the nonlexical route[1] would harm the reading of

---

1. As noted in the legend for Figure 3.10, the subdivision of the grapheme-phoneme correspondence (GPC) component of the dual-route cascaded (DRC) model into the sequence of graphemic parsing, phoneme assignment, and phoneme assembly components sketched in that figure raises issues that currently are under investigation.

those pseudowords which need such parsing—pseudowords such as *thob*—but would still permit correct reading aloud of pseudowords that did not need such parsing—pseudowords in which each individual letter corresponded to a correct phoneme, such as *trob*. This would result in a patient whose pseudoword reading was worse for pseudowords containing multiletter graphemes than for pseudowords where every individual letter corresponded to a phoneme. Derouesné and Beauvois (1979) used both types of pseudowords with their four patients with acquired phonological dyslexia. Two patients were significantly less accurate at reading aloud the multiletter-grapheme pseudowords; the other two patients showed no difference. Hence, one might take the view that the impairment of the nonlexical route in two of these patients was an impairment of graphemic parsing, and that in the other two it was something else. What could that something else be?

Pseudohomophony and phonological dyslexia. Suppose that, in these other two patients, the impairment to the nonlexical route was in the pathway from the GPC module to the phoneme system in Figure 3.10, so that activation of phoneme units by the nonlexical route was so weak that it could not always support correct pseudoword reading. This would result in worse reading of non-pseudohomophonic pseudowords (those that are not pronounced exactly like words, such as *sape*) compared to pseudohomophonic pseudowords (those that are pronounced exactly like words, such as *sope*). That is because weak nonlexical activation at the phoneme unit level would get a boost from interactive activation from the phonological lexicon so long as the phonemic representation was linked to a unit in that lexicon. Derouesné and Beauvois (1979) obtained this result. Two of their patients were better at reading pseudohomophonic pseudowords *(sope)* than non-pseudohomophonic pseudowords *(sape)* while showing no effect of the presence of multiletter graphemes, whereas the other two also showed better reading of pseudowords which had no multiletter graphemes (as mentioned above), but showed no pseudohomophone advantage.

This pseudohomophone experiment also was carried out by Berndt, Haendiges, Mitchum, and Wayland (1996) with 11 patients with acquired phonological dyslexia. Again, about half of their patients (6/11) showed better reading of pseudohomophonic pseudowords than non-pseudohomophonic pseudowords, and half (5/11) showed no difference.

Finally, Coltheart (1985) mentioned a patient with acquired phonological dyslexia, consequent on a head injury, whose problems in pseudoword reading seemed to be of a third type. The patient could translate graphemes to phonemes, even multiletter graphemes. However, she had great trouble blending individual phonemes into coherent syllables, so her responses in a pseudoword reading task sometimes consisted of uttering a string of unblended—though otherwise correct—phonemes. Such behavior supports the idea that one component of the nonlexical route is a phoneme assembly system, as sketched in Figure 3.10. To flesh out this idea properly, however, one would need to offer an adequate account of the way in which this phonemic assembly system com-

municates with the phoneme unit level of the dual-range cascaded (DRC) model. The question is important because the kind of blending difficulty seen in this case of acquired dyslexia also characterizes some children having difficulty learning to read (Whitehurst & Lonigan, 1998).

It seems quite clear, then, that brain damage can produce in previously literate people a selective impairment of the ability to use the nonlexical route. It also seems clear that there are at least three different loci within the nonlexical reading route at which this impairment can arise: graphemic parsing, activation of the phoneme system, and blending. It might well be that difficulties in acquiring the nonlexical route in the course of learning to read also might arise at any of these loci. We discuss the developmental form of phonological dyslexia in chapter 6.

Surface Dyslexia

If brain damage of one kind can selectively impair the nonlexical route, can brain damage of another kind selectively impair the lexical route, sparing the nonlexical route? A reading system with this impairment would still be able to read regular words and pseudowords aloud, but would make errors (specifically, regularization errors) with exception words, on those occasions when the lexical route failed. This form of acquired dyslexia does in fact occur: It is known as surface dyslexia (for review, see Patterson, Marshall, & Coltheart, 1985). Two particularly clear cases are patients M.P. (Bub, Cancelliere, & Kertesz, 1985) and K.T. (McCarthy & Warrington, 1986). They differed widely in etiology (distal cause), since M.P. had received a head injury when hit by a car, whereas K.T. had progressive brain deterioration of unknown origin, probably Pick's disease. Both could read pseudowords and regular words aloud with normal accuracy and even near-normal speed. Both made abundant regularization errors in reading aloud exception words: for example, *have* → /hʌv/, *yacht* → /yach°t/ and *bowl* → /bowl/.

M.P. and K.T. illustrate the general pattern of surface dyslexia. However, just as with phonological dyslexia and the nonlexical route, there are various loci along the lexical route where damage would cause surface dyslexia. Two of these in particular are the orthographic lexicon and the phonological lexicon.

Input versus output surface dyslexia. Consider the surface dyslexic error in response to the word *gauge*: "That is something about a railway. . . . [T]hat's as much as I've got, train, /gawj/" (patient E.S.T.; Kay & Patterson, 1985). This surface dyslexic patient clearly accessed the correct semantics of the word he was reading, so he must have accessed the correct entry in the orthographic lexicon. Therefore, his regularization error must have been due to a failure to activate the word's pronunciation in the phonological lexicon, compelling a reliance on the nonlexical route for reading aloud. One could call this *output surface dyslexia*.

In contrast, consider the behavior of the surface-dyslexic patient EE (Coltheart & Byng, 1989) when he was given the task of defining printed homophones. He produced such definitions as *doe* → "something you cook with" and *blew* → "a color." What must be happening here is that a patient like this cannot access the representations of these words in the orthographic input lexicon (representations that would activate the correct semantics of the words). He can attempt this reading comprehension task only by using the nonlexical route to convert print to phonology. However, because these words are homophones, their meaning is ambiguous when only their phonology is considered; hence E.E.'s errors. One could call this *input surface dyslexia*.

It seems quite clear, then, that brain damage can produce a selective deficit of the nonlexical reading route (phonological dyslexia) or a selective deficit of the lexical reading route (surface dyslexia). In addition, there are different loci within the lexical reading route at which surface dyslexia can arise, just as there are different loci within the nonlexical reading route at which phonological dyslexia can arise. Perhaps it is also true that in some children difficulties in learning to read consist of difficulties in acquiring the lexical route in the course of learning to read. This would be developmental surface dyslexia; we discuss it in chapter 6.

Lexical Nonsemantic Reading

Brain damage sometimes affects the semantic system and so impairs the comprehension of written or spoken words. This can happen as a consequence of head injury, but it more commonly is due to a progressive brain deterioration such as dementia of the Alzheimer's type. Schwartz, Saffran, and Marin (1980) studied the reading performance of W.L.P., a patient with this kind of progressive brain impairment. At a point in the evolution of her disorder where she could no longer understand written words reliably, she could still read aloud very well—and that competence included the ability to read aloud exception words such as *blood, shoe,* and *sweat.* Since these are exception words, they must have been read via the lexical route; that is, via communication from an orthographic lexicon to a phonological lexicon.

Because there must be a pathway from orthographic lexicon to semantics (needed for reading comprehension) and a pathway from semantics to phonological lexicon (needed for meaningful spontaneous speech), it might be supposed that the communication from an orthographic lexicon to a phonological lexicon in reading aloud is via these two pathways; that is, via semantics. But, if that were so, exception-word reading would not survive a severe semantic impairment such as that which W.L.P. had, and W.L.P. read exception words very well.

Therefore, it seems necessary to postulate a direct lexical pathway from orthographic lexicon to phonological lexicon that bypasses semantics, as there

is in Figure 3.10. This conclusion is supported by other reports of patients with severe semantic impairment but good exception-word reading (Cipolotti & Warrington, 1995; Coslett, 1991; Ralph, Ellis, & Franklin, 1995), and this form of acquired dyslexia has come to be called *lexical-nonsemantic reading*. It is what is to be expected, given the reading system in Figure 3.10, from an impairment of only the semantic component of that system. There also are reports of children with excellent reading aloud yet very poor comprehension; we discuss this developmental condition, often referred to as hyperlexia, in chapter 7.

Visual Dyslexia

Two cases of acquired visual dyslexia were discussed by Marshall and Newcombe (1973). Both patients made two types of error in reading-aloud tasks: errors involving confusions of one letter with another, such as reading *dug* as /bug/ or *rid* as /rig/, and letter order errors, such as reading *was* as /saw/ or *broad* as /bawd/. The letter-confusion errors sometimes consisted of replacing one letter with another similar in overall shape (e.g., reading *car* as if the print were *oar*), sometimes consisted of right-left reversal errors (e.g., *dug* → /bug/), and sometimes consisted of up-down inversion errors (e.g. confusing *b* with *p* or *u* with *n*). Marshall and Newcombe proposed the use of the term *visual dyslexia* to refer to cases of acquired dyslexia in which the prominent forms of reading error were these types of letter confusions and these letter-order errors, and they pointed out that all three types of between-letter confusion seen in the reading errors of these two patients with acquired dyslexia are also seen in young children who are normal readers, as well as in developmentally dyslexic children. Recently, Valdois, Gerard, Vanault, and Dugas (1995) reported a case of developmental dyslexia which seems to fit the category of visual dyslexia as it was defined by Marshall and Newcombe.

Marshall and Newcombe (1973) also made an important observation concerning letter-order errors. Errors such as *rut* → /tug/ are sometimes taken to occur as a result of a perceptual error: The reader actually misperceives the order of the three letters in the word he or she is trying to read. That possibility can be assessed by asking the reader to spell the word aloud after reading the whole word. Here, Marshall and Newcombe found that the spelling aloud was often correct even when the prior reading response was a letter-order error, for example, *rut* → "tug, R, U, T." The same result was reported by Coltheart, Masterson, Byng, Prior, and Riddoch (1983) in their study of a 17-year-old developmental dyslexic C.D., who also made these kinds of letter-order errors. For example, in the read-then-spell-aloud task, C.D. produced such responses as *bowl* → "wind . . . blow . . . B, O, W, L" and *enigma* → "a picture . . . image . . . E, N, I, G, M, A." Since in these cases the letters are produced in their correct positions when the stimulus is being spelled aloud, it cannot have been the case that the letter-order errors of these acquired and developmen-

tally dyslexic readers occur because of incorrect perception of letter position; that is, they are not due to some basic difficulty with spatial perception.[2]

Deep Dyslexia

The characteristic reading error of patients with deep dyslexia is the semantic error in reading aloud—a response which is similar in meaning to the stimulus word even though it may be dissimilar in all other ways (for a review of deep dyslexia, see Coltheart, Patterson, & Marshall, 1980).[3] Thus, G.R. read *city* as /town/ and *berry* as /grAps/. An English deep dyslexic called K.U. read *news* as /pA-p°/ (i.e., as if it were *paper*) and read *diamond* as /nek-l°s/ (Marshall & Newcombe, 1973).

The semantic error is not the only reading symptom shown by deep dyslexics. They also show the following:

- very poor ability to read function words, even those which are short and of high frequency;
- visual errors such as *gallant* → /gal-°n/ or *sour* → /sOOp/;
- derivational errors[4] such as *wrestle* → /res-ler/ or *invite* → /in-v°-tA-sh°n/;
- complete inability to read aloud even the simplest pronounceable pseudoword; and
- much better reading of concrete words than of abstract words.

We mention deep dyslexia here for the sake of completeness and also because of its intrinsic interest; but it is not of direct relevance to our book for two reasons. First, it does not exist in developmental form: No child has been reported who was having developmental difficulty in learning to read and who showed just this spectrum of symptoms. Second, there is no evidence that deep dyslexia reflects reading by a partially impaired version of the normal reading system, located in the left hemisphere (i.e., a partially impaired version of the system shown in Figure 3.10). In this way, deep dyslexia is unlike phonological dyslexia, surface dyslexia, and lexical-nonsemantic reading. Instead, there is good evidence (Coltheart, 2000a; Michel, Henaff, & Intrilligator, 1996; Patterson,

---

2. This type of error—a letter order error when a word is read but not when its individual letters are being read aloud sequentially—has not been investigated formally, and no explanations of how it might arise have yet been proposed.
3. This is a remarkable kind of reading error, so it is worth emphasizing here that (a) deep dyslexic patients making these errors understand that what they are being asked to do is read as accurately as possible, (b) the words are presented as single words with no context, and (c) there is no time pressure to respond.
4. A derivational error is one where the response retains the root morpheme of the stimulus correctly, but differs from it with respect to a derivational suffix (or prefix).

Varga-Khadem, & Polkey, 1987; Weekes, Coltheart, & Gordon, 1997) that deep dyslexia represents reading that involves right-hemisphere mechanisms which may play little or no role in normal reading and learning to read.

Letter-by-Letter Reading

Letter-by-letter reading is the modern name for the form of acquired dyslexia also known as pure alexia, originally reported by Déjerine (1892). The term *pure alexia* refers to the fact that these patients may have intact writing despite their impaired reading. The term *letter-by-letter reading* (Patterson & Kay, 1982) refers to the behavior that is characteristic of these patients when they are trying to read aloud. It is typical for them, when attempting to read a word or pseudoword aloud, to name[5] the letters of the stimulus aloud, slowly and left to right. If all the letters are named correctly, the patient usually will be able then to utter the whole word or pseudoword correctly. Letter naming, however, is not always accurate (that will cause the word or pseudoword to be read incorrectly), and even when accurate, is often very slow.

Abnormality of input to the reading system (i.e., of input to Figure 3.10) rather than a defect within the system itself is the proximal cause of letter-by-letter reading. Patients with this form of acquired dyslexia have damage to the portion of the left hemisphere involved in early processing of visual input. Therefore, they must rely solely on the right hemisphere for this input, transferring information about letters to the reading system (which is in the left hemisphere) via the corpus callosum. However, letter-by-letter readers also have damage to part of the corpus callosum that would allow fast and parallel transmission of information about letters from the right to the left hemisphere. Hence, the reading system receives letters slowly, one at a time (Coltheart, 1983).

Figure 4.1 shows the time taken to produce a correct reading-aloud response by a letter-by-letter reader as a function of the number of letters in the word. It can be seen that this time is a linear function of word length, with a very large slope (4.36 seconds per letter). Patients like this can have normal spelling and writing, even though they cannot read what they have written; furthermore, spoken language, both in comprehension and production, can also be entirely normal. For a review of recent work on letter-by-letter reading, see Coltheart (1998).

ACQUIRED DYSGRAPHIA AND ITS RELATION TO ACQUIRED DYSLEXIA

Acquired dysgraphia, by analogy with acquired dyslexia, refers to the presence of a writing impairment in someone whose writing had previously been normal.

---

5. We say *name* rather than *sound* advisedly. The patients do not sound out the letter or graphemes' sounds; they utter the names of the letters. Thus *seat* → "/es/ . . . /E/ . . . /A/ . . . /tE/ . . . /sEt/," not *seat* → "/s/ . . . /E/ . . . /t/ . . . /sEt/," nor *seat* → "/s/ . . . /e/ . . . /a/ . . . /t/ . . . /sEt/."

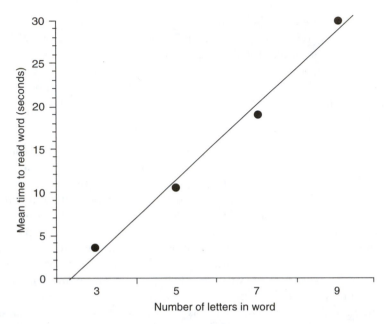

FIGURE 4.1. Effect of number of letters on word-reading latency in a case of letter-by-letter reading.

Very little is understood yet about its relationship to acquired dyslexia. We have mentioned that writing and spelling can be intact in letter-by-letter reading; but writing and spelling are always impaired in all of the other forms of acquired dyslexia that we have discussed, for reasons that are obscure and often counterintuitive.

For example, most patients with surface dyslexia also exhibit surface dysgraphia, a form of writing impairment in which the writing to dictation of pseudowords and regular words is much better than it is with exception words. Exception words often generate regularization errors in spelling (i.e., spelling the word by rule). "Yacht" is written *yot*, and "flood" is written *flud*. And, many patients with deep dyslexia also exhibit deep dysgraphia, a form of writing impairment in which

- semantic errors are made in writing to dictation—"envelope" is written as *letter*, "argument" as *fight* (Nolan & Caramazza, 1983);
- pseudowords cannot be written to dictation; and
- other symptoms of deep dyslexic reading have their analogues in the patient's writing.

If there were always such close correspondences between the kind of acquired dyslexia a person has and the kind of acquired dysgraphia the same person has, that would be of immense importance for attempts to construct explicit

information-processing theories of reading and writing. But, there are not always such correspondences. For example, the patient with deep dysgraphia described by Bub et al. (1985) was not a deep dyslexic. She made semantic errors in writing words to dictation and scored only 1/20 correct in writing pseudowords to dictation. These errors were not a result of a difficulty in processing speech input, since she was 100% correct at repeating these words and these pseudowords. Moreover, she made no errors in reading these words aloud and few errors in reading the pseudowords aloud (85% correct).

Another example of a failure of correspondence between the type of acquired dyslexia patients have and the type of acquired dysgraphia they have is provided by the patient with phonological dyslexia described by Derouesné and Beauvois (1979), who was not a phonological dysgraphic. His ability to read pseudowords aloud was severely impaired, but he scored 109/110 correct at writing pseudowords to dictation (Beauvois, & Derouesné, 1981, p. 24). He was, on the other hand, impaired at writing exception words to dictation relative to regular words. He was surface dysgraphic, but he was not surface dyslexic, since his word reading was essentially perfect. There are many puzzles here. Bub et al.'s (1985) patient could read pseudowords well but could not write them to dictation, while Beauvois and Derouesné's (1981) patient could write pseudowords to dictation but was very impaired at reading them aloud. The relationship between acquired dyslexia and acquired dysgraphia, and indeed the relationship between the normal reading system and the normal writing system, will not be understood until such puzzles have been solved.

BEYOND THE SUBTYPING OF ACQUIRED DYSLEXIA

The seminal paper on varieties of acquired dyslexia was that of Marshall and Newcombe (1973). They made two important contributions in their paper. First, they made it clear that acquired dyslexia was not a homogeneous condition by defining certain subtypes of acquired dyslexia: surface dyslexia, deep dyslexia, and visual dyslexia. (Later investigators added three more subtypes: phonological dyslexia, lexical nonsemantic reading, and letter-by-letter reading.) Second, they showed that it was possible to relate various subtypes of acquired dyslexia to a single theory of normal skilled reading by interpreting each subtype as arising from a particular pattern of preserved and impaired components of that theory.

This work revolutionized the study of acquired dyslexia; yet, within a decade after the appearance of Marshall and Newcombe's (1973) paper, the subtyping approach had been abandoned. Why? The motivation for abandoning the subtype approach was as follows:[6]

---

6. Note that in these quotations the term *syndrome* is used where we have been using the equivalent term *subtype*.

The concept of the syndrome has been a useful one in developing work relating dyslexic syndromes to reading models. However, its usefulness is likely to be short-lived. The reason is that, if a dyslexic syndrome is a specific pattern of preservations and impairments of reading abilities . . . and if a modular model of reading is appropriate, it follows that there are many different possible dyslexic syndromes. Any unique pattern of impairments to the boxes and arrows of (the model) will produce a unique syndrome; since (the model) has enough boxes and arrows to produce a large number of different unique patterns of impairments, it generates a large number of different syndromes. (Coltheart, 1984a, p. 370)

Following this logic (see also Marshall, 1984, and Howard and Franklin, 1988) pointed out that, since their model of language processing contained 27 components (boxes or arrows), the number of possible syndromes according to this model is $2^{27} - 1$, which is more than a hundred million.[7] If there are more than a hundred million possible syndromes, the concept of syndrome will not be a useful one. Reasons for abandoning the subtyping approach were spelled out further by Caramazza (1986), M. Coltheart (1987), and Ellis (1987).

Abandoning the subtyping approach seems a drastic methodological move. When the subtyping approach is being used, the object of study is the subtype, and one generalizes findings from one patient to findings from another when the two patients are being treated as representative examples of the same subtype. Abandoning the subtype approach means treating every patient as unique. How, in that case, can research be cumulative? How is generalization of one's findings achieved?

The generalizations do not take the form of claiming that there exists a single syndrome which many patients exhibit. Instead these generalizations take the form of claiming that there exists a single theory of the relevant cognitive system which can offer interpretations of the various sets of symptoms exhibited by various different patients. (Coltheart, 1984b, p.6)

Hence,

even if every patient exhibited a unique reading disorder, it might still be possible to interpret every patient's behaviour in the context of a single theory for reading. The assumption that a single theory should be applicable to all patients allows each new patient to be an appropriate source of data for testing

---

7. This argument still holds even if a theory is a connectionist style involving sets of nodes and links between these (e.g., Plaut et al., 1996; Seidenberg & McClelland, 1989; Zorzi et al., 1998) rather than one involving boxes and arrows such as the Howard-Franklin theory (1988). In both cases, the required complexity of the theory is such that the number of distinctive patterns of preserved and impaired components is too large for each different pattern to be conveniently accorded a different syndrome label.

the theory; and this permits one to generalize from previous to future patients even if one has rejected the policy of thinking in terms of syndromes. (Coltheart, 1984a, p. 371)

Here, the subtyping policy is replaced by a different research policy—the policy of seeking the proximal cause of each new patient's acquired dyslexia.

PROXIMAL CAUSES OF ACQUIRED DYSLEXIA

Figure 4.2 is the same as Figure 3.10 (i.e., it is a diagram of the theory of reading we use throughout this book) except that the grapheme-phoneme conversion is not subdivided and we have numbered each box and arrow so that we can conveniently refer to them individually. This theory of the reading system contains 15 boxes or arrows. If any one of those 15 elements is not functioning normally, reading by the system will be affected in some way or other. Following the Howard and Franklin (1988) example discussed above, we therefore could point out that the number of different patterns of impairment (one or more boxes or arrows malfunctioning) is, for this system, $2^{15} - 1 = 32,767$. Consequently, if this theory of reading at the single-word level were correct, any new patient with an acquired dyslexia would have to belong to one of those

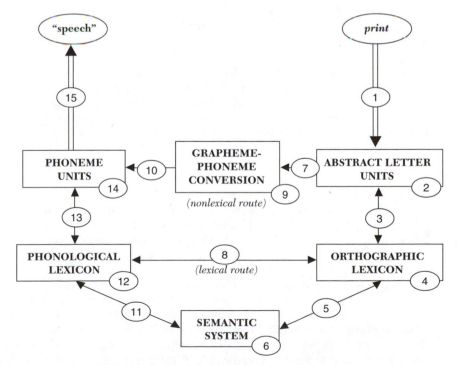

FIGURE 4.2. A labeled model of the reading system.

32,767 categories. Obviously, the probability of any two patients belonging to the same category here is vanishingly small. Hence, the cognitive-neuropsychological method of testing this theory of the normal reading system is not to seek to categorize patients with acquired dyslexia; instead, it is to see whether the reading symptoms of every patient with an acquired dyslexia always correspond to the reading symptoms that this system would exhibit when a specific subset of one or more of the system's boxes and arrows is malfunctioning.

Let us work through some examples—some possible lesion configurations. Here, we extend the kind of analyses that we began by considering how two different patterns of phonological dyslexia could be caused by damage at different points along the nonlexical route. We do this for two reasons. One is to show how relationships are established between particular "lesions" of Figure 4.2 (i.e., particular proximal causes of acquired dyslexia) and particular patterns of impaired and preserved reading abilities. The second is to illustrate that the same single symptom—a specific impairment in reading aloud exception words, that is, surface dyslexia—can arise from many different kinds of "lesion" of Figure 4.2 (i.e., can have many different possible proximal causes). For each example, we imagine that a particular arrow, or a particular box, or some combination of boxes and arrows is damaged, and then consider what the consequences would be for reading behavior.

Arrow 3

If arrow 3 is malfunctioning, the system would still be able to read pseudowords aloud because pseudoword reading does not use arrow 3; it uses the pathway 1, 2, 7, 9, 10, 14, 15. Reading exception words, on the other hand, does need arrow 3, because such words can be read correctly only via access to the orthographic lexicon, which permits subsequent access to the phonological lexicon. With arrow 3 impaired, exception words will at least some of the time have to be read via the intact 1, 2, 7, 9, 10, 14, 15 route; but that will produce a regularization error when the input is an exception word. Hence, arrow 3 damage will cause exception word reading to be impaired, with regularization errors, but will leave pseudoword reading (and regular word reading) intact. We have already discussed this pattern of acquired dyslexia: It is surface dyslexia as defined by Marshall and Newcombe (1973).

Arrow 13

Because reading an exception word aloud requires that its pronunciation be retrieved from the phonological lexicon and transmitted to the phoneme unit system via arrow 13, whenever this arrow fails, an exception word will have to be read aloud via the nonlexical route. However, arrow 13 is not required for correct reading of pseudowords or regular words. Hence, arrow 13 damage will cause exception word reading to be impaired, with regularization errors, but will leave pseudoword reading (and regular word reading) intact; that is, will

cause surface dyslexia. So, two quite different impairments of this reading system will yield the same pattern of reading-aloud symptoms.

Arrow 3 Compared to Arrow 13

Although a patient with an arrow 3 impairment and a patient with an arrow 13 impairment will show identical symptoms when tested on reading aloud of pseudowords, regular words, and exception words, these two patients can be distinguished if other tests are used. The ability to name a picture and the ability to produce spoken words in conversation both require arrow 13. So, the arrow 3 surface dyslexic will have intact picture naming and intact conversational speech, whereas the arrow 13 surface dyslexic will be impaired on these tasks (this kind of impairment of spoken-word production is known as *anomia*) as well as on reading aloud of exception words. Marshall and Newcombe (1973, p. 182) noted of their surface dyslexic patient J.C. that "his spontaneous speech was unimpaired, fluent and grammatical," whereas of their other surface dyslexic patient they wrote (p. 184) that "ST's speech is reasonably fluent and grammatical although occasional word-finding and dysarthric difficulties[8] are apparent." An even more pronounced anomia was noted in the surface dyslexic patient E.S.T. (Kay & Patterson, 1985), most dramatically shown by examples where he correctly understood a printed exception word even though he made a regularization error in reading it aloud: *gauge* → "That is something about a railway. . . . [T]hat's as much as I've got, train, /gawj/." and *foot* → "Body, and it's my shoe . . . F, O, O . . . or is it /f/ . . . /fOO/, eating? . . . /fOOt/."

Thus, Figure 4.2 offers a plausible interpretation of why some surface dyslexics are also anomic and some are not, and permits the realization that there can be two different kinds of surface dyslexia. Indeed, there are more than two ways of generating surface dyslexic reading in relation to Figure 4.2. There are seven in all,[9] the remaining five being as below.

Box 4

Damage to box 4 causes surface dyslexia with impaired visual lexical decision ability and impaired single-word reading comprehension (because both tasks need Box 4).

Arrow 8 and Arrow 5

Damage to arrow 8 and arrow 5 causes surface dyslexia with retained visual lexical decision ability (because that uses the pathway 1, 2, 3, 4) but impaired single-word reading comprehension (because that task needs arrow 5).

---

8. Dysarthria is a condition in which there is mispronunciation of some phonemes when a word is being spoken.
9. Not all of these different forms of surface dyslexia have actually been reported; some remain simply theoretical possibilities at this stage.

Arrow 8 and Box 6

Damage to arrow 8 and box 6 causes surface dyslexia with retained visual lexical decision ability (because that task uses the pathway 1, 2, 3, 4) but impaired single-word reading comprehension (because that task needs box 6).

Arrow 8 and Arrow 11

Damage to arrow 8 and arrow 11 causes surface dyslexia with retained visual lexical decision ability (because that uses the pathway 1, 2, 3, 4) and retained single-word reading comprehension (because that uses the pathway 1, 2, 3, 4, 5, 6).

Box 12

Damage to box 12 causes surface dyslexia with retained visual lexical decision ability and retained single-word reading comprehension but accompanied by anomia. (That is, there are difficulties in producing spoken words when doing such tasks as naming pictures or conversing, because box 12 is required for both of these tasks.)

THE HETEROGENEITY OF SURFACE DYSLEXIA AND OTHER ACQUIRED DYSLEXIAS

It is clear from the eight examples we have just worked through that surface dyslexia— defined as a selective difficulty in reading aloud exception words—is an extremely heterogeneous condition. Sometimes it is accompanied by anomia, sometimes not; sometimes it is accompanied by a generalized comprehension deficit, sometimes not. That is yet another reason for abandoning the subtyping approach; if there is such heterogeneity within a subtype, there is little that one is going to be able to say that holds for all patients assigned to that subtype.

In contrast, this heterogeneity is a positive advantage if one has adopted the policy of seeking the proximal cause of each new patient's acquired dyslexia. Each different pattern of symptoms provides a fresh way of testing a theory such as that shown in Figure 4.2. For example, if a patient gives the correct meaning of a printed exception word but makes a regularization error when reading it aloud (as patient E.S.T. sometimes did), the theory in Figure 4.2 demands that the impairment responsible for the patient's surface dyslexia be somewhere along the route 11, 12, 13, 14, 15. An impairment at any point on that route must also affect picture naming and the production of speech in conversation. If it were found that this particular patient had no anomia, that directly refutes the theory. Here is clear evidence that this theory, though it may seem complex, is nevertheless eminently falsifiable by cognitive-neuropsychological data.

We have shown, then, that one recognized subtype of acquired dyslexia can be easily interpreted in terms of this theory of reading. This conclusion holds equally for other recognized subtypes of acquired dyslexia. For example, an impairment of arrow 7, or of box 9, or of arrow 10 will compromise pseudoword reading while sparing word reading, and so will result in phonological dyslexia.

This way of using Figure 4.2 also allows previously unreported forms of acquired dyslexia to be predicted. Consider, for example, arrow 5. This arrow is needed to access meaning from visual word recognition, so an impairment here would compromise single-word reading comprehension. However, it would not affect reading aloud at all, because pathway 1, 2, 7, 9, 10, 14, 15 (which allows accurate reading aloud of pseudowords) would still be intact and pathway 1, 2, 3, 4, 8, 12, 13, 14, 15 (which allows accurate reading aloud of all words, whether regular or exception) would also still be intact. So, here we might expect to discover a patient with

- a disorder of single-word reading comprehension; but
- intact reading aloud of words, even exception words, and of pseudowords;
- intact comprehension of words when these are heard rather than seen.

Just such a patient was discovered by Lambon Ralph, Sage, and Ellis (1996).

At this point, readers might ask the question, Why cannot this patient comprehend printed words via the pathway 1, 2, 3, 4, 8, 12, 11, 6? Lambon Ralph and colleagues (1996) asked themselves the same question. They found that the patient's single-word reading comprehension, poor when the task was done silently, was good if the patient read the printed words aloud. In that case, why could not the patient use inner speech to succeed in silent reading comprehension via the pathway 1, 2, 3, 4, 8, 12, 11, 6? Perhaps this was because, in addition to the impairment at arrow 5, the patient also had an impairment of the process of inner speech itself. That could be tested by asking the patient to make judgments based on the phonological properties of printed stimuli—to perform tasks such as judging whether printed word pairs such as *shoe* and *screw* or *hoe* and *screw* rhyme, or judging whether or not printed pseudowords such as *chuze* or *thuze* sound exactly like words. Lambon Ralph and colleagues found that their patient was very poor at these tasks when performing them silently, though very competent when encouraged to read the items aloud before making the judgments. That result provides direct evidence that the arrow 5 impairment in this patient was accompanied by an impairment of the process of inner speech, evidence which provides an answer to the question with which this paragraph began, Why cannot this patient comprehend printed words via the pathway 1, 2, 3, 4, 8, 12, 11, 6?

DISTAL CAUSES OF ACQUIRED DYSLEXIA

At the beginning of this chapter, we allowed ourselves to discuss the possibility that a previously literate person might suddenly lose the ability to read without an examination of the person's brain revealing any abnormality. However, in practice, examinations of the brains of patients with acquired dyslexia always have revealed such abnormalities, and these abnormalities represent distal causes of the acquired dyslexias shown by these patients.

Deep Dyslexia and the Right Hemisphere

Cases of deep dyslexia all have very large left-hemisphere lesions generally involving the frontal, temporal, and parietal lobes. According to the view that, in deep dyslexia, right-hemisphere reading mechanisms are being used (Coltheart, 1980, 2000a; Saffran, Bogyo, Schwartz, & Marin, 1980), the effect of these very large left hemisphere lesions is to abolish any form of orthographic processing in the left hemisphere, so that letter and word recognition has to be done by the (undamaged) right hemisphere, insofar as that is possible. As we mentioned earlier, there is good evidence for this proposal regarding the distal cause of deep dyslexia (Coltheart, 2000a; Michel et al., 1996; Patterson et al., 1987; Weekes et al., 1997).

Letter-by-Letter Reading

Patients exhibiting letter-by-letter reading generally have two brain lesions, one of the left occipital cortex and the other of the splenium of the corpus callosum. The left occipital lesion means that printed words can be visually processed only by the right hemisphere's occipital cortex. That in itself would not cause reading to be abnormal, however. Intact readers also have no difficulty in reading words briefly presented in the left visual field, words which must be visually processed by the right hemisphere's occipital cortex. Normal readers read promptly under these conditions by transferring information from the right occipital cortex to language systems in the left hemisphere. Letter-by-letter readers cannot do that, and the reason must be that the splenium of the corpus callosum is the pathway by which such interhemispheric transfer for reading is normally done. In the patients, the splenial lesion means that some other callosal pathways have to be used for this transfer, and the use of these other pathways may impose a slow and serial letter-by-letter transfer process.

Interestingly, some patients with pure alexia, as this syndrome also is called, exhibit a phenomenon known as *covert reading*. Letter strings are presented at durations too short for the patient to be able to read them aloud, two seconds or so, for example. The patient is asked to judge whether the letter string is a word or not, or, in other studies, whether it is the name of an animal or not. Performance on these classification tasks can be well above chance, and even some-

times perfect, even though the stimuli cannot be read aloud and the patient may even claim not to have seen them at all (see, e.g., Saffran & Coslett, 1998). It has been argued that, in pure alexia, "the right hemisphere supports performance in covert reading tasks, and . . . letter-by-letter reading is the product of the left hemisphere operating on information transferred from the right" (Saffran & Coslett, 1998, p. 141).

Surface and Phonological Dyslexia and the Left Hemisphere

Patients with acquired surface dyslexia generally have left-hemisphere lesions (see Vanier & Caplan, 1985), but "surface dyslexia occurs with a wide variety of . . . lesion sites. . . . It is impossible to generalize with confidence from these scans" (Vanier & Caplan, 1985, p. 521). It is clear why this is so, of course. As we have explained earlier, surface dyslexia can result from a number of different lesions in different parts of the functional reading system. If the functional modules of that system map onto different anatomical modules, then lesions in a number of different parts of the brain can be distal causes of surface dyslexia. So, there is no reason at all to expect, in a group of acquired dyslexics all belonging to the subtype *surface dyslexia*, any consistency in the region of brain that is impaired. Exactly the same argument applies to acquired phonological dyslexia, since we have shown that this subtype of acquired dyslexia also can arise via impairments at various different points in the reading system.

If we are to learn more about the distal causes of surface and phonological dyslexia in the sense of learning what regions of the brain will, when lesioned, result in each of these forms of acquired dyslexia, it will be necessary to precede any brain-imaging study of any such acquired dyslexic patient with a careful assessment of the patient's reading system in order to identify in which of the functional modules of that system an impairment that is responsible for the acquired dyslexia exists. That will prevent brain-imaging investigators from lumping together heterogeneous patients with the same subtype of acquired dyslexia (a group in which the brain lesions will be heterogeneous). Thus, going beyond the subtype approach is as essential for the study of distal causes of acquired dyslexia as it is for the study of proximal causes.

SUMMARY

In chapter 3, we developed a dual-route theory of reading aloud and single-word reading comprehension and showed how it was able to account for various results from experimental studies of skilled reading. In this chapter, we have shown that the same model is applicable to results from studies of people with various forms of acquired dyslexia. For any such patient, that patient's pattern of preserved and impaired performances on various reading tasks can be explained in terms of a pattern of preservations and impairments of the mod-

ules comprising the theory of reading developed in the previous chapter. In the next two chapters, we consider how this theory might be extended to beginning reading and to patterns of developmental rather than to acquired reading difficulties. We explore the idea that, for any child who is having difficulty learning to read, that child's pattern of preserved and impaired performances on various reading tasks can be explained in terms of a pattern of adequately and inadequately acquired modules of the theory of reading we adopt in this book.

5

Reading Acquisition

N ow that we have laid some groundwork concerning the dual-route theory of reading and the research on acquired dyslexia that has been a primary impetus for the development of this general theory and the dual-route cascaded (DRC) model, we turn to the literature on children's beginning reading and reading acquisition. Rather than attempting a comprehensive overview of current theories, we first define the boundaries of our problem. Then, we present a sketch of beginning reading based on one popular theory, comment on some others, and contrast these with a developmental extension of dual-route theory. We then go beyond a static description of the beginner's reading system to a more speculative account of the processes by which change from a beginner's to a skilled reader's system might occur. In this dynamic context, we briefly consider other aspects of experience and cognition that are related to reading acquisition, including the development of oral language and spelling.

HOW SHOULD WE CONCEPTUALIZE THE DEVELOPING READING SYSTEM?

In order to propose connections between a theoretical model of the mature reading system and the developing reading systems of children, we need to consider several fundamental developmental questions. At what point does the evidence indicate that beginning readers first have a reading system? When does that system attain a mature form? What form of change occurs from the beginning to end of this developmental sequence? By what mechanisms does change occur?

When Do Children First Have a Reading System?

Recent conceptualizations of reading acquisition have emphasized that the roots of literacy can be found in things that most children in literate homes learn well

before beginning formal instruction in reading (e.g., Adams, 1990; Pressley, 1998). We agree it is important for young children to learn that reading has useful purposes, that the language used in written discourse differs from that used in conversation, that English words are written from left to right and separated by spaces, and so forth. However, we think that children are not likely to have a reading system in the sense we have conceived one in dual-route theory until they begin to be able to read words without support from context and by relying in some way on letter sequences. For many children, this kind of reading begins in kindergarten or first grade, but it may begin earlier for precocious readers and may be delayed for children with reading problems.

When Is Development of the Reading System Complete?

By fifth grade, that is, by age 10 or 11, children who are acquiring English reading skill at an average pace show patterns of performance indicating that they have all the components of a mature reading system in place, if not yet functioning at peak levels. For example, by Grade 5, accuracy in reading monosyllabic pseudowords is almost at adult levels, indicating near-adult mastery of basic grapheme-phoneme correspondences (GPCs) (Coltheart & Leahy, 1996). The pseudoword reading accuracy norms of many standard reading tests confirm that, beyond the elementary school years, individual differences become more pronounced than age differences and items difficult enough to challenge good GPC users are likely to be polysyllabic or include unusual or complex patterns. Stage theories of reading often top out at about the fifth grade reading level, or perhaps a little higher if they consider reading acquisition more broadly than we have (e.g., Chall, 1983). Many readers continue to enlarge their phonological and orthographic lexicons and to read ever more efficiently after this point (Perfetti, 1985). More and more words are likely to be read by the lexical route. However, the way in which the system works does not seem to change in any fundamental way.

How Do the Reading Systems of Beginning and Skilled Readers Differ?

Many early theories of reading acquisition were stage theories. According to such theories, children's reading acquisition can be described by Piaget-like models in which the nature of the reading process becomes qualitatively different as the child becomes older and more skilled (e.g., Chall, 1983).

An extreme alternative view is the item-based (i.e., individual-word-based) conceptualization of reading acquisition proposed by Share and Stanovich (1995b). Development is continuous and children at successive skill levels differ from one another primarily in the distributions of processes they use to read different words. A child at any point in the process of reading acquisition is likely to read different words in different ways. For example, a first grader might recognize her name and a few short, very common words as sight vocabulary,

sound out a few others by accurate application of rudimentary, position-limited GPC correspondence rules, but use less reliable heuristics such as guessing from the word's first letter on others. An item-based approach captures the variability of a particular child's performance in a way that is consistent with some information-processing theories of cognitive development (e.g., Siegler, 1996).

A traditional stage theory of reading acquisition would be hard to reconcile with a developmental extension of dual-route theory. By definition, a stage theory requires that a different reading system be postulated for each stage of development. The end point of development can be important to such theories, but it need not imply much about the nature of earlier stages. In contrast, an item-based theory suggests a reading system whose structures and functions are fundamentally similar throughout development, but incompletely realized. For example, such a theory suggests that one thing which might happen as children get older is that, with practice in reading, their orthographic lexicons will grow larger and they will become able to read more words by the lexical route.

Although we could consider reading acquisition as an item-based process, we find part of another, similar, conceptualization recently proposed by Ehri (1999; Ehri & McCormick, 1998) congenial because it incorporates summary descriptions of performance. These descriptions allow us to draw inferences about how well components of the lexical and nonlexical routes are likely to function as a child's reading acquisition progresses.

Ehri refers to her account as a phase theory of reading acquisition. It includes elements that seem to us to be central to the current reading acquisition literature. It emphasizes the kinds of reading typical at each successive phase but acknowledges the item-based theory premise that a child is likely to read different words in different ways. We return to this theory in more detail as a context for our own proposals about how beginning and skilled readers' reading systems differ.

How Does the Reading System Develop?

Cognitive developmentalists studying reading and other aspects of cognition consistently have found it easier to present a series of pictures of what a child's thought is like at a succession of ages than to show exactly how change from, say, 4-year-old to 6-year-old thinking patterns takes place. Identifying mechanisms of cognitive development is difficult (Share & Stanovich, 1995b; Siegler, 1996; Sternberg, 1984). Nonetheless, understanding these mechanisms is critical to forging links between theories of reading acquisition and recommendations for instruction. Therefore, at the end of this chapter, we briefly consider research suggesting the kinds of experiences that contribute to reading acquisition and how the reading system might respond to these inputs. Here, of course, we are reaching out into the realm in which distal causes of reading success and failure operate.

As we noted in chapter 3, drawing boundaries between the reading system

and other cognitive systems can be difficult. Two sets of tasks seem to draw on knowledge and processes that come especially close to this boundary. Spelling and phonological awareness tasks do not involve reading as a response, but the development of both sets of skills is related to reading acquisition in interesting ways. Therefore, we consider both spelling and phonological awareness in the final section of this chapter, when we take a dynamic look at how the reading system might develop.

TWO ACCOUNTS OF DIFFERENCES BETWEEN BEGINNING AND SKILLED READING SYSTEMS

We now offer a more complete summary of Ehri's (1999) account of phases in reading acquisition and then contrast her account of what a beginner's reading system looks like with our own proposal.

Ehri's Phase Theory

Pre-alphabetic reading. According to Ehri's (1999) theory, children begin reading in a pre-alphabetic phase, during which they use partial visual cues for word identification. This earliest form of reading sometimes has been called the logographic stage, but the term *visual cue* reflects the finding that children reading this way, who may be preschoolers or kindergartners, are likely to use only part of the visual information available in a word to identify it. In one classic study, Gough, Juel, and Griffith (1992), showed that this visual cue could be as arbitrary as a thumbprint on the card on which a word was printed. Similarly, Seymour and Elder (1986) found that very young readers read by relying on partial visual cues such as word length, an approach that could lead to reading *rhinoceros* or *children* as /tel-°-vizh-°n/.

To read using the partial visual cues of the pre-alphabetic phase, children do not need to know anything about letter sounds or even the identity of letters. Indeed, central to the definition of this earliest phase of reading is the conclusion that pre-alphabetic readers are not encoding words in terms of letter sequences. When they do seem to get letter sounds correct, this may be fortuitous. For example, Seymour and Elder (1986, as cited in Harris & Coltheart, 1986) quoted a child who read *smaller* as /yel-O/ as reasoning that this was the word "because it has two sticks" (p. 91). This particular error might seem at first glance like accurate recognition of the /l/ sound that is in the middle of both words. However, note that the child identified the words' common feature as "two sticks," not "two *l*'s," suggesting reliance on a strategy in which letters are not recognized as such, and the identity of, say, capital and lowercase *l* and *L* was not acknowledged. It also probably was fortuitous that this pre-alphabetic reader equated two words whose *l*'s were in the middle. It would be typical of this stage for a child to read words with "two sticks" in different ordinal positions, such as *yellow, llama,* and *finally,* the same way.

Ehri (1999; Ehri & McCormick, 1998) has presented pre-alphabetic reading as the first phase in her developmental sequence, but she also has acknowledged that this phase actually is a qualitatively different stage, distinct from those that follow. We agree. Pre-alphabetic or visual cue reading does not require a reading system as we have conceptualized it. Therefore, we have not tried to model the system that might underlie this primitive form of reading and will not discuss it further.

Partial-alphabetic reading.   Reading interests us more at Ehri's second phase, which she most recently has called partial-alphabetic reading. In this phase of development, which also has been called phonetic-cue reading, "readers use their rudimentary knowledge of letter names or sounds to form partial connections between spellings and pronunciations" (Ehri, 1992, p. 108). A child in this phase might read *slug* as /snAl/, attending only to the word's first letter and a picture or sentence context. In contrast to readers in the pre-alphabetic stage, children now are attending to letter order (at least for the more salient beginning and end positions) and recognizing that letters imply sounds. As this kind of reading becomes a bit more skillful, "words [still] are often misread as other words having similar letters; for example, *man* for *men, this* for *that, horse* for *house*" (Ehri & McCormick, 1998, p. 145). Later in this chapter, we consider what kind of reading system might support this partial-alphabetic reading.

Full-alphabetic reading.   The third phase in Ehri's model has been called full-alphabetic, cipher, or spelling-sound reading (e.g., Ehri, 1992; Ehri & McCormick, 1998; Gough & Hillinger, 1980; Juel, 1991). In this phase, the child is assumed to have an essentially complete system for reading words and pseudowords. This system must include components that allow the segmentation of written words into graphemes and fluent mappings of letter sequences onto phoneme sequences. Also, in Ehri's terms, the child has a substantial sight-word vocabulary of frequently occurring words. Ehri (1998, 1999) has described sight-word reading as a process of reading words from memory. "Alphabetic connections linking all of the letters in spellings to their pronunciations enable mature readers to represent thousands of words uniquely in their mental lexicons and to locate the pronunciations and meanings of these words accurately and automatically when seeing them in print" (Ehri, 1998, p. 17). Unlike the DRC model of skilled word reading summarized in chapter 3, Ehri's description has not been specified completely enough to be instantiated in a computational model, although it seems roughly consistent with some such models (e.g., Plaut et al., 1996). In contrast to the DRC model, it seems to assume that the representations used to generate the pronunciation and meaning of a familiar word always include sublexical phonology; that is, GPCs

Consolidated-alphabetic reading.   Ehri (1999) has proposed a fourth and final phase in the development of skilled reading, which she has called the consolidated-alphabetic phase. Subsequent to the full-alphabetic phase, reading

continues to become more fluent. What we call lexical processes become more dominant (Ehri, 1999; Ehri & McCormick, 1998). In other words, children's sight vocabularies continue to grow. However, what made Ehri call this a new phase of development was her conclusion that children (and adults) in the consolidated-alphabetic phase become able to chunk and rechunk letter patterns in subword units that are larger than individual graphemes, such as commonly occurring onsets and rimes, syllables, affixes, and root words. For example, Ehri and McCormick (1998) suggested that a child who has moved from the full-alphabetic to the subsequent consolidated-alphabetic phase would be able to read the word *interesting* in terms of its component grapho-syllabic units rather than as a sequence of 10 phonemes. However, Ehri also has asserted that the reader in this final phase of development "has not lost touch with the grapho-phonic nature of these chunks" (L. C. Ehri, personal communication, October, 2000)

Ehri's consolidated-alphabetic phase takes reading acquisition into a realm that is controversial and, to some extent, beyond the scope of current dual-route models of reading. These models were designed to account for the reading of monosyllabic words and pseudowords, so the parsing of a polysyllabic, polymorphemic words such as *interesting* or *prematurity* is beyond their scope. As Taft's (1992) review of this literature makes clear, there is as yet no consensus as to whether the evidence is strong enough to justify a commitment to the view that the relevant units in the reading system are morphemes rather than words. If such a commitment were made, however, that would involve modifying rather than abandoning the model shown in Figure 3.10, the modification simply being to interpret the elements of the two lexicons as morphemes rather than words.

More at odds with our preferred dual-route theory is Ehri's argument that skilled readers may process words in chunks intermediate between the grapheme and the whole word, using units such as the orthographic body (corresponding to the rime, or rhyming part) to map connections between familiar and novel words. For example, Ehri (1999) suggested that a child in the consolidated-alphabetic phase might read a new word, *string*, by dividing the word into onset and rime chunks *str-* and *-ing* and connecting these with the same chunks in already known words such as *strip* and *ring*.

Ehri herself (Ehri & Robbins, 1992) has differed from theorists (e.g., Goswami & Bryant, 1990) who have argued that very young readers use these onset-rime units to map letters patterns onto pronunciation *before* they become competent at using GPCs. Others also have supported the position that rimes are not particularly salient to young children (Bowey, 1999; Muter, Snowling, & Taylor, 1994; Nation & Hulme,1997; Savage, 1997; Savage & Stuart, 1998; Uhry & Ehri, 1999). So, we are in agreement with Ehri and many others that ability to read words by onset-rime analogies is not an early developing reading skill. Where we differ from Ehri is in our evaluation of the evidence that this process ever becomes part of normal reading.

As far as skilled adult readers are concerned, there is very little evidence

indeed that the rime is a unit used in skilled reading, once one has controlled for other important variables such as regularity of spelling-to-sound correspondence, number of orthographic neighbors, and the "whammy effect" described in chapter 3 (Rastle & Coltheart, 1998). So, as was the case with the morphemic level of representation, there is as yet no consensus as to whether the evidence is strong enough to justify a commitment to the view that the rime is a relevant level of representation in the reading system. If such a commitment were made, however, that would once again involve modifying rather than abandoning the model shown in Figure 3.10, as we said in chapter 3.

Our disagreement with Ehri about the use of supra-grapheme sublexical units in skilled reading may rest in the distinction we have drawn between reading and learning to read a word. Large-unit correspondences may indeed be helpful in learning new words, which is not our concern at this point.

What we accept from Ehri's theory. So, we have agreed with Ehri that pre-alphabetic reading is a phenomenon qualitatively different from more sophisticated forms of reading. We have disputed her controversial claim that skilled reading involves reliance on supra-grapheme nonlexical as well as GPC and whole-word (lexical) units. Therefore, we have truncated her four-phase theory of reading acquisition to two phases. The second of these, full-alphabetic reading, is skilled reading that we find consistent with operation of the DRC model as described in chapter 3. For example, Ehri (1999) describes the reader in the full alphabetic phase as "able to read sight words by remembering their spellings" (p. 100) and as someone who

- Knows letter names and sounds;
- [Is] able to segment words into the smallest sounds, phonemes;
- Invents fully phonetic spellings of words;
- Remembers the correct spelling of shorter, regularly spelled words;
- [Is] able to use known words to read unknown words;
- Reads practiced words accurately and automatically; and
- Reads text comprised of familiar, decodable, or predictable words independently. (p. 100)

This sounds to us like the skilled reading that is described by dual-route theories. However, fifth graders and college graduates are not likely to use the two routes in the same proportion. Readers who have just entered the full-alphabetic phase encounter many real words on the same basis as adults encounter pseudowords, or perhaps more precisely, as pseudohomophones of real words. When a skilled reader sees *rane* and uses the nonlexical route to identify its pronunciation as /rAn/ and associate this with the meaning as liquid precipitation, he or she is doing what intermediate readers do when attempting to read words that are in their oral but not written lexicons. Therefore, we think it is reasonable to characterize readers who have attained fairly complete mastery of the GPC code as using a rudimentary dual-route reading system to read, per-

haps one with a relatively small orthographic lexicon and rather slow and error-prone operation of the nonlexical route.

By equating Ehri's (1999) full-alphabetic reading with the kind of skilled reading system defined by dual-route theories, we further simplify the task of creating a model of beginning reading. We can use our existing model (Figure 3.10) to describe reading that is typical of readers making normal progress from the middle elementary school years onward. We are left with the task of specifying only one immature system, one that will account for partial-alphabetic reading.

A Dual-Route Conceptualization of Partial-Alphabetic Reading

Our account of partial-alphabetic reading draws primarily from the same data as Ehri's (Ehri, 1998, 1999; Ehri & McCormick, 1998), but our interpretation of the data has been informed by dual-route theory. As we have shown in chapter 3, all current models of skilled reading aloud involve dual routes. Hence, differences between models of skilled word reading are in details that are not particularly relevant for choosing among theories of beginning reading or reading acquisition. People directly concerned with developing a dual-route theory of the skilled reading system have not specifically discussed what an immature system might look like. Therefore, we are venturing into new territory. Our primary goal in this chapter is to venture some hypotheses about what an immature reading system might look like, so that we can compare this model with what we know about skilled reading and its disruption in acquired dyslexia.

Assumptions.   In proposing an initial model of partial-alphabetic reading, we make some bold, but plausible and parsimonious, assumptions. First, we assume that the immature partial-alphabetic system does not contain any procedures that skilled adult readers do not use. As Ehri (1992) once suggested, it would be highly inefficient for young children to devote considerable time and effort to developing procedures that will not continue to serve them as their reading becomes more skilled. The reading processes of the pre-alphabetic stage may be of this dead-end sort. However, recall that these are the wholly inadequate processes that children rely on when they do not yet know anything about the alphabetic system and are floundering about. In contrast, we propose that the partial-alphabetic reader does have a functional, but imperfect, reading system, one in which further change could be any of several types: (a) adding components and processing connections that initially are missing, such as the components of the nonlexical route in Figure 3.10; or (b) increasing the knowledge available and efficiency of operation within each system component; or (c) doing both of these things.

Any of these three descriptions is plausible, but Ehri's summary description of partial-alphabetic reading and other accounts of the imperfect, but diverse, skills that these beginning readers show (e.g., Share & Stanovich, 1995b)

lead us to suggest that (b) is the best description. We propose that all elements of the mature reading system exist in at least rudimentary form among partial-alphabetic readers, and that this system can be characterized by something like the diagram in Figure 5.1.

Figure 5.1 is similar in its overall structure to Figure 3.10, our model of the mature reading system. However, the contents of some of its components are different. What follows is our account of how the reading system of a child who is in the partial-alphabetic phase of reading as depicted in Figure 5.1 differs from the mature system specified in the DRC model.

The semantic system, phonological lexicon, and phoneme units. By the time the typical beginning reader, at perhaps 5 or 6 years of age, enters the partial-alphabetic phase, some aspects of his or her existing cognitive systems are ready to function as part of a new reading system. The child will not know all the word pronunciations and meanings that an adult does, and knowledge of word meanings will not be as rich, but native speakers of English already will a have substantial semantic system and phonological lexicon in place by age 5 or 6. When these system components do not include the pronunciations and meanings of the words used in reading instruction, as may be the case for children who are dialect speakers or whose parents have little formal education, learning to read is likely to be more difficult (Catts, Fey, Zhang, & Tomblin, 1999; Ehri, 1984), and require more change of the "adding knowledge" type specified above. We address this issue further in discussing reading acquisition failure in chapter 6. The point key to our current argument is that some forms of phonological lexicon and semantic system are available to all native speakers when they begin reading instruction.

In addition to everyday oral language vocabulary, the partial-alphabetic reader's phonological lexicon also is likely to include letter names, such as [em] for *M* (e.g., Ehri & Wilce, 1985). By Ehri's definition, which is consistent with abundant empirical evidence, even beginning partial-alphabetic readers can identify most, if not all, letters by name. Children who do not have letter names in their phonological lexicons at the beginning of reading instruction are likely to have more difficulty learning to read (e.g., Adams, 1990; Ehri, 1999); it is a general point that any kind of material which cannot be verbally encoded will be harder to learn.

Although the phonological lexicon in Figure 5.1 contains entries for only nine words, that is just to save space. The real number of entries would be several thousand, since children at the age characteristic of partial-alphabetic reading have spoken vocabularies of several thousand words.

The content of the phoneme units component of the reading system in Figure 5.1 has not been specified because we think it is essentially the same as that for skilled readers. We agree with the traditional view (see Metsala & Walley, 1998, for an alternative view) that normal native speakers of this age will have all the phoneme units of their native language in place and use them, perhaps

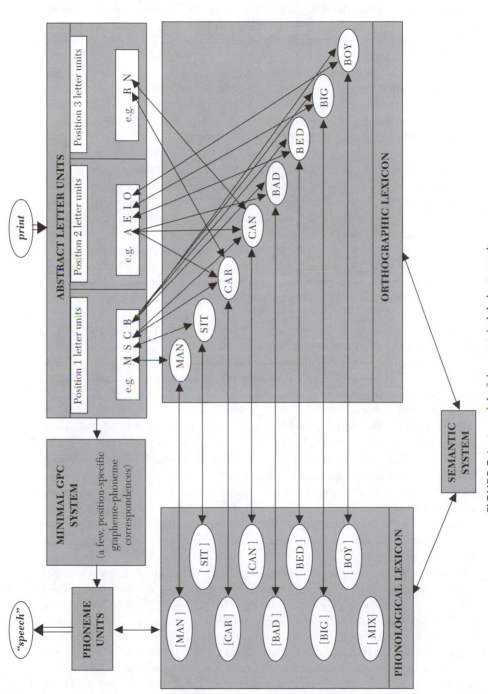

FIGURE 5.1. A model of the partial-alphabetic reading system.

with an occasional error, in speaking and listening. Pre-readers may not be aware consciously of sound patterns within words, but they can comprehend and produce speech sounds with a high degree of accuracy.

Given all the attention that has been devoted to links between reading acquisition and the development of phonemic awareness, our claim for the prior existence of a phoneme units system may seem surprising, but it is quite conventional. The phoneme units to which we refer are based on discriminations of the kind studied by Werker (1989), which develop in infancy. As Whitehurst and Lonigan (1998, p. 851) have noted, "normally developing children in the late preschool period can discriminate among [phonemes]." A young child's or dialect speaker's pronunciations of phonemes within particular word contexts may become more standard with age and reading experience (Ehri, 1984), but the set of phoneme units should be present from oral language experience.

Abstract letter units. Although most beginning readers do know letter names, they also "know" these written forms in a more fundamental sense that does not require being able to name them (e.g., Adams, 1990; Thompson, 1999). Recall that, in our conception, the system of abstract letter units contains no information whatsoever about phonology. That part of the reading system does not know about letter names, and it does not know about letter sounds. This is important because, as we indicated in Figure 3.10, the abstract letter units component of the reading system is the gateway to both the lexical and the nonlexical routes. If this component contained information about letter sounds, the distinction between the two routes would be muddied in ways inconsistent with the DRC model tests reported in chapter 3. Like skilled readers, partial-alphabetic readers can respond to letters as abstract units, recognizing their categorical identities regardless of the particular visual forms in which they are presented. Although abstract letter units are not themselves named in that component of the reading system, the demonstration of ability to name letters in forms such as capital and lowercase is evidence sufficient to prove that these abstract forms must exist in the child's mind. Typical beginning readers can name most letters well before they finish kindergarten, and most children have learned most of the capital letters before entering school (Adams, 1990). Therefore, we can conclude that partial alphabetic readers have an abstract letter units component in their reading system, although the knowledge therein may not be as complete or as efficiently accessed (Wolf & Bowers, 1999) as it is in skilled readers. In the sets of abstract letter units for each position in Figure 5.1, only a few letters are indicated. However, that is only to save space; we assume that partial-alphabetic readers have a full complement of abstract letter units for each position.

The orthographic lexicon and lexical route. We propose that the lexical route does a great deal of the work for partial-alphabetic readers. As Share and Stanovich (1995b) have observed, even a beginning, partial-alphabetic reader is likely to be able to read some short, highly familiar words, such as his or her

own name, correctly by using the lexical route. This suggests that a child is likely to have some orthographic lexicon, albeit a tiny one, very early in beginning to read. It also suggests that the partial-alphabetic reader has an operational lexical route. Beginners' reading errors confirm this. When partial alphabetic readers encounter an unfamiliar word, perhaps even a pseudoword, that they are not able to read correctly, their error is likely to be a word that is familiar to them and that is orthographically similar to the letter string they are trying to read (Ehri, 1999). According to our model, they are reading by selecting that word in their current orthographic lexicon which most closely matches the letter string, and then retrieving that word's pronunciation from their phonological lexicon.

Interestingly, this reading strategy is also seen in previously fully skilled readers with acquired phonological dyslexia who, when attempting to read pseudowords produce orthographically similar real words as responses, despite imperfect letter-by-letter matches. For example, as we noted in chapter 4, a person with acquired phonological dyslexia might read *soof* → /soot/ and *klack* → /slak/, /blak/, or /flok/ (Patterson, 1982).

Recall the example presented previously of a partial-alphabetic reader reading *slug* as /snAl/ when reading text. It appears that, like many beginning readers, this child responded based on the initial consonant of the word read plus contextual information that suggested the response /snAl/ (e.g., Biemiller, 1970). In children's texts, semantic information to support reading of a new word often is available via sentence context, accompanying pictures, or both. By definition, the partial-alphabetic reader's reading system as a whole is not yet functioning well enough to enable a complete mapping between letter units and words in his or her phonological lexicon. If either route in the system worked perfectly, the child would read better than he or she does.

The roles of semantic context and the phonological lexicon in partial-alphabetic lexical-route reading. We propose that, for the partial-alphabetic reader, mappings between letter units and units in the orthographic lexicon are incomplete. Suppose that there are several words in this child's orthographic lexicon that began with S and so were activated by an *s* in position 1, and that SNAIL was one of these but SLUG was not. Without context, the child might just have to guess between the initial-S words present in the orthographic lexicon, so might read *slug* presented in isolation as /sun/ or /snAl/. The context would allow selection of the more contextually appropriate of these; hence, *slug* → /snAl/. In the slow and effortful word recognition processes typical of beginning and poor readers, time is available for semantic information provided by sentence context or an accompanying picture to feed backward to support a lexical-route link between the child's mapping of one letter unit, S, incorrectly but plausibly, and an existing orthographic lexicon entry that might be only partially connected with the letter-unit level (e.g., Perfetti, 1999). This orthographic lexicon entry maps to the word [SNAIL] in the phonological lexicon, eliciting the pronunciation /snAl/.

The guessing from context characteristic of beginning readers in the partial-alphabetic phase (e.g., Biemiller, 1970) indicates that all the components of the mature lexical route must be operational, even if some components exist only in miniature. What the child knows about oral language mediates a connection from abstract letter units, via a rudimentary orthographic lexicon, to the phonological lexicon and pronunciation of the word.

There is nothing particularly novel about this argument in its general form. What distinguishes it from Ehri's (1999) and some other accounts is the absence of sublexical phonology in the use of this route. According to the model depicted in Figure 5.1, lexical-route reading in the partial-alphabetic reader is not logographic or pre-alphabetic. It requires mapping between abstract letter units and the orthographic lexicon. We have shown the orthographic lexicon as containing entries for only eight words, and that is not to save space: a small orthographic lexicon is what we propose is characteristic of readers at the beginning of the partial-alphabetic stage. Also, there is only limited connectivity between the abstract letter units and the orthographic lexicon. In the mature system, the letter unit for I in the second position would be connected to the unit for SIT in the orthographic lexicon. But, this partial-alphabetic reader does not need such a connection. The only word beginning with *s* that this reader has learned so far is *sit*, so all that is needed for reading *sit* is a connection from the letter unit for S in the first position to the entry for SIT in the orthographic lexicon. That will produce correct reading of the word *sit*. It will of course also cause the child to read the real word *sun* or the pseudoword *sev* as /sit/. But that, of course, is just the kind of thing that partial-alphabetic readers do. For the same reason, *mix* will be read as /man/. Similarly, although there are letter units for A in the second position and N in the third position, and although connections from these units to MAN in the orthographic lexicon would be correct, there are not such connections, because they are not needed. This child's orthographic lexicon contains only one word that begins M, so all that is needed to activate MAN uniquely in the orthographic lexicon is a connection from the letter unit for M in the first position.

We've included [MIX] in the phonological lexicon to make the point that its presence there is not sufficient to allow it to be read aloud by the lexical route; that is prevented by its absence from the orthographic lexicon. The child knows what "mix" means and how to say it; but nevertheless cannot recognize its printed form as a word, or read it aloud by the lexical reading route.

But note that the absence of MIX from the orthographic lexicon does not mean that it cannot be read aloud correctly at all; it is only reading via the lexical route that is not possible for MIX. It is a perfectly regular word, so it would pose no problems for reading via the nonlexical route, if such a route were reasonably well developed. It follows that children in the partial-alphabetic phase of reading do not routinely use the nonlexical route for reading aloud. If they did, they would not misread simple pronounceable pseudowords as orthographically similar words (*bov* → /boy/); nor, as we have said, would they read *mix* as /man/. About all the beginning partial-alphabetic reader might be able to

accomplish via his or her rudimentary nonlexical route would be reading *mix* as /m/, which, in the context of reading any real text, would be immediately recognizable as wrong. At this point, the lexical route is likely to operate more successfully.

A reader whose reading system was exactly as shown in Figure 5.1 would read *mul*, *mug*, or *man* as /man/, either *bag* or *bad* as /bad/, *sat*, *suf*, or *she* as /sit/, and so forth. Most of these errors reflect incomplete but correct mappings from abstract letter units to the orthographic lexicon. Reading *she* as /sit/ indicates a particularly interesting kind of error, one that ignores the fact that *sh* is a two-letter grapheme linked to the single phoneme /sh/. Because graphemic parsing and GPCs are not part of the partial-alphabetic reader's lexical route, such errors are predicted.

A key point here is that "pre-alphabetic" or "logographic" reading as described by Ehri (1999) is not the only alternative to using letter names or letter sounds in reading. Partial-alphabetic readers consistently use abstract letter identities in their reading. Their frequent word-substitution errors suggest that they often map these letter identities as well as they can onto entries in their orthographic lexicon, as illustrated in Figure 5.1. In our model, this kind of mapping does not involve any letter name or letter-sound knowledge. *Boz* or *box* activates the entry for BOY in the orthographic lexicon because *boz* and *box* activate the same abstract letter units as *boy*, B and O in the first and second position. Hence, the response *boz* → /boy/ or *box* → /boy/ is not mediated by a commonality in letter names or letter sounds—not mediated by anything phonological, in fact.

The partial-alphabetic reader also might map only the abstract letter unit B from *boz* or *box* onto orthographic and phonological lexicon entries to yield the letter-name pronunciation /bE/, which likewise would be wrong, but also an instance of lexical-route reading. Finally, a partial-alphabetic reader might have in his or her rudimentary GPC system the knowledge that initial *b* is pronounced /b/ and generate this letter sound as an alternative incorrect response, using the nonlexical route.

Whichever of the three processes the child uses to generate an initial incorrect response, use of context and feedback from the semantic system may enable the child, given enough time, to self-correct and generate the correct response.

Grapheme-phoneme correspondences and the nonlexical route. We have debated whether partial-alphabetic readers have any nonlexical route at all and have concluded that they do. The clearest evidence of such a route is ability to read pseudowords. Other signs are generating nonword errors and showing an advantage in reading regular rather than exception words. Data such as the norms for standard tests of pseudoword reading (e.g., Woodcock & Johnson, 1989) and experimental results (Thompson, Cottrell, & Fletcher-Finn, 1996) have indicated that average readers of kindergarten or first grade age are

likely to be able to read a few two- or three-letter pseudowords accurately. Since this is the age range at which partial-alphabetic reading is typical (Ehri, 1999), we have proposed a very rudimentary nonlexical route as part of the partial-alphabetic reading system.

We would expect the nonlexical route to become gradually more complete as a child moves toward the full-alphabetic reading phase. While the nonlexical route is still in its most primitive form, we would not expect its use to be prominent in the child's everyday reading of real words. Recall that the reading system postulated in chapter 3 allows for strategic, adaptive shifts in balance between routes. Therefore, nonword errors should be rare, as they are, in partial-alphabetic readers with incomplete and slowly activated GPC knowledge (Adams, 1990; Ehri, 1999).

If partial-alphabetic readers had a complete GPC conversion system in operation, they would be full-alphabetic readers and able to read many pseudowords, the skill that is the litmus test for existence of a nonlexical route. Because they are unable to read pseudowords at any but the most trivial level, are they reading without any nonlexical system at all? This is one of those questions about origins that always are difficult for developmental theorists, and our answer must be tentative. However, we know from test norms and other sources that a child in this phase knows the names for all or most abstract letter units. Many beginning readers also are likely to know something about individual letters' sounds, whether these have been explicitly taught, inferred from reading experience, or inferred from letter names (Adams, 1990; Ehri, 1999; Thompson et al., 1996).The reading acquisition literature suggests which GPCs are most and least likely to be within the beginning partial-alphabetic reader's repertoire. For example, Ehri and McCormick (1998) reported that these readers may not know the sounds of *h, w,* and *y* or the correspondences between the letter *c* and the sound /k/ and *g* with /g/. These authors also noted other limitations of the partial-alphabetic reader's knowledge. Mastery of the importance of left-to-right sequencing in letter processing may be shaky. Letters in medial positions may be ignored or processed incompletely, and vowels may be confused. Diphthongs and consonant clusters also are likely to be read incorrectly (Adams, 1990).

Comparison of the DRC-based model of partial-alphabetic reading with Ehri's model.   The point on which we differ most clearly from Ehri is with regard to how this incomplete GPC knowledge is used when the partial-alphabetic reader reads; that is, when his or her reading system operates. We think that cascading activation along the nonlexical route occurs routinely but rarely determines the pronunciation a partial-alphabetic reader gives a word. If it did, partial-alphabetic readers would generate many nonword errors when they read text, and they do not. Therefore, we are uncomfortable with Ehri's conclusion (e.g., 1992, 1999) that grapho-phonemic connections are essential to all partial alphabetic reading.

Ehri's blending of past learning (distal cause) and the current state of the reading system (proximal cause) makes some contrasts between our model and her model awkward. Ehri has stated that "partial alphabetic readers are reading words from memory by accessing connections that were previously formed when these words were read. This is a lexical route paved with grapho-phonemic material connections" (L. C. Ehri, personal communication, October, 2000). In Ehri's model, letter-sound correspondences are vital because she has considered these to be the only means by which word spellings are likely to stick in memory. Her theory does not include the concept of abstract letter units mapped to an orthographic lexicon without intervening phonology as a means of learning new words. Those sublexical phonological representations also are represented as being inextricably linked with the reading of familiar words

Ehri has proposed that partial-alphabetic "readers use their rudimentary knowledge of letter names or sounds to form partial connections between spellings and pronunciations" (Ehri, 1992, p. 108) rather than reading "logographically, as pre-alphabetic readers do." Putting her argument into the context of the DRC model, she seems to have proposed that letter-name knowledge enables partial-alphabetic readers to use a rudimentary nonlexical route in which letter names can stand in for letter sounds. In a subsequent section of this chapter, we will argue that the phenomena that Ehri (e.g., Ehri & Wilce, 1985) and others (Rack, Hulme, Snowling, & Wightman, 1994) have observed when young children are taught to read new words by relying on letter names or GPCs bear on the dynamic question of how the reading system might change with experience rather than on how it operates in a particular moment of reading. In other words, we agree with Ehri that letter-sound connections may be important, over time, in bonding written words with their pronunciations and meanings in episodic memory, as an aid to storing this information in lexical memory (the reading system). We do suspect that these connections may not be absolutely necessary for learning new words, but that is a relatively minor point of disagreement. In contrast, we differ substantially from Ehri in the role we give GPCs when a child reads a word at a particular time. As we showed in chapter 3, we think that role varies depending on whether the letter string read is a real word with an exceptional spelling pattern, a regularly spelled real word, or a pseudoword. Where Ehri sees a bonding of letters and sounds, we see cascading activation along dual routes. Although both models are consistent with the same basic data on partial-alphabetic reading, ours has the advantage of suggesting testable links between this kind of normal beginning reading and the phenomena in skilled reading and acquired dyslexia for which the DRC model has given a precise account.

A primitive system.   In conclusion, the performance of partial-alphabetic readers suggests that all of the elements of their juvenile reading system are also elements of the mature dual-route system shown in Figure 3.10, albeit sometimes in primitive, incomplete form.

HOW DOES THE READING SYSTEM DEVELOP?

Limits of the Evidence

Some computational models of the reading system (models that have been instantiated as computer programs) "develop" by the operation of a neural net learning mechanism known as back propagation (see, e.g., Hinton, 1989, for a review of neural net learning procedures). However, this learning procedure, and the kinds of database on which it operates, have little in common with the input that real children encounter as they learn to read, and the cognitive mechanisms that might plausibly account for change in their reading systems. For example, the models of Seidenberg and McClelland (1989) and Plaut et al. (1996) were trained by repeated exposure to their entire vocabulary of about 3,000 words, and hundreds or thousands of exposures to each word were needed before the words were correctly read aloud; the attractor network described by Plaut et al. (1996) required 1,900 training epochs to learn all the words.

When children are learning to read, they are not exposed to huge word sets, nor are words presented to them a great number of times. Instead, beginning readers are exposed to small sets of words, and learn them with few exposures if they are progressing normally in reading acquisition. Words that they have mastered they do not subsequently need to relearn, and here is the most flagrant difference between how children learn and how back propagation learns. Suppose one trained a neural net by back propagation to read a set of 100 words. When this task was mastered, the network was trained on a second set of 100 words. Then, without any further training, the original 100 words were tested. The network would fail with these words which it once could read. This is the problem of "catastrophic forgetting" (McCloskey & Cohen, 1989). When learning the second set of words, the adjustments to connection strengths originally made to permit correct reading of the first set of words are undone, since the strengths are set so that the second set of words can be read correctly. Children do not forget already learned words when learning new ones. Indeed, they learn new words with a facility that has been called "spongelike" (Reitsma, 1983, as cited in Adams, 1990). Therefore, we conclude that neural network models that learn by back propagation (e.g., Harm & Seidenberg, 1999) are not reliable guides to understanding how children learn to read. Neither is the DRC model.

The DRC model does not tell us anything about how reading skill is acquired. It does not "develop" even in the artificial sense in which neural nets trained by back propagation "develop," so it cannot offer us any direct guidance about the mechanisms by which children learn to read. Therefore, although we have drawn together research that is relevant to this question, the following proposals are extrapolations that should be interpreted as first approximations of ideas to guide future research. We do not yet know anything about mechanisms of change within the reading system itself, but we speculate about both these and the more distal environmental inputs that might influence them.

Our speculations about development are further constrained by the realization that all dual-route theories of skilled reading have a great deal in common. As noted in chapter 3, their differences are likely to be in fine points. One of these is whether they emphasize the regularity or consistency of spelling patterns as a determinant of the route used. Another is whether relations between graphemes and phonemes are represented explicitly (in the form of GPC rules) or implicitly (in the form of weighted connections linking grapheme input units to phoneme output units). None of these distinctions among cognitive models of skilled reading has any great bearing on the proposals about reading development that follow.

In general, the following accounts of developmental mechanisms acknowledge that learning can occur both by direct tuition and by inference from patterned experience. Children are sensitive to, and learn from, spatial-temporal contiguity (Siegler, 1998). Another thing we know is that many children will learn to read (i.e., eventually acquire a mature reading system) regardless of whether they are taught by "whole language" methods or by direct instruction in GPCs (Pressley, 1998). In this chapter, our account is of a large set of changes that are likely to happen with greater or lesser speed depending on the nature of the environment in which a child learns to read, the child's own predispositions, and the match between these.

We divide our speculations about the environmental inputs to and mechanisms of reading system development into accounts of development for related sets of cognitive system components that include but extend beyond the reading system. Therefore, we consider the development of extrasystem entities such as general oral language knowledge, phonological awareness, and spelling, in addition to reading system development. As we explain later, changes within each set of components are likely to contribute to changes within the others.

How Do Oral Language Components of the Reading System and Related Systems Develop?

As we noted in chapter 3, finding the boundary between the reading and the oral language system, if indeed there is one, is not easy. At any given moment, a child's oral language knowledge influences and sets limits on the operation of the reading system. The semantic system and phonological lexicon of Figure 5.1 are present in a child's oral language system even before the child begins to learn to read. The cognitive-linguistic mechanisms by which a child's oral vocabulary begins to grow rapidly even before age 2 are beyond the scope of our book, but are described well by de Villiers and de Villiers (1999). However, several features of oral language acquisition may be especially pertinent to understanding reading acquisition.

Growth of a child's phonological lexicon and semantic system is an active constructive process that draws on the child's exposure to words in the context of potentially matching perceptual experiences. Pre-readers learn words from oral language interactions with people around them. Joint adult-child book read-

ing is an effective context for oral vocabulary learning, even if a child is not yet using this experience to learn to read (de Villiers & de Villiers, 1999; Senechal, LeFevre, Thomas, & Daley, 1998).

As reading acquisition progresses, growth of the phonological and semantic lexicons eventually is enhanced by reading experience (Jenkins, Stein, & Wysocki, 1984; Fukkink & de Glopper, 1999) and no longer constrains the operation of the reading system so absolutely. A reader in the full-alphabetic phase might use the nonlexical route to pronounce a word that had not previously been in his or her phonological lexicon, then seek information from the text, prior knowledge, or other sources to identify or confirm its meaning and perhaps check its pronunciation. Most of us know from experience that failure to do the pronunciation check can be embarrassing when one's only contact with a word has been in print. For example, at an educational conference in San Diego, California, attendees from Australia repeatedly amused the more Spanish-savvy Americans present by giving a regularized English pronunciation of La Jolla (/la hoy-ya/), the name of a nearby town.

Ability to access phoneme units is different from phonological awareness. As we noted earlier in this chapter, the phoneme units that are part of both the reading and oral language systems represent implicit or procedural knowledge about language sounds that should be part of any normal native speaker's linguistic competence well before reading begins. The skills assessed on phonological awareness tests—identifying words that rhyme or begin with the same sound; isolating, counting, segmenting, blending, deleting, or transposing phonemes, onset or rime segments, or whole syllables—all require declarative or metacognitive awareness of oral language sounds. Even at the phoneme level, this awareness is something quite different from the knowledge in the phoneme units component of the DRC model. For example, the child who can say that "ball," "bike," and "button" all begin with the /b/ sound, or, at a more advanced level, that "slit" without the /l/ sound is "sit," is demonstrating knowledge about oral language sound patterns that is not intrinsic to reading.

We agree with the many researchers who have demonstrated that phonological awareness is associated with, facilitates, and probably is increased by experience in reading (e.g., Byrne, 1998; National Reading Panel, 2000b; Stahl & Murray, 1998; Torgesen & Burgess, 1998). Schatschneider, Francis, Foorman, Fletcher, and Mehta (1999) found that phonological awareness is a unidimensional construct for which the best measures change with development. We think of the acquisition of phonological awareness as beginning at an initial level, Level 1, that is indexed by ability to identify and produce rhymes and to segment words by syllables, separate initial sounds, or segment syllables into onset-rime segments (Stahl & Murray, 1998; Uhry & Ehri, 1999; Wagner, Torgesen, & Rashotte, 1999). More sophisticated, Level 2, phonological awareness often does not appear until a child already can read to some extent and involves representation of and operations on individual phonemes occurring at various positions in a word (e.g., Stahl & Murray, 1998; Wagner et al., 1999).

Our proposal is that both levels of phonological awareness are part of the context in which a reading system develops, but neither is part of the system itself.

An example of beginning reading may help show how we have drawn the boundary between the reading system and metacognitive operations that lie just outside it. Changing their notation to conform to the system we specified in chapter 1, we quote Whitehurst and Lonigan's suggestion (1998, p. 849) that

> a child just learning to read conventionally might approach the word *bats* by sounding out /bᵊ/ . . . /a/ . . . /tᵊ/ . . . /s/. Not infrequently, one can hear a beginning reader get that far and be stumped, even though the letters have been sounded out correctly. A teacher or parent might encourage the child to blend the sounds for each letter by saying the letter sounds more rapidly. Whereas adults would understand this phonological rendering, beginning readers can get this far and still not recognize that they are saying "bats." To them these are still four isolated sounds.

A child who can pronounce sounds for individual letters but not blend the sounds appears to have the same problem as the acquired phonological dyslexic patient described in chapter 4, who also could not blend phonemes. The third stage of the nonlexical route is not working properly. Both the child and the patient try to solve this problem by sounding out the isolated phonemes. These phonemes were created on line by the use of the reading system (nonlexical route thereof), but the overt sounds of the phonemes were not (e.g., the schwa that you would have to have with the /b/ is not coming from the GPC procedure). Therefore, this overt sounding out and attempt to create a syllable from the sounded-out phonemes is metacognitive and involves phoneme awareness. What prompts this behavior, which as a whole involves phoneme awareness, is a defect of the reading system; but the behavior itself does not solely reflect operations that all go on inside the reading system. The sounds metacognitively constructed and pronounced by this reader are *not* the sequence of phoneme units that would be generated from the phonological lexicon entry [BATS] or the phonological assembly of the nonlexical route. Therefore, there is no automatic way for the child to make the connection between the pronounced string of four sounds and "bats," and it is a considerable achievement. Indeed, "one frequently sees the look of pleasure or relief on the child's face at this resolution" (Whitehurst & Lonigan, 1998, p. 849).

This example could represent a beginning reader, an older child with developmental dyslexia, or, as we noted earlier, someone with a type of acquired phonological dyslexia discussed in chapter 4. That link interests us in itself. However, another reason we find Whitehurst and Lonigan's (1998) example interesting is that someone who is attempting to read a word by pronouncing letter sounds individually is doing something very close to what is required by one kind of phonemic awareness test, a phoneme blending test (e.g., Wagner et al., 1999). Therefore, this kind of reading behavior helps to define, at the operational level, the boundary between behaviors dependent on the reading system itself and those dependent on phonemic awareness.

How Does Phonological Awareness Develop?

By arguing that phonological awareness is something distinct from the reading system, we do not mean to dismiss its importance. Beginning in the preschool years, explicit instructional programs may focus a child's attention directly on sound patterns within words. Not surprisingly, such programs contribute to the development of the child's awareness of phoneme units within words (Bus & van IJzendoorn, 1999). Most children bring prior knowledge that words' sounds can be divided into syllables (and, within syllables, into initial and remaining sounds) to the task of learning to read. Preschoolers who have not acquired this understanding at home can be helped by brief instruction (Bus & van IJzendoorn, 1999; Byrne, 1998).

Full awareness of how words can be segmented into phoneme sequences may be a consequence of learning to read (Adams, 1990; Ehri, 1979), but this level of development also may be influenced by oral language exposure. Indeed, Metsala (Metsala & Walley, 1998) has suggested that the extent of a child's oral language exposure during the preschool and early school years may contribute to fundamental changes in how analytically words' sounds are represented in the child's phonological lexicon. "For example recognizing the word 'big' will require a more fine-grained representation for a child who also knows the words 'bag,' 'bug,' 'bib,' 'bit,' 'dig,' and 'wig,' than for a child who does not" (Metsala & Walley, 1998, p. 101). Our slant on this argument differs from Metsala and Walley's in that it emphasizes awareness rather than representations themselves, or perhaps declarative rather than procedural representations. However, we agree that knowing a lot of words should help draw a child's attention to the words' commonalities and differences.

For us, developing phonological awareness is a phenomenon that may interact with the development of the reading system (Stahl & Murray, 1998), but that occurs outside the boundaries of that system. As we have explained, even a 5-year-old with a very restricted oral English vocabulary should know all of its phonemes in the sense of being able to discriminate and produce them, albeit with some glitches possible in the pronunciation of difficult phonemes such as /j/. This knowledge is all that is essential to operation of the phoneme units component of the DRC model. However, children with larger vocabularies are likely to have had more opportunities to reflect on, and therefore to become aware of, subword phonological patterns. If this is so, oral language exposure and oral vocabulary size could influence a child's readiness to acquire the declarative, metacognitive phoneme knowledge that could facilitate (although it is not part of) use of the nonlexical route in our reading system.

Knowing the pronunciations of too few words also reduces the number of whole-word sound-spelling pairs a child knows, constraining operation of the lexical route. Furthermore, as we suggest in the subsequent section, this database reduction also might reduce the child's opportunities for inducing GPCs from whole-word spelling-sound matches.

How Do Components of the Lexical Route Develop?

We now move on into issues of reading system acquisition that are at the heart of our emerging theory. Our proposal about how the lexical route might develop is more radical, relative to dominant theories, than our proposal about development of the nonlexical route. Therefore, we consider this part of the system first.

Abstract letter units and the orthographic lexicon. Knowledge of abstract letter units is the gateway to both the lexical and the nonlexical routes of the reading system. Partial-alphabetic readers have a full complement of letter units for each position.

It is not surprising that the ability to name letters (the first stage of which task is the activation of the letter's representation in the abstract letter unit system) is one of the best predictors of children's subsequent success in reading acquisition (Adams, 1990; Ehri, 1999; Pressley, 1998). Most children in technologically advanced English-speaking countries know a lot about letters by the time they begin kindergarten (Adams, 1990). Children in print-filled homes have many opportunities to learn to identify letters and often begin to do so before they are 3 years old (Jackson & Roller, 1993). Letters as visual symbols and their names are taught explicitly in preschoolers' books, on educational television programs, in day care programs, and by parents who value literacy (Jackson & Roller, 1993; Pressley, 1998).

We already have argued that abstract letter units exist in the reading system as orthographic units without names or sounds attached. We also propose that children can begin to acquire an orthographic lexicon while, or soon after, acquiring a full complement of abstract letter units, even if they cannot yet identify individual letter sounds (Fletcher-Flinn & Thompson, 2000). As Thompson (1999, p. 27) has written,

> the child will learn that each letter has a range of variants, for example, that the letter *b* can appear as any one of many visual shapes, such as b, *b*, **b** and so forth. The child will also learn that each letter has upper-case forms that also have their variants, for example B, *B*, **B** and so forth. The child will soon learn that each of the 26 letters of our English alphabet does not have one particular visual shape but a range of various shapes. Hence the child learns that each of the 26 letters is an abstract category of variant shapes called an abstract letter unit (ALU). . . . As this occurs, the orthographic representation of a word gradually becomes a complete representation comprising ALUs, one for each letter position of the word.

In a previous section, we showed how partial-alphabetic readers may accept partial mismatches between the letter string they are trying to read and an existing entry in the orthographic lexicon. One consequence of this is that they will mistake words with similar letter strings for one another. However, children's texts often are constructed to help a child avoid such errors, and at least some

matches between letter units and the orthographic lexicon are likely to lead to correct pronunciations. In such cases, intrinsic or extrinsic reinforcement could reasonably be expected to strengthen the connection, thus more completely linking an entry in the child's orthographic lexicon to the letter units. We agree with Ehri (1992, 1999) that letter sounds can be very effective in the process of bonding a letter sequence with a word's pronunciation and meaning. However, we are not convinced that sounds are absolutely essential to this process.

An analogy with beginning reading of Chinese. Another way to think about how partial-alphabetic readers can build up their lexical routes is to consider a recent theory (Ke, 1996, as cited in Ke & Everson, 1999) of how Chinese children and foreign-language readers of Chinese learn to identify characters. Although there are some rough syllable-level correspondences between most characters' visual forms and their pronunciations (Jackson, Lu, & Ju, 1994), nothing like the nonlexical route is available to readers of Chinese characters. Nonetheless, young Chinese school children do learn to read hundreds of characters in each school year.

Most characters are composed of two distinct parts, and many, such as the character in Figure 5.2, have parts nested within parts. Some of these components can stand alone and be named when they occur in isolation, but others cannot. Even when a character component can be named in isolation, that name often has nothing to do with the pronunciation of the character as a whole (Perfetti & Tan, 1999). Indeed, characters' orthographic structures can be decomposed into individual strokes, of which there are 8 forms; into 31 slightly more complex basic stroke forms; and into still more complex component elements, which at their highest subcharacter composite level may suggest the character's pronunciation or meaning (Law, Ki, Chung, Ko & Lam, 1998).

The character in Figure 5.2 has meanings that include "invite" and "please" and is pronounced in a way that sounds like /ching/ to English speakers, with an intonation called the third tone. To someone who is not at all familiar with written Chinese, the character in Figure 5.2 seems like dense tangle of lines, and it

FIGURE 5.2. An example of a Chinese character whose orthography consists of several levels of component units.

may be almost impossible to recall. According to Ke (Ke & Everson, 1999), beginning American students of Chinese try to remember such characters much as pre-alphabetic readers encode English words, using idiosyncratic strategies such as in our example, "it has a box on the left and a table with a bent leg at the lower right." Like pre-alphabetic readers' attempts to read English words by noting that they contain features such as "two sticks," these primitive attempts are inefficient and unlikely to be accurate for distinguishing any substantial number of characters from one another.

According to Ke (Ke & Everson, 1999), Chinese children learning to read characters move rather quickly (and foreign-language readers more laboriously) into something like the lexical-route reading of the partial-alphabetic phase. They might recognize that a character such as the one in Figure 5.2 can be decomposed into a pattern of 15 strokes and 4 larger units (at each corner) that are written in a fairly standard sequence, much as English letters are strung from left to right. However, their mental representation of the character's orthography might be incomplete (Law et al., 1998). For the skilled reader, the components of this character most important for reading it are the whole left and right halves, which suggest its meaning and pronunciation. Each of these halves also could stand alone, as could the two bottom components.

Being able to identify these abstract patterns within characters, even though they may have no sounds (or no relevant sounds) associated with them, greatly facilitates further acquisition of a Chinese orthographic lexicon. Relying on these abstract orthographic patterns, the reader of Chinese who is operating at a skill level roughly comparable to that of Ehri's (1999) partial-alphabetic reader may acquire an orthographic lexicon without access to a nonlexical route.

When children learning Chinese are in kindergarten or first grade, they know enough about the orthographic structure of characters to be fairly accurate in identifying whether an unfamiliar character looks legitimate or if it is wrong because it has been presented as a mirror image or upside down (Lu, 1992). In kindergarten, measures of visual-spatial ability predict reading success better than measures of phonological awareness, which become more predictive during first grade (Ho & Bryant, 1997b).

Ho and Bryant (1997a) have described the character reading of Hong Kong kindergartners as logographic (i.e., as comparable to the reading of English by children in Ehri's (1999) pre-alphabetic stage). However, given that Hong Kong 5-year-old kindergartners are likely to have begun learning to read at age 3 or 4 and are expected to know more than 100 characters by the time they enter first grade (Law et al., 1998), what they are doing does not strike us as being like the arbitrary pattern finding of pre-alphabetic readers. These children are not likely to recall a character by a thumbprint presented with it. Rather, they seem to be doing lexical-route reading that draws on their knowledge of the multiple levels of lawful stroke patterns within characters.

The reason we have wandered off to consider how people learn to read Chinese is to emphasize by analogy that partial-alphabetic readers can make matches between letter units and the orthographic lexicon without relying on

letter sounds or letter names, or indeed anything phonological about letters. All they need to know is that different words are made up of different strings of the same finite set of orthographic symbols—letters—and, crucially, that the same letter can have alternative visual forms (as in capital and lowercase English letters or different Chinese scripts). Children reading English or Chinese can use these lawful, sequential patterns in their reading even though they cannot map them directly onto a sequence of sounds.

Print exposure and lexical-route development.　At a more distal level, a major influence on the growth of a child's orthographic lexicon and ability to use the lexical route efficiently to read many words is simple practice in reading, or exposure to print. For children learning to read English, estimates of print exposure are more strongly related to success in reading exception words than to success in reading pseudowords (e.g., Castles, Datta, Gayan, & Olson, 1999). These findings suggest that the most direct impact of whole-word reading experience is, as one would expect, on the lexical route.

Relying only on the lexical route to learn to read words almost certainly does not create the ideal context for rapid development of the reading system, but it can work and, as we shall show in chapters 6 and 7, sometimes does. Note that here again we are distinguishing between how a child reads a word, which falls within the purview of our partial-alphabetic reader's DRC system, and what each of those instantaneous experiences might contribute to how the reading system changes over minutes, days, months, or years.

How Do Components of the Nonlexical Route Develop?

Most children progress from pre-alphabetic to full-alphabetic reading within a few years (Ehri & McCormick, 1998) and, as we shall see in chapter 7, some do so in only a few months. Therefore, development of the nonlexical route during the partial-alphabetic stage must be fairly efficient for normal readers. In general, we agree with a variety of previous accounts of how this learning might occur (e.g., Ehri, 1999; Rack et al., 1994; Thompson, Fletcher-Finn, & Cottrell, 1999). However, here as in our discussion of development of the lexical route, we propose that evidence others have presented as bearing on how children learn to read better does not bear directly on how they are reading at any particular moment. This is the proximal-distal distinction we introduced in chapter 2, and it has enormous consequences for interpreting studies of beginning readers in which the phenomenon analyzed has been how children learn to read new words. Another way of looking at this distinction is to think of learning to read as dependent on the encoding in episodic memory of what is to be learned, while reading at a particular moment draws on nonepisodic (i.e., lexical) memory. Letter sounds may be more important in the former than in the latter.

In a series of short-term instructional experiments, Rack et al. (1994) have shown that 5-year-old children whose reading was in the partial-alphabetic stage learned to read new words more easily if the abbreviated novel spellings they

were presented, together with the words' pronunciations, corresponded closely to phonemes in the word than if they did not. For example, children learned to read *kvi* as /ko-fE/ more easily than they learned to read *ksi* as /ko-fE/. The contrasting sets of spellings were chosen to show that children gained a learning advantage at the level of a match between individual features of phonetic contrasts. For example, /v/ differs from the /f/ in /ko-fE/ only in terms of a voicing contrast, but /s/ differs from /f/ in multiple ways. Rack et al. (1994) concluded that their findings supported Ehri's theory (e.g., Ehri & Wilce, 1985) that partial-alphabetic readers read words by using directly mapped visual-phonetic connections of the kind we would call nonlexical. They further suggested that their data indicated that beginning readers are mapping letters onto phonemes rapidly, easily, and unconsciously.

Rack et al. (1994) bolstered their argument by showing, in another experiment, that children learned to read real spellings for what they called transparent words more quickly than they learned spellings for opaque words. Both sets of words were ones the children knew as oral vocabulary but could not read before the experiment began. The word sets were comparable in frequency and other relevant characteristics, but the transparent words had regular, more closely one-to-one letter-sound mappings. In contrast, opaque words included complex mappings such as a silent final *e*. Transparent words included *march* and *forest*. Opaque words were, roughly but not exactly, of the sort we could call exception words, such as *watch, biscuit*, and *giant*. Children learned the transparent words more easily. This sounds like the regularity advantage that, from our perspective, is one of the signs that a reader is using an effective nonlexical route. However, here as in the other Rack et al. experiments (and as in studies by Ehri & Wilce, 1985, and Scott & Ehri, 1990 that were less well controlled with regard to contrasting possible roles for abstract letter units vs. letter sounds), we make two distinctions that the investigators have not drawn.

First, we point out that all of these instructional experiments are, by definition, studies of how children learn to read new words, which puts us in the realm of what we have called distal cause and episodic memory. Yes, the children's learning indicates attention to letter sounds, which is not part of our account of lexical-route partial-alphabetic reading as depicted in Figure 5.1. However, their reading of a word at a particular moment may not depend on those sounds. Second, it appears to us that what the children are learning to do in these experiments is what might be called partial-phonemic, or partial-GPC reading. They are functioning at a level consistent with Ehri's (1999) description of partial-alphabetic readers, yet, in this experiment, they are doing something that is not typical of on-line reading in this phase of development.

Recall that word-substitution errors but not pseudoword errors, as shown in Figure 5.1, are characteristic of partial-alphabetic readers. If what partial-alphabetic readers do in everyday reading when they misread *mix* as /man/ involves use of the GPC *m* → /m/, why do they make this word-substitution error? Why do they not make errors that show some knowledge of the sounds of *i* or *x*? We acknowledge that the child's GPC knowledge may be position-specific and

incomplete, so that sound correspondences for *i* and *x* are not generated, but this becomes awkward if the child sometimes does read medial *i* correctly, perhaps when encountering it in *sit*. Could the explanation be that the child knows (i.e., has in his or her orthographic lexicon) the words MAN and SIT, but not MIX, and hence reads them but not *mix* correctly? This is an explanation in terms of lexical-route reading that does not fit with Rack et al.'s (1994) or Ehri's (1992, 1999) accounts.

But, let us try to account for a child reading *mix* as /man/ via the nonlexical route or Ehri's (1992, 1999) letter-sound mappings. Even if we concede that these mappings are so incomplete that the only phoneme that gets to the phonological lexicon from either *man* or *mix* is /m/, that phoneme must be present in many words in the child's phonological lexicon. A 5-year-old child can produce and understand many words beginning with the phoneme /m/ (even though this hypothetical child can only correctly read aloud one word beginning with the letter *m, man*). How does the child select, from the many words in his or her phonological lexicon that are activated, which one to say? Why is "man" always chosen?

In Rack et al.'s (1994) study this question does not come up because the three experiments involved teaching children a restricted vocabulary of new words by traditional paired-associate techniques. All of the words the children were taught to read already existed in their phonological lexicons, and the words in the set each child learned were different enough from one another that partial lexical-route mappings of the sort suggested in Figure 5.1 should have been sufficient for correct readings. But why did these children learn better with *kvi* rather than *ksi* for /Ko-fE/ or with *bzn* rather than with *bfn* for /bA-sin/? We suggest that this experimental finding has nothing to do with children's use of phonology on-line when they are trying to read the two items; it is because it has been easier to *learn* the relevant letter to orthographic lexicon connections for *bzn* → BZN → [BASIN] → /bA-sin/ than for *bfn* → BFN → [BASIN] → /bA-sin/. The children who participated in these studies were generally quite good at sounding out individual letters, which they had been taught to do in school. Therefore, many would have been able to sound out *z* → /z/ and *f* → /f/. As we indicated in chapter 3, the first of these processes contributes some activation to [BASIN] in the phonological lexicon via the nonlexical route, the second does not.

Recall that, in the DRC model as presented in chapter 3, activation cascades as best it can along both routes, even though one route's activity, facilitated or interfered with by what is happening on the other, will determine the word's pronunciation. The more activation there is in the relevant word's entry in the phonological lexicon via either route, the easier it will be to learn the relevant connections involving a printed letter string and that entry in the phonological lexicon. Therefore, as children learn a phonologically regular or transparent word, on each paired-associate trial they will be generating one or more letter, to letter sound, to phonological lexicon connections that will, across time, strengthen the lexical-route connections between those letters and the word

that includes them. But none of this suggests that the child who has learned to read *bzn* as /bAsin/ is performing this reading (as opposed to learning from a sequence of readings) task in a way that depends on GPCs.

Our account of the implications of Rack et al.'s (1994) data differs from theirs in ways that, to our knowledge, have not yet been tested empirically. Doing so will require research in which learning, over time, to read words not previously in a child's orthographic lexicon is distinguished from the child's readings of such words when they are presented initially. On a single presentation, do a child's errors (or correct pronunciations) require the use of letter-sound correspondences? A major claim following from our extension of the DRC model to partial-alphabetic reading is that it does not. Some data presented in chapters 6 and 7 support this claim.

Teaching Children to Use Dual Routes to Read

The more directly a skill is taught, the more likely it should be that children will learn it well, and the less likely it should be that the less able children in a group will fail to learn. "Distances" between taught skills and related ones that we want children to learn have been hard to conceptualize in a way that makes them measurable. Nonetheless, it is plausible to consider "synthetic phonics" or "code-based" instruction as targeted at the nonlexical route and, therefore, most likely to facilitate its development, relative to the nonlexical route. As we shall show in chapter 6, the instructional intervention literature provides abundant evidence that children who have been identified as at risk for reading failure and who have been taught by instructional programs directed explicitly to the nonlexical route generally do learn to read pseudowords exceptionally well. They also often become good readers overall, although other aspects of reading may show smaller or less persistent gains (Foorman, Francis, Fletcher, Schatschneider, & Mehta, 1998; Manis et al., 1996; Olson, Wise, Ring, & Johnson, 1997, Thompson & Johnston, 2000; Torgesen et al., 1999). Furthermore, what we know about the consequences of different kinds of reading instruction suggests to us that many children fail when the correspondences of the nonlexical route are not taught to them explicitly (e.g., Foorman et al., 1998; Torgesen et al., 1999). Therefore, our remarks about how operation of the lexical route may contribute to development of the nonlexical route are not meant as a case for "whole language" as opposed to "phonics" instruction.

However, we do think it is important to acknowledge that partial-alphabetic readers whose nonlexical routes are still very rudimentary, and who probably are reading predominantly by the lexical route, may be able to use correspondences induced from this experience to help build up their knowledge of GPCs. Work by Thompson and his colleagues provides the best evidence for this (e.g., Thompson, 1999; Thompson et al., 1996; Thompson & Fletcher-Flinn, 1993).

As soon as partial-alphabetic readers have some familiarity with abstract letter units, and perhaps, but not necessarily, with their names or a few of their

sounds, all that might be absolutely required for further development of the nonlexical route is that children be exposed simultaneously to written words and their pronunciations. As Thompson and his colleagues have suggested (Thompson & Fletcher-Flinn, 1993; Thompson et al., 1996) these nonlexical-route connections (they use the term *sublexical relations*) may be induced from reading experience. The child reads words and is corrected as necessary, or looks at the corresponding print while an adult reads, and lexical-route connections are made. From these, at least some children can induce the relationships that create the nonlexical route. However, this route, as indexed by ability to read pseudowords, may be weaker in children who develop it from induction rather than direct instruction (Thompson & Johnston, 2000).

Thompson et al. (1996) have shown that children's ability to read novel two-grapheme pseudowords (i.e. to use rudimentary nonlexical processes) is influenced by whether the novel pseudoword preserves order patterns common in the child's reading experience. They found that *b* and *th* occurred only rarely as a word-final consonants in 5- and 6-year-old New Zealand children's school texts, although many words began with *b* and *th*. In contrast, *t* and *m* occurred fairly equally as first or last consonants in the texts. Children with this pattern of word-reading experience had much more difficulty reading aloud pseudowords such as *ib* or *ith* than *et* or *im*. There was no comparable disadvantage for *b* and *th* relative to the other graphemes when all were presented as initial sounds in pseudowords. What these data show is that the GPCs that are learned are, at least initially, position specific. So they learn: "*b* → /b/ at the beginnings of words." Furthermore, the data suggest that GPC information key to development of the nonlexical route can be induced, without formal analytic instruction, via the lexical route from letter patterns encountered in reading.

What we add to the Thompson group's account (e.g., Thompson, 1999) of children's ability to induce nonlexical patterns from whole-word orthographic-to-phonological correspondences comes from our explicit statement of the partial-alphabetic system as the dual-route system of Figure 5.1. It follows from this system architecture and their data that, across development, the two routes to reading may each help the other to develop, perhaps via a mechanism that is not part of our static model but that should be included in a dynamic one.

Once the nonlexical route has developed fairly well, perhaps late in the partial-alphabetic phase of reading acquisition, GPC use does provide readers of an alphabetic orthography with a key developmental mechanism for acquiring an orthographic lexicon (e.g., Ehri, 1992; Share & Stanovich, 1995b). When a child uses the nonlexical route to sound out a word that is unfamiliar in print but familiar in speech, that word may be added to the child's orthographic lexicon and become accessible by the lexical route after as few as two or three exposures (Share, 1999). Therefore, improvements in function of the lexical route can be rapid once the nonlexical route is functioning smoothly. Indeed, this "self-teaching" mechanism is the great advantage of an alphabetic orthography (Share & Stanovich, 1995b).

Learning to Spell and Learning to Read

Ehri (1997) has suggested that reading and spelling are "one and the same, almost" (p. 237). She has pointed out that reading a word involves noting that its spelling is or is not correct, and that spelling often involves reading what one has written and making changes if the pronunciation of that letter string is not the one intended. Furthermore, poor readers also are likely to be poor spellers. Thus, there is abundant evidence suggesting that, in the terms of the DRC model, acts of reading and spelling might draw on common orthographic and phonological lexicons and a common GPC conversion system. Ehri (1997) and Perfetti (1997) agreed that a lexicon should be common to the two processes, although they have not drawn our distinctions.

However, the two processes are not entirely the same. Spelling using standard English GPCs is harder than reading using the same correspondences, because about 40 phonemes map onto about 70 graphemes, allowing more opportunities for error when one goes from sound to spelling than when one does the reverse. Furthermore, a word often can be read correctly even from an incomplete mental representation of its graphemes, but spelling correctly requires complete representation. The contrast is striking in words containing schwa vowels. Reading /lett°ce/ or /lim°sine/ is easy, but these words are difficult to spell (Ehri, 1997). Therefore, it is not surprising that practice in reading is not always sufficient to enable children to learn to spell the words read (Ehri, 1997) and that good readers can be poor spellers, but very good spellers are rarely poor readers (Perfetti, 1997). As Perfetti has suggested, the few exceptions could be individuals for whom a pathway from the spoken word to the lexicon (we would specify a series of links to the orthographic lexicon) and production of letter units is intact, but the pathway that begins with the written word to that lexicon is damaged.

A question that interests us more is whether or how practice in spelling helps young children learn to read. Children of preschool and kindergarten age often use their rudimentary knowledge of letter names and sounds to generate idiosyncratic but phonetically plausible spellings such as *gnys* for "genius" or *jl* for "jail." They sometimes are able to read what they have written, but sometimes are not (Bissex, 1980). Ehri, (1992, 1999) has argued that generating spontaneous spellings requires, and therefore draws, children's attention to the letter-sound correspondences that she has proposed are central to partial-alphabetic reading. We agree with her that such attention may help children learn to read, but we are not convinced that the literature on spontaneous spelling is relevant to how partial-alphabetic readers read words at any particular moment. Here again, we are distinguishing between proximal (reading system) and distal causes of current reading performance differences.

SUMMARY AND A LOOK AHEAD

In summary, we are espousing a view of beginning reading and reading acquisition in which most children very early begin to use a reading system like that

depicted in Figure 5.1. This system is structured generally like the skilled reading system in Figure 3.10, but it will be enhanced as the child gradually acquires more complete system components and more efficient connections among them. As so often is the case in cognitive development, improvements in multiple components facilitate improvements in others, with no clear precedence. We take this to be a mainstream and balanced view, although others have not spelled it out exactly as we have.

The sketch of beginning reading that we have presented was intended to create a context for linking the literature on acquired dyslexia with the accounts of developmental dyslexia and precocious reading that follow in chapters 6 and 7. For such links to be made between proximal causes of reading failure in skilled readers, and failure or unusual success in developing readers, we needed some way of comparing skilled and beginning reading systems. We have argued that these are sufficiently similar for principled comparisons of proximal causes of acquired and developmental reading failure to be possible. The reading system of partial-alphabetic readers is complete in its general form, its orthographic lexicon is tiny, mappings to that lexicon from the abstract letter units are incomplete, and the nonlexical route functions only in a rudimentary way.

As we shall show in chapter 6, many children with developmental dyslexia seem to operate from a system whose overall structure yields performances like those Ehri (1999) describes as typical of partial-alphabetic readers. To us, the connection is easier to make if one separates reading acquisition from current performance. However, even after one does this, the parallel might not be exact. The sketch of normal beginning reading that we have presented has ignored individual differences by indicating patterns based on data averaged across many children. This suggests more uniformity in the developing status of the nonlexical and lexical routes to reading than is likely to be the case when one's goal becomes accounting for the performance of individual poor readers.

When we introduced the dual-route theory in chapter 3, the two components of the reading system on which we focused were the lexical and nonlexical routes for reading aloud. But, it is important to reiterate that these components are both composed from smaller processing components.

Each of these smaller components needs to be learned, and so each might be a temporary locus of difficulty for beginning readers in general and a more enduring source of problems for some developmental dyslexics. For example, efficient reading by the lexical route might involve (a) visual feature analysis, then (b) letter recognition, then (c) access to an orthographic lexicon, then (d) access to a phonological lexicon, then (e) activation of appropriate phonemes (Coltheart, Curtis, Atkins, & Heller, 1993; Coltheart et al., 2001) And, efficient reading by the nonlexical route might involve (a) visual feature analysis, then (b) letter recognition, then (c) parsing the letter string into graphemes, then (d) application of grapheme-phoneme rules, then (e) activation of appropriate phonemes (Coltheart, 1985). There will be individual differences between children in how well each particular component of each of the two routes of the reading system is being learned.

Some children with developmental dyslexia, like readers with acquired

dyslexia, could show poor performance on tasks requiring operation of the nonlexical route because of weaknesses at any point along the way. Moreover, others may have a poorly developed lexical system, which also may be dysfunctional for a number of different reasons. Finally, we shall show in chapter 6 that many poor readers seem to have reading systems in which both routes function poorly.

In the latter part of this chapter, we engaged in extended speculation about the process of reading acquisition. We shall extend this speculation in our consideration of poor and precocious readers in chapters 6 and 7. However, our most important reason for sketching our own theory of reading acquisition was to mark off this area of inquiry as distinct from a theory of how a beginner's reading system operates at any particular moment. This distinction is critical because parallels among different types of atypical reading are likely to be closer if one sticks to the level of this reading system, the proximal cause of current performance.

6
Reading Acquisition Difficulties

A s we turn our attention to children who have had difficulty learning to read, we focus first on those issues that share three properties. These are issues that have been prominent in the study of poor reading in children (e.g., Share & Stanovich, 1995b), can be considered from the perspective of dual-route theory, and have parallels in the literature on proximal causes of acquired dyslexia presented in chapter 4. Later in this chapter, we review more distal causes of reading acquisition failure and speculate about how the process of reading acquisition might go awry.

UNSUCCESSFUL BEGINNERS' READING SYSTEMS

What range of specific reading problems characterizes children who are having difficulty learning to read or adults who have never succeeded at this task? This is a general question about the description and proximal causes of developing readers' failures. More specifically, what do the reading skills of poor readers look like? Are patterns of failure homogeneous, suggesting that all poor readers have reading systems containing the same kind of flaw, perhaps to a greater or lesser degree? Alternatively, are there subtypes of reading acquisition failure that are analogous to the surface and phonological subtypes, or syndromes, of acquired dyslexia? Or can we move beyond a syndrome approach, as we did in our discussion of acquired dyslexia, to identify many different ways in which struggling beginning readers might fail to be successful at reading, for example, pseudowords (the phonological dyslexic syndrome) or exception words (the surface dyslexic syndrome)?

In extending dual-route theory to consider beginning reading and its failures, we do need to pay careful attention to the differences between a once-typical system that has been damaged and a developing system that never has

functioned in a typical way. Nonetheless, when we consider causes of individual differences in reading performance at the proximal level, we can, with some confidence, draw connections between people having difficulty learning to read and people with acquired dyslexia.

Drawing connections between acquired dyslexia and reading acquisition failure demands that we keep clearly in mind the distinction between proximal and distal causes of reading failure. Indeed, we shall conclude in chapter 8 that theorists who have dismissed the literature on acquired dyslexia (and, often, cognitive neuropsychology) as irrelevant to understanding poor reading in children have failed to make this distinction. Acquired and developmental dyslexia obviously differ with respect to distal cause, but that does not mean they cannot share proximal causes.

Distal Causes of Reading Acquisition Failure

A second set of questions about the causes of children's reading acquisition failures goes beyond proximal cause (and dual-route theory) to considerations of distal cause. As we noted in chapter 2, distal causes of reading failure can be biological or environmental, or they can be cognitive causes that influence reading performance indirectly via their impact on the reading system. Furthermore, any cause that operates over time is a distal cause. Therefore, when we ask what it means for the further development of a child's reading if the immature system is defective, we are asking about distal cause.

We briefly summarize what is known about the cognitive, environmental, and biological distal causes of poor reading that are most relevant to our dual-route perspective on beginning reading and its acquisition. We cover the environmental literature, in particular, less thoroughly than is typical in comprehensive reviews of poor reading in children (e.g., Adams, 1990; National Reading Panel, 2000a, b; Pressley, 1998; Snow, Burns, & Griffin, 1998). However, we do consider how analyses of distal causes of poor reading might lead us toward a dynamic model of reading acquisition failure.

Before we present our analyses of proximal and distal causes of poor reading, we need to deal with a critical issue. Exactly what population are we describing in this chapter about reading acquisition difficulties? In chapter 4, we distinguished between acquired and developmental dyslexia and focused on the former condition. Therefore, it might seem reasonable to devote this chapter to developmental dyslexia. However, that term is not synonymous with reading acquisition failure. Many people who have failed to learn to read, or who have struggled through the process with great difficulty, do not meet the exclusionary criteria used to define developmental dyslexia. Because the composition of the population of readers considered is central to our arguments about both proximal and distal causes of reading acquisition failure, we next consider how this group should be defined.

DEFINITION OF THE POPULATION OF POOR READERS

Research about children having difficulty learning to read has focused on a group with no clear boundaries and, indeed, no universally accepted name. We refer to this broad population as poor readers. Furthermore, because most of the studies we review have involved children and adolescents, poor readers can be interpreted as shorthand for "children and adolescents who have had difficulty learning to read English and do so poorly." Difficulty in translating individual words (or pseudowords) from print to speech is central to difficulty in reading English (e.g., National Reading Panel, 2000a; Perfetti, 1985; Share & Stanovich, 1995b). Therefore, poor reading of words and pseudowords, which defines reading in the sense we are using it throughout this book, also implies poor comprehension of text, which defines reading in much of the applied educational literature.

The population of poor readers has been defined differently by different psychological and educational communities and by different investigators. Many studies have involved only a subgroup of poor readers, children selected for intraindividual discrepancies between their weakness in reading performance and their comparative strength in other aspects of their cognitive development. The children typically are described as having developmental dyslexia or a specific reading disability. These terms are synonyms, although the first tends to be used more often in medical-psychological contexts and the latter in educational settings, especially in the United States. When not constrained by our sources' usage, we use *developmental dyslexia* (or simply *dyslexia*) in this chapter because, of the two terms, it is less awkward to pair with *acquired dyslexia*. In using this term, we make no assumption that the primary cause of the observed reading failure was organic or intrinsic to the child.

Other investigators have studied the larger population of children defined as poor readers by virtue of their reading performance alone. For such children, the only discrepancy in skills is across individuals—between the child's own reading performance and that of some other group of children similar in age and instructional history. Poor readers are, in most studies that use this term, children who earn reading test scores in the lowest ranges relative to age or grade norms. Exact cutoffs vary across studies (e.g., Fletcher et al., 1994; Foorman, Francis, Fletcher, & Lynn, 1996; Stanovich & Siegel, 1994). We use the term *poor readers* when referring specifically to studies of this broader population or when we draw general conclusions about reading acquisition failure.

We agree with those who have proposed that defining poor reading without reference to intraindividual performance discrepancies generally provides a better base for describing patterns of poor readers' skills. However, like so much else in the study of reading, the question of how to define the population of poor readers raises issues of how to deal with questions of proximal and distal cause.

Arguments For and Against Discrepancy Definitions

Assumptions that propose exclusionary criteria based on certain distal causes have been central to intraindividual discrepancy definitions of poor readers. Children identified as having developmental dyslexia traditionally have been those showing subnormal achievement in reading despite (a) normal intelligence, (b) normal access to instruction, and (c) the absence of known sensory or neurological impairment. In a review of definitions of learning disabilities (including reading disability) proposed since the early 1960s, Hammill (1990, p. 77) advocated a 1988 definition that describes these disorders as conditions that are "intrinsic to the individual, presumed to be due to central nervous system dysfunction, and [that] may occur across the lifespan." This focus on using distal causes as exclusionary criteria sets up a definition of reading disability that makes no reference to the nature of the child's reading system itself—to what we have called proximal cause. Therefore, we would expect this definition to be problematic, and it has been.

Despite the tradition of treating children with special difficulty in learning to read as a population distinct from the broader population sometimes called "garden variety" poor readers (Stanovich, Nathan, & Zolman, 1988), an increasing number of researchers have challenged the scientific and educational utility of this distinction (e.g., Coltheart & Jackson, 1997; Foorman et al., 1996; Francis, Shaywitz, Steubing, Shaywitz, & Fletcher, 1996; Share & Stanovich, 1995b; Torgesen, 1989). We agree that thus far it has been more of an impediment than an aid to understanding. Because discrepancy definitions do not address issues of proximal cause, it is not surprising that children selected by exclusionary criteria and those identified simply as poor readers sometimes seem to have indistinguishable reading systems. However, we also acknowledge that children's individual cognitive profiles may be relevant for designing appropriate intervention programs (e.g., Berninger et al., 1999; Vellutino et al., 1996; Wise, Ring, & Olson, 1999).

In the review that follows, we consider both studies of children selected for a specific reading disability and studies of the broader group of poor readers. The putative distinction between these two populations remains central to our concerns only in that it highlights a problem we introduced in chapter 2. A reliable description of the prevalence of various reading skill pattern deficiencies would be a logical starting point for considering proximal and distal causes of reading acquisition failure. Deficiency patterns would be expected to vary across eras and places in which different reading instructional programs have been used (e.g., Thompson & Johnston, 2000), so some degree of uncertainty is inevitable. However, the nature of the population of poor readers also seems to vary depending on how that population has been defined and sampled. Variation in the sex ratio within samples of poor readers can be used as a marker for this phenomenon.

The research community has not yet agreed on even so straightforward a question as the extent to which poor readers are more likely to be boys than

girls. Sex ratios vary widely from sample to sample, at least in part because of variations in the methods by which the children are identified, the demographics of the larger population from which they are drawn, and whether dyslexia or garden-variety reading failure is being described (Flynn & Rahbar, 1994; Morris et al., 1998; Stevenson, 1992). Thus, one set of investigators may draw a sample of children with developmental dyslexia who are all boys and contrast their performance with that of boys who are readers of average ability (e.g., Castles & Coltheart, 1993). Another study, designed to address a similar theoretical question, might include samples of poor and average readers in which boys and girls are about equal in number (e.g., Catts et al., 1999; Stanovich, Siegel, & Gottardo, 1997). With this much uncertainty about an obvious demographic characteristic of poor readers, we must view with caution any conclusion that a particular performance pattern characterizes "most" or "only a few" poor readers, particularly when a rare pattern is dismissed as unimportant theoretically because of its apparent low prevalence.

What Comparison Group?

Definitions of poor readers and strategies for sampling from the defined population are not the only choices that influence how that population is described. Poor readers' skills are described relative to some group of more able readers. The nature of the comparison group is central to considering how well a dual-route approach characterizes the skill patterns of poor readers.

Traditionally, some researchers studying poor reading have chosen a comparison group from more able readers of the same chronological age and grade level, in what is known as a CA match (e.g., Castles & Coltheart, 1993). Others have compared poor readers to younger, more able readers matched with them on some aspect of current reading level, an RL match (e.g., Rack et al., 1992). Some studies have included both comparisons (e.g., Stanovich et al., 1997). As you proceed through this chapter, you will see why we devoted so much of chapter 2 to discussion of the complexities involved in implementing and interpreting CA and RL matches.

The RL-match design has been central to descriptions of poor reading in children because it permits comparison of poor readers with younger children, some aspect of whose reading has been developing at an average rate. Descriptive statements about special performance characteristics of poor readers depict reading as (a) an even, overall lag in development of all aspects of reading; as (b) lagged development in which there is a discrepancy, unevenness, or differential deficit in performance of different reading tasks relative to the profile of the comparison group; or as (c) deviant development. We reserve the last for instances in which a poor reader's performance has shown features never seen in better readers at any age or stage of reading acquisition. Because such a pattern is virtually unknown, the question becomes one of whether a lag or discrepancy description fits the data more closely. As we use these descriptions, any of these patterns, even a developmental lag, may be consistent with a per-

manent reading deficit (see Francis et al., 1996, for a more restrictive use of this term).

In attempting to understand poor reading in children, we are trying to hit a moving target. Reading acquisition is dynamic, and reading acquisition failure means failure to keep up with age- and grade-mates. Those who study acquired dyslexia are accustomed to a more stable baseline. Perhaps this is one reason why developmentalists and cognitive neuropsychologists may have difficulty finding a common language for discussing reading failure. We have worked through these differences in our own collaboration. Although the two of us together represent the developmental and cognitive neuropsychological perspectives, we agree that questions about developmental change fall within the realm of distal cause and should be kept distinct from proximal cause explanations of reading performance.

DESCRIPTION AND PROXIMAL CAUSES OF POOR READING

Choosing the best description of poor readers' skills is critical to understanding the phenomenon. As we noted in chapter 2, a description of skill patterns sets limits on what kind of deficit of the reading system can be assumed to be the proximal cause of a child's poor reading. Characterization of that proximal cause, in turn, may suggest possibilities for remediation. Studies of children with dyslexia, and of poor readers in general, have been moving toward a consensus description, but that consensus is not complete, and we are among those who deviate from the current majority view in some fundamental ways.

In this section, we blend an account of descriptions of poor reading with the investigators' and our own interpretations of those performance patterns at the level of proximal cause. As we indicated in chapter 2, reading tasks have been chosen, and have taken their meaning, from explicit or implicit models of proximal cause. Therefore, linking our discussions of these two levels is convenient. We have tried to defer discussion of distal causes of poor reading to a subsequent section of this chapter, but we have not been able to do so completely. The investigators whose work we are describing have so often entangled proximal and distal cause arguments with one another that we find ourselves compelled to do some disentangling here.

Nonlexical-Route Deficit

Many researchers have come to agree on a discrepancy description of poor readers, both dyslexic and garden variety, as a group whose most common and prominent weakness manifests as a deficit in pseudoword reading (e.g., Foorman et al, 1996; Manis et al., 1996; Stanovich et al., 1997; Rack et al., 1992; Torgesen et al., 1999). Moving to the proximal cause level, we would describe these chil-

dren as having a deficit at some point along the nonlexical route in their reading system. By analogy to the patterns of acquired phonological dyslexia described in chapter 4, we would expect developmental phonological dyslexics to have difficulty parsing letter strings into graphemes, matching graphemes with phonemes, blending a string of phonemes together, or all of the above. Indeed, these difficulties are seen in children who are poor readers (e.g., Whitehurst & Lonigan, 1998). Other authors (Share & Stanovich, 1995b) have described poor pseudoword reading as part of a problem they call a phonological core deficit. This term suggests a broader deficit that incorporates what we would call proximal causes (i.e., current competence of the nonlexical route) and distal causes (current and perhaps past oral language skills). Deficits in oral language knowledge and skills have been studied as concurrent (e.g., Metsala, 1999) and prior (e.g., Bus & van IJzendoorn, 1999; Byrne, 1998; Catts et al., 1999) correlates or determinants of poor reading, and we will consider them later in this chapter as potential distal causes (and outcomes) of reading acquisition failure.

Whatever specific cognitive model of the reading system is invoked to account for poor pseudoword reading, most researchers would agree that, when something is wrong with what we call the child's nonlexical route, he or she may never catch up with more able beginning readers (Byrne, Freebody, & Gates, 1992; Francis et al., 1996). Children who are poor at using grapheme-phoneme correspondences (GPCs) are likely to remain poor at pseudoword reading even if they eventually acquire adequate skill in reading real words (Bruck, 1998; Manis et al., 1996). Furthermore, poor readers often lag behind even younger RL-matched groups on measures of pseudoword reading and related tasks (e.g., Rack et al., 1992).

Do Some Poor Readers Have a Lexical-Route Rather Than a Nonlexical-Route Deficit?

Since the 1970s, investigators have acknowledged that there are some poor readers whose most extreme word-level skill deficit, relative to CA-matched comparison groups, is in reading exception words rather than pseudowords (Baron, 1979; Boder, 1973; Coltheart, Byng, Masterson, Prior, & Riddoch, 1983). Poor exception-word readers also have been identified in three more recent studies that have been especially prominent in the literature (Castles & Coltheart, 1993; Manis et al., 1996; Stanovich et al., 1997). In these studies, all three sets of investigators used regression-outlier designs to define the limits of what levels of difference between pseudoword and exception-word reading could be considered normal. The study samples were drawn from different age ranges and from three different English-speaking countries (Australia, the United States, and Canada). Two of the studies involved poor readers who had been identified as dyslexic by discrepancy criteria and who had received special education services (Castles & Coltheart, 1993; Manis et al., 1996). The poor readers in the remaining study were younger, garden-variety poor readers—third graders whose accuracy in reading words aloud was below the 25th percentile on a standard

test (Stanovich et al., 1997). In all three studies, investigators first defined a group of poor readers and then used the regression-outlier technique to identify children within that group who were especially poor readers, relative to others of the same CA, at pseudoword reading, exception word reading, or both. The results of these screenings are summarized in Table 6.1.

One group of children, the poor pseudoword readers, could be called phonological dyslexics. These children showed, at least on one set of measures, the performance pattern widely acknowledged to be prototypical of poor readers. Another group, largest in the youngest sample (Stanovich et al., 1997), was poor at reading both pseudowords and exception words. Like the original investigators, we set these broadly deficient readers aside to focus on those with more specific patterns of strengths and weaknesses, and we have not listed them in Table 6.1. Of special interest here is a third group, poor exception-word readers who were relatively good at reading pseudowords, children whose skill pattern could be called surface dyslexia. At the proximal cause level, their performance pattern indicates a defect in what we have called the lexical route of their reading system

As indicated in Table 6.1, poor exception-word readers were identified relative to their CA peers in numbers roughly equal to children who were especially poor at pseudoword reading. One might think these data would be strong evidence for diversity in the skill patterns of poor readers similar to that found in cases of acquired dyslexia. However, some investigators have dismissed the existence of these poor exception-word, adequate pseudoword readers as saying nothing of great interest about proximal or distal causes of reading failure (Bryant & Impey, 1986; Manis et al., 1996; Stanovich et al., 1997).

Table 6.1. Phonological and surface dyslexic cases (as percentages of total poor readers) identified relative to CA and RL comparison groups in three studies

Study (N poor readers)	Phonological subtype[a]	Surface subtype[b]
CA comparison		
Castles & Coltheart (1993) (N = 53)	55	30
Manis et al. (1996) (N = 51)	33	29
Stanovich et al. (1997) (N = 68)	25	22
RL comparison		
Castles & Coltheart (1993) (N = 40);		
re-analysis by Stanovich et al. (1997)	38	5
Manis et al. (1996) (N = 51)	24	2
Stanovich et al. (1997) (N = 68)	25	1

Note. The percentages are for "soft" subtypes reported on the basis of pseudoword and exception-word reading only. In the Manis et al. (1996) and Stanovich et al. (1997) studies, percentages of individuals with a "hard" subtype designation, based on validation criteria beyond these classification tests, also were calculated and were smaller.
[a]Cases whose pseudoword reading was exceptionally poor relative to their exception-word reading, based on 90% or 95% confidence intervals for a chronological age (CA) or reading level (RL) control group.
[b]Cases whose exception-word reading was exceptionally poor relative to their pseudoword reading, based on 90% or 95% confidence intervals for a CA or RL control group.

As you can see in Table 6.1, the prevalence of exception-word reading deficits diminishes much more than the prevalence of pseudoword reading deficits when one switches from CA- to RL-match comparisons. In an RL match, instances of differential exception-word reading deficits tend to disappear. In other words, when matched on general word-reading level with younger children, older surface dyslexics no longer seem especially poor at exception-word reading. Instead, their overall word-reading performance pattern looks like that of younger average children. (Although we have shown only the data for exception word reading, something similar happens, in a CA- to RL-match shift, to deficits in performance on other measures thought to reflect lexical-route processing, such as the lexical choice task, in which the reader is asked which of two homophonous letter strings, such as *rane* and *rain*, is a real word.)

How should we think about children whose exception word reading is especially poor and whose pattern of reading skills is the same as that of average readers several years behind them in school? To such children and their parents and teachers, this delayed development surely is a serious problem. However, some investigators have interpreted it in ways that suggest that surface dyslexia is less fundamental than phonological dyslexia.

Because an exception-word reading deficit does not remain apparent in an RL match, some investigators have drawn inferences about its proximal causes that are different from their causal inferences about a pseudoword deficit (Manis et al., 1996; Stanovich et al., 1997). For example, Stanovich et al. (1997, p. 121) concluded that

> surface dyslexics defined by CA comparisons appear to be children with a type of reading disability that could be characterized as a developmental lag. The performance of surface dyslexics is in no way unusual, at least in comparison to other normal readers at the same level of overall ability. In contrast, phonological dyslexia defined by comparison with a CA control group seems to reflect true developmental deviance.

These investigators went on to conclude that surface dyslexia occurs as a result of the convergence of two causal factors, arising "from a milder form of phonological deficit than that of the phonological dyslexic, but one conjoined with exceptionally inadequate reading experience. . . . In our view, it is misleading to describe such children as having an aberrant 'lexical' but intact 'nonlexical' mechanism" (Stanovich et al. 1997, p. 123). Taking a somewhat different tack, Manis et al. (1996) suggested that surface dyslexia reflects the developmental consequence of a general resource limitation operating over time: "the surface dyslexic pattern derives from an underlying deficit that causes a general delay in the acquisition of reading skills" (p. 187). They admitted that such a global deficit could arise in many ways.

So, others have used the results of RL-match comparisons to qualify their interpretation of CA-match comparison. Because the same pattern does not show up in an RL match, a CA-match deficit in exception word reading has

been discounted; the data in the top half of Table 6.1 have been disregarded as evidence that poor readers might sometimes be characterized as having a lexical-route deficit rather than (or in addition to) a nonlexical-route deficit. According to Manis et al. (1996), Stanovich et al. (1997) and others, one deficit (pseudoword reading) is important, the other (exception-word reading) is artifactual. In order to evaluate this conclusion, we first need to consider whether these RL and CA matches have the same meanings for children identified with pseudoword and exception-word reading deficits. We agree with Stanovich et al. (1997) that they do not. However, we think that those who dismiss the importance of the surface dyslexia pattern observed in CA-match comparisons have overinterpreted their correlational data.

It seems to us that Stanovich, Manis, and others (e.g., Bryant & Impey, 1986) who have dismissed the developmental surface dyslexia performance pattern as unimportant for understanding the reading system, are raising distal cause issues where they do not belong. Therefore, we need to digress for a moment to the level of distal cause. Different reading subskills have different developmental trajectories across the time span of reading acquisition. As Ehri (1999), Stanovich et al. (1997), and many others (e.g., Byrne et al., 1992) have correctly noted, the early elementary school years are a time when most children rapidly master the basic GPCs that make pseudoword reading possible. In Ehri's (1999) terms, they become "full-alphabetic" readers. Mastery of all but the most common exception words (what we would call growth of the orthographic lexicon and use of the lexical route) is likely to develop more gradually. According to Stanovich, Manis, and their colleagues, this difference in developmental trajectories makes evaluating the different kinds of word reading skills of poor readers against much better readers of their own age fundamentally unfair. Of course, they have said, poor readers who are marginally able to use GPCs to pronounce pseudowords will fail to keep up with better readers of their own age on reading exception words. This is what one would expect if children have marginal mastery of GPCs. Only if one has built up very good knowledge of GPC patterns, is one likely to be able to deal with words that have unusual patterns. From this perspective, the cases that appear in CA matches as surface dyslexic are simply showing the reading skill pattern expected for their current point in reading development, and this pattern is not specific to being a poor reader. Hence, it usually disappears in an RL match, and, hence, it is of trivial interest.

At the descriptive, performance level, we quite agree with this argument, as far as it goes. Indeed, we shall show in chapter 7 that some young children who have learned to read at exceptionally rapid rates also show unevenness in their skill patterns like the discrepancies that define surface or phonological dyslexia. Our disagreement is with the argument that a word-reading performance pattern of relative strength in one area and weakness in another becomes irrelevant to understanding poor reading in children if the pattern is seen in both normally developing and poor readers. To make this inference is to go from an observed performance pattern to an observation about changes across

age (the realm of distal cause) and then to inferences about the current reading system (back to proximal cause).

We propose that an appropriate way to evaluate the data in Table 6.1 is to consider the CA- and RL-match comparisons as two alternative descriptions of poor readers' performance, each influenced by the characteristics of the measures used and by how children's skills change with age. These performance patterns could have a variety of distal explanations. Children's lexical-route mechanisms could be poorly developed because of lack of oral vocabulary (Metsala & Walley, 1998), limited exposure to print (Cunningham & Stanovich, 1997, 1998), a reading system with "too few computational resources" for adequate learning (Manis et al., 1996, p. 187; see also Harm & Seidenberg, 1999) to permit good learning of exception words, or for some other reason. The distal cause of a problem in reading exception words (or pseudowords) could be different in every child.

We prefer to take the full pattern of data in Table 6.1 as a reminder of the distinctness of pseudoword and exception-word reading skills, a distinctness we are quite happy to admit occurs in average readers (Coltheart & Leahy, 1992) and even precocious readers (Chapter 7) as well as among poor ones. Within this context, Stanovich et al.'s (1997) observation that pseudoword reading and exception word reading have different developmental trajectories) (i.e., that pseudoword reading accuracy approaches its asymptote at a much earlier age than exception-word reading) could be part of the evidence for rather than against a distinct lexical mechanism in the reading system.

From our perspective, the reason that surface dyslexia appears rarely in RL matches between older poor readers and younger average readers probably is that the younger average readers have had very little time to build up their orthographic lexicons. Therefore, a comparison of their exception word reading with that of older poor readers is not particularly meaningful. A general conclusion about these issues is that the final answer to the question of which account is better cannot come from the weak evidence available in either RL- or CA-match designs.

Other Proximal Causes of Reading Acquisition Failure

In chapter 2, we noted that proximal causes of reading failure include, in addition to defects within the reading system, cognitive deficits that lie outside that system but also contribute directly to poor reading performance. Such defects might be manifest in problems in attending to, comprehending, or remembering oral directions for a reading task. Children who are poor readers often have such problems (Catts et al., 1999; Swanson, Mink, & Bocian, 1999; Torgesen et al., 1999). However, they are beyond the scope of our discussion except as a reminder of the possibility that group and individual performance pattern differences that are attributed to functions of the reading system may arise from other sources. No study of organismic differences is ever fully experimental. Therefore, the conclusions about the reading systems of poor readers in which

we can have most confidence are those that are supported by replicated and triangulated research findings. Fortunately, the conclusions about nonlexical- and lexical-route failures that we have drawn in this section are indeed well grounded.

DISTAL CAUSES OF READING ACQUISITION FAILURE

In moving from discussion of proximal to discussion of distal cause, we also shift our focus from a static construct, poor reading, to a developmental one, reading acquisition failure. Distal causes of reading acquisition failure lie in several realms and span both conceptual and temporal distances. We could think of distal cognitive, environmental, and biological causes of reading failure as affecting the operation of a reading system at a particular moment, causing poor reading. For the most part, however, the literatures from which we have drawn this section have been developmental literatures and the constructs studied have been hypothesized, explicitly or implicitly, to influence the process of reading acquisition. Therefore, these causes are distal temporally as well as conceptually. We start with cognitive distal causes because these operate in the realm that is conceptually closest to the reading system. We then consider hypothesized environmental and, finally, biological causes of reading acquisition failure from which these cognitive distal causes, and defects in the reading system itself, might arise.

Cognitive Distal Causes of Reading Acquisition Failure

In this section, we review evidence for a range of cognitive mechanisms that have been proposed as sources of children's failure to develop a normal reading system.

A nonlexical-route deficit that prevents self-teaching. In our discussion of proximal causes of poor reading in children, we already have noted that many poor readers show patterns of word and pseudoword reading that most prominently indicate a poorly functioning nonlexical route. Such children may have managed somehow to build up a vocabulary of familiar words that they can read by the lexical route, but their overall reading ability is poorer than that of their classmates.

Problems with the nonlexical route may be especially important for developing readers because of their impact on learning. According to Share and Stanovich's (1995a, b) self-teaching hypothesis, children who are not able to read words seen in print for the first time by assembling their pronunciations using GPCs have no efficient means to learn such words independently. This should be the case even for words which the child has often heard before and would recognize if spoken rather than presented in print. Any ordinary English text encountered by a child in the middle elementary or later grades is likely to

contain a great many words that have never been seen before (even though often heard before) and that cannot be predicted from their sentence context. Therefore, children whose nonlexical route functions poorly are likely to fall far behind their classmates in overall reading ability as early as the third grade. A large body of correlational data supports this conclusion (e.g., Byrne et al., 1992; Share & Stanovich, 1995). In our terms, the self-teaching hypothesis is an example of how a proximal cause of poor reading at a particular time, a poorly developed nonlexical route, also can be a distal cause of poor reading in the future. In its latter role, poor nonlexical route functioning interferes with the development of the lexical route, whose accumulated deficiencies, in turn, become a second proximal cause of poor reading performance later on.

Failure of nonlexical self-teaching to support lexical route development. Although a reading system with a defect in the nonlexical route is common among poor readers, some seem to have more trouble reading exception words that can be read only by the lexical route than they do reading pseudowords (Table 6.1). What do these findings imply about the process of reading acquisition?

Apparently some poor readers are able to use the nonlexical route to read unfamiliar words but do not make the links required to build up the lexical route from this experience. They may have difficulty adding an orthographic string whose pronunciation they have identified to their orthographic lexicon. Poor readers seem to require more exposures to a word before its reading becomes lexicalized (Ehri & Saltmarsh, 1995). Moreover, as we argue in our discussion of environmental causes of reading failure, poor readers are likely to get even fewer exposures to printed words than the average readers who need less input.

In discussing proximal causes of poor reading, we mentioned that some theorists have argued that a pattern of poor reading performance in which exception-word reading is more impaired than pseudoword reading is not a separate phenomenon. According to these theorists, poor exception word reading is a consequence of a child's nonlexical route not being quite good enough to support the timely acquisition of an orthographic lexicon of exception words. This argument assumes that exception words can be read and learned via the same route as regular words and pseudowords, but with greater difficulty (Harm & Seidenberg, 1999; Manis et al., 1996; Stanovich et al., 1997). Although this argument is admirable for its parsimony, we find it inconsistent with dual-route theories of reading (chapter 3), evidence from cases of acquired dyslexia (chapter 4), and the whole body of data about distal causes of poor reading in children that we are beginning to summarize here. Each of these bodies of evidence suggests that reading acquisition failure cannot be reduced to a single cause.

Both of the above. Although reading failure may take different forms and have different causes, it also may be overdetermined. Many poor readers are

rather evenly poor at a wide range of reading tasks, including pseudoword and exception-word reading (Castles & Coltheart, 1993; Harm & Seidenberg, 1999; Manis et al., 1996; Stanovich et al., 1997). This is hardly surprising. In chapter 4, we explained the scarcity of cases with pure forms of any particular type of acquired dyslexia by observing that brain damage affecting one part of the reading system is likely to be sufficiently widespread to also damage other system components. This argument should hold even more strongly for cases of poor reading in children. One of the most regular patterns in all fields of child development is the tendency of adverse biological and environmental influences to co-occur. Some of these may have the greatest impact on nonlexical-route development, others on lexical-route development. Also, as we suggested in chapter 5, a deficit in operation of either route may have a long-term impact on development of the other.

However, we do acknowledge that failure to master GPCs may be an especially important piece of what keeps a child with multiple impairments from developing adequate reading skills. An effectively functioning nonlexical route is an excellent tool for a developing reader to have. We show later in this chapter that development of components of the nonlexical route may be tied to oral language development in multiple ways. Therefore, development of this route may be especially vulnerable to those organic, home environment, and instructional conditions that also could interfere with other aspects of reading acquisition, and poor readers who are relatively good GPC users should be rare, as they have been in RL comparisons (Manis et al., 1996; Stanovich et al., 1997). A secular trend emerging in the United States in which beginning reading programs emphasizing "whole language" are being supplanted by those emphasizing "phonics" may change that pattern to some degree (National Reading Panel, 2000a: Torgesen et al., 1999).

A deficit in processes that permit rapid automatized naming. An increasing number of researchers agree that some poor readers may have a second deficit in addition to, or instead of, weakness in GPC use. This group of researchers has operationalized that second deficit in terms of children's performance on tasks that do not involve reading words, but seem to reflect cognitive processes that also are involved in reading acquisition (e.g., Catts et al., 1999; Manis, Seidenberg, & Doi, 1999; Wolf & Bowers, 1999). Hence, we treat this hypothesized processing deficit as a distal cause of reading acquisition failure.

Some poor readers respond slowly, relative to average readers their age, on tasks requiring rapid, presumably automatized, naming (RAN) of familiar visual stimuli such as letters, digits, and, sometimes, familiar pictures or colors. Letter- and digit-naming speeds generally are stronger correlates of reading and are the preferred measures, but picture- or color-naming tasks sometimes are used with children who are not expected to be familiar with letter or number names (Catts et al., 1999; Wagner et al., 1999; Wolf & Bowers, 1999).

Some researchers (Kail & Hall, 1994; Torgesen & Burgess, 1998; Wagner et al., 1994) have treated RAN as a measure of a broadly defined phonological

processing construct, which suggests that RAN performance might be linked to nonlexical-route development. However, others have suggested that RAN performance reflects a relatively broad set of cognitive processes whose integration and execution may have diverse effects on reading acquisition (Catts et al., 1999; Wolf & Bowers, 1999). In one study of an epidemiologically representative sample of good and poor readers, poor RAN (of familiar animal pictures by kindergartners) was more extreme in garden-variety poor readers with low full-scale IQs than in poor readers with normal IQs (Catts et al., 1999). The data suggest to us, as they have to some other researchers, that RAN performance reflects cognitive processes that are most strongly involved in development of the lexical route (Wolf & Bowers, 1999).

RAN deficits are somewhat independent of deficits in pseudoword reading, are more closely linked with problems in exception-word reading accuracy and general word-reading speed and text comprehension speed (Wolf & Bowers, 1999), contribute independently to later success in reading (Catts et al., 1999; Manis, Seidenberg, & Doi, 1999; Scarborough, 1998), and may remain when pseudoword reading deficits have been reduced by instruction (Breznitz, 1987; McBride-Chang & Manis, 1996; Morris et al., 1998; Vellutino et al., 1996; Wolf & Bowers, 1999). Manis et al. (1999) linked poor RAN performance with the surface dyslexia pattern of relatively poor exception-word reading.

Descriptions of these secondary or alternative performance deficits are just beginning to be drawn together theoretically. We speculate, as have others (Manis et al., 1999; Wolf & Bowers, 1999) that the deficits poor readers show in RAN task performance may reflect deficits in processes on which the growth of the orthographic lexicon also depends. However, descriptions of other things children with slow RAN speeds do poorly are just beginning to be drawn together by reading system explanations.

Manis et al. (1999, p. 137) have written that, in the dual-route model they prefer, "degrading the orthographic input has a larger effect on exception words than regular words or nonwords." Similarly, Wolf and Bowers (1999) have proposed that inefficiency in the processes that underlie RAN performance makes it difficult for children to build up appropriately sequenced mental connections between graphemes and phonemes, such that "deficits in processes underlying naming speed impede lower level perceptual requirements that, in turn, prevent increases in fluency in word identification" (p. 430). What the development of the lexical route and the development of rapidity in letter, number, color, or picture naming all have in common may be a learning mechanism that children use when learning associations between arbitrary visual symbols (letters, digits, printed words, pictures) and their names. A child in whom this particular learning mechanism is not very good will be slow at acquiring the lexical route and also slow at acquiring an efficient symbol or picture naming route.

A deficit in the phonological lexicon. The intimate involvement of language in reading is evident in statements like this one from Perfetti (1985): "the essential processes of reading are essentially mental operations on linguistic

structures that begin with visual input" (p. 5). Similarly, Harris and Coltheart (1986, p. 9) wrote that, "psychological models of language processing have to be able to explain how spoken *and* written language is processed." Recognizing the sounds of spoken words is not the same as recognizing the visual forms of printed ones, but much of what we do when we read is tied to the knowledge we have about the oral language we encounter in print. As we noted previously, finding the boundary between the reading and the oral language system, if indeed there is one, is not easy.

For many years, poor reading in children has been recognized as a phenomenon linked closely with deficiencies in oral language knowledge and processes (e.g., Catts et al., 1999; Perfetti, 1985; Vellutino, 1977). We focus here on specific aspects of oral language competence that have been linked with concurrent word-reading performance.

As we saw in chapters 3 and 4, knowledge of written words is part of the reading system itself. However, this knowledge is derived in part from what a person knows about word sounds and meanings in the realm of oral language. Readers will have more difficulty pronouncing, and are not likely to know the meaning of, a written word that is not part of their oral vocabulary. The extent to which oral vocabulary deficits are characteristic of poor readers depends on whether one considers those who are identified as dyslexic or the larger, garden-variety group.

By definition, dyslexic children have general cognitive performance levels, and sometimes verbal IQs, substantially higher than their reading levels. Therefore, a child with dyslexia is likely to have a phonological lexicon far larger than his or her orthographic lexicon This is true of normal younger readers, too. However, on the average, poor readers tend to have less knowledge of word pronunciations and meanings than good readers have. Many poor readers have broad deficits in both receptive and expressive oral language in addition to, or instead of, a phonological processing deficit (Catts et al., 1999). In the later elementary school years, as good readers begin to add many words to their lexicons and gain familiarity with complex grammatical structures from their reading experience, this gap widens.

At any given moment, a child's oral language knowledge influences and may set limits on the operation of the reading system. As we noted in chapter 5, the semantic system and phonological lexicon of Figure 3.10 are components of the reading system that are present in a child's language system even before the child begins to learn to read. However, for some children, these system components may not include the words and meanings needed for learning to read. Eventually, a deficit in either of these parts of the language system may become a proximal cause of poor reading for such a child.

A deficit in phonological awareness.   One of the most robust findings in the literature on poor reading in children is that both those identified as dyslexic and the broader group of poor readers are likely to perform poorly on tests of ability to identify, classify, segment, combine, and manipulate sound seg-

ments within words. The correlational literature (e.g., Torgesen & Burgess, 1998) shows stable, substantial relationships between performance on tests of phonological awareness and pseudoword reading ability. As we observed in chapter 5, findings that these relationships are stronger than those between phonological awareness and ability to read exception words support the argument that phonological awareness contributes to and is enhanced by development of the nonlexical route. Indeed, both correlational and experimental data suggest that causal paths go both ways (Adams, 1990; Byrne, 1998; Stahl & Murray, 1998; Thompson et al., 1999).

Looking ahead to biological and environmental causes, we conclude that a child could have difficulty acquiring phonological awareness because of a genetically determined difficulty in processing sound patterns within words (Olson, Forsberg, & Wise, 1994; Scarborough, 1990), because he or she has not heard enough words to become aware of these segmental contrasts (Metsala & Walley, 1998), because he or she has not been directly taught to identify phonemes (Byrne, 1998; Bus & van IJzendoorn, 1999), or because he or she has not induced phoneme identities as an adjunct to developing a nonlexical route (Thompson et al., 1999).

A cognitive mechanism that compensates for a defective self-teaching mechanism? There is flexibility in how the two routes of the dual-route cascaded (DRC) model work together. For example, if items to be rapidly read aloud are predominantly exception words, readers can slow the use of the nonlexical route (which causes difficulties for exception-word reading), thus strategically favoring the lexical route (Rastle & Coltheart, 1999; Zevin & Balota, 2000). In other words, some opportunities for compensatory processing, in the weak sense of the term, exist proximally, within the reading system. However, there is no compensatory mechanism in the DRC model in the stronger sense of one route being able to do the other's job. Correct pseudoword reading cannot be achieved by the lexical route no matter how it is used, and correct exception-word reading cannot be achieved by the nonlexical route no matter how it is used. Words and pseudowords are simultaneously processed by both the nonlexical and lexical routes in a cascading fashion, and any item's pronunciation depends on the joint input from the two routes to a common phonemic output stage.

However, when we move to consideration of developmental, distal causes of different patterns of reading failure, it is possible to imagine that the repeated operation of each route influences the other in ways that might be called compensatory. Share and Stanovich (1995b) invoked compensatory processing during acquisition when they argued that self-teaching via reliance on the nonlexical route gives beginning readers an efficient mechanism for adding new words to their initially sparse orthographic lexicons, enabling children to learn to read thousands of new words each year.

A more controversial question is whether, during reading acquisition, greater-than-usual use of the lexical route can compensate for difficulties in

acquisition of the nonlexical route. In chapter 5, we suggested that it can, and that it does this routinely as normally progressing children are beginning to build up their nonlexical routes and induce an implicit understanding of GPCs from lexical knowledge of the spellings and pronunciations of whole words (Thompson et al., 1996, 1999).

However, the Thompson group's studies of normal beginning readers do not directly address the question of what, if any, compensatory development might occur over several years of reading instruction in children who never seem to develop a fully functional nonlexical route. Are they developing enough of an orthographic lexicon to get by using the lexical route? Share and Stanovich (1995b) argued that it is implausible to suggest that this could happen, given that English texts include many infrequently occurring and unpredictable words. Furthermore, several investigators have concluded that the lexical processing abilities of poor readers, even when better than expected from their GPC use, are nonetheless likely to be poor (e.g., Shankweiler et al., 1999), or even "abysmal" (Foorman et al., 1996, p. 650). Perhaps any compensation for a poor nonlexical mechanism is not likely to be very effective in reading acquisition.

However, some compensation does occur. For example, Greenberg, Ehri, and Perin (1997, p. 272) summarized Siegel's proposal that "in learning to read, disabled readers compensate for their weak phonological skills by relying more heavily on orthographic processes than normal readers in learning to read words. That is, they concentrate on remembering letter sequences apart from their phonological function, more so than normal readers do."

Breznitz's (1997) findings from a study of dyslexic Israeli children reading Hebrew are consistent with the idea that children with developmental phonological dyslexia do acquire some sort of compensatory lexical-route reading strategy. Her study of on-line reading addresses flexibility within the reading system. However, we cite it here in our discussion of distal causes of reading failure because it also suggests conditions that impede or facilitate poor readers' ability to use the lexical route for reading acquisition.

In a typical RL-match design, Breznitz (1997) compared 52 dyslexic children who, on the average, fit the profile for phonological dyslexia, with a group of younger normal readers matched with the dyslexic group on real-word reading. The children read a set of short text passages at their natural or an accelerated pace and with or without auditory masking (the melody of a well-known children's song). As one would expect, this auditory masking, presumed to interfere with use of the nonlexical route, impaired the ability of Israeli children who were normal readers to read Hebrew. However, it had the opposite effect on the children with dyslexia. "During fast-paced reading under auditory masking, dyslexic readers increased their comprehension scores and decreased their average number of decoding errors by approximately 23%" (p. 108). Breznitz concluded that compelling the dyslexic children to read slightly faster than they would normally do while suppressing phonological processing forced them to "shift the emphasis away from the slow phonological route to other, possibly compensating, routes of information processing during reading" (p. 111). In

the context of the DRC model, Breznitz's results suggest that reading conditions that further impair the operation of phonological dyslexics' already inefficient nonlexical route may induce them to make the kind of strategic shift between routes described by Rastle and Coltheart (1999) and Zevin and Balota (2000), and discussed in chapter 3.

In similar vein, Hendriks and Kolk (1997) studied the reading aloud of single words and of text by 20 Dutch dyslexic children under three conditions: Neutral (no particular emphasis on speed or accuracy), Speed (read aloud as quickly as possible, even if this causes errors), and Accuracy (read aloud as accurately as possible, even if this makes reading very slow). They focused on analysis of two types of reading responses. One type was "sounding-out responses" (S); whether right or wrong, the response was made by sounding out individual components of the letter string. The other type was "word substitutions" (W); the response was a real word different from but visually similar to the stimulus item. S errors could be construed as the kinds of errors that a developmental surface dyslexic would make. (One cannot look for regularization errors in Dutch because there are too few exception words.) W errors could be construed as the kinds of errors that a developmental phonological dyslexic would make.

In the Neutral condition, 7 of the 20 children (35%) made more than the average number of W errors and less than the average number of S errors; roughly, they might be classified as developmental phonological dyslexics. In this condition, 6 of the 20 children (30%) made less than the average number of W errors and more than the average number of S errors; roughly, they might be classified as developmental surface dyslexics. When the same children read the same material under the Speed condition, applying the same classification method led to 85% classified as phonological dyslexic and 15% classified as surface dyslexic. And, when the same children read the same material under the Accuracy condition, applying the same classification method led to 5% classified as phonological dyslexic and 55% classified as surface dyslexic.

We must acknowledge that we are making a huge leap here by our equation of "more W than S errors in Dutch" with phonological dyslexia, and "more S than W errors in Dutch" with surface dyslexia. But, if we are permitted this speculation, which has at least a certain face validity, it allows us to imagine a version in English of the experiment in Dutch. When children dyslexic in English are asked to emphasize accuracy, their nonword-reading performance improves; they become less phonologically dyslexic. When they are asked to emphasize speed, they make fewer regularization errors (i.e., their exception-word reading accuracy improves); they become less surface dyslexic. If that result were obtained, we would think very differently about these two forms of developmental dyslexia. They would be reflecting, not how well a child can use each of the reading routes, but how much the child elects to use each. If a child regularizes the word *yacht* under normal conditions but reads it correctly under speeded conditions, the regularization error cannot be explained as occurring because this word is absent from the child's orthographic lexicon. If a child

reads the nonword *saib* as /sed/ under normal conditions but reads it correctly under accuracy conditions, the lexicalization error cannot be explained as occurring because of a deficient GPC route.

Be that as it may, the results reported by Hendriks and Kolk (1997) are consistent with the conclusion of Breznitz (1997). Emphasizing speed, or using auditory masking, causes dyslexic children to increase their reliance on the lexical route, decrease their reliance on the nonlexical route, or both. Emphasizing accuracy causes the same dyslexic children to decrease their reliance on the lexical route, increase their reliance on the nonlexical route, or both.

A compensatory reliance on lexical processing skills for acquisition of reading may be part of a diverse package of cognitive distal causes of individual differences in reading acquisition success. It may be evident not only in children with nonlexical-route deficits, but also in children whose instruction has included little emphasis on GPCs, but who have had extensive exposure to print (e.g., Connelly, Johnston, & Thompson, 1999; Cunningham & Stanovich, 1997; Manis, 1997; Stanovich, West, & Cunningham, 1991).

In some intervention studies, children with reading disabilities have learned to read new words in both GPC-based and sight-word-based instructional programs without showing any evidence that they have mastered the generalizable principles of the GPC code (Lovett, Warren-Chaplin, Ransby, & Borden, 1990). Therefore, we suggest that mastery of GPCs is not absolutely necessary, just as it is not sufficient, for acquiring an orthographic lexicon. This argument about distal cause parallels, but is not derived from, our previous contention that a nonlexical route alone is not sufficient as a mechanism for reading all kinds of word. We make this argument about distal cause directly from the literature on poor reading in children. It is not dependent on our preferred model of the reading system.

The argument that "mastery" of GPCs is not necessary for successful reading acquisition opens up the question of what rudimentary level of knowledge or efficiency of nonlexical route functioning is sufficient for a child to learn to read. Recall that, in chapter 5, we proposed that the knowledge about letter names, letter sounds, and a few GPCs in salient positions that is characteristic of what Ehri (1999) has called the partial-alphabetic phase of reading should permit some very rudimentary functioning of a nonlexical route. How well does this route have to function for a child to learn to read? Is the threshold lower if the child has other cognitive strengths?

Perhaps readers whose lexicons grow fairly well even though they show little ability to read pseudowords are those whose inferences about GPCs are incomplete, implicit, or remain context bound (Thompson, 1999; Thompson & Johnston, 2000). In such readers, the task of reading pseudowords may underestimate ability to use the nonlexical route in normal text reading.

We do think that the evidence for cross-route compensatory processing in reading acquisition is strong enough to require some such mechanism. Others' arguments that any effects on reading acquisition of compensatory lexical-route processing must be minimal are circular when they are based on studies of poor

readers, as is often the case. If compensation had been effective, these children would not have been identified as poor readers. Konold, Juel, and MacKinnon (1999) have suggested that compensatory processing is more likely in children who have some cognitive strengths to compensate for weaknesses in the kinds of auditory processing that are associated with development of the nonlexical route.

Adult university students who are poor pseudoword readers but competent word readers do exist, although such highly effective compensators seem to be rare (e.g., Campbell & Butterworth, 1985; Holmes & Standish, 1996). In one study, undergraduates at an American public university were screened to identify poor pseudoword readers whose text comprehension was at levels as good or better than was typical for their classmates (Jackson & Doellinger, 2001).

None of the poor pseudoword readers in Jackson and Doellinger's (2001) study were completely unable to do this task, so they must have had at least some minimal degree of nonlexical-route functioning. However, their pseudoword reading performance ranged down to primary grade levels. Despite this apparent nonlexical-route defect, most of the effectively compensated poor pseudoword readers in this study had never been identified as dyslexic.

A single case illustrates this pattern of effective compensation for poor nonlexical route functioning at its extreme. The poorest decoder in Jackson and Doellinger's (2001) sample, who was a young man, had a mean score on three pseudoword tests more than 2 SDs below the mean for his peer group of 194 university sophomores and juniors. His estimated verbal intelligence was average. On real-word reading measures, his performance was erratic. He achieved an average level of accuracy in reading a list of real words from a standard test. Some of the words he read correctly were relatively uncommon, up to five syllables in length, or had exceptional spelling patterns. Therefore, it seems reasonable to consider him to be an adequate word reader. Indeed, we would have done so if all we had available had been his performance on a standard test of word-reading accuracy (Woodcock & Johnson, 1989). However, the young man's performance deteriorated dramatically when he was required to read a word list quickly or to read lists of extremely uncommon words. He may, like another successful college student who was a poor pseudoword reader (Campbell & Butterworth, 1985), have been able to read only those words that were in his oral vocabulary and, hence, in his phonological lexicon.

The student studied by Jackson and Doellinger (2001) also struggled with spelling. However, his text comprehension showed a high degree of compensatory processing at a superordinate level. His ACT Reading Composite score (American College Testing [ACT], 1997) was 26, slightly above the mean for his university classmates, as was his score on an individually administered text comprehension test. He perceived himself to be an average reader, but he indicated that he spent more time studying than his classmates.

Effective compensators like this young man may be rare, but a theory of reading acquisition that cannot account for them probably contains some fundamental flaw (Underwood, 1975). This is one reason why we find Share and Stanovich's (1995b) account of reading acquisition incomplete.

Environmental Causes of Reading Acquisition Failure

A diverse array of environmental factors has been found to be associated with reading acquisition failure. These include constructs that are conceptually remote from any cognitive model of reading acquisition, such as an insecure parent-child attachment pattern (Bus & van IJzendoorn, 1995). However, other constructs that are prominent in the literature reflect aspects of the child's oral language and reading experience and can be more directly related to reading acquisition.

We consider only four aspects of the literature that fit most clearly with our cognitive conceptualization of reading and its acquisition. These are the literatures that link reading acquisition failure to (a) aspects of children's oral language exposure, (b) their print exposure, (c) the nature of their instruction in phonological awareness, and (d) the nature of their beginning reading instruction. We consider each of these environmental causes rather briefly to extend our discussion of cognitive causes of reading acquisition failure.

Oral language exposure.   The garden-variety poor reader is a child whose poor progress in reading is consistent with his or her limited oral vocabulary and verbal knowledge. On the average, children whose parents rank low in socioeconomic status expose their children to many fewer words than middle-class parents do. For example, Hart and Risley (1995, as cited in Pressley, 1998) estimated that, across a period of 2½ years beginning in late infancy, a child in an American welfare family hears only one sixteenth as many utterances as a child in a professional family does.

As we suggested in chapter 5, limited exposure to oral language may influence the development of the reading system in several different ways. Recall Metsala and Walley's (1998) suggestion that having a large oral vocabulary increases the likelihood that children will become aware of phoneme contrasts. Taking another tack, some investigators have argued that more specialized kinds of home language experience have special relevance for preparing a child to learn to read. For example, Bryant and his colleagues (Goswami & Bryant, 1990) have proposed that experience in listening to nursery rhymes creates an awareness of rhyming patterns that should facilitate reading acquisition.

Instruction in phonological awareness.   There is strong evidence that children may fail to learn to read because their prior oral language experiences did not enable them to become aware of sound patterns within words. This evidence has come from experimental and quasi-experimental studies in which some aspect of phonological awareness was taught to preschoolers or children in the earliest years of schooling. Bus and van IJzendoorn (1999) conducted a meta-analysis of 34 such studies and concluded that phonological awareness can be taught to very young children, but that long-term effects of phonological awareness training on subsequent reading of real words are extremely modest.

One of the few preventive interventions, limited to phonological awareness training, to show generalized long-term effects has been Byrne and Field-

ing-Barnsley's "Sound Foundations" program (1995; Byrne, 1998). This program taught preschoolers the concept of phoneme identity by having them learn to identify pictures whose names contained seven consonant and two vowel sounds in initial or (for consonants) final position (Byrne, 1998). In general, phonological awareness training has been more effective when it has been extended to include the beginnings of GPC instruction by linking sounds with letters and their names (Stahl & Murray, 1998).

Type of beginning reading instruction.   Experimental intervention studies have shown that "code emphasis" early reading instruction, designed to create solid knowledge of GPCs, works well for many children in the primary grades. These programs seem to be especially beneficial for children who, because of their family backgrounds or oral language skills, are at greatest risk for reading failure (Lovett et al., 2000; Foorman et al., 1998; Pressley, 1998; Stahl & Miller, 1989; Torgesen et al., 1999). Unfortunately, a few children fail to learn GPCs even with intense and explicit instruction. Even more unfortunately, the benefits of code-based instruction often do not generalize to substantial gains in aspects of reading such as identification of exception words or effective reading comprehension (e.g., Foorman et al., 1997; Lovett et al., 2000; Torgesen et al., 1999). The general pattern in the results of these studies is that instruction in GPCs, often preceded or accompanied by phonological awareness instruction, has substantial effects on children's ability to read pseudowords; more moderate effects on their ability to read regular real words; and still less effect on exception-word reading and text comprehension. As Lovett and her colleagues (Lovett et al., 2000) have concluded,

> phonologically based approaches alone are not sufficient for achieving optimal remedial outcomes with reading disabled children. Although phonologically based and deficit-directed remedial approaches appear necessary to achieve gains, generalization of gains is more probable if a multidimensional approach to disabled readers' core reading-related deficits is adopted. . . . The importance of strategy instruction and the promotion of a flexible approach to word identification and text reading challenges cannot be overemphasized in our approach to remediating developmental reading disorders. (p. 281)

The performance of poor readers whose deficits have been partially remediated by intensive code-based instruction reminds us that it would be a mistake to consider a well-functioning nonlexical route sufficient for successful word reading. It also takes us back to our argument earlier in this chapter that the surface dyslexia pattern (Table 6.1) seen in some poor readers has theoretical and practical significance. A fundamental rule of education applies here. Children are most likely to learn those things to which the most instructional time and attention have been devoted. If acquiring a nonlexical route and acquiring a lexical route are distinct processes, as we think they are, perhaps instruction should be directed explicitly to both.

Exposure to print.   Most young children cannot avoid being exposed to print in the signs, labels, and other printed material cluttering their homes and neighborhoods. Some parents and day care providers draw children's attention to this environmental print; others do not. Many children also begin school with extended experience looking at print while listening to stories read by an adult; others do not. These experiences are associated with individual differences in beginning reading success, although the causal connection between home experiences and reading achievement in this predominantly correlational literature cannot be made unambiguously. The connection may be through vocabulary development, which seems to be directly affected by storybook exposure (Senechal et al., 1998). Furthermore, effect sizes for preschool book-reading experience have been modest at best (Pressley, 1998; Scarborough & Dobrich, 1994; Senechal et al., 1998).

As children begin to read independently, their exposure to printed letters and words increases, and those children whose knowledge of children's literature indicates that they have not read widely are less likely to become good readers (e.g., Cunningham & Stanovich, 1998). There may be a specific association of print exposure with growth of the child's ability to read words via the lexical route (Castles et al., 1999; Olson et al., 1994).

The kinds of texts that beginning readers are exposed to in school also may influence which reading route develops better. Hiebert (1998) and Brown (1998) have argued that children profit from a balanced diet of texts in which words have regular, consistent letter-sound patterns; texts in which words are high in frequency but often have exceptional spelling patterns; and texts in which contexts help children predict what a word will be.

Biological Causes of Reading Acquisition Failure

Genetic causes.   At least for some children, risk for reading failure may begin at the moment of conception. Reading ability, like many other aspects of children's behavior, is influenced by both genotype and environment. Poor reading runs in families, and that pattern is substantially attributable to genetic transmission. In behavioral genetics studies of a very large sample of identical and fraternal twins, Olson and his colleagues in Colorado have shown that, for poor readers as a whole, deficiencies in both nonlexical-route and lexical-route processing are somewhat independently linked to variation in genotype, although nonlexical-route processing seems to be more heritable (Olson, Datta, Gayan, & Defries, 1999). In contrast, these authors found that poor readers' deficits in processing speed were not significantly heritable.

Other analyses of data from the Colorado twin sample have shown that the heritability of poor reading depends on what definition of "poor reader" is being considered. Poor reading that fits the IQ discrepancy definition of developmental dyslexia is more heritable than garden-variety poor reading that occurs in conjunction with low IQ (Wadsworth, Olson, Pennington, & DeFries, 2000). As suggested by analyses of the heritabilities for specific reading subskills, the

distal causes of poor reading also vary according to whether children are classified as developmental phonological dyslexics or developmental surface dyslexics. Castles et al. (1999) found that, for phonological dyslexics, poor performance on a composite set of word-reading measures was determined most strongly by genetic variance, ($h^2g = .67$), but also was influenced significantly by shared environment ($c^2g = .27$). (The g in h^2g and c^2g indicates that the genetic and shared environmental influences being estimated are for deviant group membership.) Shared environment includes experiences common to both children in a pair of twins, such as access to books in the home.) For surface dyslexics, the importance of these two contributors was reversed, with shared environment dominating ($c^2g = .63$) and genetic variance contributing half as much to the prediction ($h^2g = .31$).

As these analyses suggest, genotype is not destiny. Relations between particular genetic or environmental distal causes of poor reading and particular reading system or other cognitive deficits remain the subject of continued research and debate. Performance deficiencies that can be traced to genetic causes are, in principle, just as remediable as those whose origins are wholly environmental.

The kind of environmental help a child needs might vary depending on the specific nature of his or her reading problem (Vellutino et al., 1996). If a girl fails to grow because she has had no food, we can help by feeding her. If another girl fails to grow because she has a genetically influenced condition such as Type I diabetes, food alone will not be enough, but the condition is still treatable. However, this medical metaphor might be misleading as a basis for linking specific types of reading interventions with types of reading failure. Whether the distal cause of a child's reading problem is genetic, environmental, or both may have nothing to do with the nature of the intervention needed. The proximal reading system cause of the child's problem and, perhaps, the child's other cognitive characteristics, may be a more appropriate basis for designing instruction (Berninger et al., 1999).

Whether distal causes are relevant to intervention or not, psychologists and educators are likely to become increasingly able to identify children at genetic risk for reading failure. Therefore, it is important to remember that attribution of a child's difficulties to "bad genes" is no excuse for an educational system that fails to teach a child to read.

Visual pathway abnormality. The visual system contains two specialized pathways, the magnocellular (M) pathway and the parvocellular (P) pathway. The M pathway is specialized for the processing of rapidly changing visual stimuli and for low spatial frequencies in the visual input, is relatively insensitive to color contrasts in the visual input, but responds well even when input luminance is low. Responses of cells in the M pathway are very brief (hence, this pathway is sometimes referred to as the transient pathway). The P pathway is specialized for processing high spatial frequencies in the visual input, is relatively poor at tracking rapid changes over time in the visual input, responds well

to color contrasts in the visual input, but is relatively insensitive when input luminance is low. Responses of cells in this pathway are relatively long lasting; hence, this pathway is sometimes referred to as the sustained pathway.

Many authors have reported an association between difficulties in learning to read and performance on psychophysical tasks which specifically assess the operation of the M system (see, e.g., Breitmeyer, 1992; Cornellison, Hansen, Hutton, Evangelinou, & Stein, 1998; Galaburda & Livingstone, 1993; Lovegrove, Martin, & Slaghuis, 1986). This is a correlational result, and hence one must be careful about drawing causal inferences from it; specifically, about concluding that an M pathway deficit is the distal cause of difficulty in learning to read in some children. Given just these data, it might be correct to conclude distal cause here, but the results might instead reflect a cause in the other direction: It is conceivable that extensive early reading experience causes improved functioning of the M pathway. There also may be no direct causal link, but some third variable that independently affects both the development of the M pathway and the development of reading skill.

If an M pathway deficit is indeed a distal cause of difficulty in learning to read in some children, why might this be so? That is, what is the proximal cause that is a consequence of the M pathway deficit? One possibility was proposed by Breitmeyer and Ganz (1976): The M pathway inhibits the operation of the P pathway as the eyes are moving from one fixation point to the next during reading, and that this is beneficial for reading since it prevents visual information from one fixation from interfering with visual information from the next fixation. However, this turned out not to be correct, because, as Burr, Holt, Johnstone, and Ross (1982) and Burr, Morrone, and Ross (1994) showed in psychophysical studies that the M system is inactive during eye movements.

However, four recent studies (Borsting et al. 1996; Cestnick & Coltheart, 1998; Spinelli et al., 1997; and Talcott et al., 1998) have all provided evidence, from both dyslexic children and from children who are normal readers, that the association between the M system and reading is an association specifically with the nonlexical reading route, there being no association between the M system and the lexical reading route. In good readers, exception-word reading ability is not associated with performance on tasks tapping the M system, whereas pseudoword reading ability does show such an association. Dyslexic children with surface dyslexia (impaired lexical-route reading) do not differ from normal readers on M system tests; and dyslexic children with phonological dyslexia (impaired nonlexical-route reading) do differ from normal readers on M system tests.

Other biological causes of reading failure.   Technology that would permit fine-grained studies of relations between brain function and reading behaviors in children did not become available until the late 1990s, and, as we write, has been used for only a few years to investigate developmental dyslexia. Therefore, despite our assertion in chapter 2 that the biological level should, in theory, be considered in any full model of the causes of individual differences in read-

ing performance, few conclusions about relations between brain function and cognitive function during reading can be drawn with confidence. However, important discoveries are beginning to be made in this area.

For example, Shaywitz and his colleagues (2000) carried out a functional magnetic resonance imaging (fMRI) study of developmentally dyslexic and control children, imaging their brains while they carried out various reading tasks and control tasks. They also studied correlations between their imaging results and the children's performance on word- and pseudoword reading tests. These data led the authors to link different areas of brain function with what we call the nonlexical and lexical processing routes: They used these neurobiologic data as a basis for proposing a developmental model of reading and of dyslexia. In their model, the temporoparietal circuit is associated with rule-based word recognition. This is the nonlexical route of the model of the reading system we depict in Figure 3.10. In turn, the occipitotemporal area constitutes a fast, memory-based word identification system, which is akin to the lexical route of the model of the reading system in Figure 3-10. A gratifying convergence thus appears to be developing between the theoretical ideas about the nature of the reading system that we expounded in chapter 3 and work on brain imaging and reading.

CONCLUSIONS AND QUESTIONS ABOUT READING ACQUISITION FAILURE

What We Can and Cannot Conclude About Proximal Causes of Poor Reading

In considering proximal causes of poor reading in children, we have argued that developmental dyslexia and other forms of poor reading in children and adults show a diversity that indicates multiple locations of breakdowns of a complex dual-route reading system. However, both our own conclusions from this literature and those we have disputed are based on a database that is limited in an important way. Neither we nor anyone else can be quite sure of the parameters of the performance problem we are trying to describe and explain.

The study of poor reading and reading acquisition failure is beginning to be informed by solid estimates of the current prevalence of particular patterns of performance in children making slow, average, and good progress in learning to read (e.g., Foorman et al., 1996; Stanovich & Seigel, 1994). However, such estimates must remain imprecise, because the prevalence of difficulty in using GPCs varies depending on factors such as what alphabetic language children are learning to read (Comeau, Cormier, Grandmaison, & Lacroix, 1999; Wimmer, 1995; Wolf, Pfeil, Lotz, & Biddle, 1994) and how they have been taught (e.g., Byrne & Fielding-Barnsley, 1995; Manis, 1997). Therefore, it may not be possible to generate any simple and enduring picture of the exact proportions of good and poor readers who have special difficulty with GPC use or other as-

pects of reading. Nonetheless, we believe that the literature on poor reading in children, especially when considered in conjunction with the literatures on acquired dyslexia and precocious reading, supports the fundamental argument of dual-route theory: A functional nonlexical route is neither sufficient nor necessary for real-word reading to be competent. This argument applies to beginning as well as skilled or once-skilled readers.

Beyond Subtyping of Poor Reading?

We have challenged the conclusion that poor reading can be described by a single type of proximal cause, some defect in what we call the nonlexical route and others have called phonological recoding or GPC use. Instead, we have suggested that children who are poor readers are best described as having reading systems with a variety of different defects—sometimes along the nonlexical route, but also sometimes in the lexical route or in abilities to use one route to assist development of the other. The available literature supports the usefulness of continuing to think of developmental dyslexia as a phenomenon characterized as having at least two subtypes, akin to phonological and surface dyslexia. The same can be said of poor reading in children, broadly conceived.

At present, the developmental literature does not permit us to go far beyond subtyping to a more fine-grained analysis of the many ways a developing reader may be poorly acquiring the reading system. However, the need to move beyond subtyping is clear. Poor readers' skill patterns tend to fall along a normal distribution, which suggests the operation of multiple causal factors (Olson et al., 1994). Furthermore, Berninger et al. (1999) and others who have taught children with developmental dyslexia have pointed out that individual differences in children's skill patterns and in what instructional approach works best for them become striking as soon as one gathers information from a broad range of tasks. As was the case in the examples of acquired dyslexia we presented in chapter 4, we should be able to identify a myriad of ways in which different children's reading systems have been imperfectly acquired.

It seems plausible that the model of the beginning reader's system that we proposed in chapter 5 (Figure 5.1) could be imperfectly acquired in diverse ways, with potentially distinct effects from imperfection at each locus. However, in a developing system, single deficits might be more likely to have broad implications than is the case when a previously intact system has been damaged. Thus, the theoretical and practical effectiveness of attempts to go beyond subtyping in understanding poor reading may be constrained.

Thinking about this approach to modeling an imperfectly acquired reading system in a particularist way requires us to take distal, developmental effects into account. Localized reading system dysfunctions may be easier to identify in children just beginning to show reading acquisition failure than in those whose problems have been compounded and obscured across several years of instruction.

Early identification of children likely to have difficulty learning to read is

one advantage of the behavior genetics research and of longitudinal studies of the predictive power of oral language deficits. Some poor readers apparently cannot be identified early (Catts et al., 1999), but studying those who can might tell us something about how different specific impairments in the just-forming reading system can be identified, remediated, and perhaps prevented.

Toward a Model of Reading Acquisition Failure?

We can be less sure of how the dual routes of Figure 5.1 might operate when transformed into a dynamic model of reading acquisition. Here, neither computer simulations nor observations of people with acquired dyslexia provide any data that are directly relevant. Although reading acquisition failure can be modeled in a computer simulation whose ability to learn by a back propagation mechanism has been impaired by changing system parameters (e.g., Harm & Seidenberg, 1999), this device is too artificial for us to have confidence in its relevance to real children's learning failures. Therefore, we prefer to propose a very preliminary model on the basis of the literature we have reviewed in this chapter.

Our conclusions about the process of reading acquisition failure have been drawn from a number of literatures. We have considered laboratory studies of children's concurrent performances on a variety of reading and nonreading tasks, classroom-based instructional interventions, behavior genetic analyses of twin data, and observations of localized brain activity during reading. In reasoning from this eclectic database, we are far from the relatively tidy deductions that supported the development of dual-route theory and its application to acquired dyslexia as presented in chapters 3 and 4. Nonetheless, we have come to some preliminary conclusions.

How can we become more specific about varieties of reading failure? To do this, we need to consider the developmental data on multiple varieties of reading acquisition failure, including the phonological core deficit emphasized by Share and Stanovich (1995a, b), the visual processing problems described earlier in this chapter, orthographic lexicon impairments with and without corresponding deficits in the phonological lexicon (Catts et al., 1999), and so on. Each of these deficit patterns should suggest a way in which a cooperative dual-route acquisition process could be impaired.

For example, the abstract letter unit component of the partial-alphabetic reading extension of the DRC model, as depicted in Figure 5.1, is the gateway to both the lexical and the nonlexical route. Therefore, either a visual impairment that interferes with perception of an ordered string of letter units or lack of exposure to the letters of the alphabet would be expected to have a general depressing effect on reading acquisition. Repeated failures of the reading system would lead to retarded development of the system. An entirely different specific problem also could have general effects. Difficulties in making GPC connections could also lead to general reading acquisition failure by reducing the speed with which a child acquires an orthographic lexicon via GPC-based

self-teaching. In another scenario, this time for more localized failure, a child who could use GPCs adequately to pronounce novel words might fail to encode the results of that process in a way that bonds the abstract letter-unit string with orthographic and phonological lexicon entries (Ehri & Saltmarsh, 1995). A luckier child might have difficulties in making GPC connections, but show little or no delay in acquisition of an orthographic lexicon if his or her acquisition of a complete set of letter-unit representations is on schedule, he or she has an adequate phonological lexicon, and he or she has been given extensive exposure to print.

Designing a simulation that will model varieties of the reading acquisition process without relying on the problematic mechanisms used by the Seidenberg group (e.g., Harm & Seidenberg, 1999) presents an interesting challenge. We expect that such modeling will be the next step in understanding reading acquisition failure.

7

Precocious Reading

*I*t is both parsimonious and plausible to assume that children's reading systems vary in a consistent way across the full continuum of ability. Therefore, we would expect that both performance level and proximal cause conclusions about differences between poor and average readers could be extended to contrasts between average and precocious readers. For example, if all poor readers are best characterized as having a core deficit in phonological processing (e.g., Share & Stanovich, 1995a, b) or, more narrowly, in ability to use the nonlexical route, then all precocious readers should have an advantage in such processing. However, the alternative dual-route conceptualization of poor reading we introduced in chapter 6 suggests a more complex image to be mirrored.

If poor readers are best characterized as a diverse group with a variety of specific processing deficits (e.g., Castles & Coltheart, 1993), then our expectations about precocious readers also should stress diversity. Individual precocious readers would be expected to have reading systems with different kinds of strengths. Some might be especially good at nonlexical processing and others at lexical processing. Whatever picture emerges of the patterns of precocious readers' observable skills and of the reading system characteristics likely to be the proximal causes of those patterns should be related in some lawful way to a description and proximal-level explanation of poor reading.

Parallels with regard to distal causes might be expected to be less close. After all, both environmental and biological causes of poor reading might operate according to a threshold level—a language-impoverished home environment, haphazard reading instruction, or the absence of certain alleles in a child's genotype might have adverse effects on reading acquisition that cannot be extrapolated to predict precocious reading. Nonetheless, the literature on precocious reading can be informative with regard to distal conditions that might result in exceptional reading. This is most likely to be so when one thinks of distal cause in terms of the timing of effects and of relations that lie within the cognitive level of our model but extend either beyond the reading system or across time. For example, if lack of timely exposure to explicit instruction in grapheme-phoneme correspondences (GPCs) is associated with higher rates of

reading failure, is early instruction in these correspondences predictive of precocious achievement? If spoken vocabulary growth is the basis of the development of phonological awareness (Metsala & Walley, 1998) and, hence, success in beginning reading, do precocious readers have exceptionally large oral vocabularies and perform well on tests of phonological awareness? Because the literature on precocious reading is less widely known than that on poor reading, we consider distal causes more fully here than we did in chapter 6.

Focusing on the upper end of the continuum of individual differences presents especially interesting opportunities to test hypotheses about conditions that are necessary for successful reading acquisition. For example, identifying even a single child who learns to read exceptionally early and well despite poor oral English skills proves that the language skills typical of 6-year-olds are not prerequisite for successful reading acquisition.

The literature on precocious reading addresses a number of issues that are not directly relevant to our current purpose of developing an intergrated model of individual differences in reading and reading acquisition. This broader literature has been reviewed elsewhere (Coltheart, 1979; Jackson, 1992; Jackson & Klein, 1997). We restrict our current review to studies that bear on questions related to word-level reading and spelling.

DEFINITION OF THE POPULATION

In any culture in which formal instruction in reading begins at a standard age, unusually early acquisition of oral word-reading skill defines the upper end of a rate-of-acquisition continuum bounded at its low end by poor readers. Children who have learned to read before the usual age of formal instruction sometimes have been called early readers (e.g., Durkin, 1966). However, this term also has been used more broadly to describe all children in the initial stages of reading acquisition. Therefore, we prefer the more precise term, *precocious readers*.

The literature on precocious readers includes studies of children who have acquired considerably advanced competence in both oral reading and text comprehension by the end of kindergarten or beginning of first grade (e.g., Durkin, 1966; Jackson et al., 1993). It also includes studies of younger children whose word-reading skills may be just beginning to emerge (Fletcher-Flinn & Thompson, 2000; Henderson, Jackson, & Mukamal, 1993; Jackson & Myers, 1982).

No age- or grade-referenced deviation standard exists beyond which a young child's advanced reading qualifies as precocious, and criteria have varied across studies and eras. However, researchers consistently have used standards that would identify only the top few percent of children surveyed at a particular age as precocious readers, and some have been more stringent (Jackson, 1992). In most recent studies, precocious readers are reading words with accuracy levels

typical of children in second grade or beyond when they have not yet entered first grade. At age 2, 3, or 4, children might be considered precocious readers by reading at the first grade level.

Unlike studies of children designated as having developmental dyslexia, studies of precocious readers have been inclusive with regard to the educational histories of the children studied. Children usually have not been excluded from large-sample studies because they have participated in intensive or advanced reading instruction, although such instruction has not been typical of the children considered (Jackson, Donaldson, & Cleland, 1988; Jackson et al., 1988, 1993; see Tobin & Pikulski, 1988 for an exception).

Precocity in reading is a healthy, useful accomplishment that is not freakishly rare among children learning to read English (Clark, 1976; Durkin, 1966; Jackson, 1992; Stainthorp & Hughes, 1998). Becoming literate to the extent of having solid word-reading skills before beginning first grade is not typical in the English-speaking countries in which precocious reading has been studied. However, this precocious behavior occurs often enough that many kindergarten teachers are able to identify at least one such child in their current classes, and studies have included samples of as many as 116 precocious readers (Jackson et al., 1993).

Like poor reading, precocious reading occurs in children whose cognitive characteristics range widely and vary according to the context in which they are identified, age at identification, and degree of atypicality specified. However, a survey of the literature suggests that the mean IQ of precocious readers, identified as such at about age 5 or 6, is about 130 (Backman, 1983; Jackson, 1992; Jackson et al., 1993), although it may be lower (Tobin & Pikulski, 1988). Precocious readers' academic achievement is likely to continue to be good throughout their elementary school years (Jackson & Kearney, 1999; Mills & Jackson, 1990; Tobin & Pikulski, 1988).

There is no clear evidence indicating that precocious reading is the particular turf of either boys or girls. Gender differences in numbers of precocious readers identified have been in different directions in different studies (Jackson, 1992), and some of the largest samples (Jackson et al., 1988, 1993) have included approximately equal numbers of boys and girls.

A Special Subgroup of Precocious Readers?

Precocious readers generally have not been divided by researchers or educators into subgroups designated as showing specific reading precocity or more general cognitive advancement. Therefore, studies of reading precocity directly complement studies of the broad group of poor readers. However, one subgroup of precocious readers sometimes has been identified as a distinct population, albeit with criteria varying from one source to another. These children could be characterized as having a specific reading ability that is discrepant from other aspects of their cognitive development.

Just as poor reading acquisition sometimes occurs in children of above-average intelligence, precocious ability to read words aloud sometimes appears spontaneously (i.e., without unusual formal instruction) in children whose verbal intelligence, oral language ability, and reading comprehension all are both below average and below the level expected from their word reading. This phenomenon is called *hyperlexia*. Others have used a more broadly inclusive definition of hyperlexia (e.g., Silberberg & Silberberg, 1967; Snowling & Frith, 1986). However, we prefer to use this label only to describe the reading of children whose cognitive or language development is in some way pathological and whose reading has developed precociously (Aaron, 1989; Healy, 1982; Sparks, 1995). The hyperlexic pattern of reading skills (Pennington, Johnson, & Welsh, 1987) should be considered unusual only in the context of poor oral language or general cognitive development.

Children whose word-reading skills are much more advanced than their oral language or text comprehension usually are developing in ways that are entirely healthy, and their uneven skill patterns may be temporary. We see no reason to call such children's reading hyperlexic. Indeed, advancement in word reading more extreme than advancement in text comprehension is not uncommon among precocious readers tested during their preschool or earliest elementary school years. For example, in one sample of 16 normal precocious readers who all had average or above-average Stanford-Binet IQs, the median Reading Recognition grade-equivalent score on the Peabody Individual Achievement Test (Dunn & Markwardt, 1970) was 4.75, but the median Reading Comprehension grade-equivalent score was 3.20 (Jackson, Krinsky, & Robinson, 1977). One preschooler typical of this sample had a Reading Recognition grade-equivalent score of 4.8 and a Reading Comprehension grade-equivalent score of 2.9.

Discrepancies like these between written word pronunciation and text comprehension scores tell us that a child who breaks the GPC code at an unusually early age can leap years ahead in word reading, even though he or she might not yet have gained the general linguistic knowledge required to comprehend text at the same advanced level. To call such children hyperlexic suggests that their skill patterns are peculiar, when they are quite common and plausible. Furthermore, experience soothing the panic-stricken parents of bright, normal children who have been labeled hyperlexic by clinicians has made one of us (Jackson) alert to the danger of using a label with pathological connotations when nothing about a child's development is poor relative to age expectations.

When a child's word reading is truly precocious by a chronological age (CA) standard despite cognitive and language development that would be characterized as retarded or autistic, that discrepancy seems solid enough to suggest a phenomenon that merits a special label and is worth evaluating for potential distinctiveness. Therefore, one of the questions we address in this chapter is whether there are differences in the observed reading performances of normal precocious readers and children who fit this narrow definition for hyperlexia. Could it be that here, as in the case of poor reading, the garden-variety precocious reader and the hyperlexic have more in common than not?

CONNECTING STUDIES OF PRECOCIOUS READING TO STUDIES OF ACQUIRED DYSLEXIA AND POOR READING

Studies of precocious reading have not been guided by explicit theories of either proximal or distal causes hypothesized to be unique to precocious reading. Instead, those who have studied both normal precocious reading and hyperlexia have considered these phenomena from the perspective of theories designed primarily to account for poor reading. Researchers working from cognitive-psychological perspectives have paid more attention to proximal than distal causes of precocious reading. Therefore, fitting the available data into a framework in which this distinction is emphasized could be particularly helpful in future studies of precocious readers.

Research Designs

Like the literature on acquired dyslexia, that on precocious reading contains a number of case studies, some of them sufficiently extensive and sophisticated to permit strong conclusions about the reading of the individual described (e.g., Fletcher-Flinn & Thompson, 2000). Unlike case studies of people with acquired dyslexia, studies of precocious readers often have extended over several years and have been concerned with describing how the individual's reading improves with age.

Most other studies of precocious reading have been correlational, and only a few of these have been longitudinal. Both CA and reading level (RL) matches have been made, depending on the variables of interest. Researchers interested in cognitive characteristics of precocious readers that fall outside the reading system, such as oral language skills, phonological awareness, or letter-naming speed have favored CA matches (Crain-Thoreson & Dale, 1992; Jackson & Myers, 1982; Singson & Mann, 1999; Stainthorp & Hughes, 1998). All of these skills can be tested in nonreaders. In contrast, researchers concerned with evaluating the extent to which precocious readers are advanced in skills that reflect the operation of reading system components and therefore are measurable only in children who can read have favored RL-match designs (e.g., Fletcher-Flinn & Thompson, 2000; Jackson et al., 1988, 1993).

Imagine a group of preschoolers identified as precocious readers because they can read at least some words on a list of real words that includes a mixture of regular and exception words, as is typical of the standard tests used for screening in these studies. Asking whether these precocious word readers surpass their nonreading preschool age-mates on other, more specialized tasks, such as reading pseudowords or exception words, would be a rather silly exercise. Of course, they would. The other preschoolers already have shown that they cannot read by either route, because they scored zero, or near zero, on the task of reading regular words. In cases like this, an RL match becomes more interesting than a CA match. It compares readers with readers (not apples with or-

anges) and asks the question of whether the precocious preschoolers are keeping up with, or perhaps even surpassing, older average-ability word readers on tests that assess use of the nonlexical or lexical route, or both.

However, there also are many cases in which using both a CA and an RL match might facilitate interpretation of precocious readers' performance. For example, it makes sense to ask whether precocious readers perform better than their nonreading preschool classmates and better or worse than RL matches on tests of phonological awareness or oral vocabulary knowledge. Studies in which both comparisons have been made directly have been rare (Backman, 1983). However, some CA-match or case study designs have approximated an RL match by comparing precocious readers' performances against standard test norms for older children (e.g. Fletcher-Flinn & Thompson, 2000; Henderson et al., 1993).

Whichever contrast has been used, investigators have explored the general question of whether performance discrepancies between precocious and average readers' reading systems are mirror images of those between average and poor readers (with precocious readers being especially strong in performance on tasks with which poor readers have most difficulty) or whether precocious readers show behavior patterns that are not predictable from theories of poor reading acquisition (e.g. Fletcher-Flinn & Thompson, 2000; Jackson et al., 1993; Stainthorp & Hughes, 1998).

Instructional experiments designed to create precocious reading ability have been done (see Coltheart, 1979; Jackson, 1992 for reviews), albeit not in ways that address theoretical issues of concern to us in this book. However, we do consider instructional experiments briefly as part of our exploration, toward the end of this chapter, of distal causes of precocious reading.

Questions About Precocious Reading

Like studies of poor reading in children, studies of precocious reading have dealt with a set of related questions about patterns and possible proximal and distal causes of exceptional development. These have taken the following forms.

Description.   How can the component reading skills of precocious readers be described? Are these readers, as a group, more or less advanced in some skills than in others? How consistent are these patterns? Are there diverse skill patterns among precocious readers? How are various reading skills related to one another among precocious readers?

Proximal cause.   What do precocious readers' skill patterns imply about the nature of their reading systems? Are these systems different from those of more typical readers? Are these children reading words and pseudowords in ways that suggest strength or weakness in the lexical or nonlexical route? Are some of their reading system components especially well developed? If the reading sys-

tems of precocious readers are unusual, are they all unusual in the same way? To our knowledge, no one has hypothesized the existence of distinct patterns of phonological and surface reading precocity that would complement descriptions of phonological and surface dyslexia. However, the possibility of a continuum of word-reading skill patterns has been of interest (e.g., Backman, 1983; Jackson et al., 1988, 1993).

Distal cause. As in the literature on poor reading, questions about distal causes of precocious reading can take many forms. The focus of our discussion of the distal causes of precocious reading will be at the cognitive level, both within and across time. How are cognitive structures or processes that lie outside the reading system, such as those that underlie performance on phonological awareness and rapid automatized naming (RAN) tasks, related to a precocious reader's current and future performance? How do the reading systems of precocious readers change over time, and what can we conclude, even if in a preliminary way, about the mechanisms of such change? Do these proposed mechanisms of change match those we have hypothesized to account for typical or poor reading acquisition?

Family characteristics and home experience correlates of precocious reading have been reviewed elsewhere (Coltheart, 1979; Jackson, 1992). We present only those aspects of this literature that bear on our task of linking the literatures on precocious reading to studies of acquired and developmental dyslexia.

We know of no neuropsychological or behavior genetic studies of normal or hyperlexic precocious readers, so questions of biological causes of these conditions cannot be answered at this time.

DESCRIPTION AND PROXIMAL CAUSES OF PRECOCIOUS READING

In preceding chapters, we have raised the issue of whether individual differences in English word reading can be described in an essentially unidimensional way and explained at the proximal level by a reading system in which there is one mechanism for word reading. In any account of poor reading in children in which failure to master GPCs is the fundamental cause of failure (e.g., Ehri, 1999; Manis et al., 1996; Share & Stanovich, 1995b), a reader who has not failed, but who is successful enough to read a substantial vocabulary of real words quickly and accurately, is expected to have reached Ehri's full-alphabetic stage. Any full-alphabetic reader should, therefore, have basically the same kind of reading system, one that includes a well-developed nonlexical route. Extrapolating this conceptualization to precocious readers suggests that these exceptionally successful beginners all should have an especially well-developed nonlexical route.

*Word and Pseudoword Reading: Evidence for Nonlexical-
and Lexical-Route Functioning in Precocious Reading*

Beginning readers use GPCs to sound out new words, often overtly and laboriously. According to variants of the phonological core deficit hypothesis, more skilled readers have established complete sets of bonds between grapheme and phoneme strings that permit fluent reading of familiar words with both regular and exceptional spelling patterns (e.g., Ehri, 1999). Therefore, according to this hypothesis, every intermediate or skilled reader should have a reading system that contains what we call a nonlexical mechanism for matching grapheme and phoneme units. Because we believe that separate mechanisms are responsible for correct pronunciations of pseudowords and exception words, and that both mechanisms contribute to pronunciation of regular words, we focus on how well precocious readers pronounce pseudowords and exception words. This is one way to analyze whether their reading skills are what one would predict from alternative models of beginning reading.

The word and pseudoword reading of precocious readers can be described and explained at the proximal level with reference to two kinds of analyses: (a) RL comparisons of their mean performance levels with those of less precocious, older readers; and (b) correlational analyses of the extent to which precocious readers' word-reading (especially exception words) and pseudoword reading abilities vary independently. Comparisons of mean performance levels are informative, but studies of variation among precocious readers are more critical to testing hypotheses about whether they all have the same kind of reading system.

Mean performance levels of normal precocious readers. Findings regarding the reading subskill profiles of precocious readers have not yielded a single pattern of strengths or weaknesses that distinguishes these children from those progressing at a slower rate. Like average readers, precocious readers who have progressed beyond the earliest stages of reading acquisition generally can read pseudowords as well as older, RL matched readers. Therefore, precocious readers, on the average, seem to have a functioning nonlexical route in their reading systems.

Two case studies have suggested that at least some precocious readers progress with amazing rapidity from performance that suggests the partially formed nonlexical route of Ehri's (1999) partial-alphabetic stage to performance indicating a well-developed nonlexical route. According to his mother, precocious reader Max (no relation to Coltheart) began to sound out unfamiliar words at about age 2 1/2 years (Henderson et al., 1993). One of us (Jackson) observed Max at age 2 years 7 months hesitantly but successfully pronouncing the unfamiliar name *Pam Bullard* on a desk nameplate. Max was not given any tests of pseudoword reading ability, but another very young precocious reader was tested.

When tested on a list of real words at 28 months, Maxine (Fletcher-Flinn & Thompson, 2000) sometimes refused to read unfamiliar words, but her be-

ginning sensitivity to within-word patterns of the sort we locate on the lexical route (Figure 5.1) was evident. Except for the refusals, all her errors involved substituting one real word for another, graphemically similar one. For example, she pronounced *my* as /mE/. Between 32 and 37 months of age, Maxine's performance on several tasks suggested rapid development of the nonlexical route in her reading system. She became less likely to refuse to attempt unfamiliar words, and her pronunciation errors were more likely to be nonwords with GPCs close to those of the real word she was reading. For example, at 35 months, she read *nurse* as /nOrs/ and *shelves* as /shOOvs/. During this same period, Maxine was given formal tests of pseudoword reading. The number of pseudowords she read correctly increased dramatically between 33 and 37 months and was, at both ages, far superior to the norm for middle-class New Zealand 7-year-olds making typical progress. At 40 months, Maxine's reading of a list of one-syllable pseudowords was almost perfect and comparable in accuracy to the performance of adults in another study. Moreover, she read these pseudowords faster than adults had. Therefore, Maxine demonstrated that she had a fully functional nonlexical route well before she reached her fourth birthday.

Maxine's lexical route also was well developed at age 40 months. At this age, her reading was 100% accurate for phonologically irregular one-syllable words with both relatively consistent (e.g., *blind*) and inconsistent (e.g., *done*) spelling patterns in their rime units. These scores compared favorably with those for third graders. At the same age, Maxine was highly accurate, performing at about the same level as 8-year-olds, on an orthographic choice task that also reflects lexical-route use.

Not all precocious readers have pseudoword or word reading skills as advanced as Maxine's, but they typically do perform at advanced levels on such tasks. In her study of 24 precocious readers selected from among beginning kindergartners, Backman (1983) found that the group's mean Woodcock Reading Mastery Test Word Attack (pseudoword) reading score was at grade level 2.61, which was consistent with their word-reading level. The precocious readers' pseudoword reading level was a bit less advanced than that of a group of older readers matched on word-reading level. However, this relative disadvantage was not statistically significant and would be expected by regression toward the mean.

These single case and small *N* results are consistent with those of a much more comprehensive study. By the time they have completed kindergarten and are reading at or above the second-grade level, precocious readers typically are well able to read all kinds of words, including exception words and unfamiliar pseudowords (Jackson et al., 1988, 1993). Differences in word frequency and regularity affect precocious readers' pronunciations in the same ways as they affect those of RL-matched second graders (Jackson & Donaldson, 1989b).

Jackson et al. (1993) directly compared 116 precocious readers and 123 second graders' performances on a broad array of reading tasks. The RL match between these samples was done in a somewhat unusual way. Precocious readers were tested first, and second-semester second graders then were selected as

an approximate RL matching group. The second graders whose parents were willing to have them participate in the study tended to be above-average readers. However, because of the investigators' desire to maximize external validity (Jackson & Butterfield, 1989), the pool of second-grade volunteers was not culled to create an apparent exact match on any measure. Without any forced matching, the second graders were closest to the precocious readers in their reading levels on a standard test of text comprehension and generally less advanced than the precocious group in their performances on various measures of word reading. More precise matching was accomplished by statistical adjustments.

On the average, the 116 precocious readers in Jackson et al.'s (1993) study were strong in their performances across a variety of word-reading tasks. Their most advanced word-reading performance, relative to the second graders, tended to be on a nonlexical-route processing factor defined about equally by (a) accuracy in reading pseudowords, (b) accuracy in reading real words with regular GPCs, and (c) a negative split loading for a measure of orthographic matching speed. However, precocious readers also surpassed the second graders in performance on a lexical-processing factor defined by exception-word reading accuracy and speed in making orthographic matching judgments. Finally, although they were not as remarkable in this respect as Maxine, these precocious readers also were quick in doing all of the word-reading tasks they were given. In another study, a small group of precocious readers maintained an advantage in nonlexical route reading over comparably intelligent children who had not been precocious readers when both groups were 8 to 9 years old. By this time, the children who were not precocious readers had caught up on measures of real word reading and text comprehension (Burns, Collins, & Paulsell, 1991).

Performance levels of hyperlexic readers. Like normal precocious readers, hyperlexic children as a group seem to be skilled at using the nonlexical and lexical routes to read pseudowords and words (Healy, 1982; Seymour & Evans, 1992; Sparks, 1995). All 12 hyperlexic autistic children in a sample studied by Healy (1982) were able to pronounce pseudowords with accuracy at least at the second grade level. Three performed at the top of the scale on which they were tested, earning scores at the 12th-grade level by pronouncing pseudowords with multiple syllables and unusual letter patterns.

Seymour and Evans (1992) conducted a 3-year study of a boy they called M.P., who was diagnosed with mental retardation and whose hyperlexia was first apparent when he began reading at age 4. These investigators found that M.P.'s skill pattern differed consistently from those of his classmates, who were slightly younger. Across a series of assessments that began early in first grade, M.P. consistently performed pseudoword and word reading tasks in ways that reflected fast and accurate use of the nonlexical route. Furthermore, his pronunciations were fluent, showing no evidence that he was sounding out words or pseudowords bit by bit. In this respect, his word reading and pseudoword reading were similar to Maxine's. In contrast, at the beginning of first grade, M.P.'s classmates often pronounced words and pseudowords with a laborious

sounding-out strategy or made lexical substitution or refusal errors that suggest they had poorly developed nonlexical routes, as one would expect for normal first-grade "partial-alphabetic" readers.

Like Nation (1999), we conclude that "the weight of the evidence suggests that hyperlexic children read nonwords satisfactorily" (p. 343). M.P.'s performance, like that of the hyperlexic readers studied by Healy (1982), demonstrates that a nonlexical-route component is likely to be part of the reading systems of children with hyperlexia, just as it is part of the systems of precocious readers who have no developmental impairments. The very limited evidence available is ambiguous with regard to the extent to which children with hyperlexia also have a well-developed lexical route, as would be indicated by strength in reading exception words (Nation, 1999).

Individual differences in normal and hyperlexic precocious readers' word and pseudoword reading.   Mean levels of precocious readers' performances on various word-reading tasks tell only part of the story. As we have already suggested, individual precocious readers have shown rather diverse patterns of strength in reading pseudowords, regular words, and exception words. The substantial individual differences found both within and across studies cast doubt on the conclusion that strong nonlexical-route use is a universal feature of precocious readers' reading systems.

For example, Backman (1983) found that kindergarten precocious readers were, on the average, advanced in their ability to read pseudowords, although perhaps not quite as advanced as older children matched with them on real-word reading level. However, Backman also identified two subgroups of 7 precocious readers each (14 of the total sample of 24) with extremely different patterns of reading skills. One group was proficient at reading real words but poor at both phoneme deletion and pseudoword reading. The other, equally proficient at reading real words, was good at phoneme deletion and pseudoword reading. Children in the second group also tended to be better spellers. In other words, some of Backman's precocious readers appeared to have relatively well-developed nonlexical routes, while others did not.

By the summer following the end of their kindergarten year, precocious readers still vary in the extent to which they excel in performance on measures of nonlexical-route use, such as pseudoword reading, or in performance on lexical processing indicators such as exception-word reading and homophone choice. Jackson et al.'s (1993) latent-variable factor analysis of the component reading skills of postkindergarten precocious readers revealed substantial individual differences in the extent to which children showed greater or lesser strength in each route. In an analysis of data for the full model of word and text reading, the correlation between the nonlexical-route and lexical-route latent variables was .42. This value is consistent with findings from an earlier study of 87 postkindergarten precocious readers. In that study, the correlations between observed scores for accuracy in reading exception words and two lists of pseudowords were .42 and .46 (Jackson et al., 1988, Table 2).

Both of Jackson's studies suggest more independence between exception-word and pseudoword reading than generally is found in unselected samples of readers from the early elementary grades (e.g., Byrne & Fielding-Barnsley, 1995; Ehri, 1992; Jackson et al., 1993). One would expect correlations to be weaker within samples (and a population) restricted in range of ability. However, the relative independence of exception-word and pseudoword reading in precocious readers is theoretically important because it points to variability in the relative strengths of the lexical and nonlexical routes in neurologically normal, highly successful beginning readers. Both kinds of processing are related to precocious readers' overall text-reading effectiveness (Jackson et al., 1988, 1993).

Reanalysis of Jackson et al.'s (1988) data gives another perspective on this issue, replicating Backman's (1983) finding that there is a small subgroup of precocious readers whose pseudoword reading accuracy is extremely poor both in absolute level and relative to their accuracy in reading real words. When we looked back at the regular-word, exception-word, and pseudoword reading scores of the entire sample of 97 postkindergarten precocious readers in this study (not just the 87 with complete data included in the original analyses), we found 5 children who were able to read only a few one-syllable pseudowords (range 3 to 7 correct out of 36). Despite the apparent underdevelopment of their nonlexical route, these children read from 11 to 21 out of 36 regular words and from 14 to 19 out of 36 exception words correctly. Their Peabody Individual Achievement Test Reading Comprehension grade-equivalent levels (Dunn & Markwardt, 1970) ranged from 2.2 to 3.4.

The most extreme example of this phenomenon, a girl, performed like the partial-alphabetic readers described in chapter 5 despite a reading comprehension grade-equivalent level of 2.9. She refused to attempt most of the pseudowords and read only 4 correctly. In contrast, she read 21 regular words and 19 exception words correctly. Her errors on real words were all real word substitutions, as were some of her pseudoword errors. The pseudowords she read correctly included *tive* (pronounced /tiv/ to rhyme with *give*), *cloe* (as /klOO/, rhyming with *shoe*), and *tweat* (as /twEt/, rhyming with *seat*).

We also scanned this data set for examples of precocious readers who were exceptionally poor at reading exception words, despite strong ability to read pseudowords. There were a few children who read pseudowords better than they read exception words, the most extreme case being a boy with a reading comprehension grade-equivalent score of 3.7 who read 29 pseudowords and 27 regular words but only 18 exception words correctly. However, the minimum number of exception words any child read correctly was 9.[1] Therefore, none of these normal precocious readers could be described as unable to use the lexical route.

Variation in the relation between word- and pseudoword reading skills also can be seen among hyperlexic precocious readers (Nation, 1999). In Healy's

---

1. The minimum exception word score for 87 cases is reported incorrectly as 2 in Jackson et al. (1988, Table 1).

(1982) study, two of the three most advanced readers were substantially better, relative to test norms, at pseudoword than at real-word reading, but the rest had scores with no more than small deviations in one direction or the other. Overall, six children read pseudowords better, five read words better, and two had tied scores. One cannot give any clear cut interpretation to differences in grade-equivalent scores from different tests, but this pattern is noteworthy in that it mimics the diversity shown in the skill patterns of precocious readers who are not autistic and have not been called hyperlexic. Sparks (1995) also found that two hyperlexic boys differed substantially in their ability to read pseudowords. Nation (1999) summarizes other studies suggesting that some hyperlexics read pseudowords very poorly.

Lexical- and nonlexical-route use and reading speed. Recall the experimental results reported in chapter 6 suggesting that children who are poor at reading via the nonlexical route can do better if forced to read more quickly, which may increase their reliance on the lexical route. Some findings suggest that precocious readers may spontaneously use this adaptive strategy.

Jackson et al. (1988, Table 2) found that exception-word reading was more strongly related than pseudoword reading to text and word-reading speeds among normal precocious readers. In their final analysis (Table 3), the subordinate latent factor Speed was negatively correlated ($r = -.71$) with the subordinate latent factor Decoding Rule Use. This finding can be interpreted as indicating that, among precocious readers with the same overall General Reading Ability (the superordinate factor in this analysis), those who were the poorest decoders were the fastest readers of words and text passages. In a later study involving a different set of measures and a nonhierarchical analysis, the pattern of results was less clear cut. Nonetheless, it remained the case that a latent factor reflecting what we would call nonlexical-route use (Phonological Word Identification Accuracy) tended to be less strongly associated than a factor reflecting lexical-route use (Orthographic Processing) with word- and text-reading speed factors (Jackson et al., 1993, Table 3).

Semantic-System Facilitation of Word Pronunciation

As we noted in chapter 3, the semantic-system component of the reading system can influence word pronunciations. One way that the influence of this component can be detected is in the extent to which the speed with which a reader identifies a word is facilitated by a prior context that makes the word predictable. When a sentence starts out *"The king sat beside the . . .* , the word *queen* will be read more quickly than it would be on its own, although the difference may be trivial for skilled readers. Poor readers are more dependent on context for word pronunciation than good readers are (Jackson & Donaldson, 1989a).

Little evidence is available about this aspect of precocious reading, but what there is suggests that precocious readers' use of context is what might be expected. Like typical first graders (e.g., Biemiller, 1970), precocious readers

who are just beginning to read words sometimes will guess at word identity from context alone (Jackson, 1992) and may read words more accurately in text than in isolation (Fletcher-Flinn & Thompson, 2000). As their reading skills develop, precocious readers would be expected to make diminishing use of context for word identification, showing contextual facilitation effects no greater than those for older, RL-matched average readers.

One way to measure contextual facilitation of word pronunciation is to compare the speed with which children read a list of words presented in scrambled, meaningless order with the speed with which they read the same words in normal connected text. Two studies using this method have found that, compared with RL-matched readers, precocious readers are relatively slow at reading scrambled words and relatively fast at reading text (Jackson & Biemiller, 1985; Jackson & Donaldson, 1989a). Such results are consistent with others showing that precocious readers are exceptionally fast at reading text (Jackson et al., 1993; Fletcher-Flinn & Fletcher, 2000; Tobin & Pikulski, 1988). However, the scrambled list versus text-reading contrast probably does not provide a good measure of contextual facilitation effects across age groups (Jackson & Donaldson, 1989a).

Better tests of precocious readers' use of prior context to identify individual words were conducted by Jackson and Donaldson (1989a). In two similar studies, kindergarten-age precocious readers and RL-matched second graders, both with median Spache (1981) grade-equivalent reading comprehension scores of 3.5, were asked to read a series of sentences presented on a computer screen. As the child finished pronouncing the last word of the sentence context, which always was *the,* the experimenter triggered presentation of a concluding target word, which always was a noun. The child's latency to pronounce this word was recorded automatically.

In Jackson and Donaldson's (1989a) studies, easy and more difficult target words were paired with different kinds of sentence contexts. Sometimes the sentence context made the target word predictable, as in these examples:

> *The pillow was on the (bed).*
> *The girl sat down to play the (piano).*
> *To reach the ball, we had to go to the garage to get the (ladder).*
> *The gold coins and jewels were the most important part of the (treasure).*

The authors verified that these sentences did make their target words predictable in a preliminary study with adult subjects. Mean probabilities of the adults' correct guesses were .57 for the simpler context sentences and .63 for the longer ones. On other trials, the sentence context was neutral, always taking the form in this example:

> *They said it was the (king).*

On a third set of trials, the sentence context was more or less incongruous with its target:

The cook burned the (dog).
The driver started the (closet).

As expected, both the precocious readers and the second graders read the target words with a very high degree of accuracy, so data analyses focused on latencies for correct trials. The second graders were slightly faster word readers than the precocious postkindergartners. It took the precocious readers about 100 to 150 milliseconds longer to pronounce target words. Therefore, one might expect that they would show more contextual facilitation than the second graders. However, there was not even a trend in this direction. Rather, when the analyses in two experiments were controlled statistically for group differences in neutral context word pronunciation speed, the precocious readers showed, or tended to show, less contextual facilitation of word pronunciation than the older average readers did. Effects were similar for simpler and more complex facilitative contexts and for easier and harder target words.

In one of Jackson and Donaldson's (1989a, Study 3) studies, the three different kinds of sentence contexts were presented in blocks, so that children would have opportunities to learn that context would or would not be helpful for the next set of trials. This was done to determine whether the facilitative effects of context were under the readers' control. Another manipulation designed to maximize the use of strategic word identification processes in this study was introduction of a delay of 1,000 milliseconds between the child's pronunciation of the final word of the sentence context and the target word. The results were complicated by order effects, but they showed that both precocious readers and second graders were able to reduce the interfering effect of incongruous contexts as trials within this block accumulated. In other words, they were able to learn not to use prior context for word pronunciation when experience revealed that this information was misleading. These results are consistent with previous findings by Stanovich (Stanovich & West, 1978; Stanovich, West, & Feeman, 1981) indicating that among beginning readers, unlike skilled adult readers, contextual facilitation of word pronunciation at least partly based on a time-consuming and controllable expectancy mechanism. In this respect as in so many others, precocious readers are like other beginning readers.

Spelling and Precocious Reading

As we indicated in chapter 5, some researchers have suggested that spelling requires more complete lexical representations than reading (Ehri, 1997; Perfetti, 1997). In order to spell a word, one must be able either to (a) recall its graphemic representation as a whole or (b) assemble the representation bit by bit using GPCs, or (c) combine these processes. To use any of these mechanisms, a

speller needs to be able to assemble or access a complete mental representation of how the word as a whole should look or of what its sounds are and how these should be written. Therefore, studies of precocious readers' spelling should tell us something about the nature of their lexical and nonlexical representations. These are likely to be incomplete and inaccurate in poor readers. Are they consistently good in precocious readers?

In her classic study of precocious readers, Durkin (1966) described these children as "pencil and paper kids" who were interested in and proficient at drawing and writing as well as reading. However, more recent studies suggest that this is another area in which precocious readers differ dramatically from one another. Some precocious readers do fit Durkin's description well. One such child was given the pseudonym Bruce in several accounts of his precocious development (Jackson, 1988, 1992). Examples of Bruce's drawing and writing at ages 3 years 0 months, 3 years 7 months, and 5 years 9 months are given in Figure 7.1.

Bruce began writing before age 3, at about the same time as he began reading. Other comparably precocious and equally intelligent young readers have shown a dramatically different pattern, with delays of 2 years or more between the time they show substantial word-reading skill and the emergence of their ability to write and spell. This does not seem to be simply an issue of motor control, because some of the late spellers also have shown little or no ability to generate spellings with materials such as alphabet blocks or magnetic letters (Henderson et al., 1993; Jackson, 1992; Fletcher-Flinn & Thompson, 2000). For example, Max was reading words at the late first-grade level shortly after his third birhtday. At that age, he did produce what he called "silly words" with magnet letters, but these were nonwords that seemed to have haphazard

(A)

FIGURE 7.1. (A) Bruce's writing in response to the instruction to draw a square during a standard test adminstration at age 3 years 0 months.

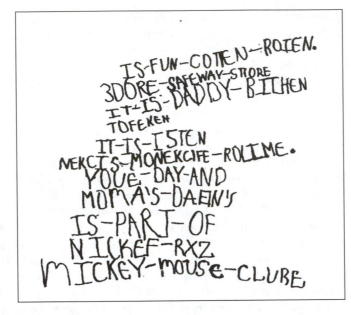

FIGURE 7.1. (B) A sample of Bruce's writing at age 3 years 7 months supplied by his mother with the comment that this was typical of ihs interest in playing with words. (C) An excerpt from an illustrated book, "All About Apples," written by Bruce in kindergarten at age 5 years 9 months.

letter patterns and which he could not pronounce accurately. He seemed to be playing with arranging the letters and then attempting to read them rather than intentionally spelling any words or sounds. Max's writing ability remained dormant until about age 4 years 6 months. At that time, his mother reported that he learned to print all of the alphabet and began asking her for help with spelling. He then began to spell and write words freely and incorporate them in his drawings, much as Bruce had begun doing at age 3 (Henderson et al., 1993).

Max's development recalls that of another precocious reader, Susan. Susan was a preschool classmate of Bruce and also began reading before she was 3 years old. However, Susan did not show any interest in spelling or writing until she was about 5 years old (Jackson, 1992).

Maxine also showed a substantial deficiency in spelling relative to her extremely precocious reading. Fletcher-Flinn and Thompson (2000) described her development through the age of 40 months. We already have commented on the highly accurate and fluent word reading she was able to do at that age. However, even at 40 months, she still could spell very little. Fletcher-Flinn and Thompson linked this performance deficit to Maxine's lagging phoneme awareness development and surprisingly poor ability to pronounce the sounds of isolated letters and digraphs, even though she could use those sounds in combination to read pseudowords. They suggested that reading requires only implicit understanding of GPCs, which Maxine had. However, spelling requires explicit knowledge of these relations, and Maxine's accuracy on a test of letter and digraph sounds was only 50% (Fletcher-Flinn & Tompson, 2000, Table 3)

The different patterns of spelling achievement illustrated in these case studies also are represented in Backman's (1983) data. As a group, her precocious readers were less advanced in spelling than in reading. Their spelling grade-equivalent scores ranged from 0.5 to 4.8. The poor spellers in Backman's sample were like Maxine in their poor performance on a sound deletion task. However, they also were relatively poor, which she was not, at pseudoword reading.

The few children with hyperlexia whose spelling has been studied seem to have attained spelling levels commensurate with their word-reading ability. On a series of tests that began when he was 6 years old and continued for 3 years, M.P. earned spelling accuracy scores that generally were at or near the top of the distribution for a group of his somewhat younger classmates. His spelling precocity matched his precocity in word reading. M.P. also was excellent, again relative to his classmates, at spelling pseudowords. This finding suggests that M.P. was able to draw on GPCs to spell, and it is consistent with his superior performance on a test in which he was asked to write letters in response to individual sounds (Seymour & Evans, 1992).

Of the two school-age boys with hyperlexia studied by Sparks (1995), one was able to spell both regular and exception words at levels roughly commensurate with his word and pseudoword reading. The other boy, who was not nearly as advanced in pseudoword reading as in real word reading, also was very poor at spelling regular words. He was somewhat better, relative to age norms, at spelling exception words. This suggests that his ability to draw on an orthographic lexicon to generate a spelling may have been better than his ability to generate sound-to-letter correspondences. The third child in Sparks's sample, a girl whose verbal intelligence was average, spelled regular words at a level consistent with her pseudoword reading ability and was somewhat worse at spelling exception words.

As a whole, these spelling data suggest that precocious readers sometimes

may be reading well but have spelling systems whose lexical or nonlexical routes, or both, are not as complete as those average readers have when they have reached the same level in word reading. However, some precocious readers clearly are also excellent spellers.

Summary: Proximal Causes of Precocious Reading and Spelling

Precocious readers' performances on reading and reading-related tasks generally indicate that, on the average, they have effective reading system components where, on the average, poor readers have dysfunctional ones. However, this broad conclusion must be qualified in two important ways.

In chapter 6, we argued that it is wrong to reduce a description of poor readers' reading system deficiencies to universal problems in nonlexical-route use. We suggested that it is possible to identify children who are poor lexical-route readers, despite having an apparently adequate nonlexical route. These children tend to be especially poor at reading exception words rather than at reading pseudowords. We argued that poor reading in children, like acquired dyslexia, can take different forms. We can make the same argument about precocious readers. Recall that exception-word reading and pseudoword reading in this group are only modestly correlated and that the pseudoword reading skills of precocious readers range widely. It appears that there may be more than one set of reading system parameters associated with exceptionally successful beginning reading, just as there are multiple ways to read poorly. Furthermore, findings that precocious readers are characteristically fast, and that this may especially true for those whose lexical route is stronger than their nonlexical route, suggest that precocious readers may take exceptionally full advantage of the flexibility in a dual-route system.

Very young precocious readers also vary dramatically in their spelling ability, and some do not begin to spell until years after they have begun reading. Spelling may depend on cognitive structures or processes that are not always available to precocious readers of preschool age.

DISTAL CAUSES OF PRECOCIOUS READING

Like proximal causes, distal causes of precocious reading can be examined in terms of questions about typical patterns and individual differences. Individual case reports may have a special role in identifying conditions that are not prerequisite for successful reading development, just as they may not be necessary for successful operation of a reading system.

Design Issues

What little is known about the distal causes of precocious reading comes from a variety of research designs, most of which yield evidence that is more sugges-

tive than it is conclusive. These sources of evidence are best considered as parts of an overall fabric in which no individual thread is particularly strong but the whole meshes together well.

As we noted in chapter 2, RL-match designs do not provide direct or strong evidence on questions about distal causes of individual differences in development. However, their results can suggest possibilities that merit further investigation. In this context, the results of RL-match comparisons of precocious and average readers bear on speculation about distal causes of poor reading and ways in which a GPC-based self-teaching mechanism such as that proposed by Share and Stanovich (1995b), or alternative learning mechanisms (Thompson, 1999), might work.

Ideally, the strongest evidence regarding the developmental sources and consequences of, for example, learning GPC rules exceptionally early, would come from experimental studies in which these rules, or their alleged phonological awareness prerequisites, were taught to very young children. Here, as in the literature on poor reading in children, theoretically complete instructional experiments have not been done (see Coltheart, 1979; Durkin, 1970, for examples from this literature). However, some prospective longitudinal studies have identified earlier-emerging skills related to precocious reading. These are described below.

Single case histories conducted while children were developing into precocious readers have special importance in this literature because they are well suited to answering questions about prerequisites for reading (e.g., Henderson et al., 1993; Sparks, 1995; Fletcher-Flinn & Thompson, 1999). Precocious reading offers special opportunities to test some kinds of hypotheses about maturational limits on the operation of the reading system. By definition, precocious reading emerges during the preschool years, when any maturational limits on fundamental, broadly relevant, aspects of cognitive performance are likely to be stronger than in later years (Case, 1991). Studies of reading in even a single child age 2, 3, or 4 have given developmentalists opportunities to test hypotheses about chronologically determined maturational limits on cognitive performance, such as those in Piagetian and neo-Piagetian theory (e.g., Briggs & Elkind, 1973; Case, 1991; Fischer & Pipp, 1985).

Cognitive Distal Causes of Precocious Reading

Precocious phonological awareness?   In samples of average and poor readers, phonological awareness skills have been found to be substantially related to concurrent and future reading skill (Ehri, 1992; Share & Stanovich, 1995a; 1995b; Stahl & Murray, 1998; Wagner et al., 1994). As we noted in chapter 5, Level 1 measures such as rhyme recognition and onset deletion tend to be most strongly associated with word reading in young, beginning readers, when performance on more challenging Level 2 tasks such as deleting a medial phoneme is still at the measurement floor. In samples of average and poor readers who are older and more advanced in their word-reading levels, Level 2 mea-

sures are stronger correlates of reading, perhaps because these skills both facilitate and benefit from reading acquisition (e.g., Torgesen & Burgess, 1998). As we noted in chapter 5, abundant correlational data suggesting a causal relation from Level 1 phonological awareness to word reading have been partially confirmed by intervention studies (Bus & van IJzendoorn, 1999). These findings give us good reason to expect that all precocious readers would perform well on phonological awareness tasks.

At the reading levels characteristic of most precocious readers who have been studied (typically second grade or higher), one would expect thorough mastery of Level 1 phonological awareness and, at least in the more advanced individuals, good performance on Level 2 tasks that seem to be influenced by experience in reading. However, the emerging evidence on precocious readers' performance on various phonological awareness tasks is inconsistent and inconclusive. Findings from seven studies are summarized in Table 7.1. Five of these studies involved children of average or above-average intelligence who could be characterized as normal precocious readers; the remaining two studies involved children with hyperlexia or otherwise anomalous advanced word reading. None of the studies included large samples, and only two could be considered anything other than case studies.

The results most consistent with the conclusion that precocious readers are about as advanced in phonological awareness as one might expect from their advanced word reading have come from studies of intellectually normal precocious readers age 5 or older at the time their phonological awareness was assessed. Even at this age, performance was inconsistent on some Level 2 tasks such as sound deletion and phoneme tapping or segmentation (Backman, 1983; Singson & Mann, 1999; Stainthorp & Hughes, 1998).

Among very young normal precocious readers and older children with hyperlexia, phonological awareness task performance has been generally poor on Level 2 tasks. These children also have performed unevenly on Level 1 tasks usually mastered by much less skillful readers, such as matching words on their orthographic body (rime), onset consonant sounds, or naming sounds for single letters.

Two normal precocious readers both showed sensitivity to onset and rime patterns in at least some contexts by age 3 or earlier (Fletcher-Flinn & Thompson, 2000; Henderson et al., 1993), but performance on phonological awareness tasks sometimes has been astoundingly poor relative to a child's advanced word-reading skills (Fletcher-Flinn & Thompson, 2000; Henderson et al., 1993; Sparks, 1995). For example, Maxine, the child studied by Fletcher-Flinn and Thompson (2000), did poorly at age 37 months on most phoneme-level phonological awareness tasks and on a test of her ability to pronounce individual letter sounds. At that age, her pseudoword reading performance was better than that of the average 7-year-old in her country, her word-reading accuracy was at the norm for children age 8 years 9 months, and her reading rate was comparable to that for children age 10 years 6 months.

These findings might suggest that there is no necessary close relation be-

TABLE 7.1. Performance of precocious readers on tests of phonological awareness (PA)

Study	Sample	Measures	Findings
Backman (1983)	24 children in kindergarten, mean age 69 months; word identification GE range 1.5 to 4.0.	Syllable and phoneme tapping, sound deletion, syllable and phoneme blending; speech sound discrimination.	Mean scores generally between those of CA and RL comparison groups; performance variable on sound deletion and phoneme tapping.
Seymour & Evans (1992)	1 child, a 6-year-old with language and other developmental delays and hyperlexia.	Rhyming, phoneme deletion (no specifics given).	Poor at rhyme; good at phoneme deletion.
Henderson, Jackson, & Mukamal (1993)	1 boy, advanced in oral language development; age 2 years 7 months and 3 years 2 months at PIAT-R testing.	PA items from PIAT-R Reading recognition subtest; informal observations.	Failed matching words on initial sounds at both ages; played spontaneous word games with onset and rime matches.
Sparks (1995)	3 children with developmental problems: 2 boys with hyperlexia, ages 8 and 9; one girl with IQ in low normal range and advanced word reading, age 10.	Lindamood Auditory Conceptualization test and 10 other rhyming and phoneme matching or manipulation tests.	Below expectation for both CA and RL on Lindamood Auditory Conceptualization test; variable on other tasks; difficulty with directions and attention.
Stainthorp & Hughes (1998)	15 children, tested 3 times at ages 5 years 0 months, 5 years 11 months, and 6 years 11 months; mean RL at first assessment was 8 years 8 months.	Rhyme production and detection; phoneme blending, addition, deletion, and segmentation	Consistently good performance, better than CA-matched nonreaders of similar verbal IQ; phoneme segmentation most difficult.
Fletcher-Flinn & Thompson (2000)	1 girl whose intellectual development was generally accelerated; age 33, 37, and 40 months at PA testing.	Rime and "onset + nucleus" matching, syllable and phoneme segmentation (tapping), oddity, phoneme deletion, pig latin, phoneme synthesis.	Only rhyme awareness at 33 months.; by 37 months did both rime and onset+ nucleus matching; at 40 months did syllable counting and onset deletion but not phoneme counting, segmentation, or synthesis.
Singson & Mann (1999)	22 children, mean age 65 months., mean word RL about second grade.	Alliteration production and judgment, initial sound deletion and substitution.	Better than nonreaders of same CA, especially on single consonant onset deletion and substitution. Difference nonsignificant for alliteration judgments.

Note. GE = grade equivalent; PIAT-R = Peabody Individual Achievement Test-Revised; PA = phonological awareness; CA = chronological age; RL = reading level.

tween phonological awareness and word or pseudoword reading. Unfortunately, the typical phonological awareness task takes a form that may not be valid for very young or cognitively impaired readers, who may have difficulty following instructions to change a word they have heard or to select the odd-sounding word from a string of three. Several investigators have commented on the difficulty that their precocious readers had in understanding task directions or maintaining focus on a task. For example, Max, a bright and verbally adept 3-year-old, could not seem to get the point of test items requiring him to choose which of a set of spoken, pictured words matched on their initial sound, even though he was well able to do more advanced word recognition items on the same test (Henderson et al., 1993). This failure contrasts with the child's enjoyment of informal word games that required awareness of onset letters (and possibly, but not necessarily, their sounds). For example, when his mother asked Max where his shoes were, he replied, "Think of a room that begins with b." His shoes were in the bathroom. He also enjoyed playing rhyming games.

At least part of very young and hyperlexic precocious readers' failure on phonological awareness tasks may be an artifact of cognitive limits outside the reading system. Another possibility, which we raised in chapter 5, is that the measurement problem is more fundamental. Perhaps precocious readers' failures on some phonological awareness tests may indeed suggest lack of declarative or metacognitive knowledge about phoneme and other within-word units that might facilitate and be enhanced by acquisition of a nonlexical route. However, this knowledge might not be as tightly linked with reading acquisition as is often supposed. Perhaps there is some fundamental way in which understanding of phoneme identity (Byrne, 1998) or some other substrate of phonological awareness is essential to the acquisition of an effective word-reading system. If so, the indirect phonological awareness measures from which we infer the existence of such a component must then be insensitive its existence in at least some successful beginning readers.

The theoretical significance of studies of precocious readers' phonological awareness is weakened by the inconsistency and ambiguity of their findings. However, these results do remind us of the practical limits of reading readiness tests based on phonological awareness (Stahl & Murray, 1998; Torgesen & Burgess, 1998). Our concern about this issue is grounded in experience with precocious readers and their parents. One of us (Jackson) has been appalled at how often school personnel will deny the existence of a child's demonstrated precocity in reading because the child has not done well on some measure supposed to predict that outcome. Such decisions represent an abuse of logic and deviation from the ethical use of predictive tests, but they do happen. Therefore, we reiterate that children may be exceptionally precocious readers without passing tests of phonological awareness skills that sometimes are supposed to be necessary for word reading.

Letter-naming speed and precocious reading. Recall that some poor readers seem to have a double deficit, performing poorly both on tasks such as

pseudoword reading that reflect GPC use and on tests of RAN speed, which may reflect cognitive processes outside the reading system that contribute to its development, and particularly to the development of the lexical route (Manis et al., 1996; Wolf & Bowers, 1999). If precocious readers are the mirror image of poor readers, we might expect them to be advanced, relative to CA peers, and comparable to older RL matches on RAN performance.

Studies of naming speed in precocious readers have not involved the variety of measures and converging findings that are available in the literature on poor reading in children and that have come together to define the construct "rapid automatic naming" (e.g., Wolf & Bowers, 1999). However, the available studies have shown that children who are precocious readers name letters more rapidly than nonreaders of the same age who also know letter names (Jackson & Myers, 1982). Furthermore, within samples of children who are all precocious readers, degree of reading precocity is moderately correlated with letter-naming speed (Jackson & Biemiller, 1983; Jackson & Donaldson, 1989a; Jackson et al., 1988, 1993).

RAN involves processes that track chronological age as well as some that covary with ability within an age group. Therefore, young precocious readers are not as fast as older children matched on reading level (Jackson & Donaldson 1989a; Jackson et al., 1993). However, the finding that reading precocity is consistently associated with rapid letter naming supports the argument that naming familiar visual stimuli rapidly may reflect processes key to the efficient development of the reading system (Manis et al., 1996; McBride-Chang & Manis, 1996; Wolf & Bowers, 1999).

Longitudinal data also support the conclusion that the cognitive processes underlying rapid letter naming may contribute to precocious readers' early progress in word reading. Jackson and Myers (1982) conducted 6-month longitudinal studies of two groups of children attending a preschool for intellectually advanced children. The participating children all passed a screening test by naming capital letters with at least 95% accuracy. In the first sample ($N = 21$), a cross-lagged panel correlation analysis revealed that letter-naming speed at the first testing time predicted performance on an untimed word recognition test 6 months later, but the converse was not true. This suggests that the mechanism underlying rapid letter naming causes later success in word reading. The results for the second, slightly younger sample ($N = 17$) were less clear cut as a causal analysis because the children's letter-naming time scores were not as stable over the period of the study. However, these results also indicated that letter-naming time is associated with later word-reading accuracy. Therefore, it seems likely that, just as slow RAN may be associated with the slow progress of poor readers (Wolf & Bowers, 1999), fast RAN may be associated with precocious readers' accelerated growth.

Working memory.   Many investigators have reported that poor readers are likely to perform poorly on tests of working memory, although this aspect of cognition may not contribute uniquely to reading failure (Torgesen & Burgess,

1998). Here again, precocious readers seem to be strong where poor readers are weak. Analyses of data from five overlapping samples of children who attended the same preschool across a period of 4 years found modest positive relations, controlled for CA, between backward digit span and word-reading accuracy in four of the five analyses (Jackson & Myers, 1992).

Results of studies of slightly older precocious readers have been less consistent. In a study of 87 postkindergarten readers, 56 of whom had completed forward and backward digit span tests, Jackson et al. (1988, Table 3) found that forward digit span was correlated with General Reading Ability ($r = .35$) and a subordinate factor measuring precision in oral text reading ($r = .29$). Forward span also was correlated with Peabody Individual Achievement Test (PIAT) Text Comprehension ($r = .44$). Backward digit span, which is a better measure of working memory and would be expected to be more strongly related to success in reading, was not correlated with general measures of reading ability. However, backward span was negatively correlated with a subordinate factor measuring speed of word and text reading ($r = -.39$) and positively correlated with the subordinate Decoding Rule Use factor ($r = .26$). Interpreting these correlations is tricky because, in this analysis, the subordinate reading factors indicate specific skills that were independent of the superordinate factor, General Reading Ability. Therefore, the subordinate factor correlations with backward digit span mean that those children who were slow readers and good decoders relative to their overall reading ability had larger backward spans. (If a precocious reader's working memory is especially good, he or she may also be a relatively slow reader who is particularly good at nonlexical route use.) These results are intriguing, but they were not replicated. In another study, precocious readers' working memory spans were not significantly related to individual differences in their word reading. However, the 116 precocious readers in this study, on the average, performed almost at the level of the second-grade RL comparison sample on span tasks (Jackson et al., 1993, Table 2).

Aspects of oral language competence.   Children whose oral language development during the preschool years is delayed in other aspects of oral language production and comprehension besides phonological awareness are likely to have difficulty learning to read (Catts et al., 1999). Is the converse also true? Is precocious oral language acquisition, in sum or in certain aspects, necessary or sufficient for precocious reading to emerge during the preschool years?

By their very existence, children with hyperlexia show that oral language precocity cannot be necessary for precocious reading acquisition. Furthermore, even among children with average and superior oral language skills, there is surprisingly little association between precocity in oral language and precocious reading. For example, in one group of 24 children who were all intellectually advanced in some way but whose verbal IQs varied widely around a very high mean, verbal IQs were independent of scores on a standard test of word recognition (Jackson & Myers, 1982, Table 1).

Crain-Thoreson and Dale (1992) looked for precocious reading acquisi-

tion among 25 children whose performance at age 20 months on any of three measures of oral language development was 2 *SD*s above the scale mean. The language measures were parent-reported vocabulary, mean length of utterance, and the language subscale from an infant development test. These children remained verbally precocious on repeated assessments through 4½ years of age. However, at that age, their mean performance on a standard test of word reading was about at the kindergarten level. Only 3 children were able to read more than a single word on the test and only 1 of the 25 was reading at a level that would be considered precocious by most investigators. Their ability to do a phoneme deletion task was minimal, again at about the kindergarten norm, and their performance on an invented spelling task was well below that shown by kindergartners in another study. Furthermore, the most advanced talkers in the group were not the most advanced readers.

Crain-Thoreson and Dale's (1992) results are dramatic because they focused on children who all were extremely precocious in their oral language development. However, their results are quite consistent with those from studies of the vocabulary knowledge of children selected for precocity in reading. As we noted earlier in this chapter, most precocious readers are not hyperlexic, and they are likely to be rather high in verbal intelligence. However, the range of their oral language performance is wide, and the correlation between verbal ability and degree of precocity in reading is modest. For example, in Jackson et al.'s (1988) sample of 87 postkindergarten precocious readers, the mean Wechsler Intelligence Scale for Children-Revised (WISC-R) Vocabulary scale score was 14.8 (*SD* = 2.6). These scores are standardized with a mean of 10 and an *SD* of 3, and the precocious readers' scores ranged from below average (8) to the upper scale limit (19). In a latent-variable factor analysis, the correlation between a composite WISC-R Verbal factor and General Reading Ability was a modest .42.

Oral language precocity and reading precocity clearly are distinct constructs. However, one would expect early talkers eventually to become good readers, and this appears to be what happens. In a later study of 21 children remaining in their sample of early talkers, Dale, Crain-Thoreson, and Robinson (1995) found that, by 6½ years of age, these children had become superior readers. However, as in the Jackson studies (Jackson et al., 1988, 1993), the most advanced talkers were still not particularly likely to be the most advanced readers.

Evidence from a study of bilingual precocious readers further supports the conclusion that children can become precocious readers of a language that they do not speak particularly well. Of the 116 postkindergarten precocious readers in Jackson et al.'s (1993) sample, 12 came from homes in which English was not the primary language spoken, although most were described by their parents as speaking English better than their home language. European languages (French and Croatian) were spoken in only 2 of the 12 homes, and the most common home languages were Chinese (*n* = 4) and Korean (*n* = 3). Other children came from homes in which Arabic, Hebrew, or a language of the Philippines was spoken.

Jackson and Lu (1992) compared the mean reading skill levels of these bilingual children with those of the 104 monolingual precocious readers in the sample. The bilingual precocious readers' scores were significantly below those of the monolingual readers on all three tests of English oral language ability, and they were especially low on tests of sentence memory and ability to supply the missing word in a sentence. In contrast, the bilingual children's scores on all of the text reading speed and accuracy measures fluctuated around the monolingual precocious sample's mean. Their best performance, relative to the monolingual group, was in the speed with which they made orthographic choice judgments about which of a pair of homophones was the real word (the *rain/rane* task). This advantage was especially strong (1.2 *SD* above the monolingual mean) for children whose home language was Chinese. The bilingual children did tend to be less accurate in reading isolated exception words, regular words, and pseudowords than the monolingual group, but these relative deficiencies in pronunciation accuracy were not significant.

Reflectivity.   Yet another aspect of cognition sometimes associated with primary grade success or failure in reading and other realms is perceptual reflectivity, which most often is measured by some version of the Matching Familiar Figures test (Cairns & Cammock, 1978). As children grow older, they become better able to scan a set of similar, complex drawings thoroughly enough to identify the only one that matches a standard. Younger children, and less able students at a given age, are more likely to respond quickly but inaccurately. Therefore, one might expect precocious readers to perform like their elders on this task, and they do. Jackson et al. (1993, Table 2) found that postkindergarten readers performed as well as (indeed, a nonsignificant smidgen better than) RL-matched second graders on this test. Within the group, those who were the best readers were not likely to be more reflective.

Environmental Causes

The issue of what kind of beginning reading instruction is most effective came up in chapter 6, where we presented evidence that programs that include explicit instruction in phonological awareness and GPCs seem to be, on the average, the most effective for poor readers. What about children who learn to read words (and sometimes pseudowords) and to comprehend text prior to beginning formal instruction in school? Have they had tutorial experiences like those that seem to work best for children who are at risk for reading failure? If children of average ability receive early, explicit instruction, do they become precocious readers?

This seems to be an area where there is an implicit aptitude-by-treatment interaction. The extended, structured experiences that are most effective in helping children who are at risk for reading failure avoid that fate, and in helping poor readers catch up, do not seem to be associated with reading precocity.

Home experiences.   Correlational studies comparing the home experiences of precocious readers with those of otherwise similar children who did not begin to read early have yielded surprisingly few differences between the groups (Durkin, 1966; Jackson, 1992; Jackson et al., 1988; Thomas, 1984). Parents of precocious readers provide the kinds of support that generally are associated with prevention of reading failure. They teach letter names and sometimes letter sounds, they read to their children, and so forth. However, middle-class parents of children who do not read early do pretty much the same things, with the same frequency (Burns et al., 1991; Jackson, 1992). Those few differences that have turned up have suggested that parents of precocious readers may have spent more time at home with their children (Thomas, 1984). Other occasionally reported differences, such as precocious readers' greater interest in reading-related activities and television programs, may be effects rather than causes of precocious reading.

Some, certainly not all, precocious readers have had a parent who had formal training in how to teach reading (e.g., Henderson et al., 1993). This training may have helped make the parent a good observer and facilitator of his or her child's development. However, years of extended interactions with parents of precocious readers has convinced coauthor Jackson that most such parents are following and supporting their children's precocious interests, not pushing their development.

Early formal instruction.   Interventions in which extensive reading instruction has been offered during the preschool years generally have not produced lasting gains in reading comprehension among middle-class children who would be expected to read well without any special interventions. Instead, they seem to have had a hothouse effect, giving participants in the experimental programs an initial advantage in word reading that was lost after a few years of schooling. Most of these studies were done in the 1970s or earlier and they have been reviewed elsewhere (Coltheart, 1979; Jackson, 1992). Early formal instruction in reading can be very effective in minimizing the rate of illiteracy among children at risk for reading failure (e.g., Hanson & Farrell, 1995; Rescorla, Hyson, & Hirsch-Pasek, 1991), but such instruction is neither necessary nor sufficient to turn capable pre-readers into precocious readers.

One feature of effective interventions for poor readers may have an important parallel in the home experiences of many precocious readers. The automatization of basic skills such as word identification proceeds most easily when a child can practice repeatedly with immediate feedback and support to minimize or correct errors, a situation that is likely to occur with one-on-one tutoring (Siegler, 1996; Torgesen et al., 1999). The support that at least some precocious readers receive from their parents or other family members (Durkin, 1966, 1984) is likely to create just this kind of efficient context for learning.

How Does Precocious Reading Develop? Overview of Distal Causes of Precocious Reading

Taken together with what little longitudinal information is available, descriptions of precocious readers' current skill patterns and hypothesized reading systems also suggest that individuals have relied on a variety of different strengths in the process of learning to read. In other words, this is a population in which interactive-compensatory processing, almost by definition a failure in poor readers (Stanovich & Siegel, 1994), actually works. How have precocious readers, whose diverse patterns of excellent word-reading skills are compatible with a dual-route model, developed their present reading competence? The literature suggests several different answers, which eventually may be integrated into a comprehensive model of precocious reading acquisition.

Routes to precocious reading?   Case studies of preschool-age precocious readers have suggested that children vary in the rapidity with which they progress through increasingly complete versions of partial-alphabetic reading and begin to demonstrate full-alphabetic reading (Clark, 1976; Jackson, 1988). Bruce seemed aware of GPCs from very early in his reading (and simultaneous spelling) acquisition, perhaps because he had learned these from watching the television program *Sesame Street* several times a day (Jackson, 1992). Both Max and Maxine initially seemed unaware of GPCs, but both moved quickly to a point at which they seemed able to use the nonlexical route to pronounce unfamiliar words or pseudowords (Fletcher-Flinn & Thompson, 2000; Henderson et al., 1993; Jackson, 1988). Other precocious readers seem to amass a considerable orthographic lexicon, perhaps by relying on an immature lexical route and the other resources available in the reading system depicted in Figure 5.1, before showing clear evidence of a well-developed nonlexical route (Clark, 1976; Jackson, 1988, 1992; Jackson et al., 1988). The possibility of substantial individual differences in the extent to which precocious readers' progress depends on mastering GPCs also is suggested by the result of Backman's (1983) study of 24 kindergarten-age precocious readers and by the studies of hyperlexic children described previously.

Those precocious readers who have large oral vocabularies and who have had extended experience in reading predictable texts that allow strong semantic-system support for development of the orthographic lexicon may show faster development of the lexical route. Others, perhaps those like Bruce and some hyperlexic readers whose early interest in reading has focused on the alphabetic code (Jackson, 1992, 2000), might show faster development along the nonlexical route.

As we suggested in chapters 5 and 6, well-developed lexical processing might act in a compensatory way as a distal mechanism of reading acquisition, allowing readers to induce sublexical relations (Thompson & Johnston, 2000). Fletcher-Flinn and Thompson (2000) suggested that Maxine's remarkably precocious development might be similar to that of more typical children who have

learned to read without explicit instruction in letter sounds or GPCs. Recall that, by 3½ years of age, Maxine was extremely accurate and fluent in reading both words and pseudowords. However, she performed poorly on phonological awareness tasks and was unable to name the sounds for individual letters. The small amount of instruction she received in these correspondences seemed to have been forgotten. She could not spell at all.

Max's early reading experiences suggest that he began learning to read much as Fletcher-Flinn and Thompson (2000) proposed that Maxine did. Max's mother began teaching him to read after she noticed him, at age 2, reading words on signs. She first confirmed that he could read these words, such as *pizza*, without supporting context. She then began giving Max opportunities to read text that she knew he would find interesting. She started making a diary of his daily activities, and the two of them read these entries together over and over again. Max's mother made no effort to restrict the vocabulary in these texts. For example, one sentence read as follows in the all-capitals script she used:

WHEN WE PASS THE FIRE STATION ON THE WAY TO
PLAYGROUP MAX ALWAYS SAYS, WITH VIGOR, "TWO FIRE
ENGINES. I CAN'T STAND IT."

Max's mother did not explicitly teach Max to sound out the words in this diary. However, after about 6 months of such text-based reading practice, Max began to sound out novel words.

Fletcher-Flinn and Thompson's (2000; see also Thompson, 1999) model of reading acquisition raises the possibility that precocious readers may be especially good, whereas poor readers are especially bad (Ehri & Saltmarsh, 1995), at forming complete linkages between strings of letter units and entries in an orthographic lexicon. However, the Thompson group's work takes this proposal an important step further by suggesting that at least some children can use these lexical-route connections to induce sublexical GPC relations. We suspect that Fletcher-Flinn and Thompson's model accounts well for the development of those precocious readers whose acquisition of reading and related skills does not seem to fit the phonologically driven self-teaching model.

Filling in gaps?   Some precocious readers, especially the youngest and the least intellectually able, appear to have gaps in cognition outside the reading system that have been associated with reading failure in other groups. Hyperlexic children are, by definition, limited in the oral language semantic-system knowledge they can draw on to support word identification. The youngest precocious readers do not seem to be as fully aware of sound patterns within words as one might expect successful beginning readers to be.

Superior metacognitive understanding of the nature of reading and superior executive control of their own reading processes are obvious candidates for mechanisms to explain how precocious readers of above-average intelligence make their reading systems work well and develop rapidly, despite some miss-

ing or minimally functional internal or supporting external components. After all, the ability to learn effectively with partial information is a hallmark of intellectual giftedness (e.g., Jackson & Butterfield, 1986). However, metacognition seems much less plausible as a component of the rapid reading acquisition of children with hyperlexia. Many such children have autism, and all, by our definition, are below average in verbal intelligence. Therefore, this is a group in which intellectual flexibility and self awareness are much more likely to be deficient than superior.

Perhaps the quality that all precocious readers most clearly have in common is strong interest, sometimes to the point of obsession, in print (e.g., Dale et al., 1995; Durkin, 1966; Fletcher-Flinn, 1999; Jackson, 1992; Nation, 1999). Precocious readers vary in the kinds of things they like to read and in whether they seem most interested in breaking the GPC code or in using this code to gain access to the stories, baseball news, or dinosaur trivia available in text. Boy and girl precocious readers have different reading interests that remain stable across their elementary school years (Jackson, 1992; Mills & Jackson, 1990). However, whatever their individual goals in reading might be, precocious readers do gobble up print.

Another consistent finding about precocious readers' skill patterns is that they read text quickly (Jackson & Biemiller, 1995; Jackson & Donaldson, 1999a; Jackson et al., 1993; Pikulski & Tobin, 1989; Fletcher-Flinn & Thompson, 2000). Rapid reading reduces working-memory load and can facilitate comprehension (Perfetti, 1985). It may be especially helpful to readers with nonlexical-route deficiencies (Breznitz, 1987; Hendriks & Kolk, 1997). Recall the finding (Jackson et al., 1988) that precocious readers who are the poorest decoders, relative to their general reading ability, are also the fastest readers. Rapid text reading may affect operation of the reading system to take maximal advantage of the lexical route. In the long run, rapid reading also may help a child learn new words, both by increasing total exposure and by allowing a child to chunk a lot of semantic context information into working memory that can be used, if needed, to bolster incomplete decoding.

We know from studies of other populations (chapters 5 and 6) that print exposure is an important element in successful reading acquisition, and that it seems to contribute to lexical processing independent of phonological processing and GPC use (e.g., Cunningham & Stanovich, 1998). When passion fuels the system, sustained and reflective engagement with printed words, coupled with simultaneous access to parallel information about the words' sounds or meanings, may be sufficient for children to learn to read by using whatever incompletely formed reading system they have available.

8

Conclusions

Our central goal in writing this book was to look across several different populations of atypical readers and to use this broad perspective as a context for testing and extending a particular theory of reading. In framing this synthesis, we have paid special attention to some conceptual and methodological issues that often are muddled in discussions of reading and reading acquisition. We have summarized our favored dual-route model of skilled reading, the dual-route cascaded (DRC) model, and considered its application to acquired dyslexia, beginning reading, poor reading in children, and precocious reading. Now, the time has come to review our arguments and see whether we have reached our goal.

THE READING SYSTEM

People can read only when they possess a mental information-processing system that can accept print as input and can create semantic, syntactic, and phonological representations as output. Throughout this book, we have referred to this system as the reading system, and we have conceived of it as comprising numerous different components, each dedicated to just one of the many different information-processing jobs that must be done if reading is to be accomplished.

Some of these jobs have to do with processes beyond the single-word level—processes such as determining the syntactic structure of printed sentences, or integrating the semantic representation of a just-read sentence into a conceptual representation of the whole text read so far. Our book says very little about how readers accomplish such tasks, and even less about atypical difficulties, or atypical expertise, in performing or learning to perform them. These are important issues, but doing them justice would require a different book by different authors.

However, some of the jobs that the reading system must also perform are at more basic levels—the levels of the single printed letter, or the single printed

letter string. Much is known about how readers accomplish such tasks, and much is also known about atypical difficulties or atypical expertise in learning or performing them. Such knowledge does not constitute all that there is to know about reading and learning to read, but it does constitute an important part, on which our book has focused.

A theory that specifies these basic components of the reading system is thus a partial theory of the processing architecture of the system. The partial theory of reading we have adopted uses dual-route conceptions. As applied to the explanation of how we read aloud, this conception proposes that there are two processing routes from print to speech. One involves consulting a mental lexicon and retrieving a word's pronunciation from that lexicon: That is the lexical reading route, and it permits the reading aloud of any word familiar to the reader, but not the reading aloud of unfamiliar words or pseudowords. The other route for reading aloud involves applying rules that specify relationships between subword-sized orthographic segments and the pronunciations of these segments. This is the nonlexical reading route, and it permits the reading aloud of pseudowords and of regular words (those containing no violations of the spelling-to-sound rules). Exception words, those words that do contain such violations, are misread ("regularized") by this route. We assume that the nonlexical route uses just grapheme-phoneme correspondence (GPC) rules, but it is possible that rules about larger segments might also be involved. Since the skilled reader can correctly read aloud both exception words and pseudowords, acquiring reading skill must involve acquiring both of these procedures for reading aloud.

As applied to the explanation of how we comprehend single printed words, the dual-route conception also specifies two mechanisms. Comprehension thus can be "direct" (a matter of contacting semantics directly from print) or "indirect" (a matter of deriving phonology from print and then using the resulting phonological representation to access the word's meaning).

Chapter 3 outlined a specific dual-route theory of the reading system consisting of six processing components and their connections. The first of these components to be activated when a reader encounters print is a system of abstract letter units. There is a separate set of these for each different position in a letter string, and within each set there is one unit for each letter the reader can recognize. These units are abstract in the sense that they do not contain any information about the pronunciations of letters and also in the sense that they are indifferent to the specific visual forms of letters. A letter activates the same unit in this system regardless of its font, case, or size.

There are two forms of output from the abstract letter units. Information as to which letters are present in the input is transmitted sequentially, from left to right, to a GPC conversion system. Letter units activated at the abstract letter units level also activate word-specific units in an orthographic lexicon. These word-specific orthographic-lexical units also have two forms of output. One is to a semantic system, so that a word's meaning can be activated; the other is to a phonological lexicon, so that a word's pronunciation can be activated. Activa-

tion of a word's meaning in the semantic system can also activate its pronunciation in the phonological lexicon. Finally, there is a system of phoneme units that is activated by the output of the GPC system or from the phonological output lexicon.

We have used this proposal about the nature of the reading system to think about skilled reading and the ways in which it can be impaired after brain damage. We also have used it to think about beginning reading, reading in children having difficulties in learning to read, and reading in children who have shown unusual proficiency in learning to read. We also have gone beyond the scope of even this extended DRC model to speculate about the processes by which poor, average, and precocious readers learn to read.

Acquiring the Reading System

We agree with other developmental researchers (e.g., Ehri, 1999) that there is a very early stage of reading in which children, typically when they are of pre-school age, use distinctive visual properties of words such as word length or visually distinctive letter configurations to identify words. In our theory of reading acquisition, we explicitly exclude this "pre-alphabetic" reading (e.g., Ehri, 1999) from the kinds of reading performance to be accounted for by any version of our proposed system. Pre-alphabetic (or logographic) reading does not use the reading system, not even in its most primitive form, because reading this way does not involve use of abstract letter identities.

The following phase of reading acquisition does, however, involve use of a primitive version of the reading system: This is the phase of reading acquisition that we, adopting Ehri's (1999) term, have referred to as "partial-alphabetic reading."

When normal children come to the task of learning to read, they already possess three of the six components of the reading system in Figure 3.10 and connections between these three components. Having already mastered oral language, beginning readers must have a semantic system, a phonological lexicon, and a phoneme units system. So, learning to read involves acquiring the abstract letter units system, the orthographic lexicon, the GPC system, and the connections between these components; and interfacing these with the already-existing components of the reading system.

We have proposed that at the partial-alphabetic phase of reading, there is an orthographic lexicon that contains entries for just a small number of words, and that these entries are only partially connected to letter units at the abstract letter unit level, as suggested in Figure 5.1. For example, there may be only one word beginning with the letter *m* which the child has learned to read—the word *man*, say. Here, the only connection that the child has acquired from abstract letter units to the entry for MAN in the orthographic lexicon is a connection from the letter M in the first-position set of abstract letter units. So, the child is likely to read any word beginning with the letter *m* as "man"; and that is the kind of reading behavior one observes in children who are at the partial-alphabetic phase of reading acquisition.

Of course, even if the links from abstract letter units to orthographic lexicon were as we have just described, reading *mix* as /man/ would be prevented if the GPC system were also being used, because such use would yield the correct pronunciation for the word *mix*. So, we propose that a second property of the reading system as it is present at the partial-alphabetic phase of reading acquisition is that little or nothing of the GPC system has been acquired yet. If so, children at this stage should be unable, or almost completely unable, to read pseudowords aloud. If they read any word beginning with an *m* as /man/, they should do the same with any pseudoword beginning with an *m*. As we showed in chapter 5, this, too, is the kind of reading behavior one observes in children who are at the partial-alphabetic phase of reading acquisition.

Children at this phase of reading acquisition have rather few entries in the orthographic lexicon, but very many entries in the phonological lexicon. Therefore, they frequently will encounter words in print which are visually unfamiliar to them. These words are not yet in their limited orthographic lexicons, and hence cannot be read via the lexical route, which goes through that lexicon (see Figure 5.1). However, children can recognize these words from speech because the words are present in their phonological lexicons. Therefore, what children need to do is convert the printed letter string to the phonology they already know, which they can do via the nonlexical route, using the GPC system.

The way out from the partial-alphabetic phase of reading acquisition is therefore to seek mastery of the GPC conversion system. If that is achieved, the child will be able to sound out many visually unfamiliar words, and thus achieve access to their pronunciations and hence their meanings, which will help the child to learn these words; that is, to add them to the orthographic lexicon. The idea that such use of the nonlexical route aids acquisition of the lexical route is expressed well by the self-teaching hypothesis proposed by Share and Stanovich (1995b).

We also have proposed, on the basis of the work of Thompson and his colleagues (e.g., Thompson et al., 1996), that the converse also occurs—use of the lexical route to aid acquisition of the nonlexical route. The claim here is that one of the ways in which GPCs are learned is by induction from what is known about the spellings and pronunciations of words that are already in the orthographic and phonological lexicons.

ATYPICAL ACQUISITION OF THE READING SYSTEM

The Concept of Proximal Cause

Many children encounter difficulties in acquiring the reading system; some, on the other hand, acquire the system with abnormal ease. Both kinds of children exhibit atypical patterns of reading acquisition. What causes such atypicalities? A critical distinction, central to most of what we have to say in this book, is between what we have called proximal and distal causes of atypical reading behavior.

Reading behavior relies directly on the use of the reading system. Therefore, if reading behavior is in any way atypical, that reader's reading system must also be atypical in some way; and it is that atypicality that is the proximal cause of the abnormal reading. Furthermore, something, or some things, have caused the reading system to be atypical; these things are distal causes of the atypical reading. A complete account of why reading is atypical in a particular person requires that something be said about both proximal and distal causes.

Consider the often-discussed relationship between phonemic awareness and learning to read. Suppose a child is very poor at "sounding out" as measured by pseudoword reading, and also performs very poorly on tests of phonemic awareness, which we and others have conceptualized as metacognitive awareness of phoneme-level sound patterns within words. One might propose that the reason the child reads pseudowords so badly is because he or she lacks phonemic awareness (e.g., Byrne, 1998; Harm & Seidenberg, 1999; Olson et al., 1999; Torgesen et al., 1999). This would be a mistake, however, because as one is reading a pseudoword aloud, phonemic awareness is not used or needed. Such awareness probably facilitates learning how to read pseudowords aloud. It also may be generated and drawn on as an epiphenomenon by hesitant readers, as in the example of the child struggling to read *bats* that we presented in chapter 5. However, phonemic awareness is not directly involved in on-line performance in which graphemes are linked to phonemes to pronounce a written word. Hence, poor phonemic awareness is a distal, but not a proximal, cause of the atypical reading behavior. Proximal causes are atypicalities of some component or other of the reading system, and phonemic awareness is not a component of that system.

Any account of atypical reading that does not refer to some specific atypicality of the reading system itself is therefore necessarily incomplete. There are many such accounts. For example, the influential phonological core deficit hypothesis (Jorm & Share, 1984; Share & Stanovich, 1995b; Torgesen & Burgess, 1998), according to which pervasive phonological impairment is at the heart of developmental reading difficulty, is incomplete in itself because it is a proposal primarily about distal causes. It does not explain at the level of specificity we have given in the DRC model and our extrapolations from it what kind of atypicality of the reading system is caused by the phonological deficit. That is also true of explanations of difficulties in learning to read that refer to abnormalities of the magnocellular component of the visual pathways in the brain (e.g., Cornellison et al., 1998; Lovegrove et al., 1986) and many other such explanations.

This is not at all to say that incomplete accounts cannot be valuable and informative—they certainly can be—but it is essential to acknowledge that any account of atypical reading performance that does not include any statement about exactly how the reading system itself is atypical is missing a critical link in the causal chain: the proximal cause.

Some developmentalists have indeed proposed distinct accounts of both skilled reading and learning to read (distal cause). For example, Ehri (1998) built on Rumelhart's interactive model of word reading and other sources to

distinguish between the processes of sight word reading and decoding and to describe features of skilled and beginning reading. She also described the process of reading acquisition. However, she did not specify a model of what is happening on line when, for example, a child misreads a pseudoword as if it were a real word. Neither has she linked that momentary behavior with an equally specific account of how it might change over time. Indeed, to our knowledge, no one previously has laid out a full scheme of links between particular patterns of observed deficits in on-line reading, an explicit model of reading, and hypothesized developmental processes such as we have attempted in this book.

Proximal Causes of Atypical Reading in Children Learning to Read

To define "atypical" one must make reference to what is typical. In chapter 2, we discuss two ways one can do that, with respect to reading acquisition: the chronological age (CA) match and the reading level (RL) match. The CA-match approach is to compare a child's reading to the reading of other children of the same chronological age. The RL-match approach is to match the focal child with younger normal readers on some particular reading task, and then to compare the child with this level-matched control group of typical readers on other reading tasks. These and other correlational designs can suggest hypotheses about proximal causes of atypical reading. If two groups, say older poor readers and RL-matched younger average readers, have quantitatively distinct reading systems, they should show different patterns of strong and weak performances on tasks that depend on different components of the reading system. For example, one group might be relatively stronger at pseudoword reading and the other at exception word reading.

There are six different components of the reading system. Given that a proximal cause of reading atypicality is an atypicality of one or more of these components or of the connections between them, one might expect to interpret the atypical reading behavior of any child learning to read as due to an atypicality of just one of the system's components or connections. That expectation is clearly met when one studies reading in people who had been skilled readers but then had a reading impairment due to brain damage. But, if what we have said about the normal course of reading acquisition is correct, this expectation is in fact unlikely to be met when one studies children as they learn to read. To understand what to expect regarding proximal causes of atypical reading in developing readers, one must move to the distal level and consider the process of reading acquisition.

Distal Causes of Atypical Reading Acquisition

Suppose, for example, a child has a very poorly developed orthographic lexicon, relative to either children the same age (CA match) or children at the same estimated reading level (RL match). The poorly developed orthographic lexicon will be the proximal cause of poor exception-word reading, relative to the

comparison group. Since the reading of pseudowords does not use the ortho-graphic lexicon, might such a child be perfectly normal (again, relative to a comparison group) at pseudoword reading? This depends on the importance, for acquiring the GPC system, of the lexical process of inducing GPCs from knowledge of the spellings and pronunciations of a body of known words (Thompson et al., 1996). If this induction process makes a significant contribu-tion to GPC acquisition, then an underdeveloped orthographic lexicon will be the proximal cause of poor exception word reading and a distal cause of future poor pseudoword reading. Conversely, if the self-teaching mechanism described above, which depends on good ability to use the GPC system, is a substantial contributor to the development of the orthographic lexicon, then poor GPC ability will be the proximal cause of poor pseudoword reading and a distal cause of future poor exception-word reading.

If the self-teaching mechanism is the more important of these two, then one would expect poor pseudoword reading to be the most prominent deficit in samples of children who are having difficulty learning to read, as it has been in many, but not all, studies (e.g., Rack et al., 1992). The amount and kinds of instruction a child receives and the kinds of text to which he or she is exposed would be expected to influence how efficiently each of these mechanisms is acquired, but it should not change our fundamental argument about the mecha-nisms by which GPC use can contribute to development of the orthographic lexicon or by which development of the orthographic lexicon can contribute to the induction of GPCs.

If each kind of deficit impedes development, we should not be surprised to find that children who are atypical at exception-word reading are often atypi-cal at pseudoword reading, and vice versa, even though these two tasks depend on different parts of the reading system. If what we have proposed about how learning based on each route's operations contributes to the development of the other route is true, we would expect deficits in both types of reading to be the most common, but not the invariable pattern. Indeed, this is what has been found. Poor readers generally are poor, and precocious readers generally are very good, at reading both pseudowords and exception words. However, there have been striking exceptions to this pattern, which also would be expected in a theory of development based on two mechanisms.

In chapter 6, we noted studies of people who were very poor at pseudoword reading, but who had overall levels of reading skill sufficient for them to suc-ceed at university-level reading. If a normal GPC system is a prerequisite for attaining a normal level of overall reading skill, such people should not exist. We concluded that there are compensatory mechanisms for reading acquisition that allow at least some people to succeed even when the GPC-based self-teach-ing procedure is not available to them. Conversely, children can acquire mas-tery of the GPC system even with a very impoverished orthographic lexicon (see, e.g., Castles & Coltheart, 1993). Such findings indicate that the induction of GPCs from a body of lexical knowledge, though useful for GPC acquisition, is not essential to that developmental process.

In the case where atypicality refers to superiority rather than inferiority—that is, the case of precocious reading, the subject of our chapter 7—the picture is the same. Most precocious readers are precocious at both lexical and nonlexical reading, but this is not so for all precocious readers. It is clearly the case that a child can be precocious at reading words while being very poor at pseudoword reading; and some normal and hyperlexic precocious readers are considerably better at reading pseudowords than exception words.

LOSING THE READING SYSTEM

Those who dismiss the relevance of studies of acquired dyslexia and of models like the DRC model to understanding poor reading in children often emphasize the greater specificity of deficits in acquired dyslexia. For example, Foorman (1995) wrote as follows:

> Dual-route theory predicts the pattern of impairments referred to as *phonological dyslexia* or *surface dyslexia*. . . . Nice as these pictures are of the ideal *acquired dyslexic*, they do not fit the usual picture of a *developmental dyslexic* [whose] modal pattern of impairment in irregular word and nonword reading cuts across the patterns predicted by dual-route theory. Difficulty with irregular words is the essence of *surface dyslexia* and difficult with nonwords is the essence of *phonological dyslexia*. Simultaneous difficulty with irregular words and nonwords undermines the credibility of two distinct mechanisms or routes and favors the adoption of a single mechanism approach. (pp. 396-397)

In a similar vein, Harm and Seidenberg (1999) argued that

> in principle, the dual-route model affords the possibility that exception word and nonword reading could completely dissociate, with perfect performance on one and nil performance on the other, a pattern that has not been observed. . . . The fact that most dyslexic individuals are impaired on both exceptions and nonwords also presents a problem for the dual-route model. (p. 507)

We agree, as we have said previously, that developmental reading impairments are more likely than acquired ones to be diffuse. However, we disagree with Foorman's and Harm and Seidenberg's conclusions that this difference invalidates extension of the DRC model to describe poor reading in children. Furthermore, we reiterate that acquired dyslexia and developmental dyslexia may be similar in some ways (i.e., at the proximal level of explanation), yet different in other ways (i.e., at the level of distal cause). Thus, what we learn about the nature of the reading system from studies of acquired dyslexia can sometimes be helpful in understanding developmental dyslexia. However, when making these connections, it is critical to remember the poet Robert Frost's (c. 1967) observation that "good fences make good neighbors."

Suppose we are studying two people who can read real words aloud reasonably well, but are very poor at reading pseudowords aloud. Close investigation reveals that pseudowords with one-to-one relationships between letters and phonemes (pseudowords like *trib* or *bolv*) can be read correctly, but pseudowords containing multiletter graphemes (pseudowords like *thib* or *boov*) cannot. A reasonable explanation here is that neither reader possesses a subpart of the GPC conversion system, which we called graphemic parsing in Figure 3.10, that underlies ability to group letters into individual graphemes. When such parsing is not possible, every letter is treated as a separate grapheme. This is a hypothesis about proximal cause, and the claim is that the proximal cause of the poor pseudoword reading is the same for the two readers.

Suppose it is then revealed that one of these readers is 10 years old and has never been able to read pseudowords with multiletter graphemes, while the other was a fluent and accurate reader of all kinds of pseudowords until she had a stroke. Here, the distal causes of the poor pseudoword reading are very different in the two readers. Nevertheless, the proximal cause is the same. It is because proximal causes of abnormal reading can be the same in children who have never acquired adequate reading ability and adults who once were fluent readers, but then received a brain injury which impaired their reading, that one can profitably compare developmental and acquired patterns of reading impairment.

That is the way in which developmental and acquired dyslexia are comparable. The way in which they are not comparable is that the acquisition of each reading route is aided by the other reading route, as we have argued above, but the on-line use of each route does not require the other. So, an impairment of the nonlexical route might slow the acquisition of the lexical route in someone who was learning to read. However, in a skilled reader whose reading has been impaired by brain injury, if that impairment affected just the nonlexical route, there is no reason to expect reading via the lexical route to be impaired. One would therefore expect forms of acquired dyslexias to reflect acquired impairments of just one component of the reading system much more often than developmental dyslexias. Chapter 4 shows that this is so. Six different subtypes of acquired dyslexia are reviewed there, and five are interpreted in terms of specific impairments of particular parts of the reading system or input to the system. The sixth, deep dyslexia, is argued not to involve the reading system at all; reading in this form of acquired dyslexia uses a different mechanism, one located in the right hemisphere of the brain rather than the left.

Although it thus is possible to classify subtypes of acquired dyslexia, there is great heterogeneity even within each subtype, exactly as one would expect if damage to any box or any arrow within the reading system would give rise to some specific pattern of impairment of reading. The enterprise of subtyping acquired dyslexias was invaluable as a ground-clearing exercise, but it has now been supplanted by case-by-case interpretation of individual patients in relation to some model of the reading system. That would seem to be a promising next move in relation to the study of developmental dyslexia, in which indi-

vidual differences typically are characterized in terms of quantitative multidimensional variation rather than discrete subtypes (e.g., Vellutino et al., 1991).

LEARNING AND DOING

In the introduction to their 1978 collection of Vygotsky's work, Cole and Scribner echoed his ideas by writing, "If higher psychological processes arise and undergo changes in the course of learning and development, psychology will only fully understand them by determining their origin and mapping their history" (Vygotsky, 1978, p. 12). Reading is a higher psychological process, and we agree that what Cole and Scribner say here applies to reading. But, we would like to add—well, perhaps to insist on—a second claim, which would go something like this: If any higher psychological process depends for its successful execution on the use of a particular mental information-processing system, psychology will only fully understand that process by determining the architecture of the relevant information-processing system, and by determining how the architecture varies across developmental and individual differences. We think that claim applies to cognition in general (and, hence, to reading in particular), just as Cole and Scribner's claim does.

There are two sets of mental processes that psychology needs to understand if it is fully to understand reading (or any other domain of cognition). One set prototypically operates over a time scale of years; the other operates over a time scale of tenths of a second. In 5 years, most children go from being illiterate to being skilled readers; to understand how children learn to read, we need to know exactly what goes on during those 5 years, as far as reading is concerned. Five tenths of a second after a skilled reader is shown a real word, the printed letter string's meaning and pronunciation are known by that reader; to understand skilled reading, we need to know exactly what goes on during those five tenths of a second.

We have sought in our book to discuss reading at both of these time scales. The shorter scale is the scale at which the DRC model operates, and it defines the realm of proximal cause. The longer scale defines the realm of distal cause, a realm into which we have ventured with some speculations consistent with the DRC model. However, as happens so often in psychology, these time scales are not discrete entities but ends of a continuum, and the way in which one considers the midpoints of this continuum is critical to our bifurcation of proximal and distal cause.

As Vygotsky (1978) and others (e.g., Siegler & Jenkins, 1989) have observed, "microgenetic" changes in behavior that occur over minutes, hours, or weeks as a person learns something new may represent development in miniature. Instructional experiments in which children are taught to read new words or pseudowords (e.g., Ehri & Wilce, 1985; Rack et al., 1994; Share, 1999; Thompson et al., 1996) take place within this intermediate time scale. We have found it useful to consider such short-term changes in reading behavior as dis-

tinct from on-line reading of a particular letter string in a particular fraction of a second.

The reading system operates and it develops over time. We learn to read and we read. Boundaries between these two human processes inevitably are fuzzy, and the fuzziness is most apparent in the on-line reading of a beginner for whom reading a word takes, not a fraction of a second, but several seconds to complete. What is happening here, reading or learning to read? Probably both, but we maintain that it is useful to acknowledge, as few developmentalists have, that the two processes are distinct and need to be considered separately. Raising this fence makes connections across skilled and beginning reading, acquired and developmental dyslexia, and exceptionally good and exceptionally poor reading easier to understand.

References

Aaron, P. G. (1989). *Dyslexia and hyperlexia: Diagnosis and management of developmental reading disabilities*. Dordrecht, The Netherlands: Kluwer.

ACT, Inc. (1997). *ACT Assessment: Technical manual*. Iowa City, IA: Author.

Adams, M. J. (1990). *Beginning to read: Thinking and learning about print*. Cambridge, MA: MIT Press.

Allington, R. L., & Walmsley, S. A. (Eds.). (1995). *No quick fix: Rethinking literacy programs in America's elementary schools*. New York: Teachers College Press.

Allington, R. L., & Woodside-Jiron, H. (1999). The politics of literacy teaching: How "research" shaped educational policy. *Educational Researcher, 28*, 4–13.

Ans, B., Carbonnel, S., & Valdois, S. (1998). A connectionist multiple-trace memory model for polysyllabic word reading. *Psychological Review, 105*, 678–723.

Backman, J. (1983). Psycholinguistic skills and reading acquisition: A look at early readers. *Reading Research Quarterly, 18*, 466–479.

Baron, J. (1979). Orthographic and word-specific mechanisms in children's reading of words. *Child Development, 50*, 60–72.

Baron, J., & Strawson, C. (1976). Use of orthographic and word-specific knowledge in reading words aloud. *Journal of Experimental Psychology: Human Perception and Performance, 2*, 386–393.

Bauer, D. W., & Stanovich, K. E. (1980). Lexical access and the spelling-to-sound regularity effect. *Memory and Cognition, 8*, 424–432.

Beauvois, M.-F., & Derouesné, J. (1981). Lexical orthographic agraphia. *Brain, 104*, 21–49.

Berent I., & Perfetti, C. A. (1995) A rose is a reez—The two-cycles model of phonology assembly in reading English. *Psychological Review, 102*, 146–184.

Berndt, R. S., Haendiges, A. N., Mitchum, C. C., & Wayland, S. C. (1996). An investigation of nonlexical reading impairments. *Cognitive Neuropsychology, 13*, 763–801.

Berninger, V. W., Abbott, R. D., Zook, D., Ogier, S., Lemos-Britton, Z., & Brooksher, R. (1999). Early intervention for reading disabilities: Teaching the alphabet principle in a connectionist framework. *Journal of Learning Disabilities, 32*, 491–503.

Berninger, V. W. & Corina, D. (1998). Making cognitive neuroscience educationally relevant: Creating bidirectional collaborations between educational psychology and cognitive neuroscience. *Educational Psychology Review, 10*, 343–354.

Besner, D., Twilley, L., McCann, R. S., & Seergobin, K. (1990). On the association between connectionism and data: Are a few words necessary? *Psychological Review, 97*, 432–446.

Biemiller, A. J. (1970). The development of the use of graphic and contextual information as children learn to read. *Reading Research Quarterly, 13*, 223–253.

Bishop, D. V. M. (1997a). Cognitive neuropsychology and developmental disorders: Uncomfortable bedfellows. *Quarterly Journal of Experimental Psychology. A, Human Experimental Psychology, 50*, 899–923.

Bishop, D. V. M. (1997b). *Uncommon under-*

standing: Development and disorders of language comprehension. Hove, England: Psychology Press.

Bissex, G. L. (1980). GNYS AT WRK: A child learns to read and write. Cambridge, MA: Harvard University Press.

Blazely, A., & Coltheart, M. (2001). Semantic dyslexia with and without surface dyslexia. Manuscript in preparation.

Boder, E. (1973). Developmental dyslexia: Prevailing diagnostic concepts and a new diagnostic approach. Bulletin of the Orton Society, 23, 106–118.

Borsting, E., Ridder, W. H., III, Dudeck, K., Kelley, C., Matsui, L., & Motoyama, J. (1996). The presence of a magnocellular deficit depends on the type of dyslexia. Vision Research, 136, 1047–1053.

Bowey, J. (1999). The limitations of orthographic rime analogies in beginners' word reading: A reply to Goswami (1999). Journal of Experimental Child Psychology, 72, 220–231.

Breitmeyer, B. G. (1992) The roles of sustained (P) and transient (M) channels in reading and reading disability. Schweizerische Zeitschrift Fuer Psychologie, 51, 43–54.

Breitmeyer, B. G., & Ganz, L. (1976). Implications of sustained and transient channels for theories of visual pattern masking, saccadic suppression and information processing. Psychological Review, 83, 1–36.

Breznitz, Z. (1987). Increasing first graders' reading accuracy and comprehension by increasing their reading rates. Journal of Educational Psychology, 79, 236–242.

Breznitz, Z. (1997). Enhancing the reading of dyslexic children by reading acceleration and auditory masking. Journal of Educational Psychology, 89, 103-113.

Briggs, C., & Elkind, D. (1973). Cognitive development in early readers. Developmental Psychology, 9, 279–280.

Brown, G. D. A. (1998). The endpoint of skilled word recognition: The ROAR model. In J. L. Metsala & L. C. Ehri (Eds.), Word recognition in beginning literacy (pp. 121–138). Mahwah, NJ: Erlbaum.

Bruck, M. (1998). Outcomes of adults with childhood histories of dyslexia. In R.M. Joshi et al. (Eds.), Reading and spelling: Development and disorders (pp. 179–200). Mahwah, NJ: Erlbaum.

Bryant, P. B., & Goswami, U. (1986). Strengths and weaknesses of the reading-level design: A comment on Backman, Mamen, & Ferguson. Psychological Bulletin, 100, 101–103.

Bryant, P. B., & Impey, L. (1986). The similarities between normal children and dyslexic adults and children. Cognition, 24, 121–137.

Bub, D., Cancelliere, A., & Kertesz, A. (1985). Whole-word and analytic translation of spelling to sound in a nonsemantic reader. In K. E. Patterson, J. C. Marshall, & M. Coltheart (Eds.), Surface dyslexia: Neuropsychological and cognitive studies of phonological reading (pp. 15–34). London: Erlbaum.

Burns, J. M., Collins, M. D., & Paulsell, J. C. (1991). A comparison of intellectually superior preschool accelerated readers and nonreaders: Four years later. Gifted Child Quarterly, 35, 118–124.

Burr, D. C., Holt, J., Johnstone, J. R., & Ross, J. (1982). Selective suppression of motion sensitivity during saccades. Journal of Physiology, 333, 1–15.

Burr, D. C., Morrone, M. C., & Ross, J. (1994). Selective suppression of the magnocellular visual pathway during saccadic eye movements. Nature, 371, 511–513.

Bus, A. G., & van IJzendoorn, M.,H. (1995). Mothers reading to their 3-year-olds. The role of mother-child attachment security in becoming literate. Reading Research Quarterly, 30, 998–1015.

Bus, A. G., & van IJzendoorn, M. H. (1999). Phonological awareness and early reading: A meta-analysis of experimental training studies. Journal of Educational Psychology, 91, 403–414.

Byrne, B. (1998). The foundation of literacy: The child's acquisition of the alphabetic principle. Hove, England: Psychology Press.

Byrne, B., & Fielding-Barnsley, R. (1995). Evaluation of a program to teach phonemic awareness to young children: A 2- and 3-year follow-up and a new preschool trial. Journal of Educational Psychology, 87, 488–503.

Byrne, B., Fielding-Barnsley, R., & Ashley, L. (2000). Effects of phoneme identity training after six years: Outcome level distinguished from rate of response. Journal of Educational Psychology, 92, 659–667.

Byrne, B., Freebody, P., & Gates, A. (1992). Longitudinal data on relations of word-reading strategies to comprehension, reading

time, and phonemic awareness. *Reading Research Quarterly, 27,* 141–151.

Byrnes, J. P., & Fox, N. A. (1998). The educational relevance of research in cognitive neuroscience. *Educational Psychology Review, 10,* 297–342.

Cairns, E., & Cammock, T. (1978). Development of a more reliable version of the Matching Familiar Figures Test. *Developmental Psychology, 5,* 555–560.

Campbell, R., & Butterworth, B. (1985). Phonological dyslexia and dysgraphia in a highly literate subject: A developmental case with associated deficits of phonemic processing and awareness. *Quarterly Journal of Experimental Psychology. A. Human Experimental Psychology, 37A,* 435–475.

Caramazza, A. (1984). The logic of neuropsychological research and the problem of patient classification in aphasia. *Brain and Language, 21,* 9–20.

Caramazza, A. (1986). On drawing inferences about the strucure of normal cognitive systems from the analysis of patterns of impaired performance: The case for single-patient studies. *Brain and Cognition, 5,* 41–66.

Case, R. (1991). *The mind's staircase: Exploring the conceptual underpinnings of children's thought and knowledge.* Hillsdale, NJ: Erlbaum.

Castles, A., & Coltheart, M. (1993). Varieties of developmental dyslexia. *Cognition, 47,* 149–180.

Castles, A., Datta, H., Gayan, J., & Olson, R. K. (1999). Varieties of developmental reading disorder: Genetic and environmental influences. *Journal of Experimental Child Psychology, 72,* 73–94.

Catts, H. W., Fey, M. E., Zhang, X., & Tomblin, J. B. (1999). Language basis of reading and reading disabilities: Evidence from a longitudinal investigation. *Scientific Studies of Reading, 3,* 331–362.

Chall, J. S. (1983). *Stages of reading development.* New York: McGraw-Hill.

Chapman, L.J. & Chapman, J.P. (1985). Methodological problems in the study of differential deficits in retarded groups. In D.K. Detterman (Eds.), *Current topics in human intelligence: Vol. 1. Research methodology* (pp. 141–153). Norwood, NJ: Ablex.

Cipolotti, L., & Warrington, E. K. (1995). Semantic memory and reading abilities: A case study. *Journal of the International Neuropsychological Society, 1,* 104–110.

Clark, M. M. (1976). *Young fluent readers.* London: Heinemann.

Coltheart, M. (1978). Lexical access in simple reading tasks. In G. Underwood (Ed.), *Strategies of information processing* (pp. 151–216). London: Academic Press.

Coltheart, M. (1979). When can children learn to read—and when should they be taught? In *Reading research: Vol. 1. Advances in theory and practice* (pp. 1–30). New York: Academic Press.

Coltheart, M. (1980). Reading, phonological recoding, and deep dyslexia. In M. Coltheart,, K. Patterson, & J. C. Marshall (Eds.), *Deep dyslexia* (pp. 197–226). London: Routledge & Kegan Paul.

Coltheart, M. (1983). The right hemisphere and disorders of reading. In A. Young (Ed.), *Functions of the right hemisphere* (pp. 173–201). London: Academic Press.

Coltheart, M. (1984a). Acquired dyslexias and normal reading. In R. N. Malatesha & H. A. Whitaker (Eds.), *Dyslexia: A global issue* (pp.357–374). The Hague, The Netherlands: Martinus Nijhoff.

Coltheart, M. (1984b). Theoretical analysis and practical assessment of reading disorders. In C. Cornoldi (Ed.), *Aspects of reading and dyslexia* (pp. 117–126). Padua, Italy: Cleup.

Coltheart, M. (1985). Cognitive neuropsychology and the study of reading. In M. I. Posner & O. S. M. Marin (Eds.), *Attention and performance X11* (pp. 3–37). Hillsdale, NJ: Erlbaum.

Coltheart, M. (1987). Functional architecture of the language-processing system. In M. Coltheart, G. Sartori, & R. Job (Eds.), *The cognitive neuropsychology of language* (pp. 1–26). London: Erlbaum.

Coltheart, M. (1996a). Phonological dyslexia: Past and future issues. *Cognitive Neuropsychology, 13,* 749–762.

Coltheart, M. (Ed.). (1996b). *Phonological dyslexia.* Hove, England: Erlbaum.

Coltheart, M. (Ed.). (1998). *Pure alexia (letter-by-letter reading).* Hove, England: Psychology Press.

Coltheart, M. (1999). Modularity and cognition. *Trends in Cognitive Sciences, 3,* 115-120.

Coltheart, M. (2000a). Deep dyslexia is right hemisphere reading. *Brain and Language, 71,* 299–309.

Coltheart, M. (2000b) Dual routes from print to speech and dual routes from print to meaning: Some theoretical issues. In A. Kennedy, R. Radach, J. Pynte, & D. Heller (Eds.), *Reading as a Perceptual Process* (pp. 475–492). Oxford: Elsevier

Coltheart, M. (2000c). *Strategic effects in reading aloud: Implications for computational models.* Paper presented at the annual meeting of the Psychonomic Society, New Orleans, LA.

Coltheart, M., & Byng, S. (1989). A treatment for surface dyslexia. In X. Seron & G. DeLoche (Eds.), *Cognitive approaches in neuropsychological rehabilitation: Neuropsychology and neurolinguistics* (pp. 159–174). Hillsdale, NJ: Erlbaum.

Coltheart, M., Masterson, J., Byng, S., Prior, M., & Riddoch, M. J. (1983). Surface dyslexia. *Journal of Experimental Psychology: Human Experimental Psychology, 35,* 469–495.

Coltheart, M., Curtis, B., Atkins, P., & Haller, M. (1993). Models of reading aloud: Dual-route and parallel-distributed-processing approaches. *Psychological Review, 100,* 589–608.

Coltheart, M. & Jackson, N. E. (1998). Defining dyslexia. *Child Psychology & Psychiatry Review, 3,* 12–16.

Coltheart, M., Langdon, R., & Haller, M. (1996). Computational cognitive neuropsychology. In B. Dodd, L. Worrall, & R. Campbell (Eds.), *Models of language: Illuminations from impairment* (pp. 9–36). London: Whurr.

Coltheart, M., Patterson, K., & Marshall, J. C. (Eds.). (1980). *Deep dyslexia.* London: Routledge & Kegan Paul.

Coltheart, M., Rastle, K., Perry, C., Langdon, R., & Ziegler, J. C. (2001). DRC: A dual route cascaded model of visual word recognition and reading aloud. *Psychological Review, 108,* 204–256.

Coltheart, M., Woollams, A., Kinoshita, S., & Perry, C. (1999). A position-sensitive Stroop effect: Further evidence for a left-to-right component in print-to-speech conversion. *Psychonomic Bulletin and Review, 6,* 456–463.

Coltheart, V., & Leahy, J. (1992). Children's and adults' reading of nonwords: Effects of regularity and consistency. *Journal of Experimental Psychology: Learning, Memory, and Cognition, 18,* 718–729.

Coltheart, V., & Leahy, J. (1996). Procedures used by beginning and skilled readers to read unfamiliar letter strings. *Australian Journal of Psychology, 48,* 124–129.

Coltheart, V., Patterson, K., & Leahy, J. (1994). When a ROWS is a ROSE: Phonological effects in written word comprehension. *Journal of Experimental Psychology: Human Experimental Psychology, 47,* 917–955.

Comeau, L., Cormier, P., Grandmaison, E., & Lacroix, D. (1999). A longitudinal study of phonological processing skills in children learning to read in a second language. *Journal of Educational Psychology, 91,* 29–43.

Connelly, V., Johnston, R. S., & Thompson, G. B. (1999). The influence of instructional approaches on reading procedures. In G. B. Thompson et al. (Eds.), *Learning to read: Beyond phonics and whole language. Language and literacy series* (pp. 103–123). New York: Teachers College Press.

Cornellison, P. L., Hansen, P. C., Hutton, J. L., Evangelinou, V., & Stein, J. F. (1998). Magnocellular visual function and children's single word reading. *Vision Research, 38,* 471–482.

Coslett, H. B. (1991). Read but not write "idea": Evidence for a third reading mechanism. *Brain & Language, 40,* 425–443.

Crain-Thoreson, C., & Dale, P. S. (1992). Do early talkers become early readers? Linguistic precocity, preschool language, and emergent literacy. *Developmental Psychology, 28,* 421–429.

Cunningham, A. E., & Stanovich, K. E. (1997). Early reading acquisition and its relation to reading experience and ability 10 years later. *Developmental Psychology, 33,* 934–945.

Cunningham, A. E., & Stanovich, K. E. (1998). The impact of print exposure on word recognition. In J. L. Metsala & L. C. Ehri (Eds.), *Word recognition in beginning literacy* (pp. 235–262). Mahwah, NJ: Erlbaum.

Dale, P. S., Crain-Thoreson, C., & Robinson, N. M. (1995). Linguistic precocity and the development of reading: The role of extralinguistic factors. *Applied Psycholinguistics, 16,* 173–187.

Déjerine, J. (1892). Contribution à l'étude anatomo-pathologique et clinique des differentes variétés de cécité verbale [Contribution to the anatomopathologic and clinical study of different dyslexia ("word blindness") types]. *Memoires de la Société de Biologie, 4,* 61–90.

Derouesné, J., & Beauvois, M.-F. (1979). Phonological processing in reading: Data from dyslexia. *Journal of Neurology, Neurosurgery, and Psychiatry, 42,* 1125–1132.

De Villiers, J. G., & de Villiers, P. A. (1999). Language development. In M. H. Bornstein & M. E. Lamb (Eds.), *Developmental psychology: An advanced textbook* (4th ed., pp. 313–376). Mahwah, NJ: Erlbaum.

Dunn, L. M. & Markwardt, F. C., Jr. (1970). *Peabody Individual Achievement Test.* Circle Pines, MN: American Guidance Service.

Durkin, D. (1966). *Children who read early.* New York: Teachers College Press.

Durkin, D. (1970). A language arts program for pre-first-grade children: Two-year achievement report. *Reading Research Quarterly, 5,* 534–565.

Durkin, D. (1984). Poor black children who are successful readers: An investigation. *Urban Education, 19,* 53–76.

Edwards, V. T., & Hogben, J. H. (1999). New norms for comparing children's lexical and nonlexical reading: A further look at subtyping dyslexia. *Australian Journal of Psychology, 51,* 37–49.

Ehri, L. C. (1979). Linguistic insight: Threshold of reading acquisition. In T. G. Waller & G. E. Mackinnon (Eds.), *Reading research: Vol. 1. Advances in theory and practice* (pp. 63–114). New York: Academic Press.

Ehri, L.C. (1984). How orthography alters spoken language competencies in children learning to read and spell. In J. Downing & R. Valtin (Eds.), *Language awareness and learning to read* (pp. 119–147).

Ehri, L. C. (1992). Reconceptualizing the development of sight word reading and its relationship to recoding. In P. B. Gough, L. C. Ehri, & R. C. Treiman (Eds.), *Reading acquisition* (pp. 107–144). Hillsdale, NJ: Erlbaum.

Ehri, L. C. (1997). Learning to read and learning to spell are one and the same, almost. In C. A. Perfetti, L. Rieben, & M. Fayol (Eds.), *Learning to spell: Research, theory, and practice across languages* (pp. 237–270). Mahwah, NJ: Erlbaum.

Ehri, L. C. (1998). Grapheme-phoneme knowledge is essential for learning to read words in English. In J. L. Metsala & L. C. Ehri (Eds.), *Word recognition in beginning literacy* (pp. 3–40). Mahwah, NJ: Erlbaum.

Ehri, L. C. (1999). Phases of development in learning to read words. In J. Oakhill & R. Beard (Eds.), *Reading development and the teaching of reading* (pp. 79–108). Oxford, England: Blackwell.

Ehri, L. C., & McCormick, S. (1998). Phases of word learning: Implications for instruction with delayed and disabled readers. *Reading and Writing Quarterly, 14,* 135–163.

Ehri, L. C., & Robbins, C. (1992). Beginning readers need some decoding skill to read words by analogy. *Reading Research Quarterly, 27,* 12–26.

Ehri, L. C., & Saltmarsh, J. (1995). Beginning readers outperform older disabled readers in learning to read words by sight. *Reading and Writing, 7,* 295–326.

Ehri, L. C., & Wilce, L. S. (1985). Movement into reading: Is the first stage of printed word reading visual or phonetic? *Reading Research Quarterly, 20,* 163–179.

Ellis, A. W. (1987). Intimations of modularity, or, the modelarity of mind: Doing cognitive neuropsychology without syndromes. In M. Coltheart, G. Sartori, & R. Job (Eds.), *The cognitive neuropsychology of language* (pp. 397–408). London: Erlbaum.

Ellis, A. W., & Young, A. (1988). *Human cognitive neuropsychology.* London: Erlbaum.

Fischer, K. W., & Pipp, S. L. (1985). Processes of cognitive development: Optimal level and skill acquisition. In R. J. Sternberg (Ed.), *Mechanisms of cognitive development* (pp. 45–80). New York: Freeman.

Fletcher, J. M., Shaywitz, S. E., Shankweiler, D., Katz, L., Liberman, I., Stuebing, K., Francis, D. J., Fowler, A., & Shaywitz, B. A. (1994). Cognitive profiles of reading disability: Comparisons of discrepancy and low achievement definitions. *Journal of Educational Psychology, 86,* 6–23.

Fletcher-Flinn, C. M., & Thompson, G. B. (2000). Learning to read with underdeveloped phonemic awareness but lexicalized phonological recoding: A case study of a 3-year-old. *Cognition, 74,* 177–208.

Flynn, J. M., & Rahbar, M. H. (1994). Prevalence of reading failure in boys compared with girls. *Psychology in the Schools, 31,* 66–71.

Folk, J. R. (1999). Phonological codes are used to access the lexicon during silent reading. *Journal of Experimental Psychology: Learning, Memory, and Cognition, 25,* 892–906.

Foorman, B. R. (1995). Practiced connections of orthographic and phonological process-

ing. In V. W. Berninger (Ed.), *The varieties of orthographic knowledge. Vol. 2. Relationships to phonology, reading, and writing* (pp. 377–419). Dordrecht, The Netherlands: Kluwer.

Foorman, B. R., Francis, D. J., Fletcher, J. M., & Lynn, A. (1996). Relation of phonological and orthographic processing to early reading: Comparing two approaches to regression-based, reading-level-match designs. *Journal of Educational Psychology, 88,* 639–652.

Foorman, B. R., Francis, D. J., Winikates, D., Mehta, P., Schatschneider, C., & Fletcher, J. M. (1997). Early interventions for children with reading disabilities. *Scientific Studies of Reading, 1,* 255–276.

Foorman, B. R., Francis, D. J., Fletcher, J. M., Schatschneider, C., & Mehta, P. (1998). The role of instruction in learning to read: Preventing reading failure in at-risk children. *Journal of Educational Psychology, 90,* 37–55.

Forster, E. M. (1985). *Howards End.* Toronto, Canada: Bantam. (Original work published in 1910).

Forster, K. I., & Chambers, S. (1973). Lexical access and naming time. *Journal of Verbal Learning and Verbal Behavior, 12,* 627–635.

Francis, D. J., Shaywitz, S. E., Stuebing, K. K., Shaywitz, B. A., & Fletcher, J. M. (1996). Developmental lag versus deficit models of reading disability: A longitudinal, individual growth curves analysis. *Journal of Educational Psychology, 88,* 3–17.

Frost, R. (c. 1967). *The complete poems of Robert Frost.* New York: Holt.

Frost, R. (1998). Toward a strong phonological theory of visual word recognition: True issues and false trails. *Psychological Bulletin, 123,* 71–99.

Fukkink, R. G., & de Glopper, K. (1998). Effects of instruction on deriving word meaning from context: A meta-analysis. *Review of Educational Research, 68,* 450–469.

Funnell, E. (1983). Phonological processes in reading: New evidence from acquired dyslexia. *British Journal of Psychology, 74,* 159–180.

Galaburda, A., & Livingstone, M. (1993). Evidence for a magnocellular defect in developmental dyslexia. *Annals of the New York Academy of Sciences, 682,* 70–82.

Glushko, R. J. (1979). The organization and activation of orthographic knowledge in reading aloud. *Journal of Experimental Psychology: Human Perception and Performance, 5,* 674–691.

Goswami, U., & Bryant, P. B. (1990). *Phonological skills and learning to read.* Hove, England: Erlbaum.

Gough, P. B., & Cosky, M. J. (1977). One second of reading again. In N. J. Castellan, D. B. Pisoni, & G. R. Potts (Eds.), *Cognitive theory* (Vol. 2, pp. 271–288). Hillsdale, NJ: Erlbaum.

Gough, P. B., & Hillinger, M. (1980). Learning to read: An unnatural act. *Bulletin of the Orton Society, 30,* 180–196.

Gough, P. B., Hoover, W. A., & Peterson, C. L. (1996). Some observations on a simple view of reading. In C. Cornoldi & J. Oakhill (Eds.), *Reading comprehension difficulties: Processes and intervention* (pp. 1–13). Hillsdale, NJ: Erlbaum.

Gough, P. B., Juel, C., & Griffith, P. (1992). Reading, spelling, and the orthographic cipher. In P. B. Gough, L. C. Ehri, & R. Treiman (Eds.), *Reading acquisition* (pp. 35–48). Hillsdale, NJ: Erlbaum.

Greenberg, D., Ehri, L. C., & Perin, D. (1997). Are word-reading processes the same or different in adult literacy students and third-fifth graders matched for reading level? *Journal of Educational Psychology, 89,* 262–275.

Hanson, R. A., & Farrell, D. (1995). The long-term effects on high-school seniors of learning to read in kindergarten. *Reading Research Quarterly, 30,* 908–933.

Hammill, D. D. (1990). On defining learning disabilities: An emerging consensus. *Journal of Learning Disabilities, 23,* 74–84.

Harm, M. W., & Seidenberg, M. S. (1999). Phonology, reading acquisition, and dyslexia: Insights from connectionist models. *Psychological Review, 106,* 491–528.

Harris, M., & Coltheart, M. (1986). *Language processing in children and adults.* London: Routledge & Kegan Paul.

Healy, J. M. (1982). The enigma of hyperlexia. *Reading Research Quarterly, 17,* 319–338.

Henderson, S. J., Jackson, N. E., & Mukamal, R. A. (1993). Early development of language and literacy skills of an extremely precocious reader. *Gifted Child Quarterly, 37,* 78–83.

Hendriks, A. W., & Kolk, H. H. J. (1997). Strategic control in developmental dyslexia. *Cognitive Neuropsychology, 14,* 321–366.

Hiebert, E. H. (1998). *Text matters in learning to read* (CIERA Report No. 1-001). [Online]. Available Internet: http://www.ciera.org/ciera/publications/report-series

Hinton, G. E. (1989). Learning distributed representations of concepts. In R. G. Morris (Ed.), *Parallel distributed processing: Implications for psychology and neurobiology* (pp. 46–61). Oxford, England: Oxford University Press.

Ho, C. S.-H., & Bryant, P. B. (1997a). Learning to read Chinese beyond the logographic phase. *Reading Research Quarterly, 32,* 276–289.

Ho, C. S.-H., & Bryant, P. B. (1997b). Phonological skills are important in learning to read Chinese. *Developmental Psychology, 33,* 946–951.

Holmes, V. M., & Standish, J. M. (1996). Skilled reading with impaired phonology. *Cognitive Neuropsychology, 13,* 1207–1222.

Howard, D., & Best, W. (1996). Developmental phonological dyslexia: Real word reading can be completely normal. *Cognitive Neuropsychology, 13,* 887–934.

Howard, D., & Franklin, S. (1988). *Missing the meaning? A cognitive neuropsychological study of the processing of words by an aphasic patient.* Cambridge, MA: MIT Press.

Jackson, N. E. (1988). Case study of Bruce: A child with advanced intellectual abilities. In J. M. Sattler (Ed.), *Assessment of children* (3rd ed., pp. 676–678). San Diego, CA: Sattler.

Jackson, N. E. (1992). Precocious reading of English: Sources, structure, and predictive significance. In P. S. Klein & A. J. Tannenbaum (Eds.), *To be young and gifted* (pp. 171–203). Norwood, NJ: Ablex.

Jackson, N. E. (2000). Strategies for modeling the development of giftedness in children. In R. C. Friedman & B. M. Shore (Eds.), *Talents unfolding: Cognition and development* (pp. 27–54). Washington, DC: American Psychological Association.

Jackson, N. E., & Biemiller, A. J. (1985). Letter, word and text reading times of precocious and average readers. *Child Development, 56,* 196–206.

Jackson, N. E., & Butterfield, E. C. (1989). Reading-level-match designs: Myths and realities. *Journal of Reading Behavior, 21,* 387–411.

Jackson, N. E. & Doellinger, H. L. (2001, June). *When do university students who are poor decoders comprehend text adequately?* Paper presented at the annual meeting of the Society for the Scientific Study of Reading, Boulder, CO.

Jackson, N. E., & Donaldson, G. (1989a). Precocious and second-grade readers' use of context in word identification. *Learning and Individual Differences, 1,* 255–281.

Jackson, N. E., & Donaldson, G. (1989b, April). *Effects of frequency, decodability, and versatility on word identification by precocious and second-grade readers.* Paper presented at the biennial meeting of the Society for Research in Child Development. Kansas City, MO.

Jackson, N. E., & Butterfield, E. C. (1986). A conception of giftedness designed to promote research. In R. L. Sternberg & J. E. Davidson (Eds.), *Conceptions of giftedness* (pp. 151–181). Cambridge, England: Cambridge University Press.

Jackson, N. E., Donaldson, G., & Cleland, L. (1988). The structure of precocious reading ability. *Journal of Educational Psychology, 80,* 234–243.

Jackson, N. E., Donaldson, G., & Mills, J. R. (1993). Components of reading skill in postkindergarten precocious readers and level-matched second graders. *Journal of Reading Behavior, 25,* 181–208.

Jackson, N. E., & Kearney, J. M. (1999). Achievement of precocious readers in middle childhood and young adulthood. In N. Colangelo & S. G. Assouline (Eds.), *Talent development: Proceedings from the 1995 H. B. and Jocelyn Wallace National Research Symposium on Talent Development* (pp. 203–217). Dayton, OH: Ohio Psychology Press.

Jackson, N. E., & Klein, E. J. (1997). Gifted performance in young children. In N. Colangelo & G. A. Davis (Eds.), *Handbook of gifted education,* 2nd ed. (pp. 460–474).

Jackson, N. E., Krinsky, S. G., & Robinson, H. B. (1977). *Problems of intellectually advanced children in the public schools: Clinical confirmation of parents' perceptions.* (ERIC Document Reproduction Service No. ED 143 453).

Jackson, N. E. & Lu, W.-H. (1992). Bilingual precocious readers of English. *Roeper Review, 14,* 115–119.

Jackson, N. E., Lu, W. -H., & Ju, D. (1994).

Reading Chinese and reading English: Similarities, differences, and second-language reading. In V. Berninger (Ed.), *The varieties of orthographic knowledge:, Vol. 1., Theoretical and developmental issues* (pp. 73–110). Dordrecht, The Netherlands: Kluwer.

Jackson, N. E., & Myers. M. G. (1982). Letter naming time, digit span, and precocious reading achievement. *Intelligence, 6,* 311–329.

Jackson, N. E., & Roller, C. M. (1993). *Reading with young children* (Research-Based Decision-Making Series Report No. 9302). Storrs, CT: National Research Center on the Gifted and Talented.

Jared, D. (1997). Spelling-sound consistency affects the naming of high-frequency words. *Journal of Memory and Language, 36,* 505–529.

Jenkins, J. R., Stein, M. L. & Wysocki, K. (1984). Learning vocabulary through reading. *American Educational Research Journal, 21,* 767–787.

Job, R., Peressotti, F., & Cusinato, A. (1998). Lexical effects in naming pseudowords in shallow orthographies: Further empirical data. *Journal of Experimental Psychology: Human Perception and Performance, 24,* 1–9.

Jorm, A. F., & Share, D. L. (1984). Phonological recoding and reading acquisition. *Applied Psycholinguistics, 4,* 103–147.

Juel, C. (1991). Beginning reading. In R. Barr, M. Kamil, P. B. Mosenthal, & D. R. Pearson (Eds.), *Handbook of reading research,* Vol. 2. (pp. 759–788). Mahwah, NJ: Erlbaum.

Kail, R., & Hall, L. K. (1994). Processing speed, naming speed, and reading. *Developmental Psychology, 30,* 949–954.

Kay, J., & Marcel, A. (1981). One process, not two, in reading aloud: Lexical analogies do the work of non-lexical rules. *Journal of Experimental Psychology: Human Experimental Psychology, 33,* 397–413.

Kay, J., & Patterson, K. E. (1985). Routes to meaning in surface dyslexia. In K. E. Patterson, J. C. Marshall, & M. Coltheart (Eds.), *Surface dyslexia: Neuropsychological and cognitive studies of phonological reading* (pp. 79–104). London: Erlbaum.

Ke, C., & Everson, M. E. (1999). Recent research in CFL reading and its pedagogical implications. In M. Chu (Ed.), *Mapping the course of the Chinese language field.* (Chinese Language Teachers Association Monograph No. 3, pp. 189–203). Kalamazoo, MI: Chinese Language Teachers Association.

Konold, T. R., Juel, C., & McKinnon, M. (1999). *Building an integrated model of early reading acquisition* (CIERA Report No. 1-003). [On-line], Available Internet: http://www.ciera.org/ciera/publications/report-series

Ladefoged, P. (1993). *A course in phonetics* (3rd ed.). Fort Worth, TX: Harcourt Brace.

Lambon Ralph, M. A., Sage, K., & Ellis, A. W. (1996). Word meaning blindness: A new form of acquired dyslexia. *Cognitive Neuropsychology, 13,* 617–639.

Lambon Ralph, M. A., Sage, K., & Ellis, A. W. (1998). Word meaning blindness revisited. *Cognitive Neuropsychology, 15,* 389–400.

Law, N., Ki, W. W., Chung, A. L. S., Ko, P. Y., & Lam, H. C. (1998). Children's stroke sequence errors in writing Chinese characters. *Reading and Writing: An Interdisciplinary Journal, 10,* 267–292.

Lichtheim, L. (1885). On aphasia. *Brain, 7,* 433–484.

Loftus, G. (1978). On interpretation of interactions. *Memory and Cognition, 6,* 312–319.

Lovegrove, W. J., Martin, F., & Slaghuis, W. (1986). A theoretical and experimental case for a visual deficit in specific reading disability. *Cognitive Neuropsychology, 3,* 225–267.

Lovett, M. W., Lacarenza, L., Borden, S. L., Frijters, J. C., Steinbach, K. A., & De Palma, M. (2000). Components of effective remediation for developmental reading disabilities: Combining phonological and strategy-based instruction to improve outcomes. *Journal of Educational Psychology, 92,* 263–283.

Lovett, M. W., Warren-Chaplin, P. M., Ransby, M. J., & Borden, S. L. (1990). Training the word recognition skills of reading disabled children: Treatment and transfer effects. *Journal of Educational Psychology, 82,* 769–780.

Lukatela, G., & Turvey, M. T. (1994). Visual lexical access is initially phonological: I. Evidence from associative priming by words, homophones, and pseudohomophones. *Journal of Experimental Psychology: General, 123,* 331–353.

Lukatela, G., & Turvey, M. (1998). Reading in two alphabets. *American Psychologist, 53,* 1057–1072.

Lu, W.-H. (1992). *Children's developing metalinguistic awareness of properties of Chinese characters*. Unpublished master's thesis. The University of Iowa.

Luo, C. R. (1996). How is word meaning accessed in reading? Evidence from the phonologically mediated interference effect. *Journal of Experimental Psychology: Learning, Memory, and Cognition, 22,* 883–895.

Mamen, M., Ferguson, H.B., & Backman (1986). No difference represents a significant finding. The logic of the reading-level design: A response to Bryant and Goswami. *Psychological Bulletin, 1000,* 104–106.

Manis, F. (1997, March). *Cognitive profiles in subtypes of dyslexia*. Paper presented at the annual meeting of the Society for the Scientific Study of Reading, Chicago.

Manis, F. R., Seidenberg, M. S., & Doi, L. M. (1999). See Dick RAN: Rapid naming and the longitudinal prediction of reading subskills in first and second graders. *Scientific Studies of Reading, 3,* 129–157.

Manis, F. R., Seidenberg, M. S., Doi, L. M., McBride-Chang, C., & Petersen, A. (1996). On the bases of two subtypes of development dyslexia. *Cognition, 58,* 157–195.

Marshall, J. C. (1984). Towards a rational taxonomy of the acquired dyslexias. In R. N. Malatesha & H. A. Whitaker (Eds.), *Dyslexia: A global issue* (pp. 211–232). The Hague, The Netherlands: Martinus Nijhoff.

Marshall, J. C., & Newcombe, F. (1973). Patterns of paralexia: A psycholinguistic approach. *Journal of Psycholinguistic Research, 2,* 175–199.

McBride-Chang, C. A., & Manis, F. (1996, April). *Naming speed, verbal intelligence, and phonological awareness in good and poor readers: A test of the double deficit hypothesis*. Paper presented at the annual meeting of the American Psychological Association, New York.

McCann, R. S., & Besner, D. (1987). Reading pseudohomophones: Implications for models of pronunciation assembly and the locus of word-frequency effects in naming. *Journal of Experimental Psychology: Human Perception and Performance, 13,* 14–24.

McCarthy, R. A., & Warrington, E. K. (1986). Phonological reading: Phenomena and paradoxes. *Cortex, 22,* 359–380.

McClelland, J. L., & Rumelhart, D. E. (1981). An interactive activation model of context effects in letter perception: I. An account of basic findings. *Psychological Review, 88,* 375–407.

McCloskey, M., & Cohen, N. J. (1989). Catastrophic interference in connectionist networks: The sequential learning problem. In G. H. Bower (Ed.), *The psychology of learning and motivation* (Vol. 24, pp. 109–164). New York: Academic Press.

Meehl, P. E. (1972). Second-order relevance. *American Psychologist, 27,* 932–940.

Metsala, J. L. (1999). The development of phonemic awareness in reading-disabled children. *Applied Psycholinguistics, 20,* 149–158.

Metsala, J. L., & Walley, A. C. (1998). Spoken vocabulary growth and the sequential restructuring of lexical representations: Precursors to phonemic awareness and early reading ability. In J. L. Metsala & L. C. Ehri (Eds.), *Word recognition in beginning literacyreading* (pp. 89–120). Mahwah, NJ: Erlbaum.

Michel, F., Henaff, M. A. & Intrilligator, J. (1996). Two different readers in the same brain after a posterior callosal lesion. *NeuroReport, 7,* 786–788.

Mills, J. R., & Jackson, N. E. (1990). Predictive significance of early giftedness: The case of precocious reading. *Journal of Educational Psychology, 82,* 410–419.

Morris, R. D., Stuebing, K. K., Fletcher, J. M., Shaywitz, S. E., Lyon, G. R., Shankweiler, D. P., Katz, L., & Francis, D. J. (1998). Subtypes of reading disability: Variability around a phonological core. *Journal of Educational Psychology, 90,* 347–373.

Morton, J. (1984). Brain-based and non-brain-based models of language. In D. Caplan, A.R. Lecours & A. Smith (Eds.), *Biological perspectives on language* (pp. 40–64). Cambridge, MA: MIT Press.

Morton, J., & Frith, U. (1995). Causal modeling: A structural approach to developmental psychopathology. In D. Cichetti et al. (Eds.), *Developmental psychopathology: Vol. 1. Theory and methods* (pp. 357–390). New York: Wiley.

Morton, J., & Patterson, K. E. (1980). A new attempt at interpretation, or, an attempt at a new interpretation. In M. Coltheart, K. E. Patterson, & J. C. Marshall (Eds.), *Deep dyslexia* (pp. 335–360). London: Routledge & Kegan Paul.

Muter, V., Snowling, M., & Taylor, S. (1994). Orthographic analogies and phonological awareness: Their role and significance in early reading development. *Journal of Child Psychology and Psychiatry, 35,* 293–310.

Nation, K. (1999). Reading skills in hyperlexia: A developmental perspective. *Psychological Bulletin, 125,* 338–355.

Nation, K., & Hulme, C. (1997). Phonemic segmentation, not onset-rime segmentation, predicts early reading and spelling skills. *Reading Research Quarterly, 32,* 154–167.

National Reading Panel. (2000a). *Teaching children to read: An evidence-based assessment of the scientific research literature and its implications for reading instruction* [On-line] Available Internet: http://www.nichd.nih.gov/publications/nrp/smallbook.htm

National Reading Panel. (2000b). *Teaching children to read: Reports of the subgroups* [On-line] Available Internet: http://www.nichd.nih.gov/publications/nrp/report.htm

Nolan, K. A., & Caramazza, A. (1983). An analysis of writing in a case of deep dyslexia. *Brain and Language, 20,* 305–328.

Norris, D. (1994). A quantitative multiple-levels model of reading aloud. *Journal of Experimental Psychology: Human Perception and Performance, 20,* 1212–1232.

Olson, R. K., Datta, H., Gayan, J., & Defries, J. C. (1999). A behavior-genetic analysis of reading disabilities and component processes. In R. M. Klein et al. (Eds.), *Converging methods for understanding reading and dyslexia: Language, speech, and communciation* (pp. 133–151). Cambridge, MA: MIT Press.

Olson, R. K., Forsberg, H., & Wise, B. (1994). Genes, environment, and the development of orthographic skills. In V. W. Berninger (Ed.), *The varieties of orthographic knowledge: Vol. 1. Theoretical and developmental issues* (pp. 27–71). Dordrecht, The Netherlands: Kluwer.

Olson, R. K., Wise, B. W., Ring, J., & Johnson, M. (1997). Computer-based remedial training in phonological awareness and decoding: Effects on the post-training development of word recognition. *Scientific Studies of Reading, 1,* 235–253.

Paap, K. R., & Noel, R. W. (1991). Dual-route models of print to sound: Still a good horse race. *Psychologische-Forschung, 53,* 13–24.

Patterson, K., & Kay, J. (1982). Letter-by-letter reading: Psychological descriptions of a neuropsychological syndrome. *Journal of Experimental Psychology: Human Experimental Psychology, 34,* 411–441.

Patterson, K. E., Marshall, J. C., & Coltheart, M. (Eds.). (1985). *Surface dyslexia: Neuropsychological and cognitive studies of phonological reading.* London: Erlbaum.

Patterson, K., & Shewell, C. (1987). Speak and spell: Dissociations and word-class effects. In M. Coltheart, R. Job, & G. Sartori (Eds.), *The cognitive neuropsychology of language* (pp. 273–294). London: Erlbaum.

Patterson, K., Vargha-Khadem, F., & Polkey, C. (1987). Reading with one hemisphere. *Brain, 112,* 39–63.

Pennington, B. F., Johnson, C., & Welsh, M. C. (1987). Unexpected reading precocity in a normal preschooler: Implications for hyperlexia. *Brain and Language, 30,* 165–180.

Perfetti, C. A. (1985). *Reading ability.* New York: Oxford University Press.

Perfetti, C. A. (1997). The psycholinguistics of spelling and reading. In C.A. Perfetti, L. Rieben, & M. Fayol (Eds.), *Learning to spell: Research, theory, and practice across languages* (pp. 21–38). Mahwah, NJ: Erlbaum.

Perfetti, C. A. (1999). Cognitive research and the misconceptions of reading education. In J. Oakhill & R. Beard (Eds.), *Reading development and the teaching of reading: A psychological perspective* (pp. 42–58). London: Basil Blackwell.

Perfetti, C. A., & Tan, L. H. (1999). The constituency model of Chinese word identification. In J. Wiang, A. W. Inhoff, & H. -C. Chen (Eds.), *Reading Chinese script: A cognitive analysis* (pp. 115–134). Mahwah, NJ: Erlbaum.

Pikulski, J. J., & Tobin, A. W. (1989). Factors associated with long-term reading achievement of early readers. In S. McCormick & J. Zutell (Eds.), *Cognitive and social perspectives for literacy research and instruction: Thirty-eighth yearbook of the National Reading Conference* (pp. 123–124). Chicago: National Reading Conference.

Pitchford, N. J., & Funnell, E. (1999). An acquired form of developmental phonological dyslexia. *Cognitive Neuropsychology, 16,* 573–587.

Plaut, D. C. (1997). Structure and function in

the lexical system: Insights from distributed models of word reading and lexical decision. *Language and Cognitive Processes, 12,* 765–805.

Plaut, D. C., McClelland, J. L., Seidenberg, M. S., & Patterson, K. (1996). Understanding normal and impaired word reading: Computational principles in quasi-regular domains. *Psychological Review, 103,* 56–115.

Pressley, M. (1998). *Reading instruction that works: The case for balanced teaching.* New York: Guilford Press.

Rack, J., Hulme, C., Snowling, M., & Wightman, J. (1994). The role of phonology in young children learning to read words: The direct-mapping hypothesis. *Journal of Experimental Child Psychology, 57,* 42–71.

Rack, J., Snowling, M. J., & Olson, R. K. (1992). The nonword deficit in developmental dyslexia: A review. *Reading Research Quarterly, 27,* 28–53.

Ralph, M. A. L., Ellis, A. W., & Franklin, S. (1995). Semantic loss without surface dyslexia. *Neurocase, 1,* 363–369.

Rastle, K., & Coltheart, M. (1998). Whammies and double whammies: The effect of length on nonword naming. *Psychonomic Bulletin and Reviews, 5,* 277–282.

Rastle, K., & Coltheart, M. (1999b) Serial and strategic effects in reading aloud. *Journal of Experimental Psychology: Human Perception and Performance, 25,* 482–503.

Rastle, K., & Coltheart, M. (2000). Lexical and nonlexical print-to-sound translation of disyllabic words and nonwords. *Journal of Memory and Language, 42,* 342–364.

Rescorla, L., Hyson, M. C., & Hirsh-Pasek, K. (Eds.). (1991). *Academic instruction in early childhood: Challenge or pressure?* (New Directions in Child Development No. 53). San Francisco: Jossey-Bass.

Saffran, E., Bogyo, L.C., Schwartz, M. F., & Marin, O. S. M. (1980). Does deep dyslexia reflect right-hemisphere reading? In M. Coltheart, K. Patterson, & J. C. Marshall (Eds.), *Deep dyslexia* (pp. 381–406). London: Routledge & Kegan Paul.

Saffran, E., & Coslett, H. B. (1998). Implicit vs. letter-by-letter reading in pure alexia: A tale of two systems. *Cognitive Neuropsychology, 15,* 53–92.

Savage, R. S. (1997). Do children need concurrent prompts in order to use lexical analogies in reading? *Journal of Child Psychology & Psychiatry & Allied Disciplines, 38,* 235–246.

Savage, R., & Stuart, M. (1998). Sublexical influences in beginning reading: Medial vowel digraphs as functional units of transfer. *Journal of Experimental Child Psychology, 69,* 85–105.

Scarborough, H. S. (1990). Very early language deficits in dyslexic children. *Child Development, 61,* 1728–1743.

Scarborough, H. S. (1998). Predicting the future achievement of second graders with reading disabilities: Contributions of phonemic awareness, verbal memory, rapid naming, and IQ. *Annals of Dyslexia, 48,* 115–136.

Scarborough, H. S., & Dobrich, W. (1994). On the efficacy of reading to preschoolers. *Developmental Review, 14,* 245–302.

Scarr, S. (1985). Constructing psychology: Making facts and fables for our times. *American Psychologist, 40,* 499–512.

Schatschneider, C., Francis, D. J., Foorman, B. R., Fletcher, J. M., & Mehta, P. (1999). The dimensionality of phonological awareness: An application of item response theory. *Journal of Educational Psychology, 91,* 439–449.

Schwartz, M. F., Saffran, E. M., & Marin, O. S. M. (1980) Fractionating the reading process in dementia: Evidence for word-specific print-to-sound associations. In M. Coltheart, K. Patterson, & J. C. Marshall (Eds.). *Deep dyslexia* (pp. 259–269). London: Routledge & Kegan Paul.

Scott, J. A., & Ehri, L. C. (1990). Sight word reading in prereaders: Use of logographic vs. alphabetic access routes. *Journal of Reading Behavior, 22,* 149–166.

Seidenberg, M. S. (1999, April). Presentation in the seminar, "How can theoretical models of learning to read incorporate more realistic learning environments?" *Annual meeting of the Society for the Scientific Study of Reading,* Montreal, Canada.

Seidenberg, M. S., & McClelland, J. L. (1989). A distributed, developmental model of word recognition and naming. *Psychological Review, 96,* 523–568.

Senechal, M., LeFevre, J-A., Thomas, E.M., & Daley, K.E. (1998). Differential effects of home literacy experiences on the development of oral and written language. *Reading Research Quarterly, 33,* 96–116.

Seymour, P. H. K., & Elder, L. (1986). Beginning reading without phonology. *Cognitive Neuropsychology, 3,* 1–36.

Seymour, P. H. K., & Evans, H. M. (1992). Beginning reading without semantics: A cognitive study of hyperlexia. *Cognitive Neuropsychology, 9,* 89–122.

Shankweiler, D., Lundquist, E., Katz, L., Stuebing, K., Fletcher, J. M., Brady, S., Fowler, A., Dreyer, L. G., Marchione, K. E., Shaywitz, S., & Shaywitz, B. A. (1999). Comprehension and decoding: Patterns of association in children with reading difficulties. *Scientific Studies of Reading, 3,* 69–94.

Share, D. L. (1999). Phonological recoding and orthographic learning: A direct test of the self-teaching hypothesis. *Journal of Experimental Child Psychology, 72,* 95–129.

Share, D. L., & Stanovich, K. E. (1995a). Accommodating individual differences in critiques: Replies to our commentators. *Issues in Education, 1,* 105–121.

Share, D. L., & Stanovich, K. E. (1995b). Cognitive processes in early reading development: Accommodating individual differences into a model of acquisition. *Issues in Education, 1,* 1–58.

Shaywitz, B. A., Shaywitz, S. E., Pugh, K. R., Mencl, W. E., Fulbright, R. K., Constable, R. T., Skudlarski, P., Jenner, A., Fletcher, J. M., Marchione, K. E., Shankweiler, D., Katz, L., Lacadie, C., & Gore, J. C. (2000, June). *Disruption of posterior brain systems for reading in children with developmental dyslexia.* Poster session presented at the annual meeting of the Organization for Human Brain Mapping.

Shaywitz, S. E., Shaywitz, B. A., Pugh, K. R., et al. (1998). Functional disruption in the organization of the brain for reading in dyslexia. *Proceedings of the National Academy of Science, 95,* 2636–2641.

Siegler, R. S. (1996). *Emerging minds: The process of change in children's thinking.* New York: Oxford University Press.

Silberberg, N. E., & Silberberg, M. C. (1967). Hyperlexia: Specific word recognition skills in young children. *Exceptional Children, 34,* 41–42.

Singson, M., & Mann, V. (1999). *Precocious reading acquisition: Examining the roles of phonological and morphological awareness.* Paper presented at the annual meeting of the Society for the Scientific Study of Reading, Montreal, Canada.

Snow, C. E., Burns, M. S., & Griffin, P. (1998). *Preventing reading difficulties in young children.* Washington, DC: National Academy Press.

Snowling, M., Bryant, P. B., & Hulme, C. (1996). Theoretical and methodological pitfalls in making comparisons between developmental and acquired dyslexia: Some comments on A. Castles and M. Coltheart (1993). *Reading and Writing, 8,* 443–451.

Snowling, M., & Frith, U. (1986). Comprehension in "hyperlexic" readers. *Journal of Experimental Child Psychology, 42,* 392–415.

Spache, G.D. (1981). *Diagnostic reading scales.* Monterey, CA: CTB/McGraw-Hill.

Sparks, R. L. (1995). Phonemic awareness in hyperlexic children. *Reading and Writing, 7,* 217–235.

Spinelli, D., Angelelli, P., Deluca, M., Dipace, E., Judica, A., & Zoccolotti, O. (1997). Developmental surface dyslexia is not associated with deficits in the transient visual system. *Neuroreport, 8,* 1807–1812.

Stahl, S., & Miller, P. D. (1989). Whole language and language experience approaches to beginning reading: A quantitative research synthesis. *Review of Educational Research, 59,* 87–116.

Stahl, S. A., & Murray, B. (1998). Issues involved in defining phonological awareness and its relation to early reading. In J. L. Metsala & L. C. Ehri (Eds.), *Word recognition in beginning literacy* (pp. 89–120). Mahwah, NJ: Erlbaum.

Stainthorp, R., & Hughes, D. (1998). Phonological sensitivity and reading: Evidence from precocious readers. *Journal of Research in Reading, 21,* 53–68.

Stanovich, K. E. (1998). Cognitive neuroscience and educational psychology: What season is it? *Educational Psychology Review, 10,* 419–428.

Stanovich, K. E., Nathan, R. G., & Zolman, E. B. (1988). The developmental lag hypothesis in reading: Longitudinal and reading-level comparisons. *Child Development, 59,* 71–86.

Stanovich, K. E., & Siegel, L. S. (1994). Phenotypic performance profile of children with reading disabilities: A regression-based test of the phonological-core variable-difference model. *Journal of Educational Psychology, 86,* 24–53.

Stanovich, K. E., Siegel, L. S., & Gottardo, A. (1997). Converging evidence for phonological and surface subtypes of reading disability. *Journal of Educational Psychology, 89,* 114–127.

Stanovich, K. E., & West, R. F. (1978). A developmental study of the category effect in visual search. *Child Development, 49,* 1223–1226.

Stanovich, K. E., West, R. F., & Cunningham, A. E. (1991). Beyond phonological processes: Print exposure and orthographic processing. In S. Brady & D. Shankweiler (Eds.), *Phonological processes in literacy* (pp. 219–235). Hillsdale, NJ: Erlbaum.

Stanovich, K.E., West, R.F., & Feeman, D.J. (1981). A longitudinal study of sentence context effects in second-grade children: Tests of an interactive-compensatory model. *Journal of Experimental Child Psychology, 32,* 185–199.

Sternberg, R. J. (Ed.). (1984). *Mechanisms of cognitive development.* New York: Freeman.

Stevenson, J. (1992). Identifying sex differences in reading disability: Lessons from a twin study. *Reading and Writing, 4,* 307–326.

Strain, E., Patterson, K., & Seidenberg, M. (1995) Semantic effects in single-word naming. *Journal of Experimental Psychology: Learning, Memory, and Cognition, 21,* 1140–1154.

Swanson, H. L., Mink, J., & Bocian, K. M. (1999). Cognitive processing deficits in poor readers with symptoms of reading disabilities and ADHD: More alike than different? *Journal of Educational Psychology, 91,* 321–333.

Taft, M. (1992). The body of the BOSS: Subsyllabic units in the lexical processing of polysyllabic words. *Journal of Experimental Psychology: Human Experimental Psychology, 45,* 51–71.

Taraban, R., & McClelland, J. L. (1987). Conspiracy effects in word recognition. *Journal of Memory and Language, 26,* 608–631.

Thomas, B. (1984). Early toy preferences of four-year-old readers and nonreaders. *Child Development, 55,* 424–430.

Thompson, G. B. (1999). The processes of learning to identify words. In G. B. Thompson & T. Nicholson (Eds.), *Learning to read: Beyond phonics and whole language* (pp. 25–54). New York: Teachers College Press.

Thompson, G. B., Cottrell, D. S., & Fletcher-Flinn, C. M. (1996). Sublexical ortho-graphic-phonological relations early in the acquisition of reading: The knowledge sources account. *Journal of Experimental Child Psychology, 62,* 190–222.

Thompson, G. B., & Fletcher-Flinn, C. M. (1993). A theory of knowledge sources and procedures for reading acquisition. In G. B. Thompson, W. E. Turner, & T. Nicholson (Eds.), *Reading acquisition processes* (pp. 20–73). Clarendon, England: Multilingual Matters.

Thompson, G. B., Fletcher-Flinn, C. M., & Cottrell, D. S. (1999). Learning correspondences between letters and phonemes without explicit instruction. *Applied Psycholinguistics, 20,* 21–50.

Thompson, G. B., & Johnston, R. (2000). Are nonword and other phonological deficits indicative of a failed reading process? *Reading and Writing, 12,* 63–97.

Tobin, A. W., & Pikulski, J. J. (1988). A longitudinal study of the reading achievement of early and non-early readers through sixth grade. In J. Readance & R. S. Baldwin (Eds.), *Dialogues in literacy research:. Thirty-seventh yearbook of the National Reading Conference* (pp. 49–55). Chicago: National Reading Conference.

Torgesen, J. K. (1989). Cognitive and behavioral characteristics of children with learning disabilities: Concluding comments. *Journal of Learning Disabilities, 22,* 166–168.

Torgesen, J. K., & Burgess, S. R. (1998). Consistency of reading-related phonological processes throughout early childhood: Evidence from longitudinal-correlational and instructional studies. In J. L. Metsala & L. C. Ehri (Eds.), *Word recognition in beginning literacy* (pp. 161–188). Mahwah, NJ: Erlbaum.

Torgesen, J. K., Wagner, R. K., & Rashotte, C. A. (1999). *Test of Word Reading Efficiency.* Austin, TX: Pro-Ed.

Torgesen, J. K., Wagner, R. K., Rashotte, C. A., Rose, E., Lindamood, P., Conway, T., & Garvan, C. (1999). Preventing reading failure in young children with phonological processing disabilities: Group and individual responses to instruction. *Journal of Educational Psychology, 91,* 579–593.

Treiman, R., Goswami, U., & Bruck, M. (1990). Not all nonwords are alike: Implications for reading development and theory. *Memory and Cognition, 18,* 559–567.

Treiman, R., Mullenix, J., Bijeljac-Babic, R. &

Richmond-Welty, E.D. (1995). The special role of rimes in the description, use, and acquisition of English orthography. *Journal of Experimental Psychology: General, 124,* 107–136.

Uhry, J. K., & Ehri, L. C. (1999). Ease of segmenting two- and three-phoneme words in kindergarten: Rime cohesion or vowel salience? *Journal of Educational Psychology, 91,* 594–603.

Underwood, B. J. (1975). Individual differences as a crucible in theory construction. *American Psychologist, 30,* 128–134.

Valdois, S., Gerard, C., Vanault, P., & Dugas M. (1995). Peripheral developmental dyslexia: A visual attentional account? *Cognitive Neuropsychology, 12,* 31–67.

Vanier, M., & Caplan, D. (1985). CT scan correlates of surface dyslexia. In K. E. Patterson, J. C. Marshall, & M. Coltheart (Eds.), *Surface dyslexia: Neuropsychological and cognitive studies of phonological reading* (pp. 511–525). London: Erlbaum.

Van Orden, G. C., Johnston, J. C., & Hale, B. L. (1988). Word identification in reading proceeds from spelling to sound to meaning. *Journal of Experimental Psychology: Learning, Memory, and Cognition, 14,* 371–386.

Vellutino, F. R. (1977). Alternative conceptualizations of dyslexia: Evidence in support of a verbal deficit hypothesis. *Harvard Educational Review, 47,* 334–354.

Vellutino, F. R., Scanlon, D. M., Sipay, E. R., Small, S. G., Pratt, A., Chen, R. -S., & Denckla, M. B. (1996). Cognitive profiles of difficult-to-remediate and readily remediated poor readers: Early intervention as a vehicle for distinguishing between cognitive and experiential deficits as basic causes of specific reading disability. *Journal of Educational Psychology, 88,* 601–638.

Vellutino, F. R., Scanlon, D. M., & Tanzman, M. S. (1991). Bridging the gap between cognitive and neuropsychological conceptualizations of reading disability. *Learning and Individual Differences, 3,* 181–203.

Vygotsky, L. S. (1978). *Mind in society* In M. Cole, V. John-Steiner, S. Scribner, & E. Souberman, (Eds.), Cambridge, MA: Harvard University Press.

Wadsworth, S. J., Olson, R. K., Pennington, B. F., & DeFries, J. C. (2000). Differential genetic etiology of reading disability as a function of IQ. *Journal of Learning Disabilities, 33,* 192–199.

Wagner, R. K., Torgesen, J. K., & Rashotte, C. A. (1994). Development of reading-related phonological processing abilities: New evidence of bidirectional causality from a latent variable longitudinal study. *Developmental Psychology, 30,* 73–87.

Wagner, R. K., Torgesen, J. K., & Rashotte, C. A. (1999). *The Comprehensive Test of Phonological Processing.* Austin, TX: Pro-Ed.

Weekes, B. (1997). Differential effects of number of letters on word and nonword naming latency. *Journal of Experimental Psychology: Human Experimental Psychology, 50,* 439–456.

Weekes, B., & Coltheart, M. (1996). Surface dyslexia and surface dysgraphia: Treatment studies and their theoretical implications. *Cognitive Neuropsychology, 13,* 277–315.

Weekes, B., Coltheart, M., & Gordon, E. (1997). Deep dyslexia and right-hemisphere reading—a regional cerebral blood flow study. *Aphasiology, 11,* 1139-1158.

Werker, J. (1989). Becoming a native listener. *American Scientist, 77,* 54–59.

Wernicke, C. (1874). *Der aphasische symptomenkomplex.* Breslau, Poland: Cohn and Weigart. (Translated in *Boston Studies in Philosophy of Science, 4,* 34–97).

Whitehurst, G. J., & Lonigan, C. J. (1998). Child development and emergent literacy. *Child Development, 69,* 848–872.

Wimmer, H. (1995). From the perspective of a more regular orthography. *Issues in Education, 1,* 101–104.

Wise, B., Ring, J., & Olson, R. K. (1999). Training phonological awareness with and without explicit attention to articulation. *Journal of Experimental Child Psychology, 72,* 271–304.

Witton, C., Talcott, J. B., Hansen, P. C., Richardson, A. J., Griffiths, T. D., Rees, A., Stein J. F., & Green, G. G. (1998). Sensitivity to dynamic auditory and visual stimuli predicts nonword reading ability in both dyslexic and normal readers. *Current Biology, 8,* 791–797.

Wolf, M., & Bowers, P. G. (1999). The double-deficit hypothesis for the developmental dyslexias. *Journal of Educational Psychology, 91,* 15–438.

Wolf, M., Pfeil, C., Lotz, R., & Biddle, K.

(1994). Toward a more universal under-standing of the developmental dyslexias: The contribution of orthographic factors. In V. W. Berninger (Ed.), *The varieties of ortho-graphic knowledge: Vol. 1. Theoretical and developmental issues* (pp. 137–171). Dordrecht, The Netherlands: Kluwer.

Woodcock, R. M., & Johnson, M. B. (1989). *Woodcock-Johnson Tests of Achievement.* Chicago: Riverside.

Zevin, J. D., & Balota, D. A. (2000). Priming and attentional control of lexical and sublexical pathways during naming. *Journal of Experimental Psychology: Learning, Memory, and Cognition, 26,* 121–135.

Zorzi, M., Houghton, G., & Butterworth, B. (1998). Two routes or one in reading aloud? A connectionist dual-process model. *Journal of Experimental Psychology: Human Perception and Performance, 24,* 1131–1161.

Author Index

Subject Index

ABOUT THE AUTHORS

PATRICK B. JOHNSON is Professor in the Department of Human Development and Learning at Dowling College on Long Island, New York. Before moving to Dowling, Johnson was a senior fellow and Deputy Director of the Medical Research Division at the National Center on Addiction and Substance Abuse at Columbia University. He was also Senior Research Associate at the Hispanic Research Center at Fordham University where he worked on culture and alcohol abuse for over a decade.

MICHELINE S. MALOW-IROFF is Assistant Professor in the Special Education Department at Manhattanville College located in Westchester, New York. Prior to joining the faculty at Manhattanville College, Malow-Iroff was Assistant Professor at Queens College in the Elementary and Early Childhood Education Department. In addition, Malow-Iroff is a certified school psychologist and worked in a preschool for children with special needs for eight years providing therapy and support to children, teachers, and parents.